VITA AND HAROLD

ALSO BY NIGEL NICOLSON

Two Roads to Dodge City
(with Adam Nicolson), 1987

Napoleon: 1812
1985

The Letters of Virginia Woolf
(editor, with Joanne Trautman), 1975–1980

Mary Curzon
1978

Portrait of a Marriage
1973

Alex: The Life of Field Marshal Earl Alexander of Tunis
1973

The Diaries and Letters of Harold Nicolson
(editor), 1966–1968

Great Houses of Britain
1965 and 1978

Vita and Harold on the steps of the tower at Sissinghurst, 1932.

VITA
AND
HAROLD

The Letters of Vita Sackville-West and Harold Nicolson

EDITED BY

NIGEL NICOLSON

WEIDENFELD & NICOLSON
London

First published in Great Britain in 1992 by
George Weidenfeld & Nicolson Limited
91 Clapham High Street, Longon SW4 7TA

Copyright © Nigel Nicolson 1992

A catalogue reference is available from the British Library

ISBN 0 297 81182 7

Printed in Great Britain by
Butler & Tanner Ltd, Frome and London

CONTENTS

List of Illustrations   ix

Editorial Note   3

Introduction   5

Letters   16

Index   439

ILLUSTRATIONS

Frontispiece
Vita and Harold on the steps of the tower at Sissinghurst, 1932

Following page 150
Vita in 1910, the year she first met Harold
Harold as a junior official in the Foreign Office, 1911
Lord and Lady Sackville, Vita's parents, in 1913
Vita, Harold, Rosamund Grosvenor, and Lord Sackville, 1913
Vita and Harold are married in the chapel at Knole, 1 October 1913
Violet Keppel (Trefusis) in the early 1920s
Vita at about the time of her elopement with Violet Trefusis (1920)
Vita and Harold, with Raymond Mortimer and Gladwyn Jebb, in Persia, 1926
Virginia and Leonard Woolf, Monk's House, Sussex, 1926
Vita at Long Barn in 1928
Vita's sitting room at Long Barn
The Nicolson family at Long Barn in 1927

Following page 310
Harold Nicolson in 1930 (Howard Coster)
The entrance range of Sissinghurst Castle
The Nicolsons at Sissinghurst in 1932
Vita and Harold in California, 1933
Vita and her dog, Rollo, in the orchard at Sissinghurst

The Elizabethan tower at Sissinghurst (*Country Life*)
Charles and Anne Lindbergh, 1934 (The Bettmann Archive)
Harold with Bertrand Russell and Lord Samuel in 1951 (BBC)
The yew "rondel" at Sissinghurst (L. & M. Gayton)
Vita in 1955, aged 63
Vita and Harold in 1959, outside the South Cottage at Sissinghurst
Harold, Nigel, and Nigel's son Adam (Edwin Smith)

VITA AND HAROLD

EDITORIAL NOTE

ON THE LAST DAY OF 1958, as Vita Sackville-West put away the letters that Harold Nicolson had written to her during that year, she glanced through some of the annual folders that had preceded this latest addition to her filing cabinet, and wrote to her husband, "I hope that someday Nigel may publish a selection of them." By the time of her death four years later, there were fifty such folders, containing all, or nearly all, the letters he had written to her since their engagement in 1912. He preserved her letters, too. Their correspondence totaled 10,500 letters in all, many of them pages long.

For some years after my father's death in 1968 I kept them at Sissinghurst, and made use of them in editing the three volumes of his diaries and writing *Portrait of a Marriage*. I also lent them to his biographer (James Lees-Milne), to Vita's biographer (Victoria Glendinning), and to the historians of their gardens, Anne Scott-James and Jane Brown. Their books aroused the interest of many other people, and as it was difficult to store the documents safely in a private house and make them available to students, I decided in 1983 to sell the entire collection, together with Lady Sackville's diaries, to the Lilly Library, Indiana University, at Bloomington, Indiana, where they are kept in conditions ideal both for preservation and access. I am much indebted to William R. Cagle, the Lilly Librarian, and to Saundra Taylor, his Curator of Manuscripts, for their hospitality, interest, and help.

Vita proposed a selection of Harold's letters only, thinking her own unworthy companions to them, an opinion that I have ignored because I do not share it. A one-sided correspondence is not a correspondence, and her letters are of much interest, particularly in the early years, and essential for an understanding of their remarkable relationship.

The majority of these letters have not been published before, and were selected for that reason. But it would have been foolish to omit, for the sake of claiming first publication for everything, certain letters previously quoted in full or in part by myself or the two biographers, when they are key documents in explaining important incidents or attitudes, or perhaps for no other reason than that they are interesting or very funny. Examples are Vita's apologia for her affair with Violet Trefusis (pp. 66–67) or Harold's description of his first meeting with Charles and Anne Lindbergh (pp. 258–259).

My main purpose has been to show how the companionship of two very different people developed over these fifty years, and how their marriage survived crises, sexual incompatibility and long absences to become a source of profound happiness to both. They kept their work (Vita her writing, Harold his diplomacy and politics) separate from their personal lives, and seldom wrote to each other about it, unless one of them had just published a book or an event of great national importance, like the Abdication or both world wars, had occurred. I have retained enough to indicate the impact of these events upon them, but in the main their correspondence is the story of their maturing love for each other, expressed, for example, in their joint creation of the garden at Sissinghurst.

I have not thought it necessary to print the whole of every letter. Most letter-writers deal in the same letter with several subjects, and to isolate one or two of them for publication in a book that does not pretend to be a complete correspondence is, I believe, excusable. Nor have I annotated the letters fully, because to do so in a popular edition is likely to annoy the reader by telling him what he does not need or want to know. Only the first letter is annotated in the traditional way, to show him what he has been spared in all the others.

The addresses are given in full when they first appear, but thereafter they are truncated ("Long Barn," "Teheran," "Sissinghurst," "Berlin," etc.). Sometimes the greeting and signature are given in full, but more often they are omitted, because to repeat endlessly the endearments at the beginning and end of letters written by the same two people is to render their correspondence more saccharine than it seemed to them. Family expressions, nicknames, family jokes, and their habit of referring to each other in the third person ("Mar isn't going to like this: nor does Hadji") are only tolerable to an outsider if sparingly used, and they have been reduced by judicious excision.

I am much indebted to Mary Morgan for her sympathetic typing of the letters from photocopies supplied by the Lilly Library.

NIGEL NICOLSON
Sissinghurst Castle, Cranbrook, Kent

INTRODUCTION

HAROLD NICOLSON WAS the better letter-writer of the two, and not only because he had more to write about after 1930, the watershed in both their lives, when he changed his profession in mid-career and Vita left social Long Barn for reclusive Sissinghurst. He enjoyed writing letters more than she did, was eager to share experiences that would interest or amuse her, and he used his letters, as he did his contemporary diary, not just to record, but as a literary exercise at the start of each day, much as a man might knock up in a squash court before the match began. Thus he was given to set-piece descriptions of incidents and conversations (he had an exceptional aural memory), of moods and landscapes, of other people's clothes and houses, and how accent, gesture, mannerisms, and chatter reveal a person's background and taste. His letter-writing style, in fact, was little different from that which he adopted in his most loved book, *Some People,* and developed in his broadcasts of the 1930s, but less severe, less classical, less ornate than his articles and other books. He had no thought of publication as he wrote his daily letters to Vita, but some of them, like his description of the signing of the Treaty of Versailles on 28 June 1919 or his meeting with James Joyce on 4 February 1934, were undoubtedly intended for more than her eyes.

Vita, on the other hand, had no great wish to record or share experiences. Her diary, which she kept only intermittently, was little more than a retrospective engagement book. Nor was she gifted with Harold's effortless wit, or his ability to praise without flattery and mock without offense. In writing to him she didn't choose to exercise her narrative or poetic skills, which were greater than his, as she did when writing to other intimates, like Virginia Woolf. Indeed, I find it strange that the best of her books, like *The Garden, Passenger to Teheran,* and *All Passion Spent,* reveal a quite different, profounder, cleverer Vita than her letters to Harold. Perhaps it was because he understood her so well, and she felt so certain of his love, that she saw no need to show off a little, moan a little, exult a little, as he did in his letters to her. He threw his pleasures like confetti into the air, and craved sympathy for his sorrows. She nursed hers to herself. But this had not always been so. She became more reticent as she grew older. Some of her earliest letters, when they were engaged, indulged in mock scolding and flirtatious quips that she abandoned after marriage, but that she, too, was capable of the set piece, and did it well, is illustrated by her description of Rodin in his studio on 3 September 1913, and her humor (as well as her fortitude) emerges from the account of her escape from revolutionary Poland on 13 May 1926. Her most self-revealing letters were written to Harold in Persia, when she was struggling to reconcile her concurrent love for him and for Virginia Woolf, and at least two weeks would elapse before her letter reached him, and a month before she received his reply, the interval of time and distance reassuring her that she was not trapped.

Even before their wedding, Harold referred to "our amazing marriage" (28 July 1913), and indeed it was strange, so strange that many people could not resist questioning whether it was a marriage at all. When my account of it was published in 1973, a Sunday newspaper headlined its review of the book, "Portrait of a *What?*" The critic could not believe that a marriage that renounced sex after two sons were born could be anything more than a loving friendship, and that didn't count as marriage, particularly when both partners, by mutual consent, were unfaithful to each other with people of their own sex. But in every other sense Vita and Harold achieved a relationship richer and more enduring than most couples, replacing sex by something more binding and even more gratifying—mutual support, mutual sympathy, mutual forebearance, common enjoyments (gardens, books, children, travel, friends), and the generosity to encourage in the other separate achievements, separate pleasures, separate holidays, separate lovers, without loss of trust or affection. Neither felt any jealousy, envy, or resentment of the other. While they missed each other agonizingly during Harold's long absences abroad, it never occurred to them to suggest that Vita should sacrifice her independence by joining him permanently in his diplomatic posts. They wore their separation like a hair shirt. "It is rather good for us to have a chance of thoroughly missing each other," wrote Vita before their wedding had even taken place. And thirteen years later (slightly paraphrased):

What is the point, in our enlightened world, of *marriage?* You see, if we had just lived together, we would be living together still, just as happily, and it would make no difference to our passion for our garden or our interest in the children. The whole system of marriage is wrong. It ought, at least, to be optional, and no stigma if you prefer a less claustrophobic form of contract. For it *is* claustrophobic. (26 December 1926)

Harold never found it claustrophobic. He liked marriage. It gave their union stability, legitimized their children, made Long Barn a home, not just a shared house, and their possessions common possessions. He was domesticated: Vita was not. He needed her love more than she needed his, because she was always sure of his and for many years he was not quite sure of hers. The slight tension that resulted is evident from his letters. He is always reassuring himself by dramatizing the happiness of their marriage and constantly re-examining its roots, and ultimately she caught the habit. ("I do think that we have managed things cleverly.") There is a note of self-congratulation about their correspondence that some readers have found puzzling.

Harold began by thinking that he could manage Vita. She responded with spirit, as if testing her blade against his before a duel. In his engagement letters he made tentative sallies to assert his masculinity: "I really must be the one who 'disposes' in these things . . . About big things I am to have the upper hand" (17 February 1913), but he did it in the manner of someone who, having once put his foot down, immediately lifts it up again. He ended the same letter, "Remember that whatever you do . . . I shall know that you were right." He was Victorian by birth, Edwardian by upbringing, Georgian by temperament, and the three influences conflicted in his character, the first authoritative, the third conciliatory, whereas Vita, even in childhood, had settled her priorities much more firmly. She would be liberated, iconoclastic, rebellious; and although she loved Knole with a sick passion, she was a wanderer, a gypsy—Pepita reincarnated—or so, for a time, she liked to think.

The duality of her character led to the great Trefusis affair. It has so often been described, even dramatized on film, that I need only repeat that it was the crisis of their marriage. In this volume I have included letters that tell the story from their two points of view as it was happening, and added later letters that make clear Vita's remorse for her part in it and Harold's fear of Violet's pernicious influence which persisted until the end of his life.

"You know what infatuation is," she wrote to him, soon after the crisis had passed, "and I was mad." And then, rather curiously, within two years of her death, "You were older than me, and far better informed. I was very young, and very innocent. I knew nothing about homosexuality . . . You should have told me" (23 November 1960). She was not all that young, not all that innocent. In 1920 she was twenty-eight, and although she may not have given homosexuality a name, she had had a taste of it with Rosamund Grosvenor long before her more torrid affair with Violet Trefusis began. We have no need to find excuses for her. Her behaviour was reckless and cruel. Violet's was worse. Her humiliation of her husband was an act of cynical wickedness compared to Vita's guilt-laden betrayal of Harold.

What of his part in it? As his dialogue with Vita was conducted almost entirely by correspondence (when alone together they could barely bring themselves to mention the subject), one can trace his terrible dilemma through all its mutations, undecided whether to bully Vita into submission or cajole her, act like Petruchio with his shrew or Bassanio with Portia. His nature was gentle, and it was gentleness that won in the end, but from time to time he simulated defiance, "Come back at once" alternating with "Come back when you can," and Vita took advantage of his vacillation, hating herself for doing so. But if he was gentle, Harold was not weak. It was not the performance of a weak man to woo and win, against formidable competition, so fiery a girl as Vita was in 1912, nor to gain an early reputation as the most brilliant diplomatist of his generation, the confidant of Lloyd George, Balfour, and Curzon, the adviser of Clemenceau, Venizelos, and President Wilson. He managed to retrieve Vita from Violet not just by being lovable, but because he was admirable, in spirit, intelligence, and fervor, and because, by that time, deep down, she *wanted* to be rescued from her insane adventure. Her ruthlessness had given the impression of strength, but it was she who was the weakest of the three, and afterwards the most repentant. She spent the rest of her life making up for him the brutality of those three years.

Yet a streak of mercilessness persisted in her. She could hate more violently than Harold: "Those filthy Germans! Let us level every town in Germany to the ground! I shan't care" (16 February 1944), and in the casual way she discarded lovers she displayed an arrogance worthy of generations of Sackvilles. Her shabby treatment of Geoffrey Scott is a striking example. But her short-lived affair with him was an aberration. She was born to be a lesbian lover. Though she bore three sons (one of whom died at birth), she was perpetually astonished that God should have devised such a peculiar way of begetting children, and her astonishment soon turned to disgust. With women lovers her only problem was to free herself of one love affair in order to begin the next, and she contrived this difficult task without ever inflicting a lasting wound. She did not regard sex as the most important element in her relationship with women, no more than she had with Harold, and once that phase was over, they could remain friends. Not all her lovers saw it in quite the same way. They were disconcerted by the frankness of some lines in her poem *Solitude* (1938):

> Those cheap and easy loves! But what were they,
> Those rank intruders into darkest lairs?
> We take a heart and leave our own intact.

Was that all they had meant to her?

With Virginia Woolf it was very different. Vita was flattered by her attention, awed; and it surprised her that Virginia could embark at the age of forty-four upon the only love affair of her life without trepidation, as if she didn't want to go to her grave without having done something really wicked. Vita was apprehensive (she didn't need Harold's warning) that their love making might trigger in Virginia a new attack of madness. It didn't. Both women were enriched by it. Vita found in their intimacy an inspiration that she gained from no other person. *Seducers in Ecuador* was one direct result of it, the most original of all Vita's prose works, written for Virginia, in her allusive style, and published by her, and from Virginia's side came *Orlando,* the longest and most charming love letter in literature.

Vita told Harold, who was in Teheran, a safe distance away, that she and Virginia had slept together, but it was the only occasion when she was so frank. Their unwritten marriage pact stipulated that each would tell the other about their current affairs. When it came to the point, they were too shy. They allowed the information to be surmised from dropped hints, that Harold had met "a funny new friend, a dressmaker," Edward Molyneux (15 September 1919), or Ivor Novello, the film star (14 April 1928), and Vita spoke lightly of Mary Campbell and Hilda Matheson, knowing that he would guess the true situation, just as she never needed to probe into his lifelong friendship with Raymond Mortimer, or his more casual affairs with young men like James Pope-Hennessy or John Strick. It was as if in this respect they were two unmarried friends, trained to leave each other's indiscretions unquestioned and not even to think of them as infidelities.

Vita's character changed more than Harold's as she grew older. The major transformation coincided with their move from Long Barn to Sissinghurst in the early 1930s. At Long Barn there had been weekend parties, constant expeditions to London and other people's country houses, but at Sissinghurst, a house twice the size of Long Barn, she determined to have no guest rooms, for guest rooms imply guests. Harold's gregariousness was satisfied in London during the week, and Sissinghurst with its "succession of intimacies" was his refuge as much as hers. So extreme was Vita's desire for solitude that she insisted on my brother and I sharing a bedroom until we were both at Oxford, because, she explained, if we had a bedroom each and one of us was away, Lady Colefax might find out and invite herself for the weekend. It halved the risk.

If this sounds eccentric, it gives a false impression of Vita's personality. She was deeply conservative. I have hesitated to print in this volume her letter of 7 February 1945, because her dislike of change, accentuated by the turmoil of a war that was just ending, is phrased in terms so reactionary as to defy belief. She would have preferred to call it her love of tradition, which she had expressed in very different ways in her novel *The Edwardians* and her poem *The Land*. She believed profoundly that the old order, including its class structure, was the best. People should stay in their villages, not demand buses to the nearest town. Tractors are no better than plough horses, and uglier. Retirement pensions are regrettable because they are a substitute for

savings, and family allowances odious because they encourage the
wrong people to breed. Wars, she thought, could be avoided if only
enough people wanted peace, but when the Second World War broke
out, she was exhilarated. Her love of England, the excitement of the
air battles overhead and the threat of invasion on the Kentish coast,
the involvement of both her sons on active service in Africa and Italy,
and the danger to which Harold was nightly exposed in London
cumulatively aroused her latent patriotism and induced in her a solemn
contemplation of life and death, God and nature, which in the darkness
of her tower she poured into her profoundest but most neglected poem,
The Garden. How much one can sympathize with her complaint to
Harold (1 October 1957) that, in contrast, her gardening articles in
The Observer had gained her a reputation which she neither desired nor
deserved!

Once she had written to him (26 September 1926): "What I really
like is a severe life," by which she meant application, the industry
needed to finish a book or perfect a garden, instead of frittering her
time away socially. Harold did not agree. All his life he worked
regularly and intensively, and his output on paper was doubled by his
fluency, his retentive memory and quick imagination, but his well-
regulated life allowed him equal time for conversation, parties, clubs,
committees, meetings, broadcasts, lectures and love. His activity when
he was in charge of the British Embassy in Berlin in 1928 is an example
of the pattern of life which best suited him. Deeply engaged in
analyzing for his Government the gradual resurgence of Germany as
a great power, he entertained countless visitors, taking them at considerable risk to his reputation to the sleaziest nightclubs, mixed with the
intellectual elite of Berlin, did his hated duty as host at formal
diplomatic functions, lectured in Cologne, Munich, and Frankfurt, and
yet found time to write what he considered the best of his books, his
life of his father, Lord Carnock.

On retiring from diplomacy in 1929, largely because Vita hated
it, he endured two disastrous years when he was involved first with
Lord Beaverbrook's newspapers and then with Oswald Mosley's New
Party, and only regained his poise by writing a best-selling novel,
Public Faces, and his trilogy of books on diplomacy, the last of them
a biography of an American, Dwight Morrow.

Harold's attitude to Americans was ambivalent. He could not

justly be called a snob. In England he had little sympathy with the Ascot or City sets, and chose his friends, as most people do, from among those who shared his interests, which in his case were undeniably elitist. He demanded a certain level of culture, taste, and intelligence before he could feel comfortable with them. He liked people who would recognize a Matisse on sight, quote the poets appositely and without showing off, wear a top hat without feeling or looking foolish, and when someone referred to Pinero's plays, didn't need to ask, "Who's Pinero?" In politics he hated the fake cordiality that a candidate has to assume. Therefore, he found himself as much at a loss in the workingmen's clubs of Leicester (his constituency) as in the smarter houses of Mayfair, Long Island mansions, and the drawing rooms of suburban Des Moines. His first visit to the United States, with Vita, was on a lecture tour in 1933, in the worst possible combination of circumstances for a first acquaintance with that exciting country— mid-winter, the depth of an economic depression, and an exhausting three-month tour by train and car of some of the most unappetizing of American cities. "There simply does not exist here the sort of person whom we like," he wrote to Vita. This nonsense he retracted when he went to Charleston, South Carolina, and a year later when he stayed with the Morrows and the Lindberghs, and met people like Thomas Lamont, Archibald MacLeish, and Mrs. Longworth. Yet the prejudice of the Old World against the New lingered in him. One of his funniest letters (30 August 1935) candidly describes how the New World had its revenge.

He sat in the House of Commons from 1935 to 1945, and for a year was a junior Minister in Winston Churchill's wartime government. He was an excellent speaker, a companionable colleague who never made a political enemy, and almost the only back-bench member who had had direct experience of the conduct of foreign policy. He would have risen to high office had he possessed one other quality, which Churchill once described as the most estimable in a man— mettle. Harold lacked it. He held no animosity in reserve, and displayed no political vehemence, except in one instance, his opposition to Chamberlain's attempts to conciliate the Dictators. His speech against the Munich agreement was his finest political hour. His training as a civil servant inclined him to seek compromise, see merit in his opponent's arguments, and avoid controversy. One of his parliamentary friends urged him to become more formidable. He replied that having been unformidable for fifty-five years, it was difficult suddenly to acquire the necessary techniques. In the end, he regarded his political career as a failure—too severe a verdict—and withdrew to his other life: the writing of books, the cultivation of his garden, and Vita.

They often reassured each other that the success of their marriage was due to "a common set of values," a blanket term that covered the whole range of moral and intellectual probities, an amalgam of Greek, Roman, Christian, and eighteenth-century virtues, among them, truthfulness, charity, industry, curiosity, decorum, and a capacity for friendship. Neither of them was formally religious. In one of these letters (7 July 1929), Harold expressed his astonishment at the "twaddle" that the English hymnal contained, and while Vita worried more about her lack of faith and actually wrote the lives of three saints (Joan of Arc, and the two Saints Teresa), both were content to describe themselves as good pagans. Their goodness was not quite absolute, their values not entirely common. They shared a seam of racism that could be uncovered not far beneath the surface, and the Sackvilles' "bedint" shibboleth, to which one clue was accent, often clouded their judgment. A young woman interviewed for the post of secretary at Sissinghurst ruined her chances by uttering in her nervousness the telltale phrase, "Our cow is a brown cow," and not one eye dared meet another.

Vita, like Virginia Woolf, was by temperament a pacifist and feminist, though neither satisfactorily worked out the implications of what they professed. Harold was neither. He believed unashamedly in the threat of war as an instrument of policy, and his attitude to women remained Edwardian: they were incapable of "thinking logically." There were also political differences between them. In 1948 Harold stood for Parliament as a Labour candidate: Vita's conservatism was unshakable. His "socialism" was the easy price he paid for the advantages he had enjoyed in life. Vita felt no guilt about her equivalent prejudices. Too well-bred to utter them publicly, in private she proclaimed them.

It was because she found it hard to come to terms with a changing world that her relationship with her two sons became uneasy. In our childhood her love for us was explicit and unforced (see, for example, her letter of 26 December 1926), but children were demanding, dirty, spies, pests, and disturbers of the peace. They interrupted terribly. In later life, the University, war, Parliament, scholarship, and business set us further apart from her in what she still considered male occupations, and we both drew closer to our father because he understood them better, and was more extrovert than Vita, more active, funnier, more demonstrably affectionate. I feel remorseful about this. I should have taken the trouble to know Vita better. I excused my partial withdrawal from her by what I supposed to be her partial withdrawal from me, but it was a sort of shyness on both our parts, a misguided fear of intrusion that vitiates the relationship between many parents and their children. At first it was Ben whom she loved the better; later it was me, for she considered me the rural son, Ben the urban, and though I was the younger, she bequeathed Sissinghurst to me, believing that I would care for it more. She misunderstood the adult Ben, and so did Harold, thinking his reaction against the domesticity and values of his family ungrateful, his erudition austere, and his untidiness and silences discourteous. They underestimated the position he won for himself as an art historian and his gift for friendship, and would have been surprised to know that at his memorial service in 1978, five hundred people crowded the church and Kenneth Clark gave the address.

In the last years of their marriage, their letters were shorter because they knew each other so well and spent almost every weekend together. There was nothing left to explain, and on Vita's side little to relate. "Another quiet day at Sissinghurst" became a constant refrain. Harold remained very active until her death in 1962, reporting the consequences of the war from Nuremberg and Paris, standing once again for Parliament, and writing the official biography of King George V, for which, to his slight dismay and Vita's, he was awarded a knighthood. Their bond was literature and the garden. For many years both wrote, or broadcast, reviews of current books, and published another dozen of their own. The garden was their sustained pleasure, expressive of their common attitude to nature, keeping it cool, Kentish, and indigenous, as Harold had counseled Vita from Teheran when she was making the garden at Long Barn. Flowers should not quarrel, no more than people. They had achieved at Sissinghurst a serenity that matched their own lives.

Looking back on their marriage, they came to consider it the perfect compromise. If Vita, from time to time (see, for example, her letter of 13 December 1928, a key document in this long story), confessed to a sense of inadequacy as his wife, or if he wondered (31 March 1941) whether she might not have been happier married to a more determined man, neither bothered to reply, for each knew what the reply would be. When she told him at the height of the German bombardment of London that she would kill herself if he were killed, she meant it. As it was, they lived into old age, Harold dying six years after her. He could have spoken for both of them when he wrote to her (9 April 1958), "When I die, nobody will think I failed to make the most of life."

Harold and Vita first met at a London dinner party on 29 June 1910, and he was invited by Lady Sackville to spend the following weekend at Knole. He was twenty-four, Vita eighteen, each in their different ways a young star of Edwardian society. He was a junior official in the Foreign Office, of which his father, Sir Arthur Nicolson, became head in September of that year; and she, a beautiful though reluctant debutante, was the only child of a family that in February had become notorious by winning the famous Pepita legitimacy case. Knole was restored to its full grandeur, and Harold was invited to stay there more than once. He and Vita often met at London parties, and her first surviving letter to him records their friendly but by no means intimate relationship.

VITA TO HAROLD   *Knole [Sevenoaks, Kent]*

5 November [1910]

My dear Mr Harold,

I have been asked to "ask a man" to dine on Thursday with Mrs Harold Pearson[1] and go to a dance, so would you like to come? I promise you shan't be made to dance! I think it might be rather amusing. Would you let me know as soon as possible, to the St Petersburg Hotel,[2] North Audley Street, or better still come to tea

---

1. She was Agnes Beryl, a daughter of Lord Edward Spencer-Churchill. In 1905 she had married Harold (Weetman) Pearson, a Liberal M.P. and heir to the 1st Viscount Cowdray, whom he succeeded in 1927.
2. Knole had been half closed, pending the result of the legitimacy trial which could have deprived the Sackvilles of their inheritance, and they had been living in this hotel off Grosvenor Square for the best part of two years.

tomorrow at 6 South Street with the Rubens lady,[3] who is here and tells me to ask you. We are both going up to London tomorrow to go to *Macbeth*.

Do come to the dance.

Yours very sincerely,

Vita Sackville-West

Mr Vansittart is here.[4] How is Green Archie?[5]

---

3. Rosamund Grosvenor, Vita's childhood friend and current lover. She called her the Rubens lady because of her fleshy, roseate appearance.
4. Robert Vansittart (1881–1957), an early admirer of Vita and a friend of Harold. In 1910 he was on leave from Cairo, where he was a second secretary in the British Embassy. In 1930 he became head of the Foreign Office and was a major voice in warning the Government of the Nazi threat.
5. Harold's Morris Oxford car. Although he had learned to drive, he gave it up soon after his marriage, and it was always Vita who drove when they were motoring together.

No letters survive from 1911, although it was the year when Harold fell in love with Vita. He was parted from her for six months when he was appointed to the Embassy in Madrid, but spent Christmas and New Year at Knole, where their friendship developed rapidly. Shortly afterwards he learned that he was to be posted to the Embassy in Constantinople. He was determined to propose to her before he left, and took the opportunity at a ball at Hatfield House on 18 January 1912. Vita hesitated, then half accepted him, but when he left for Constantinople a week later, it was on the understanding (imposed by Lady Sackville) that they were not to correspond as an engaged couple nor even as lovers. Hence the apparent coldness of Vita's letters, and for the first year she did not keep Harold's. In 1913 their correspondence grew warmer, and they began to break Lady Sackville's rules, but Harold, though worried by Vita's varying moods, was quite unaware of the reason for them, that she was simultaneously much in love with Rosamund Grosvenor. The crisis came in May 1913, following her visit to Spain, when she hinted that perhaps they should not marry after all, but his anguished response convinced her, and she committed herself to Harold absolutely. He returned from Turkey in July, in time to witness the Sackvilles' triumph in the Scott inheritance case, and they were married in the chapel at Knole on 1 October 1913.

Knole

23 January [1912]

My dear Harold,

   The Saint has arrived. He is quite lovely, and has a gloriously flat
nose. I like him quite, quite enormously, and he is going in the niche,
and thank you ever so much. I suppose he is old?[1]

   This letter is meant to catch you tomorrow morning between
Ireland and Constantinople, though Providence alone knows whether
it will. Anyway, if you receive it three months late you will know
from this that the intention was good. As a matter of fact, I see that
the Saint is really only a little boy, unless he is John the Baptist, who
was a man saint at first, wasn't he? I have got influenza, isn't it a
bore? Not very bad, but enough to keep me in bed with a temperature and neuralgia. This room is such fun to be ill in, there are so
many things to look at. But it makes one long to get up and finish
it.[2]

   Goodbye and *buonissimo viaggio.*

                                        Yours very sincerely
                                        Vita Sackville-West

6 South Street,
                                             London W.1
1 February [1912]

My dear Harold,

   I am writing at the Rubens lady's house, with her pen, (which is
vile), but she is not here. She is at the *Miracle,*[3] and I am by way of
coming to tea with her. I am going to the *Miracle* myself tonight,

---

1. The saint was in fact female, St. Barbara, a sixteenth-century wooden statuette, 21 ins. high,
   which Harold bought for Vita in Spain. "Barbara" became a symbol of their marriage,
   accompanied them from house to house, even to Persia, and is still at Sissinghurst.
2. Vita and Rosamund were painting her bedroom in a mock-Italian style, blue and gold.
3. Max Reinhardt's play, in which Lady Diana Manners (later Diana Cooper) played the
   leading role.

hence my being in London at all. Then I am going for balls in the country, and then Knole, and parties. Perhaps I will go to Montana [Switzerland] with Uncle Charlie, *Schlittschuhlaufen* [skating]. I lunched with him today, and they told me they had heard of me at Hatfield. Don't you dislike being told you were heard of at various places?

Why I am really writing to you, besides that the Rubens lady is late, and I have nothing to do, and know her well enough to invade her writing table, is that Mother gave me a message for you, which is that the negotiations with the solicitors are being very tedious,[4] and that nothing will be 'proven' till the summer; but I *know* it is going to be all right, and so does she. How low and base and mean and altogether horrible money questions are, and how I hate the very word 'will', and how dreadfully long anything takes that has to do with the law. One ought to have a sort of whipping-boy, like child-kings used to have, to take upon their shoulders for one all the least pleasant parts of life, and then one would be free to revel in its joys like a lizard in the sun.

The lizards that lie on the red brick wall at the bottom of *my* garden in Florence, among the roses. When I was sixteen I used to write decadent poems about them, and I haven't forgotten them now, though I don't write decadent poems. They were so green and hot. The lizards, of course. And once I had a tame one. Then there were poor little overladen donkeys who couldn't drag their carts up the hill to Fiesole, and I used to go and help the little Florentine boys to push. Usually they had left the brake on. And if they were nice to the donkey I gave them *soldi*. My villa [Pestellini] there has a big garden, and the gardener's wife was called Aosunta. You have seen the picture of Florence in my room at Knole, done from my garden. I have the key of the garden gate even now, in my bag. Isn't that a pose?

Here is the Rubens lady, so I stop.

V.S.W.

---

4. Over the disputed will of Sir John Murray-Scott. His brother and sister claimed that Lady Sackville had used "undue influence" on him to secure for herself a large part of his fortune.

21 February 1912

My dear Harold,

Thank you ever so much for the Turkish delight. It is so bad for me, and I like it so much, especially with monkey-nuts in it like this kind. I also got a distressed letter which I couldn't understand, as I *had* written. What happened? I am so glad you danced. You must learn to go round the wrong way, because you are going to lots of dances next summer, which you will hate but which will be so good for you, and you will have to dance then. Do you know by the way that Ace[1] is coming home about the same time? Muriel [his sister] told me; we met skating at Prince's. Do you and Ace still correspond volubly as you used to? It will be fun having him again.

Here I have become an architect, and go about with two carpenters and a hammer and a yard-measure, and the result of much tapping of walls is that we are going to have another bedroom for people staying. I nearly made a bathroom too, but they said the house would collapse if we dug away the wall. Besides, Dada said Mother was bad enough about bathrooms without my starting too. I agree. But it is fun digging holes and making new rooms.

Tomorrow we are going to London. Mother may go to Paris on Sunday. At Monte Carlo Dada saw Anne (Stanley) and she had already made £100. Did I tell you that before? I am going to balls. Hitherto I have avoided them by banning all the invitation cards. I foresee a terrific season next summer. The other night we went to such an odd dinner you would have liked; there were queer untidy artist people, with a sprinkling of 'clever' young men like Patrick Shaw-Stewart.[2] Do you know him? he is the ugliest thing you ever saw, but very amusing. It is a recent friendship, but we have met quite often. Then there was Granby,[3] who is a curious rather morose person. I don't think I altogether like him. And there were playwrights and sculptors

---

1. Archibald Clark-Kerr, the diplomatist who became Ambassador in both Moscow and Washington. In his youth he was Harold's closest friend.
2. Harold's most brilliant contemporary at Balliol. He was killed in France in 1917.
3. The Marquess of Granby, heir to the Duke of Rutland, who was much in love with Vita.

and novelists and painters, and it was fun. I like that sort of people, and some of them came in quite vaguely after dinner, which I like too, but they were all quite clean. My erratic friend Violet Keppel[4] is coming home in April, so you will know her; I am so glad. She will amuse you more than anybody. You are going to know such crowds of people. And it will not be any use you saying you don't want to.

Tell me something to read. I am tired of the Italian Renaissance and Ranke's History of the Popes. Is it any use sending you English books by the bag? because of course I will if you would like. Have you got a horse? Call it anything except Pegasus. Dada's horse is called Trois Quartiers, but it is too long a story to tell you why. You would put your finger in your eye. Or didn't you know that was the family gesture for saying one is bored? One does it across the table at dinner, and nobody knows. One also does it when one has had enough and wants to go away. This letter is really quite short, but my writing straggles. And isn't it bad?

I don't want to go to London tomorrow.

Yours
Vita

VITA TO HAROLD   *Knole*

27 February 1912

My dear Harold,

Mother has gone to Paris, and I am all alone here for the moment, and all this big house is mine to shut up if I choose, and shut out all the rest of the world by swinging the iron bars across all the gates. But instead of doing that I have locked all the doors of my own tower, and nobody will come near me till tomorrow morning, or even know whether I am still alive. And it is so warm, and Micky [her dog] is dreaming in front of the fire, and the gold on my blue walls gleams in places in the light. And I think I have gone back five hundred years,

---

4. Violet (later Trefusis) had been spending a year in Ceylon with her mother and sister, following the death of King Edward VII.

to the days when the paintings on my walls were new. I heard from you this evening, about the Tschamlüja [outside Constantinople], and your arty pink handkerchief fluttering on the railings. If I sent you a rag, would you tie it on for me? only probably one can't wish by proxy, and even if one could I could not tell you what I should wish. Besides I am off wishing, since the day I fell into a wishing well as a child. I was fished out with a blackberrying stick. I was not pleased. I was an unsociable and unnatural mar[1] with long black hair and long black legs, and very short frocks, and very dirty nails and torn clothes. I used to disappear for hours up high trees, and they couldn't find me till I threw the eggs out of the bird's nests down upon their heads. Then I wouldn't do arithmetic, or scales on the piano. I had a governess who used to hit me across the knuckles with a ruler; you know her, Miss Scarth. She occasionally talks of you, and calls you Harry. In those days the Rubens lady lived quite near here, and that's how I knew her. She was sent for to console me when Dada went to South Africa. (I nearly wrote South Audley Street, with visions of Spealls![2])

The other day I went to a cotillon, and met a mutual friend of ours, who instantly asked why people hated him, and said you had not written to him. I said that wasn't my fault. I really almost did hate him, except that he was so ridiculous. Then Dada and I came down here, and 500 soldiers had a terrific battle in the park, and I saw the moment when I could defend a spiral staircase with an inefficient sword. If there was a war, could diplomats volunteer?

VITA TO HAROLD   [Knole]

18 March 1912

Suddenly, I have decided to go to Italy. Telegrams are flying to people who might possibly take me. Of course I should love to throw a toothbrush into a bag, and just go, quite vaguely, without any plans

---

1. "Mar" was the Sackville word for "small," hence a child. It was the name by which her mother, and later Harold, called her.
2. Lady Sackville's shop.

or even a real destination. It is the Wanderlust. And then I want the
sun so badly, and to get away too, right away. Wouldn't you like to,
in green Archie, from one little town with red roofs perched on a hill
to another, and never minding the fleas, and making friends with the
dirty children, and taking them all for drives in green Archie? And if
it was not warm enough in the North, you would drive Archie onto
a railway truck and go away down to Sicily. Isn't that much more than
travelling luxuriously with wagons-lits, and couriers, and rooms kept
for one in the best hotels in all the big towns? Mother can't understand
why I would *rather* go without a maid.

VITA TO HAROLD

St. Petersburg Hotel,
Grosvenor Square,
London W.

March [1912]

Harold, I am *not* rich, and even if I was, it couldn't possibly jar.
It is quite easy. So don't worry.

It is a good thing that we can always talk about anything without
minding, quite brutally. I am glad we fell into that way from the first.
It could never have been otherwise, though.

VITA TO HAROLD

[Knole]

10 April 1912

I used to hate Eddy[1] when he was a baby and I wasn't much more,
because he would have Knole, and I was vaguely jealous. But now I
don't want it, and he will be an excellent person for it, and when he
is twenty-two we will marry him to someone revoltingly rich. He will
be too gentle to mind. He will have long hair, and wear very low

---

1. Edward Sackville-West (1901–65), the writer and musician, who succeeded his father as
5th Lord Sackville in 1962. He never married.

collars with a large bow, and probably a velvet coat. He will be a soul [intellectual].

Mr Vansittart was here for Easter—he plays tennis wonderfully, but otherwise I don't care much for him. Patrick Shaw-Stewart I like; he is *so* ugly, but if one dresses him (in imagination) in Louis XI clothes his ugliness does not matter. He has the gift of condensing all one's vaguest and most intricate ideas into six words. It is like a flash of lightning on a dark night. But I think his qualities probably stop there, and beyond that I don't know whether he is really nice—a horrid word, but it exactly fits what I mean, so I must use it. He is going to Dorothy Heneage's at Coker[2] next Sunday, and so am I. And to Taplow[3] the following week, so by the time I start for Italy I ought to have all my ideas thoroughly well expressed, classified, and pigeon-holed.

VITA TO HAROLD

34 Hill Street
[London W.1]

6 June 1912

My dear Harold,

This morning I came home from a ball at 4, and I slept two hours only, and I'm so tired, so I dined all alone here off a bit of dry cold beef and a banana, and nobody is here because the B.M.[4] went to Knole today, and then I came in and found a letter from you. My room (where I am) is no longer macabre and like a hearse; it is rich and full of glowing sombre colours, and the light is very soft, and I love it, and I expect everybody else will hate it because it is *outré,* but up to now no one has seen it and it is quite, quite mine. Also in some odd way you are sprawling on the sofa saying how far off August is, and how you are bored with Constantinople, and I am cross with you for interrupting me while I am writing letters, and at the same time I am

2. Coker Court in Somerset, where Vita and Harold spent the first night of their honeymoon.
3. Lady Desborough's house on the Thames.
4. Bonne Mama, the family name for Lady Sackville. 34 Hill Street was her new house in Mayfair.

telling you—aren't I?—that August isn't very far, and *I* don't mind half so much as you do, and that I do really, only I pretend not,—it is all rather involved and has no more *queue* or *tête* than a dream, all because I went to a 100-years-ago ball and stayed up till 4.

Archie [Clark-Kerr] was there, in a smock like a shepherd! and I said he reminded me of the *Et moi j'aime mes moutons* tune and he didn't like it. But it is so good for Archie to be laughed at. He introduced me to a friend of yours called [Edward] Keeling, and we talked about you and whether you were liking Constantinople. It was quite serious, because I was Arabella Diana Duchess of Dorset, and had three nodding white plumes, and ring-miniatures of John Frederick the Duke on my fingers. There were other dukes there too, live ones, or rather future ones, and we walked about the Albert Hall together,[5] and I could see *"How suitable!"* in people's eyes as we went by. And I am asked to plays and to dinner-parties every night, and we are put next to each other, and I wonder if he thinks it as funny as I do. And he came to Knole. Please don't mind. And yet please do, a little. I tell you because I would rather you knew, and you must take it as I take it, and see how funny it is.

Now I am sorry I told you, because even if Lady Lowther[6] had a daughter how I should hate her, and you will torment yourself when you needn't. I am sorry, Harold.

This is very primitive, and unsubtle for literary people like us.

How I *loathe* writing this sort of letter, I mean half and half, don't you? It would be almost better to write about the weather. When you come back we will make other arrangements—if they will let us. Because after all . . . Oh how frightfully I want you to come back! and yet you must go on being pleasant to Lady L. and I must talk to dukes, and write you letters about balls. I never minded restrictions[7] so much as I do tonight. And, by the way, I am observing them extra-ordinarily little. Are you angry with me for it? especially when the B.M. is away which makes it worse.

---

5. With Lord Granby, the future Duke of Rutland and heir to Belvoir Castle.
6. Wife of Sir Gerard Lowther, Harold's Ambassador in Constantinople. Lady Lowther, who was an American, had two daughters.
7. Lady Sackville's, on the nature of their correspondence.

Now listen, Harold. You are not to mouch, and you are to sail your boat briskly, and be hearty on it, and in little green Archie all glorious with new shiny paint. Also remember there was a time when you wrote to me, "I have a motor, may I bring it to Knole?" and that was even worse than waiting five weeks.

But I can't be really cheerful because I mind so dreadfully myself the very thing I am telling you not to mind.

Write to me often.

VITA TO HAROLD   *Knole*

21 June 1912

Will you not write to me once, a totally post-Hatfield letter? I want you to. I ought not to ask you, but I *am* asking. Write it when you are inclined.

You see, sometimes I mind the stiffness—no, not stiffness, but I can't find the word, and you will know—of our letters so much, and that would alleviate it.

Harold, do.

I'll never ask you but this once.

VITA TO HAROLD   *34 Hill Street*

4 July 1912

You asked me about rugs and yellow amber. I would love a rug. No, we will never make *des façons* about presents.

I have never given you anything. When is your birthday? Are you generous?

After all, I am not sorry not to know you better, it makes it even more fun your being a *terra incognita*. We will find each other out gradually. You will be disappointed.

There is no fun equal to being *quite* at the beginning of things. Is there?

VITA TO HAROLD   *Knole*

23 July 1912

I got a long letter from you. It was rather a startling letter. I am alone here for today so I can answer it. Shall I? Conscientiously?

You enlarged upon the disadvantages before you left England, and *then* I made very light of them, not only to you, but also to myself, and since you went I've thought them over, and I can't say they frighten me very much. So we can leave them out of the question. You see, 1) as for finding the life dull, I am never bored; 2) as for poverty we shouldn't be very poor, because the B.M. has been splendidly frank with me about that, and I know we shouldn't—rather the contrary; 3) and as for being forgotten in England, the people who matter don't forget, and those who don't, don't count. And though it would be silly to pretend I should like spending two or three years in Rio, I shouldn't mind it so very dreadfully—and anyway you wouldn't enjoy it any more than I should, and it would be just a boring thing, to be made the best of. To compensate for that, besides, there would be years in splendid places like Rome, where we should have an apartment in a palazzo, and have little parties for the people we must be civil to, and be a success. Because if I marry you, everything has got to be a success all through.

(You see I have abandoned maddening grammatical evasions quite as honestly as you did.)

But, Harold, though for months I've kept going almost entirely on plans—the delicious plans we used to write to each other—and though I have been wretched on each of the numerous and separate occasions when your leave has been delayed, and though there isn't 'anybody else' to compare with you—in spite of all that, I don't think we can marry this autumn. Don't be depressed by this; it doesn't mean anything awful, or that I am paving the way to worse! I am not. It just means this: that this is the first year I have lived at all (because last year doesn't count), and begun to make friends, and that if I let you take me away this year it will all end—after all, I am only twenty. I suppose it is selfish of me, because you are away, abroad, and not having what one calls a good time, and I am just beginning to, but let me be selfish for myself till next June, or even April, and I'll spend the rest of my life being unselfish for you. Besides, there really is

another reason. The B.M. would simply *hate* it. I know you will think
that if I wanted it sufficiently myself I should not stop to think about
that, but you are wrong: she has been wonderfully good to us both,
and we do owe her that.

Oh Harold, you must be so depressed and so disappointed by now,
but do read my letter several times as I did yours, and you will see
that it is quite sensible. But then sense is never attractive.

So when you come back in September let us be merely unspeak-
ably happy, and not think of when you have to go away again.
Someday there will be no more away.

And you will probably get quite tired enough of me then, in the
no-more-away-days, and be only too glad to have escaped six months
of it at the beginning!

Because you don't know me either, I'll give you a category too,
and then if you are frightened you needn't come home at all. What
you will mind most is my forgetfulness, which is phenomenal—I mean
I go downstairs to do something and then absolutely forget on the way
what I have come down for. This will not amuse you in the least after
a week of it. You will ask me to send the motor for you at the
Embassy, and I shall forget it. We shall have people to lunch, and I
shall forget to tell the servants. It will drive you quite crazy. That is
the worst, I think. Then I am just as untidy as you are, and disgracefully
happy-go-lucky and on the everything-will-turn-out-all-right-if-you-
don't-fuss-about-it system. This is because I am very lazy. I will come
out riding with you, but I won't gallop down hills, or jump, and do
anything like that because I am frightened—and you will get very
impatient about it. To make up for this cowardice, I don't fuss about
my health, and you must appreciate that as an inestimable blessing.
Then I am very selfish, and it bores me to do things for other people;
I like having things done for me. And of course this is a lamentable
characteristic under the circumstances.

Those are the drawbacks, to which you must add unpunctuality,
which irritates you even now. You will have to get over that by
putting the clocks on.

I don't know so much about my virtues. I'm very good-tempered
indeed, and that's about all. I'll never worry you when you are tired,
or give digs about your friends. And I shall probably like the books
you like—except that you are more *décadent* than me, and I'm essen-

tially breezy!—and I'm quite intelligent about them, and about tombs by Mino da Fiesole [1429–84]. I think that is quite a good list of virtues, all rather important ones. Up to now, too, I never have rows with the people I live with—and I'm very logical and very reasonable, and very amenable if people do it nicely, not if they try to compel. You are like that too. I think we should both *amène* each other quite easily. And of course, as we have always known, we are quite ludicrously suitable.

By the way, I'm atrociously jealous. So are you, and we may quarrel over that, especially you with me. But you mustn't make fusses about people I speak to more than once because I will always tell you about it, and we can laugh at them together.

And about your career—I will always be ready to go to dinner parties if you want me to, even if I am tired (will you be nice to me if I am ill?) and look nice, and you won't be ashamed of me.

And *surtout*—such a *surtout*—we will be wonderfully good friends.

After writing all this, and making pictures which are between the lines somewhere, I am half sorry I decided to be so firm about the autumn, but I'm going to keep to it, because it is fairer all round, to me, to you, to the B.M., and in September you will try to persuade me, and I shall say I won't. But in spite of that we will be engaged, if you like, even though people don't know about it. Then, some time we will have the tremendous fun of telling people like Anne [Sackville-West] and [Edward] Keeling—who has taken to writing me long letters about nothing at all.

If London gossip reaches Constantinople you may hear that I am engaged to someone [Lord Lascelles][1]—a new person this time—as simply everyone in London has been busy congratulating me about it, but it isn't true, and I didn't think there was anything in it at all, until to my intense astonishment he asked me (yesterday) to marry him. He must be mad; he hardly knows me, and I've never taken the slightest trouble about him. He's rather nice, poor thing, and a *parti!!* Don't tell the B.M. I told you about this episode, though. *How* I wish you were

---

1. Viscount Lascelles was, with Lord Granby, Harold's main rival for Vita's hand. He was heir to the Earldom of Harewood and the splendid house in Yorkshire that went with it. In 1922 he married Princess Mary, only daughter of King George V.

coming home on August 4th—in less than a fortnight. It's cruel, and I used awful Italian swear-words about it, which doesn't seem to have helped much.

Do you hate me for having sent such an unsatisfactory answer to your letter, or do you understand?

Goodbye, Harold, bless you.

VITA TO HAROLD   *Knole*

23 July 1912

You really won't like me much after a week or two, you know. You will hate coming home and finding me in rags and looking like nothing on earth, and you will resent my keeping beasts, and disgusting mongrel dogs. But that will only be in places like Teheran. In Rome or any decent place I should wear gorgeous clothes and jewels, and not be humble and dirty—except when we go to the one little ramshackle place which is all our own, near the sea. Harold, do you realise how happy we might be? We should bathe before breakfast on a deserted beach in the sun, and breakfast (unsociably) in the loggia, and read our letters to each other, and you would smoke horrid pipes, and I would wear green corduroy. We would take green Archie to pieces for the fun of it. And we would have a garden, because it would be in a climate where everything grows, and masses and masses of flowers. And a rather dark, very cool house. And in the evening we should sit out in the loggia, and read, or merely do nothing.

HAROLD TO VITA   *British Embassy, Constantinople*

14 January 1913

Vita darling,

This is written with a fountain pen as Reggie Cooper[1] is using my writing table. And I write badly with a fountain pen.

But it is rather fun, as I am sitting in the window seat, and it went

1. Harold's oldest friend, from schooldays, and his colleague in the Embassy.

and snowed last night and all the roofs are silent, unlike here, and it reminds me of Russia before I knew you and before I cared for life in the way I now do.

I wanted to get a frank opinion out of you about Vienna and I got it.[2] It is, of course, just what I feel myself. Even the snobbish feeling that it would be such fun to show you in a European place— sort of, "Look at this person, she is MY WIFE"—seems less attractive than having coffee with an untidy mar on the roof.

Of course Vienna is the very worst place of all socially. I mean they are all *touf touf* [snobbish] and uneducated and exclusive—and they won't at all like us taking up with grubby artists. But then we can have our two lives—one *touf touf* Embassy and one just Vita and Harold, and then we will go away often in a motor and sleep in little inns among the pines.

Vita darling, I should be happy wherever I was with you—and it is so splendid that we will always look at places in the same way—I mean you will know just what I hate, and just why I hate it, and I will know just why you are bored—and we will always want to go away at the same time.

And then, Vita—and this is to be pondered over—we will keep each other up to the mark. I don't think, poor darling, you have any conception how dull diplomatic dinners are—especially if you don't play bridge—which by the way you don't play. (Also what about golf—lazy.)

I have read this letter again up to where I have got. I see I have gone round the central subject, which is that we've jolly well got to go to Vienna anyhow. Don't you agree? More from the ghastly selfishness of it as regards my people [Sir Arthur and Lady Nicolson] than from any feeling that I would hurt my career by not going.

Anyhow there is time. If only we could get married by June we could come out to Therapia[3] for three months. Which would be awful fun—except we would have to go to the hotel. Vita, it would be fun, you and I, wouldn't it, at Therapia?

I don't think my people will go to Vienna till November.

---

2. He had written that his father might be appointed Ambassador to Austria, and he might have to go, too. Vita was appalled by the idea. In the end, neither went.
3. The summer resort of the British Embassy on the European shore of the Bosphorus.

Oh Vita, I've got such a cold in my head and I talk so funny. That's why this letter's so dull

HGN[4]

VITA TO HAROLD   *Hill Hall, Epping*

30 January 1913

I am horrid about Vienna, I know, not only because I couldn't be an Eastern potentate there, but because the whole thing would be so stodgy. And of course I shall hate diplomacy! You are always saying so, and I suppose you are right. But I love you, little Harold, so what are we to do about it? Of course the castle by the sea, and the vague expeditions in Archie, and our solitude *à deux,* were and are glimpses of perfection and Paradise, but, oh Harold, the rest! . . . And after a few years, when we had got tired of Archie, and the solitude *à deux,* and of everything being a new toy, as we *must,* there will remain— what? Rio de Janeiro, boring old diplomats, no English friends, no B.M. _ _ _ _ _ _ _ _ _ _ _ _ (as they do in French novels).

Aren't I being depressing about it?

I am wrong—aren't I, Harold? and the truth is a rose-coloured story culminating in you and me making a State entry into Delhi on an elephant with a golden howdah, and you receiving deputations of Indian princes, and me watching, and thinking, "If it hadn't been for me, he wouldn't be here now", because *j'aurai été pour quelque chose,* shouldn't I?

Write and cheer me up, and don't tell me I shall hate diplomacy. (I shall though).

HAROLD TO VITA   *British Embassy, Constantinople*

30 January 1913

There may be something happening today. It is rather complicated. You see the whole question is like this. Europe sent a letter to the

---

4. He often signed himself by his initials only, even in his most intimate letters.

Turkish Government saying 'make peace'.[1] They thought about it a long time and were just writing back "yes", when the revolution occurred[2] and the answer was never sent. The new Government were thinking what answer *they* were to send—and then they told us that the answer was to be at the Austrian Embassy by 11.0 today.

So we were all sitting with our cyphers ready to telegraph it to London when news came that the note had left the Sublime Porte and then suddenly a man ran after it and stopped it just at the door of the Austrian Embassy—and took it back.

Does this interest you? Do you know what it means? It may mean anything—war, revolution or peace.

And then again news that Romania is mobilising.

How dead and dim and distant this must all seem to you, darling: only one day it will interest you as much as it does me.

And thank God I am so busy that I have little time to sit in armchairs and ponder over big-eyed mars [Vita]—or even to write to them.

V ITA TO H AROLD　　　　　　　　　　　　　　　　　*Knole*

15 February [1913]

I got such a blowing-up from you this morning. I'm not *décadente*, you little wretch, and I *was* ill, and I *never* faint, so when I do, it matters (I'm not your grandmother, and I won't be compared to her), and if you don't like me you had better marry somebody else, and see how you like it, so there!

And you know I'm not 'cultured' (how dare you!), but essentially primitive; and not 1913, but 1470; and not 'modern'; and you know I am nicer than anybody else, and you love me more than anybody in the world,—you know you do. And you know Ozzie[3] knows

1. With Bulgaria, Serbia, and Greece, whose troops had captured Salonika and were approaching Constantinople.
2. On 23 January, when Enver Bey seized power and the Turkish army mutinied.
3. Oswald Dickinson, a lifelong bachelor and patron of the arts. He was more Harold's and Lady Sackville's friend than Vita's.

nothing about it at all, and if I don't "seem to care much about any of the others", you know why; and you know if I leave my beautiful Knole which I adore, and my B.M. whom I adore, and my Ghirlandaio room which I adore, and my books and my garden and my freedom which I adore—it is all for you, whom I don't care two straws about.

Now you dare to deny a word of all that.

I will sit on the arm of your chair and read your dispatches over your shoulder, and rumple your curls, which will make you cross. And I want to be there when you are ill, and go out though you begged me to stay with you, so that you would appreciate me more when I came in. And I want to give dinner-parties in *our* house, when we will be so bored with the people because we would rather be alone. And it will be such fun becoming familiar with each other's possessions, and you will come into my room and use my brushes with "VITA" on them.

All this will be fun.

PS. I'm *not* decadent!!! You wouldn't like me if I was. I shall revenge myself by not burning incense in *our* house when we have parties, and you'll see how you like the smell of Brussels sprouts.

HAROLD TO VITA   *British Embassy, Constantinople*

17 February 1913

I see that it would be nicer to go to Rome or Tangier or to stay here. I notice that Vienna combines everything which we will both of us most dislike.

But then I *do* feel a *duty* to go—I would think less of us if we didn't go—I would think it a lack of discipline—morally 'sloppy' if we got out of it. Besides I really must be the one who 'disposes' in these things.

I tell you this because I want you to understand that this is the basis of our life that is to be. I will be invariably weak about trifles—but about big things I am to have the upper hand.

I know that in the bottom of your heart you think, "Oh yes, it's very well for him to say that, but he doesn't know what I give up."

But I *do* know what you give up. I know that by marrying me you give up vast worldly things—but they don't matter. And then any girl by marriage gives up her girlhood—which is so much.

Of course this is common to all, but then the diplomacy thing in your case is worse. Because, Vita, you will be admired (especially at Vienna) in the wrong way. You will be admired in the way that people will be surprised to find you can't dance better.

And this (though a tiny thing) is illustrative of the general irritation which their attitude will evoke. Darling Vita.

So you see, I admit the utter weakness of my position. I see how utterly you will hate doing what I am asking you to do, and yet I ask it, because deep down I know you will give this up to me, and that you will yourself not let me run away from it when I want to.

And, Vita, pull yourself together, you vague person: pull up all the blinds in your mind—and think whether you want it.

Darling, be *sure* about it before you decide. And remember that whatever you do—if you never speak to me again—I shall know that you were right.

VITA TO HAROLD   *Knole*

24 February 1913

Violet Keppel and I gave a party. It was *the* success of the year. The Rubens lady, who is jealous of VK, was furious. Especially when Violet and I acted afterwards, and ended up in each other's arms. I disguise from the Rubens lady when Violet comes here.

HAROLD TO VITA   *British Embassy, Constantinople*

26 February 1913

No letter from you for ten days. I know you are not ill, because B.M., in her last letter, says, "V. will have told you all about our last party." I know no letters can have been lost as I have got regular ones from my family.

Oh Vita, this is so dreadful for me—being left without letters. I know, I mean I *hope,* you will be saying, "Silly boy—why does he get into a state about nothing?"

But *is* it nothing, Vita? You must see how I look on it. I know you have nothing to do—and I am busy all day and yet find time to write to you four times a week. Oh Vita! And I know that in a case like this there can be no question of indolence. You can't be too *lazy* to write to me. At least if you are too lazy it means that you don't care one fig. It can't mean anything else. You see I always come up against that granite wall.

And there are lots of little things which make me feel it also. Little absurd things which mean enormously. Things like your never telling me about things that interest me—no I *don't* mean that, because everything you write does interest me—but somehow when I get some of your letters I feel you have not thought of the many things I would like to hear of—of your room, of your clothes, of the people you see—yes even of *Rosencavalier.* [1]

Oh Vita! Vita! I am making you angry and all because I am wretched myself. Yes wretched—and so frightfully disappointed to come back here early and to wait for the post because I feel sure there *must, must* be a letter from you today. I thought you would have *at least* written to say you couldn't get the Fortnum stuff. How I should love it if you made me get *your* stuff.

And then there is another thing—*not* a little thing—which has hurt me awfully, and in a point where you might have known me frightfully sensitive. You have only been once to see my mother since I left. Of course I know that it is shy-making and very tiresome. But still you know (or you ought to have guessed) that nothing in the world would give me more pleasure than that.

Is this a foolish letter to write, Vita? But it is only because my eyes are stinging with disappointment and my heart is sore—sore, Vita—and you are so far away, and I don't know what's happening.

Oh Vita, they are playing in my sitting room. (I write this in my bedroom with your photograph there), and, Vita, they are playing, *"Il pleure dans mon coeur comme il pleut sur la ville"*—and I feel it so, and I look over the wet roofs, and Mikky [dog] is by the fire—and

---

1. Harold was virtually tone-deaf throughout his life.

No! No! No! I can't bear it, you out there laughing with strange people, people I don't know, people who may have a power over your mind—and sometimes, before dinner, you write me a letter while Rosamund is having her bath, and it is written so lightly and goes so far, and is so important when it gets there.

HAROLD TO VITA   *British Embassy, Constantinople*

3 March 1913

I went to the front on Saturday. I went dressed up as a doctor with a red crescent and a fez like this, and they were fighting just behind the field hospital  and the maxims [machine-guns] made a noise like a motor bicycle, and I got so nervous and the wounded came in, and there were heaps of them and they sobbed when they were moved, and when their coats were taken off they screamed. And there were three officers who ran away, and they hid in the launch that had brought me up. And everybody said the Bulgars would be in at any minute and that we would have to bolt. And in the garden there was a cherry tree in full blossom and under it two pails full of bits of soldiers that they had cut off.

You would have liked it all, being a callous mar with big eyes, who has special note-paper for red-cross things.

And I took 22 wounded back in the launch with me and it was awfully rough and they were so ill. And they asked me about Adrianople, and when I said it was captured, they said "as God wills," which is what is written on the bit of embroidery I gave you.

Oh Vita, I sat there in the upper room making a splint for one of the people who were groaning below, and the rain slashed against the rattling window and the cherry blossoms shimmered in the failing light, and still the rattle went on beyond the village over the hill. And I thought of you warm and secure somewhere, my Vita, secure and unsuffering, and myself callous comparatively about the people downstairs, and thinking of you while I made the splint. I was left alone in the dark with the noise of the waves and the outline of the officer at the wheel against the glow in the sky.

But it was capable of me to get out—as no foreigner has been, not even the military Attachés, since when they got to Chavalia, they said they would shoot foreigners at sight.

So who says I am not capable!!

VITA TO HAROLD   *Knole*

4 March [1913]

Harold, you wrote me a long tempestuous letter [26th February], and it upset me so, I didn't know how to answer it, though I wanted to sit down straight away and write you a letter which would have consoled you altogether. I am sorry, miserable that I have hurt you, and don't, *don't* say, "She doesn't care," because she does, only things are so difficult sometimes, and to understand it all, you must think yourself into the atmosphere in which I am living, in which I hear nothing but case, case, case,[1] and when is it coming on? and the months it will be before it is settled, and the B.M. showing me (so kindly, but so inexorably) the impossibility of contemplating anything yet for you and me—it is all drops on a stone, and I get hopeless about it, and try to put it out of my mind, and to take an interest in parties, and then I suppose I involuntarily write *agacée* letters to you, until you write to me like you have done now, which brings me to my senses. Harold—you don't know, and how am I to tell you? but you are ever-present to me, and if I am slack and bored, it is because you are not here, and if I am cross, it is for the same reason, and if people bore me, it is because I want to talk to you,—don't you see? And then sometimes (this is so silly and rather BS[2] and I hate you for making me tell you, but I suppose I must) sometimes I think you are really quite happy there with your Gerry [Wellesley] and your wars, and I am not by any means all-important, and so again I write you a beastly

1. The Scott "undue influence" case, which began on 24 June in the High Court, London.
2. "Backstairs"—Sackville jargon for common.

letter, or I don't write at all. It is this long delay and separation that
upsets our apple-cart, and gets on our nerves. I do see it is worse for
you, much worse.

Then about parties, I think it can't interest you to get a week-old
list, but since it does interest you, you shall have it, and I am glad you
wrote that letter because it clears up a lot.

Go out for a ride with the wind in your face, Harold, and don't
be morbid, and imagine I care nothing for you.

(This is me trying to be bracing.)

Of course I love you—you make untidy parcels, and read yourself
into despair over *décadent* French poets, and you want me badly; and
to other people you are just clever and someone who will get on. They
don't know how far (you and I do), and we are going to do it together,
and they will say, "She has helped him tremendously." Because I shall
have.

But not if you write me morbid letters.

I wish you were here.

HAROLD TO VITA   *British Embassy, Constantinople*

10 March [1913]

My dearest Vita,

Your letter has arrived—the answer to my beastly one of which
I am so penitent, and you have heaped more coals than ever, and I am
a perfect idiot—and you are quite right about its all being morbid,
and my oughting to go out and ride, and have the Black Sea wind in
my hair.

I will do it tomorrow and I will take your letter with me, and
I will ride to the sea's edge, and let you blow into me, and afterwards
I will ride home into the sunset. Which will be like something by your
friend [John] Masefield.

And Vita, I will wait and wait and wait for you—and be patient
unendingly—and unendingly will I resolve not to bother you again
or to be morbid.

Because you are firm and splendid, Vita—and all should be right
with my world. My world that has been rather tremulous of late.

How feeble to be tremulous, Vita, when there is a splendid mar
over there in England—with the rooks tumbled against the grey sky.
And here, in little funny corners, snowdrops are coming.

Thank you V. for your letter.

VITA TO HAROLD   *Hotel De Inglaterra, Seville*

17 April [1913]

This is the life for me[1]: gipsies, dancing, disreputable artists, bull-
fights. Oh Harold, I can't paint to you the state of mind I am in by
now, I feel I can *never* go back to that humdrum existence; I am a
different being. Last night there was dancing at the house of a French
artist; imagine the little patio, open to the sky, with the fountain
trickling, and the moonlight, and the gipsies in their coloured shawls;
I know them all intimately! and go to their houses in *such* a slum, with
a strange creature who has come to live here and has 'gone native', and
won't speak to English people, but accepts me as a kindred spirit,
irritated by the tourists in perpetual search after 'local colour', Mrs
Hunter meanwhile thinking I am sight-seeing in the cathedral. Then
I got a letter from you and it was so in tune with Seville, and we might
have two rooms here, Harold, with a roof, mightn't we?, and my
gipsies will come and dance for us while we smoke cigarettes. It is the
feria here now. We go to bull-fights, and I wear a black mantilla and
a high comb and carnations, and hang my orange *manton* over the edge
of the box, and shout "yolé! bravo toro!" You would laugh at me so,
and be awfully good for me, and say I was more Spanish than the
Spaniards, and I shouldn't care.

VITA TO HAROLD   *Grand Hotel de Russie, Rome*

10 May 1913

I am absolutely alone in Rome! Not even a maid, and this evening
I start for London quite alone. I'm so frightened, but I mean to see

1. Vita had gone on holiday to Spain with Mrs. Charles Hunter.

Rome today. Mrs Hunter left today. Shall I get into the wrong train
and come to Constantinople by myself instead of London? Or go right
away where no one would ever find me? To my Sevillian gipsies? It
is the chance of a lifetime and no one would ever hear of me again,
and it would be in the *Daily Mail.* [1]

HAROLD TO VITA   *British Embassy, Constantinople*

19 May 1913

Vita darling—darling Vita

I got a terrible letter from you today [2] and it has quite crushed me
with apprehensions. You put the fierce part into French, half because
you were a little ashamed of it and half because you felt it sounded
deadly earnest. But then it was so steely to use French.

Vita, I can't answer coherently about it. I have been trying to
diminish the effect of it to myself. I have been explaining that you
began the letter quite lazily in the garden—and quite thoughtlessly
you put that in the end because you were alone, and had come back
to England [from Spain] and found your house secure, welcoming and
comfortable, and my letters in the bustle of arrival had seemed flat and
impersonal, and you had read them in the wrong order, and while
people were asking you questions, and they had left no after-glow—
and so you ended your letter almost brutally, in an impulse of irritation
and in the reaction to the home-coming excitement and the sort of
feeling, "Well there is going to be nothing exciting now till Harold
comes home, and will that be exciting? I wonder, now."

Oh Vita Vita, but did you think that those easy cruel little French
sentences would go 1,500 miles—and knock the sun out of my days
and make even the clock tick differently.

Oh Vita, if I could talk to you now I might do something—but
what can a letter do if I have lost touch with you? I opened it in my

---

1. Harold replied: "I don't like one bit that you're going about alone like that. When you
   are my wife, I shall not allow you to go without Emily [her maid] to look after you."
2. It has not survived. Perhaps Harold destroyed it in his anguish. But obviously she was
   hinting that their semi-engagement should be ended.

room and Reggie Cooper came in and saw something was the matter, but he has no idea what is the matter, or how hard and terrible a thing it may be, and how vague and uncombatable.

And I, these last days, have been thinking, thinking, thinking, thinking about how it could be hurried up. And I was going to make a huge row about it and we were going to get married hurriedly—and quietly—and you were coming off to little autumn tours with me in Archie. And now it will be three days before I can get a letter from you and to know whether it was a mood.

I feel that you may be sounding the ground for worse news in your next letter.

Vita, surely you could not treat me like that. I feel I should kill you. And all those bright plan-edifices to be pulled down and shoved away by a few words at the end of a letter—like a Christmas tree the day after.

Vita, is it because I am flippant about us both—and don't talk heroics—that you think I won't mind? Why, it would alter the whole substance of things. You have worked in and out of the bits of me, and it would be such a fearful tangle to undo and it would hurt so awfully. (There I am using slang about vital things—which is a silly trick—but it doesn't make the things less vital.) And Vita, I was coming back so soon now—only six weeks—and I had planned it all out so. Oh Vita really really I get so angry—so repugnant about it all.

I suppose I felt too sure of you and this doubt shows me how thin the ice is. But at least, Vita, let me have some slight consolation for the moment—and wait till you see me before being really cruel.

And I love *you* so far more than ever before—the longing after you is like a stretched cord within me.

Of course it's all this damned artistic temperament that has been the muddle for both of us; the inveterate habit of seeing both sides.

And Vita, Vita, *why* on earth if the [Scott] case is won should we not get married at once? I always counted on that in my silly ass way. And now I have nothing to count on. Except that you can't have meant it, Vita; you can't have meant to write it to me out here: you would have kept it till I got home.

H.

VITA TO HAROLD   *Knole*

20 May [1913]

Mea culpa! mea maxima culpa! I come to you in sack-cloth and ashes, and humble myself to the dust at your feet, a bad naughty mar who hardly dares hope to be forgiven. Did you think, Harold, that you had at last got the much discussed terrible letter, or at least a warning? No, what you really got was just an ill-tempered storm from a wanderer who felt caged again after weeks of liberty, and was cross in consequence, and rebellious of iron bars—and, you poor, rash, ill-advised Harold, that is what you so lightly contemplate undertaking for life, something you know nothing about, which is liable to give you these frights . . . but who would at least make up for it afterwards, as you might see if you were here now. But how much happier and more comfortable you would be with something more in the nature of the Rubens lady [Rosamund], not the Rubens lady herself, *mais enfin dans ce genre-là,* very gentle and dependent and clinging.

Oh Harold darling, I *am* sorry, I didn't mean to upset you, or being strictly truthful I suppose I did at the time, but I don't now; the only real true thing was that I do frightfully want you back. It is too awful your always being away, and eight months is a lifetime, and I don't know what I shall do if it has to happen again. I did write to you the very next day, but I didn't dare send it, so I tore it up and waited to see what would happen. Now your telegram has happened, and I answered it, and by now as I write you must have got mine, which is a comfort.[1] Also I got a letter from you so pleased to come back, and in it you said you wouldn't let me travel alone (I shall, though!), and you made me feel a beast. Which I am. Harold, darling, I do want you to forgive me, you never will, and you will say I am capricious and despicable, and no more reasonable than Gwen [Harold's young sister], for all I am twenty-one. I *wish* I had never sent that letter, I do. Why do I do these mad things? and then I am sorry afterwards. If only this could get to you quickly, quickly, but it will take four days and all that time you will have only a miserable telegram, and while you are playing golf you will remember there is

---

1. Vita's telegram, in reply to his which asked her if he was to take her letter seriously, read (in French), "No. Forgive me. Don't believe a word of it."

something wrong, without quite knowing what it is. But there *isn't* anything wrong, it is all all right, and soon you will come back to me, in the summer, and we will play in the garden and make the best of our two months. Write to me, and say I am a ridiculous mar, but that you aren't angry with me. Only before that I suppose I shall get an upset letter from you,—and then I shall beat my head against the wall.

Tu me pardonnes?

VITA TO HAROLD   *34 Hill Street*
                                   Berkeley Square, W.
29 May [1913]

Today I went to such a *touf-touf* lunch at the Ritz. There were Rodin,[1] and Sargent,[2] and Mrs [Nancy] Astor, and others, and Lord Crewe,[3] whom I sat by. I love that sort of party, it is such a relief after the little silly pink and whites one sits by at dinner-parties for balls, who only ask one if one has been here, and is going there. After two days I am sick of it, except a very fine ball at Sunderland House, *un bal un peu propre,* not one of those scrimmages at the Ritz, but powdered footmen announcing duchesses. *N'est ce pas dégoutant d'être snob à ce point-là?* But I *do* like fit things, I do, I do, I do, I can't help it, and if I had the chance I would *faire les choses richement bien.* You know I would, and we will—someday. Then I went to an exceedingly amusing arty party at the Laverys,[4] given for Rodin, where I sat by a pianist called Mark Hambourg[5] who would talk to me about Bach— to *me! c'était bien trouvé.* And little Edward Keeling goes to balls, and I see him hovering shyly in corners. Next week there is an Albert Hall ball (one of the entertainments you say I shall miss in Vienna), where I am in the Louis XIV court as La Grande Mademoiselle; such good clothes, orange velvet and black, a riding dress with high boots and

---

1. Auguste Rodin (1840–1917), the French sculptor, who had fallen in love with Lady Sackville, and done several busts of her.
2. John Singer Sargent (1856–1925) had painted Lady Sackville's portrait, but she so much disliked it that he drew another in charcoal, which she thought sufficiently flattering. It is now at Sissinghurst.
3. 1st Marquess of Crewe, at that time Secretary of State for India.
4. (Sir) John Lavery, the fashionable painter.
5. Mark Hambourg, the pianist and composer. Vita, like Harold, was quite unmusical.

a *cravache* [riding-whip], and if you look in the illustrated papers you will find me probably.

Tonight there is a dinner of 70 at the Keppels to which I am going, so I am being conscientious about my season—my last? And how I hate it!

Harold, I have an awful feeling that this engagement of ours has so far brought you more worry than pleasure. Don't blame me entirely, but the exceptional circumstances. (Me too a little).

HAROLD TO VITA   *53 Cadogan Gardens, S.W.*[1]

28 July 1913

My family are in a perfect glow of enthusiasm about Knole, its owners, inhabitants and hospitality. I am glad they were so pleased. Father volunteered a statement that when you were in the room he could not look at anyone else. And I think he meant it, as it is a decorative Vita, with heavy eyes and hair as I said before.

But darling, I do feel so funny inside about you—oh my darling darling Vita who will be so absolutely mine one day—mine in a way that possession has nothing to do with—and which will be a sort of fire-fusion, darling—and there are such wonderful, terrifying abysmal things that will happen in our amazing marriage. I mean darling, that I feel giddy at the thought of you as my wife—giddy in a wider sense than the odd whirl-feeling that comes over one on your triangular piled sofa—oh my darling, you don't know how passionate I am—and how it frightens me—and how glad I am of it.

VITA TO HAROLD   *Knole*

28 July 1913

I think we are past mere words now, and I can only write to you about chairs and presents, but all the while my room is full of your

---

1. Harold returned from Constantinople on 3 July 1913 in time to hear Vita give her evidence in the Scott case, which the Sackvilles won easily. He stayed with his parents in London until his wedding in October.

presence as though you were smiling at me across my judge's desk,[1]
and every possible receptacle is full of your nasty cigarette ends.
Goodnight, my poor boy, so hating Buxton.[2] It *is* a shame, but rather
good for us to have a chance of thoroughly missing each other, which
we shan't have after this for many years.

HAROLD TO VITA   *Palace Hotel, Buxton, Derbyshire*

13 August 1913

Darling, it is so dull writing to you when I might be talking and
looking at you. Vita, there are moments when the whole wind-swept
sky seems to stagger at my happiness and at my hopes. No, it wasn't
the same with poor dear Eileen.[3] It was less 'cosmic'. I fear it was less
inspiring. Oh my darling, how I ache for that poor girl and the
abominable way I behaved. I feel it more remorsefully now than I have
ever felt it.

VITA TO HAROLD   *Hotel Meurice, Paris*

Wednesday [3 September 1913]

I have been spending the afternoon at Rodin's atelier. B.M., having worn herself out over sheets for us, and bath-mats for us to get
out on from the bath which won't exist, was too tired to go, and I
went alone (terrified) and bearded Rodin, by invitation, of course, in
his nice messy atelier which used to be a convent, and which is now
very dilapidated and where he is supremely happy. I was shown into
his room, and waited there a few minutes—do you know how sug-
gestive a person's room can be, before they come? It was rather dark,

---

1. The Italian desk given to Vita by her mother on her twenty-first birthday. It is now at
   Sissinghurst.
2. In Derbyshire, where Harold was staying with his parents.
3. Lady Eileen Wellesley, a daughter of the 4th Duke of Wellington, and sister of Harold's
   close friend, Gerald Wellesley (7th Duke). Harold had been unofficially engaged to her
   when he met Vita. Later she married Cuthbert Orde, the painter.

and there were huge roughly-hewn lumps of marble and a chisel left on a chair where he had put it down, and nothing else, and the suggestiveness of it grew on me more and more as I waited, and then he came in, very gentle and vague, and rather a commonplace little French bourgeois with long boots and the Légion d'Honneur in his buttonhole—rather an unreal little fat man, like a skit on the Académiciens in a funny paper, and the whole thing was a reaction and a come-down from the massive white marbles all round. But not when he talks about them, and points out lines to one with a real sculptor's sweep of his thumb, and he draws his finger lovingly across the marble brow of Mozart, and he and Mozart seem to smile at each other.

He gave me a bronze, signed, a statuette of a man, *une étude,* as he calls it. He has some magnificent things there at his studio. He has two people flying, which is supposed to be *l'aviation.* I admit that it sounds dreadful, but in reality it is beautiful, and rather the same idea as the Florence Mercury (that sounds like a newspaper, but I mean the Giambologna). And the head of Mozart, which is half strength and half-reverie, perfectly marvellous, and then two great clasped hands emerging out of a block of marble, and he says, *"Voyez les doigts entrelacés."*

HAROLD TO VITA   *Foreign Office*

19 September 1913

My dearest you know you have no idea how fond I am of you—because when things are really serious with me I become reserved about them. And I feel so dreadfully that you do not care nearly as much for me. There are such heaps of signs that you don't—your letting me go away so easily, and your being cross with me about getting my hair cut.

Darling, I know these things are absurd, and I don't mind really, as all I want is for you to let me adore you: and then, when we are married, perhaps you will get to care for me too. I mean really care—not just like. Except I know you care more than just like already, but it is not that absolute abandonment of self which I feel.

Darling, it was so nice when I was tired yesterday and you let me put my head on your shoulder.

Is this a depressed letter? But I am depressed.[1]

---

1. They were married, in the chapel at Knole, on 1 October 1913.

They spent their honeymoon traveling through Italy and Egypt (where they stayed with Lord Kitchener) and thence to Constantinople, where Harold resumed his duties as third secretary at the Embassy. They had their own house at Cospoli, overlooking the Golden Horn, and Vita made her first garden there. In June 1914 they returned to England, and their first son, Benedict (Ben), was born at Knole two days after the outbreak of World War I.

In 1915 they bought Long Barn, a tumbled-down fourteenth-century cottage near Knole, which they repaired and extended, and this was their country home till 1932, when they moved permanently to Sissinghurst. In London they lived at 182 Ebury Street, where their third son, Nigel (a second son was born dead in November 1915), was born on 19 January 1917. Harold was exempted from military service during the war by his essential work in the Foreign Office. Vita was beginning to write poetry and novels.

Vita to Harold   *Knole*

9 July 1914

My darling Harold,

I am writing this in case I should die when Mikki III[1] is born instead of encumbering my will with small details. I know that you will carry out everything I want, and that no one will try to interfere with you so doing.

---

1. Mikki I and II were Harold's dogs. Mikki III turned out to be Benedict (Ben), born at Knole on 6 August 1914.

By my will I leave you everything of which I die possessed: jewels, furniture, pictures, books, *everything*. I want you to distribute certain things as follows:

If our baby is a girl, and lives, you must keep for her until you esteem her old enough to appreciate them:

1) my emerald chain
2) my string of pearls
3) my rope tiara,

and all my other jewels with the exceptions I will make below.

My other tiara, the one with the leaf pattern in emeralds and diamonds, is to go to Knole and be made an heirloom.

Give my diamond crystal watch, the one Sevenoaks gave me, to Rosamund [Grosvenor], also the diamond and crystal hat-pin, and any two of my rings that she may like to choose, except my engagement ring, which I should like you, Harold, to keep for yourself. If there is any other small thing that Rosamund particularly wants, give it to her, darling; you will have so much left for yourself.

Give Irene Pirie[2] some small jewel of mine; you can choose it.

Give Muriel Kerr-Clark my diamond wrist-watch on a black ribbon; and I should like you to send some small jewel to each of the following, and say it was at my request: Dorothy Heneage, Olive Rubens,[3] Lady Connie [Constance] Hatch, Aunt Maude, Aunt Cecilie, Aunt Mary, [Aunt] Eva, Anne Stanley, your mother, Emily [maid].

Give Gwen [Harold's sister] the seven big diamonds, the emerald ornament your mother gave me as a wedding-present, and one or two of my rings.

Will you keep my red amber [necklace] for yourself? and only let your daughter wear it if you would like her to, and if she is like me.

Now if the baby is a boy, you must dispose of the surplus jewels as you think best. Keep them, if you like, for your daughter if you marry again and have one. I should like her to have them. Or

---

2. Born Irene Hogarth, a childhood friend, whom Vita always called by the Italianized version of her first name, Pace.

3. Mrs. Walter Rubens, the singer, an intimate friend of Lord Sackville.

give them to Mikki III for his wife when he marries, if he does so with your approval and if you are convinced they love each other as we do.

Give Dada [Lord Sackville] a piece of furniture; perhaps he would like the big writing-table in my sitting room; he can use it without its platform.

B.M. would not care for any of my things, except the copies of Miss Linley, the Duke of Dorset, the Duchess his wife, and the three children.[4] Give her those. And any very personal thing she would like.

Everything at Constantinople goes to you. Please never get rid of the Kuba you gave me, or of Barbara [see note, p. 19]. I should like you to have Barbara always in your own room; she knew us both so well from the very beginning. Keep Mikki I [dog] with you, *please.* If you marry again, which I expect you will, and hope you will to save you from being lonely, don't be just the same with her as you were with me; give her a place of her own, but don't let her take mine exactly. I am not jealous of her, but I should like there to be a difference somewhere, and don't teach her our [family] expressions.

Darling, it is so lovely in the garden, and I hope I shan't die; I want years and years more with you as my play-fellow. I am not morbid, but I don't want to die a bit, and somehow today it seems impossible that I should. I love you so, my own darling husband; we are so mar, and we have such fun together always, I refuse to believe that it can be cut off.

All the same, in case it is, will you take care of all my manuscripts and ask Dada to have them put away in the muniment room at Knole, except the poems I wanted to publish; please publish these for me.[5] Rosamund has two books of mine which you must put in the muniment room too, and Violet Keppel has another.

Give Violet Keppel my small sapphire and diamond ring.

I can't think of anybody else just now, but if I have left anyone out, please supplement it.

---

4. All pictures at Knole. Miss Linley (by Gainsborough) and The Three Children (by Hoppner) were sold to American collections to raise duties on the deaths of the 3rd and 4th Lord Sackvilles.
5. These poems were published by Vita herself in *Constantinople* (1915) and *Poems of West and East* (1917).

Darling, I suppose I must say goodbye, because if ever this letter comes to you it will be after a bigger goodbye than we have ever said. Anyhow we shall have had nearly a year of absolutely unmarred perfect happiness together, and you know I loved you as completely as one person has ever loved another. There hasn't been a single cloud the whole time, and at least you will never have the torment of feeling that we might have made more of each other while we had each other because that would not have been possible. If I could have these months over again I would not alter a day of them—would you? I don't think many people could say as much.

You will never know how I have loved you, Harold.

Mar

God bless you, God bless you, my darling.

HAROLD TO VITA   *Foreign Office*

15 August 1914

I am afraid I won't be able to come down tonight—and it gives me a sink which even the consciousness of virtue and efficiency won't elate. Darling Mar, you would laugh if you could feel how depressed I get when I am not going to see my own darling. No one else in the whole world matters a halfpenny compared to you my angel, and it is only near you that I feel happy and at peace. When I have to go away I feel sore and sensitive as if the whole world has T.I.[1]—and I long to get back to my little black head. I don't know what it is, I never felt helpless before when I was alone—but now when I am without you I feel I can't cope with anything.

Oh my angel, I long for this most un-through-leaves[2] period to be over, and to get my own darling to myself again.

Give a hug from me to that odd little funny [Benedict] which happened the other day.

---

1. Thin Ice—a Sackville expression for an awkward or delicate situation.
2. Another Sackville expression, meaning difficult, unpleasant.

HAROLD TO VITA   *53 Cadogan Gardens,*
                                        London S.W.
11 September 1914

My own darling Mar,

I have been blaming myself all day about my attitude to B.M.[1]
It is a tremendous tug-of-war within me and I don't know which side
is the stronger.

You see, darling, on the one hand everything in me cries out in
loathing of B.M.—of her vain empty insincere nature—and I get hot
with shame to think that I have allowed myself to pander to her vanity,
to adulate her emptiness and to abet her insincerity.

And on the other hand I think of that soft gentle little head
[Vita's], and I blame myself for even dreaming for one instant that
anything you could love could be really vile, and I feel guilty that I
have allowed my self-control to get cracks in it out of which all this
jar and jangle has escaped into our sun-lit world.

And then again I feel, with you, my own gentlest, that this is a
terrible thing to have happened, and that now at last has arisen
something which comes between us—a thing about which you and
I feel differently: on the one side your clean gentle love for
B.M., and on the other my hatred for the vain egoist who has humiliated me.

And this can't go on, my dear one. We must make a treaty about
it—a treaty of alliance not against B.M. and not in favour of B.M.,
but just a treaty of defence against the subtle difference and even
discord that B.M.'s destructive personality might in the end intrude
between us—between *us* my darling who love each other so passionately. Why the mere fact that she is the only thing on earth which
could cause a cloud on our blue sky makes me hate her with a yet
intenser loathing.

Darling, you must see that it will take me years to get over the
wounds that B.M. has dealt to my pride, and I fear that never, never
can I hope to form one of her sycophants. Without that ultimate

---

1. Lady Sackville had been insisting that Benedict be given the additional name Lionel, to
which his parents agreed under protest. She had also abused Harold's parents, and he lost
his temper, then apologized.

humbling of myself I fear that between her and me there can be no peace.

Little spirit of gentleness and love, don't think I am being a hard egoist about it: but really, darling, when I look down the vista of humiliation which my future co-operation with B.M. would entail, I realise quite calmly that I would emerge from each defeat with less self respect, and that our upper-air love for each other would get weighted with shame till it sank into the foetid atmosphere where she reigns supreme.

Darling, you are of finer stuff than I am and can afford to descend into these *bas fonds* as an administering angel. But I have not the strength of character.

And meanwhile our youth and peace are being given blows like the blows of a vulture's beak.

Oh my love I am not angry tonight, only smarting under the degrading letter[2] I wrote to her this morning.

Dear Mar, you know you used to say you would mind so fearfully if I and B.M. fell out—and darling, I do feel such a beast. In all the turmoils I go through, I get back to hearing my conscience say, "the one difficult thing you could have done for her you have failed to do."

Oh my love, my love!

Harold

VITA TO HAROLD   *Long Barn, Weald, Sevenoaks*

25 June [1915]

Somewhere I hear Detto [Ben] whimpering in his pram because he is bored, and you are in London, and it is all very workaday and commonplace, I suppose, to anyone else's eyes. One marries and has a mar, and settles down and you daily-bread. Only to you and me, darling, it does not mean that, because there is a great warm enveloping radiance, and Detto stands for wonderful things ("What does Mikki

---

2. Agreeing to the name Lionel. But Benedict never used it, and was known throughout his life as Ben only.

say?") and because every evening when you come back our minds and our hands rush together and merge and are happy to be one again instead of two, and everything which is dear and intimate to us is mutually so, and your life is mine, and mine is yours. Darling, please don't think I am sentimental, because I am not. I don't love you morbidly, but strongly, and tenderly, and passionately, and every way. It is all made up out of different sorts of love, and the result is something very companionable really, only there is something as well which makes me want to tell you about it.

VITA TO HAROLD   *[Long Barn]*

[November 1915]

Harold, I am sad, I have been thinking of that little white velvet coffin with that little still thing inside.[1] He was going to give you a birthday present next Sunday [21 November]. Oh darling, I feel it is too cruel at times. I can't help minding, and I always shall; I mind more when I see Detsey [Ben], how sweet and sturdy he is, and the other would have been just the same. It isn't so much that I grudge all the long time or the beastly end, as everybody thinks. I mind his being dead because he is a person. Darling I do mind so: I can't be really happy. I love you and I know you love me and nothing can alter that except to make it more, but I do mind this and it clouds everything and I can't be happy. It is silly to mind so much. Detsey makes it worse as well as better. I can't bear to hear of people with two children.

Oh Harold darling, why did he die?

Why, why, why did he? Oh Harold, I wish you were here—I am meant to be asleep. I haven't got any more paper.[2] I try and stave it off not to think about it, and when I am alone it rushes out at me. I am frightened of being alone now. Darling, it isn't because I am ill, because I am not ill now any more; it is real. Harold, I want you so badly, I wish I could go to sleep.

---

1. Vita's second son was stillborn on 3 November.
2. She continued on the back of a map of St. Paul's journeys, torn from her Bible.

HAROLD TO VITA   *Foreign Office*

22 May 1916

My own dearest little one,

Dear heart, I do hate to feel that at the end of my beastly bustled days here, I don't get into that soft gentle haven—when I am alone with you, my gob, and when nothing outside fusses or worries or telephones.

Dearest, how happy we two are, when one gets outside ourselves, and think of our life and our two happy homes (Ebury Street[1] rather stern and prim and quiet, and the cottage [Long Barn] all untidy and tinkly), and of our baby, and the things we do together and like together, and all the many many things we will do and will like together in the future when this beastly war is over, and all Europe becomes a playground for the Mars to spend money in.

Darling, there are no clouds, are there? my sweetest, and when and if they rise, I feel we will just go indoors a bit, and sit together in front of the fire and wait till it clears up. Sweetest, it is such a deep strong river our love, isn't it? and there are great meadows on each side of it, and cows, and babies, and guinea pigs and newts.

Dearest, I am oh so busy—and I write now as there may be a rush at the end.

Ruffle that little head for his daddy.

Goodbye my darling.

H.

HAROLD TO VITA   *Royal Automobile Club, London*

24 December 1916

You don't know how I worship you, but I can't show you when you are there and it sounds sentimental, but when you are away from me I yearn for you with every fibre in my body, and with every beat

---

1. 182 Ebury Street, the house which Lutyens had remodeled for Lady Sackville in Pimlico, London.

of my heart, and with every pulsation of my brain. Darling, you are all in all to me, and if you ceased to love me the whole sun of life would be darkened, and all my joy in life would become a mass of leaden despair. Little Vita, you are mine, mine, mine and you have been mine for three years, and you will be mine as long as life remains for either of us—and even after death.

VITA TO HAROLD *[Long Barn]*

[February 1917]

Come up and peep in at my door, and if I am asleep kiss me and creep away like a little mouse; and if I am not asleep, kiss me all the same, and then stay with me.

I shall not be asleep, and anyway you are more precious than sleep.

Darling, how undull love can be, even though it is married and has a little boy, two little boys, of its own.[1] I lie and wait for you with as much thrill as though you had never told me you loved me till yesterday, and had never kissed me, and I thought perhaps you might today, and half hoped you would, half hoped you wouldn't.

And I know you will.

HAROLD TO VITA *Foreign Office*

22 August 1917

A busy day again—but I rather like it. George Clerk[2] is such an angel to work with: so appreciative and encouraging and stimulating. He never snubs one for being uppish, and oh dear, I was so uppish today: I suggested peace with Austria against everybody's views, and instead of just turning it down, he sends for me to discuss it all, and

---

1. Nigel had been born in Ebury Street on 19 January 1917.
2. Sir George Clerk (1874–1951) had been first secretary at the Embassy in Constantinople, where Harold had got to know him well. In 1914 he was appointed head of the new War Department of the Foreign Office.

I know how busy he is and how easy it would be for him just to put, "I think the moment inopportune." I don't care what Hardinge or Balfour say now.[3]

VITA TO HAROLD   *Long Barn*

August 1917

This is only to say how I miss you—it is all black when I think I am not going to see you. I love you, and you are absolutely the only thing that counts in the world. You are the vessel which contains the wine of life. My darling, I do appreciate you, and your lovely nature and eyelashes.

HAROLD TO VITA   *Foreign Office*

19 October 1917

I was at a loose end last night, so I telephoned to Macned[4] thinking he was a widower too, but oh dear, oh dear, he wasn't, so he had to ask me to Bedford Square, and I am sure it led to a row with Emmie.[5] Anyhow I went—and a terrible Theosophist friend was there, and poor Macned was such a darling. Emmie is a devil. She nags and jeers and sniffs and sighs at Macned as if he was a naughty schoolgirl, and the poor man is snubbed before that little swine of a Theosophist, who is not worthy to tie his bootlaces. There were only a few rissoles, and the rest, veg. Poor, poor Macned. She *is* a gloom. I do understand why

---

3. Lord Hardinge, the ex-Viceroy, had succeeded Harold's father in 1916 as permanent undersecretary at the Foreign Office. Arthur Balfour had been Foreign Secretary since December 1916.

4. Lady Sackville's name for Sir Edwin Lutyens, the architect, whose intimate friend she had become.

5. Lutyens married Lady Emily Lytton, who in 1907 fell under the influence of Mrs. Annie Besant, President of the Theosophical Society, with which he had little sympathy. He consoled himself with the constant company of Lady Sackville, but remained attached to his wife until his death in 1944.

B.M. cheers him up. Really, for once, there is a great deal in what B.M. says.

I love you.

I will write again.

I love you very much.

Kiss my two babies.

HAROLD TO VITA   *Foreign Office*

7 November 1917

Vita my dearest,

I wrote this afternoon and this is just another.

I love you.

You were such an angel in the little *too-too* [car], and you nearly ran over a man in St James' Street—and you upset a cart.

But I can't laugh over it all. I am so flight [frightened] about it.[1] It will be such an awful business if the [doctor's] report is not satisfactory. I simply *dread* it. Darling if you hated me today, how much will you hate me if it really does come? I haven't the courage to face it all.

Darling, I shall be so wretched about it if it goes wrong. I shall know what you will suffer and it will be my fault, my fault:—and that eats into my brain like some burning acid.

It is too horrible. Darling, I can't believe that our love and happiness would not survive even such a disaster.

Dear one—let's face it together and bravely.

All my whole love to you Vita—all my whole soul, my darling. Nothing in this whole earth counts for me but you.

Darling Vita

Hadji[2]

---

1. Staying with Vita at a smart weekend at Knebworth House, Hertfordshire, Lord Lytton's house, Harold had contracted a venereal infection from another male guest. He confessed it to Vita, and saw a doctor. See Victoria Glendinning's *Vita,* pp. 86–7.
2. Hadji ("pilgrim") had been Harold's father's pet name for him, and Vita adopted it for the rest of her life. To him she was usually "Mar," her mother's name for her.

19 18–20 were the years of Vita's passionate love affair with Violet Trefusis, which nearly wrecked her marriage, but in a strange way stabilized it, because having jointly escaped this near disaster, Vita and Harold relied absolutely on the other's total support and love.

The story has several times been retold in books about Vita, Harold, and Violet, and was dramatized for a BBC television serial in 1990. Only its outline needs to be repeated here.

Vita and Violet Keppel had been friends since childhood, and they became lovers in April 1918, first at Long Barn and then during an extended holiday at Polperro, Cornwall. Their affair soon became a mutual infatuation. They spent months together in Monte Carlo while Harold was in Paris wrestling with the complications of the Peace Treaty, and in spite of all his efforts to reclaim her, and Violet's marriage to Denys Trefusis in June 1919, the two women eloped in February 1920, intending to abandon their families and spend the rest of their lives together. Their husbands caught up with them at Amiens and persuaded them to separate. In July of that year Vita, now repentant, wrote the whole story, which in 1973 was published with a commentary by her son Nigel under the title Portrait of a Marriage.

HAROLD TO VITA   *Foreign Office*

23 April 1918

It was rather lucky that I stayed up tonight, as I have been made to write a Memo for the War Cabinet about Holland—of which I know nothing, and I am wretched about it, and overwhelmed. Anyhow these things all straighten themselves out when one fights them. I get Saturday off and we will have a nice holiday together and get ourselves to each other.[1]

HAROLD TO VITA   *St James' Club, Piccadilly, W.1*

28 April 1918

My little girl,

You can't think what London is like on a Sunday. Have you ever been there? One's foot echoes on the pavements, and here, in the Club, stretch fearful forms of fearful men in sleep.

All this is not very cheery for a young husband who has just been deserted by his wife, and whose two infant sons are marooned in some distant village in charge of a hard featured stranger.

> Can the mother's tender care
> Cease towards the child she bore?
> Yes, she *may* forgetful be . . .[2]

Darling, you will get down there [Cornwall] and the bed will be hard and the sheets will be coarse and the sea will come in at your window full of huns and botolitis and submarines.

I lunched at home. I dine at home tomorrow. They are both [his parents] coming down for the *day* on Sunday! Thank God they don't want to sleep.

I shall dine here alone tonight and there will be the same fearful men still asleep.

Oh absence! le pire de tous les maux. [3]

But I forgive you and hope you will be very very happy with your new companion.

---

1. He did not know that Vita and Violet were alone at Long Barn, and had decided to go to Cornwall together.
2. William Cowper, *Olney Hymns 18.*
3. Paul Verlaine, 1885.

Harold imagines Violet Keppel in Cornwall.

HAROLD TO VITA   *Foreign Office*

28 April 1918

Oh darling—*how* am I to get through these heavy black days in front of me? Poor Hadji! He does so hate being without his little one, and he feels no spirit left in him to do anything but mill and mope.

So if you see that the "body of an unknown man—stout and middle-aged[1] with plentiful curly hair and a snub nose" has been picked up at Wapping Stairs, you will know it's me and you can stay at Polperro a few days more.

Dearest—I do hope it is fine and warm—and that the blister gets all right—and that you are happy. That's all I want.

Anyhow it may make you like sea and moorland, and that will be something gained.

I adore you,
            and I miss you so.

HAROLD TO VITA   *Foreign Office*

2 May 1918

I hate being a bachelor—and it is most unwise from your point of view, as I get so miz [miserable], that I go and play poker with pretty ladies and then I lose that quiet balance which makes our life so happy, and I get a taste for excitement, and wine, women and poker, and become debauched and unfaithful and undomestic, and the divorce-court and Doctor Woods are the inevitable sequel.

Anyhow I am dining at home tonight which will be a damper.

I do hope Violet is not really ill—poor dear. She will mind feeling wretched in uncomfy surroundings and on boiled eggs. I am so sorry.

Oh my sweet, please don't go away and leave me again. I suppose I should get used to it in time, but it is so bloody for a short bit.

Darling, I feel so lonely without you—and it isn't really much fun playing poker with Diana[2]; only it makes one forget.

---

1. Harold was only thirty-one.
2. Lady Diana Manners, who married Harold's diplomatic colleague, Duff Cooper, in 1919.

[11 May 1918]

Beloved, when I got home today I found your two letters, and although I shall see you this evening and all during tomorrow, I answer them because somehow it's easier.

Darling, you are such an angel, and nobody in this world will ever appreciate you more than I do. God knows I prefer your gentleness and patience and endurance to the violence you seem to covet. There is nothing, nothing, nothing I would alter in you.

Yes, I have got Wanderlust, and got it badly. I don't know if you've ever had it? It is real pain, you know—as definite as love, or as jealousy. You seem to muddle it up with what you call the desire for 'adventures'. You are wrong. I don't want that sort of adventure, having *you*. It is real Wanderlust I have—the longing for new places, for movement, for places where no one will want me to order lunch, or pay housebooks, or come with a grievance against someone else: yes, it is silly little things like that which have got on my nerves. Being interrupted, being available. I want to go away (with you) where no one knows where we are, where no letters can follow because no one knows our address. You see, it is a mixture of Wanderlust, the spring, and Westiness, and, as you say, probably liver.

Do you see now that it is not that I don't love you? Or that I want other people to love me?

I write this with my eyes fully open to the fact that to allow such things to grow upon me, of all people, is the most appalling form of selfishness—me who at this time of all others have got you safe (so far, *unberufen* [touch wood]) by an almost miracle of luck; who have you to love me; who have two little boys; a cottage; money; flowers; a farm; and three cows. It's absurd. I have everything I want, and my one real worry in life is Dada—no others. Whereas you, my darling, are tied to a beastly office, and yet you retain your sweetness, your charm, and your unselfishness for others. I feel ashamed now.

Of course I knew that you would trace it to Violet, but again you aren't right, because as I've explained, I don't covet that sort of life—in fact I should loathe it. No, I want to be free with you, that's all, a thing I can't have till the war is done. But in the meantime I feel that Violet and people like that save me from a sort of intellectual stagnation and bovine complacency, which is the very natural consequence of my present life. I *adore* my present life, but it is, after all, only one side of the medal, and on the other side is all the intellectual stimulus you and I both require and which we simply must not allow ourselves to neglect. So don't be jealous of Violet, my darling silly. You know you have always raved against the stagnation of Cadogan Gardens [Harold's parents' house].

Darling, one day we will go off with two little toothbrushes, and the bloody war will be over. If I can only keep you I am afraid I don't much care what happens to the war, if only it would stop. It is all such a fantastically tragic mistake.

HAROLD TO VITA   *Foreign Office*

16 May 1918

You have no conception how lovely the world looked this morning as I went up the hill. The fields swung great clouds of buttercups down the hillside, and every blade of grass stretched out its little green hands to the sun—and to our Weald which lay like a wet quilt below me. My walks up that hill [at Long Barn] have *qualcosa di sacerdotale*, and are indeed poems to nature and our own little nestling home there amid the meadows with the irises and the vine—and upstairs a little person who loves me like she used to, in spite of a terrible lapse within the last fortnight.

I went to lunch with Violet. Mrs K. [Keppel, Violet's mother] in a nice mood—she *raved* about you and said your yellow dress was too lovely and that never had you been so en beauté before. "She really is one of the most beautiful young women I have ever seen." Hadji put on his little face like this.

HAROLD TO VITA   *Foreign Office*

10 June 1918

Darling, I sit here and the sky is so blue and the little clouds sail across the window, so straight and direct, while underneath the trees show the whites of their eyes and bluster in all directions.

Even so, my sweet, I want our own life to sweep onwards to a clear old age, while other people's toss and touzle underneath. But that is a smug little thought, and Hadji is not going to be smug any more. He is going to be a Devil—a great blue and red devil with claws; and then his sweet one will love him again as once she did, and not feel that her own glowing youth is being wasted upon a curate.

Darling I feel dumb when I think of your 'sweet womanliness' as Gerry [Wellesley] would say. It is a sort of melody which harmonises all this jangle—and out of it all will come some assurance in the continuance of human things.

Darling, I fear it is all rather dull for you my sweet—but we will have another honeymoon at Herm[1] which will last for ever. Sweetheart, you know how I long for your happiness above all things—but it is so difficult to create the happiness of another: one can only destroy it.

HAROLD TO VITA   *Foreign Office*

18 June 1918

Darling, I did love the picture so.[2] It is so *absolutely* my little Mar: she's all there—her little straight body, her Boyhood of Raleigh manner, and above all, those sweet gentle eyes which are so familiar to me. I am really enthusiastic about it. It is, I think, one of the best portraits I have ever seen. It is so young and so grown up. It doesn't date. She is younger than the sham Chippendale chair on which she

---

1. One of the smallest of the Channel Islands, which they thought of buying.
2. A portrait of Vita by William Strang, R.A. It was commissioned by Lady Sackville soon after Vita's return from Cornwall, but she rejected it, and the portrait was sold to the Glasgow Art Gallery, where it still hangs. It is reproduced in *Portrait of a Marriage*.

sits, and the eyelids are a little weary.[3] And she has arrayed herself in strange webs from diverse merchants, and as Miss Vita has been the distant princess of my exile, and as Viti the mother of Ben and Nigel. That little head is that on which a thousand kisses have fallen—and she has been down to the sea at Polperro and come back just the same to the little cottage.

Olive [Rubens] telephoned to me about something—and she had been to see it too. She thought it wonderful but a little 'coarse'. I could see no coarseness—only a certain blatancy, which is contradicted by the beauty of the eyes. It really is a splendid achievement.

HAROLD TO VITA   *Foreign Office*

2 September 1918

Hadji has got a brilliant idea which she mustn't laugh at. It is this. Mar is to get a little cottage in Cornwall or elsewhere—and it is to be a Padlock[4] cottage: and the Padlock is to be that Hadji never goes there, or sees it. It will just have two or three rooms, and will be hers absolutely, and she can go there when she likes and be quite alone and have whom she wants. Then the Padlock is that Hadji never goes there and can't (by the rules of the Padlock) even be asked—or even know when she is there or who she has got with her. It will make it a real escape from the YOKE [of marriage]. And when I am rich, I shall have one too, just the same and on the same condition.

Darling, take the idea seriously and think over it.

HAROLD TO VITA   *Foreign Office*

4 September 1918

The following is the decision of Lord Denman's Committee[5] in my case:—

---

3. A parody of Walter Pater's famous description of the Mona Lisa.
4. "Padlock" was a Sackville term for an unbreakable promise.
5. Appointed to adjudicate on exempting civil servants from military service.

"Hon. H. G. Nicolson age 31, grade 1
Retained as indispensable.
   Reasons: "Has dealt with certain subjects from the outbreak of the war, and has an intimate knowledge of many
difficult and intricate European problems. His technical experience and facility for writing memoranda render him quite
invaluable when information on the Balkans and other problems is called for by the War Cabinet at short notice. Mr
Balfour, whose opinion was solicited, stated that he did not
know how Mr Nicolson could be replaced: that, indeed, he
had no hesitation in saying that it would be almost impossible to do so."

So that's that—and I think I am safe for this war. I can't say that
I am really glad about it, or that I feel they had the facts put honestly before them. It was true in 1917. I doubt whether it is true
now.

HAROLD TO VITA   *St James' Club, Piccadilly, W.1*

9 September 1918

My little Viti,

   I was so rushed all today that I couldn't find time to write, and
this will come late and she'll think he doesn't love her any more.

   But oh he does! he does! he does! he's never loved her so much
as in the last few months when she has been slipping away from him.
Viti, my little one, you will never get anyone to love you as I do. I
know that, and one day you will know it. You see, all I want is for
you to be happy. Really I would go and live in a Martello tower[1]
all by myself with 2 bats and six mice—if it would make you happy.
I feel oceans of abnegations as regards you, my perfect.

   But then—I know—it is not that which counts: and Violet in her
clever way has made you think I'm unromantic. And oh dear! Oh dear!

---

1. A girdle of small round towers erected round the southeast coast of England in the early
   1800s as defenses against the threat of a Napoleonic invasion.

how can an impoverished, middle-aged civil servant cope with so subtle an accusation? You see, if I was orfully rich I could have a valet, and an aeroplane and a gardenia tree, and it would all be very Byronic—but not being rich, or successful, it is just "poor little Hadji, he's such a darling and *so* patient."

But sweetheart—I am just *not* going to be a bore or touchy or sentimental. I'm not going to plant water lilies in the sea. It just *is* the sea—my love of you. My little one—you think you are so unaccountable, but you aren't.

Little one—I wish Violet was dead: she has poisoned one of the most sunny things that ever happened. She is like some fierce orchid, glimmering and stinking in the recesses of life and throwing cadaverous sweetness on the morning breeze. Darling, she is evil and I am not evil. Oh my darling, what is it that makes you put her above me? It is so difficult to realise. It is so poignant to think of. We seemed, you and I, to be running hand in hand on the downs (near Lewes), and now a fog has come and you have got into someone else's conservatory, and I am wandering about cold and rather frightened in the fog. And from the little valleys comes the laughter of past happiness and the shudders of the future (even *that* sounds forced).

Oh dear! oh dear! it was all so real and easy and natural, like the weeds on the terrace or the smell of Alyssum—and now, somehow, it isn't frank any more.

Yet I'm the same, my saint, and my love is the same. It burns so straight darling, it doesn't gutter. Oh darling, yesterday I wanted to kiss you as if I loved you, and you turned aside. Such a slight deflection—an *exiguum clinamen,* and yet it hurt me so, it sent me away so hurt, darling—and you meant to be so kind and nice and gentle.

Darling, is it all an Algy Hay[2]—or is it just a transitory thing, or is it more? You see, it may be your bloody Westie [Sackville] business, or it may be a sort of George Sand stunt [the notorious Sapphist], or it may be just that I am a bad, futile, unconvincing, evasive, unromantic husband.

And then against me I have that little tortuous, erotic, irresponsible, irremediable and unlimited person [Violet]. I don't blame her.

2. Algy Hay was an old Sackville friend who was notoriously accident-prone.

I don't hate her even—no more than I should <u>hate opium</u> if you took it.

But darling, what does it all mean?

Darling, what do your odd unconvincing bursts of affection mean? What do your intermittent and (alas) so convincing coldness mean? Little one, I am not a fool. I can forgive and forget anything, and understand a good deal.

But can't you tell me? Can't you write it to me? What has happened? You see it isn't *me*—so it must be *you*. And you, who are quite analytical too, should be able to tell—and to tell *me*.

You see, if it was tangible I could help, perhaps. But is it so untangible? I know it is more than that. Is it that I am not amorous enough? How can I even think such things? But what is it, darling?

It is raining tonight—and the winter is coming on.

Hadji

Burn this, my little friend, and don't ever speak of it.

VITA TO HAROLD *34 Hill Street, London W.1*

[1 October 1918]

I know, as I know the sun will rise tomorrow, that I love you unalterably. I know it would survive any passing liking I might have for anyone else (It's all right! don't be afraid. I *don't* like any-one else!) I know now, after five years, what a difference there is between a thing with great long strong roots, all gnarled and Rackham-like, and a love which is merely an accident of the imagi-nation, and the person one imagines one loves might just as easily have been somebody else.

You see, I don't think a love like ours often happens. Passion happens, and habit happens, but the knowledge that one is linked and welded and soldered by a mixture of passion *and* habit *and* ten-derness *and* friendship *and* circumstance *and* memories *and,* above all, by the thing one calls love, which is essentially a sense of be-longing, of choice, a sense of 'He is MINE'—I don't think that often happens.

HAROLD TO VITA *Foreign Office*

11 November 1918

A strange, hectic, flag-waving [Armistice] day today, in which I have endeavoured to work on unaffected by the cheers and jubilation outside.

It began almost directly after we heard the news: a little knot of people had gathered outside No. 10—and the Prime Minister [Lloyd George] came out and told them. There were the wildest cheers—and they were silent—and they bared their heads and sang "God Save the King"—after which throughout the morning came cries and cheers from the [Horse Guards] parade—and at one moment I looked from an upper window to see a hatless white-haired and flushed Lloyd George, pushing himself backwards through a sea of hands, faces and flags into his little garden gate.

And then by luncheon the disorder had become more organised. Motor lorries filled with soldiers, women, and gutter urchins on the mud guards flew past yelling wildly. Everyone had flags—and as I went towards the Marlborough [Club], Pall Mall was festooned as never before. Again there was a rush of crowded lorries and people on the tops of taxicabs—wild heated hatless people.

I am so busy getting peace terms ready. It is rather fun, though I feel oddly responsible. I feel that what I do is so likely to be accepted, and that one tracing of my pencil in this familiar room and on my own familiar maps may mean the fate of millions of remote and unknown people.

I feel, almost an impulse [to say], "God guide me to the right." I feel quite solemn about it.

HAROLD TO VITA *Foreign Office*

5 December 1918

You have stayed in Paris nearly a week without a word to me as to when you were going south or where.[1] The result is that I haven't

---

1. On 26 November Vita and Violet went to Paris for a week, and Vita paraded the streets dressed as a young, wounded soldier. They then went to Avignon, and from there to Monte Carlo, where they stayed for three months.

the least idea where to get hold of you. You really are quite *hopeless* about such things, and I put it all down to that swine Violet who seems to addle your brain. Oh you little idiot, I should shake you if you were here.

HAROLD TO VITA   *British Delegation, Paris*

10 January 1919

I know how extremely busy you are and how much of your time is taken up playing tennis and talking to your dirty little friend and your Persian Prince. Of course I know it is a lot to ask—but you might at least send me a postcard when you have no time to write. I am sorry to be a bore, and I know that your dirty little friend must chaff you about it a great deal, and that you must feel I am a tie and a responsibility. But try and remember that I am alone here, and anxious to settle about a flat which I can't do till I hear from you. Of course it must be much nicer in the South and I quite realise that you don't want to come up.

Damn! Damn! Damn! Violet. How I *loathe* her. I refuse absolutely to see her—and if you arrive with her I shan't meet you. I don't think I could trust myself to touch her. I feel I should lose my head and spit in her face.

HAROLD TO VITA   *Hotel Majestic, Paris*

[10 January 1919]

My own darling, dearest, sweetest one.

Another cross letter I sent you today and again I feel guilty. But darling, please don't mind them—don't think of them—it is only that at times I get quite racked with longing for you—and the slightest thing makes me angry and gives me a *crise de jalousie,* not jealous, dearest, of your loving other people (you know I am calm about that), but jealous simply of your *being* with other people—enraged, red-blood-surgingly indignant at the thought of other people, *dont je ne connais pas la puissance sur votre coeur*—of other people seeing you, hearing your dear modulated deep voice, and noting your splendid ways and movements—and oh dear the grace of you, and that little neck, that little neck with the pearl clasp all untidy, and the straight untidy tuque [cap]. And then I see red, darling, and the thought that you have spent two whole days without writing to me, running down unknown hotel steps into the sun with your racquet, and playing with unknown people on an unknown court, when you should have at least sent me a postcard.

Poor Hadji! I suppose it *is* jealousy—but I am not jealous, my own sweetheart, when you are there with me—and when I have at least a portion of your time.

Darling, I don't want to be a bore—but I do love you so. But *so* deeply darling—you understand.

VITA TO HAROLD   *Hotel Beau Rivage, Cannes*

27 January [1919]

My darling,

It is dreadful of me not to write to you. I know. Don't think it is just indifference, or forgetfulness, it is not. But as I've often said to you in talking, it's so difficult for me to write to you when I am staying with V.; it seems to me *indecent*. You can't say I have disappeared this time, because I have kept you *au courant* with my movements by means of telegrams, and I have written regularly to B.M.; this also I would much rather not do, for the same reason, but I have forced myself to. But you are different. It *is* indecent for me to write to you under these circumstances, oh, do, do, do try to see it!

Darling, I do hope you liked being in Paris.[1] It must have been rather exciting, but I am anti your conference because it has spoilt the exchange, and I hadn't yet changed any of my English money hoping it would go up! I sent you a telegram asking if you knew Lady

---

1. Harold returned to Knole, where he spent Christmas with his sons but no wife.

Lowther's[2] address in Cannes, but haven't had any answer. I am in Cannes now. I thought Lady Lowther would be a nice respectable person for me to see, and would gratify B.M. By the way, I think it is rather horrid of B.M. to be cross, when I gave up going to Spain which I was simply dying to do. It makes me feel "as well be hung for a sheep as for a lamb," and since you are in Paris I am not inconveniencing you in any way by being out of England.

Hadji . . .

Oh, nothing. But so many things, all the same.

I'm lonely, and have got a cold and wish I hadn't come here. I got an awful chill walking up a mountain and getting cold at the top. V. tried to get a cabin for Algiers and was promised one almost for certain last Monday, but it fell through. It was not her fault, or mine. It even got so far as paying for it.

What shall I do? I thought of going to Ajaccio, but thought you wouldn't like it.

Did you get dewdrops [compliments] in Paris? How could I have been any use to you there? darling. I fear you are better without me on those occasions. *C'est triste à dire* . . .

Your loving, and rather miz, and very snuffly

Mar

HAROLD TO VITA   *British Delegation, Paris*

1 February 1919

Yesterday I was at work from 9.30 to 12.30 and 1.30 to 8.0. I have generally a Committee all morning and then even lately I have been going down to the Conseil de Dix all afternoon. The latter is terrifying. A small but magnificent room, with armchairs arrayed both sides of a huge Régence writing table. At the table sits Clemenceau [France], and on his right are the 5 great Powers, Wilson, Lansing [U.S.A.]; Lloyd George, Balfour [Great Britain]; Orlando, Sonnino [Italy]; Pichon [France], and the Japanese.

---

2. Former Ambassadress in Constantinople.

Then comes Hadji—oh dear he looks so funny. In the middle are
secretaries, and an interpreter.

This, of course, is the *real* Congress, where the work is done, but
it doesn't look like one, as everyone is just sitting about, and they get
up and lean against the mantelpiece.

The wretched small powers are brought in one by one and made
to state their case. They are sat down opposite Clemenceau as if in the
dock. It is an odd spectacle.

Hadji doesn't say anything except when he's asked—and then he
gets pink.

HAROLD TO VITA   *British Delegation, Paris*

2 February 1919

I am feeling crushed, and sore, and sad today—because it's Sun-
day—and I had been packing some things to take round to the flat.[1]
I packed them so tenderly as if they were bits of you, my saint—and
I was so happy, *so* happy.

And then your letter came—and it was so dark and grim and
horrible. I have never been so disappointed in my life—I didn't know
it could come on one like that.

But it is childish, of course, and disappointment is after all a very
transitory hurt—and nothing compared to poor V.'s [Violet's] tragic
and hopeless position. Little one, don't think I am angry or sad about
you. I always dissociate these things from you—especially when you
tell me frankly what has happened.

But all the sun has gone from Paris—which has become a cold,
grey meaningless city where there is a Conference going on somewhere, a conference which meant so much to me yesterday, and today
is something detached, unreal and inanimate.

But tomorrow it will be all right again—and when you get this
I shall be all right again. Only please get a new photograph done of

1. Harold had rented a flat in Paris for himself and Vita, who had promised to come, but she
   chucked him at the last moment.

yourself and send it me. I feel you are slipping away, you who are my anchor, my hope, and all my peace.

Dearest, you don't know my devotion to you. What you do can never be wrong.

God bless you, Viti.

HAROLD TO VITA   *[Paris]*

[9 February 1919]

I have torn up the rest of this letter. It was too cross and despairing to send.

I don't want to write to you at present much—as I don't want to say things which I shall regret.

You see, I have been quite terribly over-worked and all this sorrow and confusion has made me quite unnaturally upset—so I can't trust myself to write.

I don't want to say things which I shall regret. Only day and night there is a voice in my ear, "She lied to you! She broke her promise to you! She hurts you like this to spare the other!"

Would V. have suffered as I have this dark week? I wonder. If so I am sorry for her. But I feel quite different and aged—and all my joy in life and work has left me.

What frightens me so, is that I feel now I don't *want* to see you.

HAROLD TO VITA   *[Paris]*

[18 March 1919]

I want you to think: "Well, whatever I do, there is one person whom I need never consider, who always will understand—and that is my fat, ugly, red-faced, bourgeois, sentimental but *so* loving Hadji." I want you to feel that I shall always take your point-of-view and that I realise it is all as if you had been run over by a bus and broken your leg, and however bloody, it is *not* your fault.

VITA TO HAROLD   *34 Hill St.*
                                                  [London W.1]
[20 March 1919]

My own darling,

I got so dreadfully poisoned yesterday that I stayed the night at
Folkestone. I am all right today.[1] The crossing also was beastly,
although I wasn't sick. So I came on here today—B.M. has been *quite
too foul* for words to me. Dada has scolded me too, but he is so sweet
and sensible and un-violent that one doesn't mind, and of course I
know he is perfectly right and justified in all that he says, and I haven't
tried to pretend to him that I don't accept all his criticisms as perfectly
well-founded and just. He has not really really got a down on me. But
B.M. is impossible; she talks in a voice trembling with passion (you
know), contradicts herself the whole time, and is obviously even more
furious than one had gathered from her letters—she even refused to
take the little presents I had brought her—I HATE her tonight, I hate
her too much even to be unhappy about it. I want you so dreadfully
badly. I know I have brought it all on myself, and have got only myself
to thank, and all that sort of thing, and also I know B.M. has got a
real justifiable grievance this time against me, but all the same I don't
see why she should be such an utter beast to me, and *so* hard.

Well, darling, I mustn't bore you with it; I found a darling letter
from you here, which cheered me up lots; bless you. I wanted to leave
the house, but Dada said no. Oh, she *can* be horrid when she likes. I
expect she will write you a filthy letter; put it in the fire unread.

My sweet, I shall go to Brighton[2] tomorrow. Dada and Olive
[Rubens] have both talked about Ben to me; apparently he has missed
us quite dreadfully, and it isn't just repeating what the servants have
said to him. They are both extremely urgent that I should take him
over to Paris, and I trust them, even before I have seen him. I will of
course write and tell you about them both tomorrow.

Poor little Ben, it appears that no day has passed without his asking
for me, and that whenever they saw him he said at once, "Can we go

---

1. Vita joined Harold in Paris on 15 March, and on the 19th returned to England after nearly
   four months absence.
2. Lady Sackville's house in Sussex Square, where Vita's two sons had been temporarily lodged
   with a nanny.

and find Mummy now?"—isn't it dreadfully how?[3] and it does make me feel a beast. Also he realises that there is a general theory that he is naughty (the criminal!), and he says, "I know I am naughty, but Mummy thinks I am good, and I will be good when Mummy comes." Darling, it harrows me horribly. Olive says she could never have believed it of so small a child. He is always talking of Long Barn, and of how much he loves it. They say Nigel is most attractive, but it is my own dark Ben I want,—oh I do want to see him, Hadji, and to get away from B.M. who looks at me with eyes of stone.

I shall come back to you as soon as I can—with Ben.

I can't believe I ever loved B.M., or that she ever loved me. I think Dada hates her and a good deal too.[4]

Darling, goodbye.

I could not be as hard as B.M., not to anyone.

Mar

HAROLD TO VITA   *British Delegation, Paris*

26 March 1919

My darling Vita,

I got such a sad letter from you today my dearest. What can I say, darling? You know only that I love you beyond anything in this world, and that my whole life will be devoted to shielding you against unhappiness. Poor darling, how buffetted you have been by circumstances—and how terrible it is that I should not be available when I am necessary to you: to protect you and heal you, and bring you back to calm and security.

Darling, you know that one day you will be able to tell me all about it—and that I shall love you all the more for what you have been through; and do all I can to save you from such tragedies.

Of course I blame myself chiefly. I should have helped you more from the first, and taken the decision out of your hands. I shall do so

---

3. "How" was the family expression for "pathetic," "touching."
4. It was on 19 May 1919 that Lady Sackville left her husband and Knole forever.

in the future, dearest, and not let terrible situations grow upon you and overwhelm you. But I have this excuse, that I have been so overcome by work—it is just as if I had been in the trenches. It is the war, darling, and the war is over, and now we are to have peace.

So try, my darling, to recover your confidence in yourself, and your serenity of life. Don't look upon yourself as a straw in the wind, but as a twig on some firm tree which waves and shivers in the wind but which is at least rooted somewhere to hope and solidity. My poor darling, I feel for you so. I got such a pang of sympathy when I read of Violet's engagement.[1] It is terrible for her. I hated to read it.

So try, darling, to recover *le beau calme de jadis*—and when we meet at last I shall help you, and support you and soothe you and fight all your battles for you. I promise, darling.

I feel so strong now—my work has made me feel that. I get my way about Europe by persistence. I shall get my way too about your life and mine.

Darling, I would give the world to be with you now. I feel I could help—by gentleness first, and by force later. All I want now is that you should still be strong these weeks. You are recovering from a terrible fever—and you can't quite walk across your room. But every day it will get a little easier—you will feel less tired—relapses will become less frequent. Only keep from doing anything foreign for these next weeks and you will heal.

The Council of Ten have realised their own futility and have dissolved into the Council of 4[2]—so that we really shall be at peace soon.

I have been turned on to getting an agreement out of the Americans on *all* South Eastern Europe questions. It is a *great* compliment, but also a terrible responsibility and entails appalling work. It is also a deep, deep secret, so don't say anything.

But it has made me happier about peace. I get my way with the Yanks generally.

---

1. Violet's engagement to Denys Trefusis was announced in *The Times* on this very day, 26 March.
2. The Council of Ten consisted of two delegates each from France, the United States, Great Britain, Italy, and Japan. It was now skimmed to Clemenceau, President Wilson, Lloyd George, and Orlando.

29 March 1919

My own darling,

I was so distressed by your letter today.

Let me make my own view quite clear.

(1) I don't want or expect you to 'break' with Violet. I don't expect you not to see her or write to her. I don't care how affectionate your letters are: I know how difficult is the position in which you are placed.

(2) I will not, however, allow you to go away again with Violet for any long period. I don't want you to allow her to completely monopolise your life—I don't mean it in a selfish or jealous way. What I mean is that the position is impossible—and that you simply can't go on sacrificing your reputation and your duty to a tragic passion. It is bad for you and bad for Violet—and it simply cannot be allowed.

If therefore Violet is completely unreasonable, and wants you to go away with her again, and refuses to see you unless you consent, then you are right to break with her.

If, ever, you find that seeing or writing to her leads to scenes, and leaves you both more wretched than before:—then also you are right.

But if you are taking the drastic line merely because you are not strong enough to take the middle line, then I think you are wrong.

I wish, darling, you could tell me exactly what you feel about it all. It makes me so wretched and miserable. Not so much the thing itself—but that you should be unhappy and I be powerless to help, or even to understand.

Darling, why did you ever leave our calm quiet road for this scarlet adventure? It is all a torment to me to think of—but above all that it should make you suffer. You dear gentle, loving, loyal saint—and I *did* want to make you happy, my own angel, and I have failed. I read your Constantinople poems—and they hurt me so dreadfully. Where are the happy feet that used to patter about our staircase over there? There is nothing but leaden sorrow and disease in our life now—and our love which is all that has survived is wild eyed and full of tears.

My poor poor darling!
poor poor Hadji.

HAROLD TO VITA   *British Delegation, Paris*

4 May 1919

I scribbled you a note yesterday in President Wilson's ante-room while a man was watering the lawn outside with a hose, under the eyes of an American sentry. Just as I had finished, Lloyd George burst in in his impetuous way: "Come along, Nicolson, and keep your ears open." So I went into Wilson's study and there were he and Lloyd George and Clemenceau with their armchairs drawn up close over a map on the hearth-rug. I was there about half an hour. The President was extremely nice—and so, I must say, was Lloyd George. Clemenceau was cantankerous, the *"Mais, voyons, jeune homme"* style.

But, darling, it is appalling those three ignorant and irresponsible men cutting Asia Minor to bits as if they were dividing a cake, and with *no-one* there except Hadji—who incidentally has nothing whatsoever to do with Asia Minor. Isn't it terrible—the happiness of millions being decided in that way—while for the last two months we were praying and begging the Council to give us time to work out a scheme?

Then decisions are immoral and impracticable—and I told them so. *"Mais, voyez-vous, jeune homme—que voulez-vous qu'on fasse? Il faut aboutir."*

The funny part is that the only part where I *do* come in—the Greek part—they have gone beyond, and dangerously beyond, what I suggested in my wildest moments—and everyone will think it was me.

Anyhow I was working up to 11.30, and got to bed dead to the world which was a good thing as it prevented me being miz. More Councils today—and I write this in violent haste.

HAROLD TO VITA   *British Delegation, Paris*

Saturday, 17 May 1919

There is *such* a thunderstorm brewing here against the P.M. [Lloyd George]. It is all about this Asia Minor business—and it is difficult for Hadji to guide his row boat safely in and out of these fierce Dreadnoughts.

Even A.J.B. [Balfour] is angry: "I have three all-powerful, all-ignorant men sitting there and partitioning continents with only a child to take notes for them." I have an uneasy suspicion that by the "child" he means me. Of course perhaps it may be Hankey.[1] I hope it is Hankey. After all Hankey is bald—but still he is younger by 25 years than A.J.B.

Then the P.M. had sent for the Indian Delegation from London—who took a special train—only to find that the question had been decided by the three men and the child and that Ll.G. had gone off on a motor tour.

I had better lie very low for a bit. Anyhow I have, I think, got my point. But it was playing with gun-powder.

HAROLD TO VITA   *British Delegation, Paris*

19 May 1919

When Mar has *nothing* to do, will she please think, sometimes, about the League of Nations?[2] She had better get a League temperament, ready to help Hadji and tonic him when he becomes too national and anti-dago. You see, if the League is to be of any value it must start from a new conception and involve among its promoters and leaders a new habit of thought. Otherwise it will be no more than a continuation of the Conference—where each Delegation subscribes its *own* point of view and where unanimity can be secured only by a mutual surrender of the complete scheme. But we must lose all that, and think only of the League point of view, where Right is the ultimate sanction, and where compromise is a crime. So we must become anti-English when necessary, and when necessary pro-Italian. So when you find me becoming impatient of the Latins you must snub me. It is rather a wrench for me as I like the sturdy, unenlightened, un-intellectual muzzy British way of looking at things. I fear the Geneva tempera-

---

1. Sir Maurice Hankey, Secretary to the British Delegation, and to the Council of Four. But he was forty-two, scarcely "a child." Harold was thirty-two, Balfour, sixty-seven.
2. Harold had been warned that after the signature of the Peace Treaty he would be temporarily detached from the Foreign Office to the League of Nations, which was established by the Treaty itself.

ment will be rather Hampstead Garden Suburb—but, dearest, the thing may be *immense,* and we must work for it. You can do as much as me by gentle proselytising. Think that you are a Salvation Army worker and when you hear the League abused and scoffed at, put on a gentle patient smile, and say, "But why?" They will have no *real* reason to condemn it, and you can then confound them by, "Obviously, it will fail if ignorant people attack it before its birth and without giving it a moment's thought."

But seriously, sweetest, when you hear the League thoughtlessly abused, think of yourself down in the cellar at 182 Ebury Street (without port) and with the guns going all round: and think how if there is another war that will begin again a thousand-fold: and then catch hold of the little thread of indignation which this memory awakes in you, and elaborate it to moral wrath at irresponsible gibing at what *may,* what really may, prevent all this. My feeling about the League is that it is a great experiment. And I want you to feel rather protective of it, just like you would rush to protect the unborn *Critic* [3] from the reviler and the cold-water thrower.

There is sun today—and it is splashing on the lawns at Knole, and over those gold brown roofs and into my babies' bedroom. And my darling—my sun is there—oh my sweet—how my love goes out to you, my darling. Dearest Vita, darling little one. I *do* hope you are less unhappy. Don't think of me my angel. I am feeling secure and confident again. Really I think love is the only *supreme* virtue—and covers all other ugly things. Nothing sad or beastly can do deep harm, I mean deep *moral* harm, if one loves.

HAROLD TO VITA   *British Delegation, Paris*

22 May 1919

Oh Viti—Viti—how I love you and cling to you and long to help you. But it *is* difficult and uphill work and I feel so discouraged sometimes. You see all I can do is to love you absolutely, and under-

---

3. *The Critic* was the title of a literary magazine that Vita proposed to edit in collaboration with Michael Sadleir, the publisher. The idea was stillborn.

stand you absolutely, and let you do whatever you like. That is easy. But it creates in you a feeling of debt to me, and that is in itself a bond. There are moments when I feel you would rather I gave you an excuse for going away for ever: when I think that you would rather I didn't love you and you didn't love me and that there was absolute liberty for you—moral as well as actual. I give you absolute liberty in fact—but in principle you are too loyal not to feel there remains an obligation. It is sad, because anyone else would be so easy to manage. I mean that to anyone else I should not be a burden and a responsibility. Dearest, I almost despair at times. You see, the weapons with which I can fight for you may make you hate me.

But I am feeling overworked, and stale, and depressed about this humbug peace, and I can't feel opty [optimistic] about things at present. Oh my dearest Vita, don't feel annoyed at this momentary despair of mine. But how can I, who only represent peace and security, cope with Violet who represents adventure? Of course I know that if you were wretched, or frightened, you would come to me. But by then it may be too late. You say you have no confidence in yourself. But you evidently have all confidence in me, in my patience and forebearance. I hope you are right. I think you are. But this can't go on for years! Oh darling, I have suffered so, this long dark year: have I got to go through another?

Darling, I am quite resigned to not seeing very much of you in my life. I quite see that for three months in the year you will go off alone somewhere—and you needn't even leave me your address. But does it do any good? We are getting on for half-year—and I have seen you 14 days! Do you realise that—14 days out of six months! And the babies have seen you less! You can't say that marriage is a bore to you, or motherhood a responsibility. I don't grumble at your having been away so long: what saddens me is that evidently you want to be away for longer. And we are so happy! at least *I* was. And then Violet came and all has been unrest and horror ever since.

And everybody envies me so! How little they know!

I think that V. has thrown the evil eye on all of us—on you and me and Dada and B.M. and Charlie and Maud [Sackville-West] and Walter and Olive [Rubens]. Don't let her see my babies.

Don't feel cross at this letter. My darling—it would be easier if

I didn't love you. I almost long for the peace and quiet of not loving
you or caring what you do. How awful, though, if you just became
a bore! It is funny to think of—but I suppose it will end like that.

I wish I knew where you were.

HAROLD TO VITA   *British Delegation, Paris*

23 May 1919

I read Celery[1] through from cover to cover last night in bed. It
really is good. It is difficult to get outside it—but it leaves so strong
a taste in the mouth, and the defects are merely a question of organisa-
tion, which is largely mechanical. All the un-mechanical part appears
to have come quite naturally and that is what I suppose is called 'talent'.
I have no doubt whatsoever that you will really become an important
writer. You must keep your gravity of style. It is no use you trying
to be funny—and you realise that. The only light business you could
do well would be passages about children or animals or how [simple]
people generally. I got annoyed with *The Observer* review about
Ruth! To me she is a real achievement. The best thing in the book.

I hadn't realised its value quite, or its complete originality, till I
read Celery again. In an emotional passage you really attain *Virtuo-
sité*—you do really—and it is by gravity and simplicity. The passage
when Malory tells her [Ruth] of love is as good a bit of prose as one
could wish. And there is no 'precious' word in the whole business.

VITA TO HAROLD   *Long Barn*

Sunday, 1 June [1919]

Darling, something will absolutely have to be done about my
coming to Paris, because V.'s wedding is tomorrow fortnight, and I
know that there will be some disaster if I stop here. You may say that

---

1. "Celery" was his name for *Heritage,* Vita's first novel, which was published, to great
acclaim, on 15 May.

I am superstitious, but I know, like Malory [in *Heritage*], fate will be too strong for me! I am really serious, Hadji. I am not just worried, I am ABSOLUTELY TERRIFIED. I feel as though I were being stalked. I tell you about it in order to protect myself from myself. I'm not afraid of anybody but myself. I shall do something quite irretrievable and mad if I stay in England. I shall probably try and do it even from Paris, at the last moment, but there I shall be prevented by just sheer distance.

O my Hadji, you oughtn't to have married me, I make you unhappy. But I do love you. That is the only anchor, as I told you. If it wasn't for you, I would give London something to talk about!!

Darling, the other night I sat next to Lord Hugh Cecil at dinner. He said he wondered why people didn't oftener do absolutely crazy things which would revolutionise their lives. I said probably because in doing them they would do infinite harm to the people they cared for and who cared for them. And also because most people weren't made that way, and simply didn't think about it. And Lady Hamilton joined us and said how often she had wanted to disappear, and I said how it was an instinct in people, a real instinct, which expressed itself in liking to dress-up, i.e. be somebody quite different for the time being, and they said it was quite true, and Lord Hugh got quite excited and eloquent.

O Hadji, I never ought to have married you or anybody else; I ought just to have lived with you for as long as you wanted me, because I am a pig really, and you are the dearest and sweetest and tenderest person in the whole world, and I only hurt you. I would have let you have a nice gentle affectionate wife who looked after your washing, which reminds me, have you got mine? Or else I ought not to have married till I was thirty. I think really that is the best solution for people like me, because not to marry at all is a mistake. We would have lost nothing, you and I, because we would have been every bit as happy unrespectably as respectably. Women ought to have freedom the same as men when they are young. It's a rotten and ridiculous system at present, it's simply cheating one of one's youth. It was all right for Victorians. But this generation is discarding, and the next will have discarded, the chrysalis.

You see, the mistake one makes is to expect youth to be consistent.

Youth is so fluid and impressionable that it will flow quite happily for a given time through any mould one chooses to provide. But then one's nature reasserts itself. That is why one oughtn't to bind oneself—in other words, marry—when one is very young. That is why I say that women, like men, ought to have their years so glutted with freedom that they hate the very idea of freedom. Like assistants in a chocolate-shop are allowed for the first month to eat as many chocolates as they like.

If ever we have a daughter we will bring her up to bring herself up. And she will have a floater-mar [illegitimate child] which we will have to pass off as the housemaid's.

O Hadji, if you knew how it would amuse me to scandalise the whole of London! It's so secure, so fatuous, so conventional, so hypocritical, so whited-sepulchre, so cynical, so humbugging, so mean, so ungenerous, so self-defensive, so well-policed, so beautifully legislated, so well-dressed, so up-to-date, so hierarchical, so virtuously vicious, so viciously virtuous. I'd like to tweak away the chair just as it's going to sit down.

HAROLD TO VITA   *British Delegation, Paris*

3 June 1919

The letter I got this morning was so *rotten* that I think you had better come here at once. (N.B. This is not meant to be cross.) You seem to have no will-power at all—but just to drift and attribute the muddle you have got into to the conventionality of the world. It is as much good as a kitten who has fallen into the river blaming the ground for having been too dry!

So you must come over at once and let me know by telegraph. I shall get a room for you, and meet you.

Poor Hadji. If he looks after her he is infringing on her liberty—and if he gives her her liberty she gets into a muddle. And what is the use of his loving her so dreadfully?

But come at once my poor shattered Viti—and I shall be with you, and help.

Now don't do anything excessive, but buy some black socks for me instead. And keep your head and your sense of proportion, and your self-respect, my sweet.

VITA TO· HAROLD   *Long Barn*

[8 June 1919]

O Hadji, I couldn't ever hurt somebody as tender and sensitive and angelic and loving as you—at least, I mean—I know I *have* hurt you, but I couldn't do anything to hurt you dreadfully and irrevocably. What a hold you have on my heart; nobody else would ever have had such a hold. Darling, I will tell you something which although I say it quite casually in a letter is really very true and illuminating: the fact of loving you has made of me a quite different person, or rather it has entailed the renouncement of all in me that wasn't compatible with loving you. That part isn't quite dead yet, it's flickering and struggling to live, it struggles on its knees and puts its hands together, and says "O PLEASE!" and I say "NO," and it lies down again in its corner, very sick, and I look the other way and go to a dance.

O Hadji, it is so neat, the division in me, more neat than you'll ever know.

Darling, I suppose you needn't worry: I shan't do anything 'excessive', as you say.

I love you more than myself, more than life, more than the things I love. I give you everything—like a sacrifice.

I love you so much that I don't even resent it—which is rather contradictory, but you know what I mean, you've so often said it yourself.

I want to impress on you that it is all *you*, it isn't B.M., or Dada, or even the babies, or respectability, or peace and comfort (because I don't really like peace and comfort): it is only *you*. I should be pleased and flattered, if I was you.

The reason I am not coming till Saturday is that if I came to Paris several days earlier I should never stand it, but should go back to London and stop the whole thing [Violet's wedding], but if I cross on

Saturday I simply shall not have time to, however much I may want to—willy-nilly.

Hadji darling, I wonder how much you realise?

I can't tell you what I'd give to be this time next year!

O Lord, the weariness and length and *dread* of it all—It all seems to go from bad to worse, and this is the climax.[1] However, I suppose one survives everything.

This isn't meant to be a worrying letter, but a reassuring one.

HAROLD TO VITA   *British Delegation, Paris*

20 June 1919

I went to the front yesterday—to Noyon. It is less destroyed than I imagined—not Noyon, I mean, which is like the pictures, but the woods around, which are just like other woods. There is only one little knoll with the stumps of gassed trees like the remains of one's asparagus, but otherwise there are poppies and corn blowing over what less than a year ago was the fiercest battle-field of all. They are filling up the trenches and the shell-holes—and already the barbed wire is hidden by great crops of nettles.

HAROLD TO VITA   *British Delegation, Paris*

28 June 1919

It is over—the signature [of the Treaty of Versailles]—and as I write in my room at the Astoria the Arc de Triomphe is black with people watching the cars stream up the Avenue du Bois.

We were told to leave the Majestic at 1.30, so I had a small and early luncheon, put on my tail coat, lit a cigar, and started in one of our cars. My old black slouch hat came with me, as it has seen so much of the Conference that I thought it would like to see the end. Besides,

---

1. Violet married Denys Trefusis in London on 16 June while Vita was with Harold in Paris.

my top-hat is sitting quietly at Hill Street indifferent to the fate of Empires.

Along the road—under the trees at St Cloud—were posted soldiers in their grey helmets holding red flags and waving us along our privileged way. Little knots of people stood about with flags and babies and prams and rosettes and souvenir sellers. We swung suddenly into the main avenue leading to the Château. A sudden blaze of fluttering colours flashed out from the lancer-pennants of the cavalry who lined the road—and we bumped over the pavé of the great courtyard between thick rows of cavalry and infantry at the salute.

At the door the usual battery of official photographers and cinematographers—and a sudden rush in the cool hall, out of the crowd, with only one or two silent frockcoated plenipotentiaries blowing their noses before climbing upstairs.

The staircase was magnificent—on each step stood two Gardes Républicains in their helmets with drawn swords—and a splendid Aubusson splashed down it like a waterfall. My black hat began to feel a little ashamed of itself so I hid it under my arm. The two large salons before the Galerie des Glaces had been furnished with Aubusson, Gobelins and the gems of the Louvre. It was magnificent—the sense of dignity and order. At each door stood the Gardes Républicains like caryatids, at the salute—and we strolled in talking now and then to our friends and looking out on the terrace, where a privileged and ticketed crowd had gathered behind a close row of blue soldiers.

Beyond the second Salon opened the Galerie des Glaces, looking huge and barrelled with the gilt chairs in the middle, and rows of benches and *escabeaux* [stools] at the nearer end. I found my place at once—there were printed tickets, with a pin shoved through the card. For about twenty minutes we chatted with our friends and moved about. At the further end of the room the Press were already established.

Clemenceau was already *installé* in his presidential chair—and one after the other the Delegates began to arrive—Wilson, Lloyd George. It was like a wedding: no applause, but not what you would call silence.

At about three o'clock the *officier d'ordonnance* came from bench to bench saying, *"Asseyez-vous, messieurs—la séance commence,"* and in a few seconds there was a complete hush and everyone was seated.

Four Gardes Républicains then entered and kept the aisle clear. Suddenly there was an order from the Salon outside and with a loud click the Gardes Républicains flashed their swords into their scabbards ("We shall not sheath the sword", flashed into my mind). A silence among all those people so that you could hear a pin drop and faces turned towards the door into the anteroom. Suddenly a stiffening on the part of the four guards and the sound of slow steps on the parquet outside. First came two messieurs in silver chains, and then four officers—a French, a British, an American and an Italian in single file—followed by Müller and Bell,[1] upon whom all eyes were fixed, hostile and interested.

They passed close to me up the aisle, but they held their heads high and looked to the ceiling where Louis XVI sprawled among clouds and goddesses. Hardly had they sat down when Clemenceau began, *"Messieurs la séance est levée,"* and then just a few words, "We are here to sign the peace." The moment he had finished the Germans stood up suddenly—but sat down again abruptly as Mantoux [interpreter] began to translate into English. As soon as Mantoux had finished, St Quentin advanced to the Germans and led them to the table where the Treaty was. In breathless silence they signed—and walked back, their eyes still on the ceiling. Then Wilson rose, and his plenipotentiaries with him, and then began a *défilé* of the Delegations past the table of signature, like candidates filing past the Bishop at confirmation. America, Great Britain, Italy, Japan, while the tension relaxed. Suddenly from outside came the crack of the first gun which announced to Paris the signing of the peace—and in the intervals of the salvoes rose the cheers of the crowds outside on the terrace.

We were told it would last 3 hours—but almost at once it seemed that there came a loud "Sshh" from the ushers—and while an aeroplane rattled past the great windows, Clemenceau spoke again: *"Messieurs, le traité est signé. La séance est levée."* People kept their seats while the formal procession formed out again and the Germans were led from the room in silence. Then a general exodus while I went to one of the great windows and out on to the balcony. The fountain was playing and the crowds were waiting silently behind the troops. Suddenly a great cheer—and below me a group of top hats followed by generals

1. The two German Representatives.

in gold and blue with *grands cordons*. The crowd broke the lines and rushed towards them. It was Wilson, Clemenceau, Lloyd George—and I suppose Foch but I could not see him. They went mad: they yelled, "Vive Clemenceau": they threw flowers, and the guns by the Orangerie crashed out again. It was a wonderful fusion of enthusiasm—dust, flowers and uniforms—some soldiers came up at a double and rescued Ll.G. from the crowd and piloted him to his motor car which was drawn up between the fountains.

And then back again through lanes of cheering people—*"Vive l'Angleterre"* they yelled at our car—and the roses they threw always missed us.

I smoked my pipe and was happy and thought of you, my light and love.

VITA TO HAROLD   *Long Barn*

1 July [1919]

I wrote myself nearly sick yesterday.[1] I wrote poetry too. I have got a new system of writing poetry. I get such heaps of ideas that I just scribble them all down in prose and scraps of verse, and cast them into verse in calmer moments.

HAROLD TO VITA   *British Delegation, Paris*

4 July 1919

Hardinge[2] sent for me yesterday and after a pompous exordium which made all the people in the Champs Elysées stop and take off their hats, he said, "Now why are you so determined to go to this League of Nations?" I murmured something—'interest,' 'hope,' 'the new Europe' etc. etc. and he went on, "I can tell you frankly that it had been my intention prior to your decision to offer you an appointment

---

1. Her second novel, *The Dragon in Shallow Waters*.
2. Lord Hardinge of Penshurst, ex-Viceroy of India and Permanent Undersecretary of State for Foreign Affairs, 1906–10 and 1916–20.

of real importance. I am prepared to offer it you again—if you will abandon the League—I am prepared to make you MY PRIVATE SECRETARY." At these last words the crowds which had collected outside dropped on one knee—and not an eye was undimmed—even a poilu who had been through Verdun murmured the word "chouette" [splendid!] and burst into floods of tears.

I remained unmoved however—and while my head swam—I refused it. You can never say again that I am ambitious!

HAROLD TO VITA   *British Delegation, Paris*

14 July 1919

My darling,

Well the [victory] procession was a success. In fact it was a great success. There was a wonderful moment when Foch and Joffre came through the Arc [de Triomphe] like two pigmies. I have never seen such enthusiasm. But our men would have made you weep. A bright sun, with a cold wind and the flags fluttering: a long pause: and then a quite dull naval band coming through. Suddenly out of the diagonal shade of the arch another group—flashing with an enormous white ensign carried by a naval detachment. The Astoria [British Delegation's hotel] waved with enthusiasm while the British Grenadiers came from under the arch, and behind them hundreds and hundreds of British regimental flags—stiff, imperial, heavy with gold lettering, "Busaco" "Inkerman" "Waterloo"—while the crowd roared with enthusiasm, and our own tommies on the roof yelled "Good old Blighty", and Douglas Haig passed with his generals at the salute. Mar would have sobbed. Norman[1] cried which was a good mark. Hadji pretended to be looking at the programme—but he was rather weepy too. I have never had such a patriotic feeling. I never felt less League of Nations. There they were, the flags of British regiments—of people we know— people from Sussex and Bedfordshire and Kent and Houndsditch—in this blatant foreign capital—with flags emblematic of our past victories of which this is the most glorious, the most democratic and the most

---

1. Montagu Norman (1871–1950), Governor of the Bank of England from 1920.

final. The flags hung stiffly under their gold embroidery—whereas the American flags had flattened, unweighted by history or past achievements. There were two tiny boy scouts at the head of one group, and they saluted as they passed, stiffly like a Coldstream Sergeant-Major. And behind them came the swirl of the bagpipes and the swinging of the kilts. They walked quickly and rather shyly, and the officers rode in front, and the air rocked with cheers and enthusiasm. What a *fool* you were not to come.

VITA TO HAROLD   *Long Barn*

July 1919

Hadji mine,

I've got no news. I haven't been at the cottage the last two days, I've been living on a delicious island in the Aegean, playing gooseberry to the oddest couple . . .[1]

There has been a lot of fighting there, too, and I don't care what you say: it is *damned good.* So there. Now you can think me conceited if you like. (Don't tell anybody, for pity's sake.) They are really very odd people: they have dreadful rows nearly all the time, *et comment!*

I am pleased, *really* pleased. (This cannot mean anything except that it is extremely bad, on the analogy that what *I* think bad you think good!)

VITA TO HAROLD   *Possingworth Manor, Sussex*

30 July 1919

I am at Blackboys.[2] Mrs K and Sonia [Violet's mother and sister] came down to luncheon today. It was all so ghastly, they talked about

1. She had begun to write her third novel, *Challenge,* which was the story of Julian (Vita), a rich young Englishman who becomes President of a small republic on the Greek coast and falls in love with his wayward cousin Eve, who is, of course, Violet.
2. North of Lewes, Sussex. Violet and Denys Trefusis had rented Possingworth Manor for the summer, and Vita spent much of her time there when Violet was not at Long Barn.

people's incomes, and all the usually mean little London gossip. V. and I just looked at each other in despair, it was such a contrast from the conversation we had been having just before, which had been about the Iliad and Wagner's operas. Oh I *do* hate Mrs Keppel. She is a soul-destroying woman.

I love books and flowers and poetry and travel and trees and dragons and the wind and the sea and generous hearts and spacious ideals and little children.

HAROLD TO VITA   *British Delegation, Paris*

8 August 1919

My darling Viti,

I had a terrible day yesterday. A long 2 hours interview with Balfour and the new American (Polk)[1]—about the Greek business. Mr B. was rather weak at the last moment and asked me to come to an agreement with the Yanks and present it to the Council of Five. I refused to do so without first presenting it to Venizelos.[2] He agreed. We then sat down and drew up an agreement. I then went round with my American to submit it to Venizelos. It was very painful. I simply loathed it—and it was like letting Venizelos down. He was very indignant, and stormed for an hour. It was *bloody*. We then went away and I got A.J.B. to agree that we could not force a settlement on Venizelos. But I hardly slept all night (it was like Verdun), and at 9.0 I went round again to see V. and suggested a possible compromise. This he accepted. He had not slept either, and there were tears in his eyes. I then went to Tardieu[3] and got him to agree, and then to A.J.B. who also agreed. It comes up this afternoon at the Council and it will be

---

1. Frank L. Polk, a lawyer and diplomat, was leader of the United States Delegation after the departure of President Wilson and Robert Lansing.
2. Eleutherios Venizelos (1864–1936), the Greek Prime Minister with whom Harold, an ardent phil-Hellene, had established a cordial relationship. The argument concerned the division of Thrace between Greece and Turkey.
3. André Tardieu, a leading member of the French Delegation and close collaborator of Clemenceau.

decided one way or another. It is a *bloody* solution for Greece, but better than the American one. I am unhappy about it.

HAROLD TO VITA   *British Delegation, Paris*

15 September [1919]

I had a very busy day yesterday—chiefly with Maurice Hankey. I got some things done—at least I think I have. I must say Lloyd George is a dynamic person. I wish I could have a long talk with him, but he is too busy—and I have to do it through Hankey.

I have got such a funny new friend—a dressmaker,[1] with a large shop in the Rue Royale, a charming flat at the Rond Point (where I spent the *whole* of Saturday night—sleeping on the balcony) and about 10 mannequins of surpassing beauty. I am lunching at the shop today. My dressmaker is only 27—and it is rather sporting to launch out into so elaborate an adventure at that age. Mar would like my new friend, I think—very attractive. Such a nice flat too. I think I shall stay there when and if I come back and not go to the Majestic. There is a spare room and I would pay for my board.

VITA TO HAROLD   *Long Barn*

19 October 1919

My own own darling, my own beloved darling, I scribble this for you to read when I'm gone[2] and you are having your breakfast by yourself and are perhaps wishing I was there. My own precious love, I only want to say again what I said last night, namely that I love you immutably, sacredly, and rootedly—you're all the sacred secret things of life, my beloved, that's what you are, (the cottage, the babies, and all that), and besides that, you're *all* that I think clean and sweet and

---

1. Edward Molyneux, the well-known couturier and collector of Impressionist paintings.
2. On this day Vita and Violet, with Harold's consent, left for their second long visit to Monte Carlo. They were away until early January 1920.

good (*really* good, not priggy) and fresh and *tout couvert de rosée* and like apple blossom. My darling, my darling, I haven't got words to tell you how much I think of you in that way, or with what tenderness—and love. O my darling, I wish one could tell a person how much one loves them, it's one of the aggravating things of life that one shouldn't be able to.

Nothing in this world could ever alter my love for you, I KNOW THAT.

Darling, this letter is *packed* with love.

HAROLD TO VITA   *League of Nations*
                             Sunderland House
25 October 1919   *Curzon Street, London W.1*

Darling, I've got a grievance against you—why did you tell B.M. the most intimate things about you and me? It is all right you telling her things about yourself—(though I think that very unwise)—but it is bad luck on me to tell her things about me, which are at once repeated to Ozzie [Dickinson] and via him *urbi et orbi*. But it's no use writing you grievances to 1200 miles away—and I love you.

I don't pretend that I'm happy, because I'm not. I feel I've thrown the precious vessel of my happiness into Niagara and it may either be submerged or taken out to distant and alien waters. I know that under V.'s influence you will think it very smug of me to worry. But you are all my hope, darling, and it is agony to think of your dear splendid nature being warped or hardened. You see she has all the weapons and I have none. The only ones I have represent for you what you hate. The ones she has are all that you most love and desire. So it's not a fair fight, darling, but *you* are fair and I am fair and it may be all right. I don't like the gossip—but it is only a detail and once I get over to Paris[1] it will all be easier. At present it drives me away from the haunts of man and woman. Oh darling! I feel so lonely and hopeless, and you are the only person who understands.

---

1. Harold left Paris on 21 October and began work on the International Secretariat of the League of Nations in London.

I long to get over to Paris and drench myself in work.

I feel rather selfish writing to you a grumble, when you will be so happy out there in the sun [Monte Carlo]. Darling, don't forget me—don't feel hard to me. Don't throw yourself too madly into an orgy of irresponsibility. Don't let little Smuts[2] reflect the cruelty of present circumstances. Keep Eve the little prig she is. Devotion is only really beautiful when it entails sacrifice: not when it becomes a bonfire on which the lives of others are chucked and broken.

Anyhow as you *are* there, enjoy yourself—and don't think of me as nursing grievances which I haven't got. I love you too much for that.

HAROLD TO VITA   *Paris*

4 November [1919]

I do envy you so your freedom and liberty—but don't let yourself feel it is a right, this self indulgence: it is merely a holiday. Oh darling, I am rather fussed about you—not about you or me, but about your getting sloppier and sloppier, till even having to wear stays will become a *corvée* [unpleasant duty]—and your life will become one long sluttish slatternly muddle. That's why it annoys me that you should *always* lose your luggage. It's so slovenly. I loathe slov (rather a good word that). But I know you think you don't do a slov about your work. But that's no excuse as you can sit down to that and not move, and it doesn't entail plans, arrangements, accounts, time-tables, arguments, accuracies, previsions, coming upstairs, telephoning, writing cheques, writing in the counterfoil of cheques, standing in queues, talking to bedints [servants], having to make up one's mind, pushing, having one's hair blown about in the wind—no, one just sits on a chair quite still and quiet with a cigarette, 2 tubes of lipsalve and a pot of powder.

Mind, darling, I want you back by Dec. 21—and no mistake about it.

---

2. His name for Vita's novel *Challenge*.

26 November [1919]

Oh Hadji, I don't think I am fit to love anyone, or for them to love me.

Darling, I do love your letters, and you can't think what a help your remarks about little Smuts [*Challenge*] always are, and such an encouragement. Eve is not a 'little swine', she is just all the weaknesses and faults of feminity carried to the nth power, but also redeemed by the self-sacrifice which is also very feminine. I do think she is left sympathetic at the end, in spite of what she has done. It will be fun to think you are reading it. Julian is a practical idealist. He is much better, and less a schoolgirl hero. (But still a little bit that, I'm afraid.) The end was very difficult. I have tried to keep it as simple as possible. But as a whole it is a bad book. I shall never write a good book; at least, I might write dozens of *quite* good books, but I shall never write a great one. And to be great is the only thing that really counts, whether for books or people. *The Idiot* [Dostoyevski] is great.

HAROLD TO VITA *Paris*

3 December 1919

I fear I am going downhill without you—and I get so awfully depressed that I drink too much, and I spend my time with rather low people, but I am ashamed to go into society, so I live in the demi-monde and I don't like it much.

VITA TO HAROLD *Bordighera, Italy*

5 December 1919

I feel it's such a mockery my writing you superficial letters, and I dread writing you *real* ones; that's really why I have written so little.

I hate unreality and convention, especially between you and me. It's an insult to us both. So I'm going to write you a real letter now, a long one, and, please, you must realise that I'm writing quite sanely, and not think that anything I say is hysteria or theatrical, or anything but the sober fact and truth.

You see, I don't think you realise except in a very tiny degree what's going on or what's been going on. I don't think you have taken the thing seriously. (Of course, I know you have hated my being away and all that, but I think you have looked on it all as more or less transitory and "wild oats"—your own expression.) But surely, darling, you don't think I would have gone away from you and risked all that I *have* risked—your love, B.M.'s love, Dada's love, and my own reputation—for a whim? (I don't really care a damn about the reputation, but I do care about the rest.) Don't you realise that only a very great force could have brought me to risk these things? Many little things have shown me that you don't realise it. For instance: you talked of "wild oats." You talked of my being away as a holiday. You write of V. as Mrs Denys Trefusis—don't you realise that that name is a stab to me every time I hear it? every time I see it on an envelope? Yet you write of her as that as a joke.

There is another thing you don't realise. When I come back this time, V. and I [will] give each other up for ever. It is the only thing we can do, but it is going to break me for the time being. I'm not grumbling about it, or suggesting any other course; only, simply, there it is . . . Please, darling, don't write to me and say why is this necessary? *please* don't do that, or refer to it; I know you are such an angel that you wouldn't ever want me to do anything so drastic, but you must let me decide this for myself, and I *have* decided.

This brings me to the question of my coming to Paris. It is quite true that I shan't be well, and I really won't travel sitting up all night under those conditions. Denys is coming to Cannes on the 15th. I will come back then. [She didn't.] I don't want to write any more about this. I am infinitely sorry to know B.M. will be in Paris. I should have liked to be alone with you, or failing that, by myself.

Then, oh Hadji, my darling darling Hadji (you *are* my darling Hadji, because if it wasn't for you I would go off with V.), there's another thing. You say you only want to *tromper* me with myself.[1] But that's *impossible,* darling; there can't be anything of *that* now—just now, I mean. Oh Hadji, can't you realise a little? I *can't* put it into words. It isn't that I don't love you; I do. I do! How much you will never know.

The whole thing is the most awful tragedy, and I see only too clearly that I was never fit to marry somebody so sane, so good, so sweet, so limpid, as yourself; it wasn't fair on you. If you had asked me to live with you, I would have done so. It is all I am fit for. But at least I love you with a love so profound that it can't be uprooted by another love, more tempestuous and altogether on a different plane.

Hadji, I don't want to hurt you, I can't *really* hurt you, can I, when I tell you I love you so infinitely much?

Oh dear, all the fount of anguish with which I started this letter seems to have exhausted itself and I must stop. Don't think it a 'rattled' letter, it's so much graver than that, if you only knew. And don't be afraid I shall do anything awful.

Mar

HAROLD TO VITA   *Paris*

9 December 1919

Darling, your letter was so frank and splendid. So like the real you which I know. You see my love for you rests on such firm foundations of truth and frankness, that when, for a red few days, I thought you had deceived me, the whole edifice of life appeared to totter. You know I could forgive you (it is an absurd word to use)—but I could wipe out all things except meanness. And if you were mean it would be as if you were dead, and my love would die for all except the remembrance of what you once were. But now your letter has come and you are alive again. And my love is like a forest in spring.

When you come back to me, I shall get on your nerves and so will B.M. And it will all be a nightmare. But it has got to be gone through,

---

1. In this roundabout way (for she spoke French perfectly) Vita was suggesting that Harold wanted to make love to her.

and we will go through with it together. And you can count on me to say nothing, and to go on as if nothing has happened.

And what's more, you can count on B.M. too. I really think you can. She is in her best mood and anxious only to help you. She really does love you deeply—below all the surface selfishness.

So my darling, you will have a month or two months of real torture. I am dreading it for you. But you will be brave and splendid— and you can be irritable to me and I should know it, and you can cry to me and I shall say nothing, and you can laugh, and I shall know what ashes your laughter is made of.

Oh my Vita—I know what you are sacrificing for me.

VITA TO HAROLD   *Long Barn*

[1 February 1920]

There is so much in my heart, but I don't want to write it because *à quoi bon?* Only if I were you, and you were me, I would battle so hard to keep you—partly, I daresay, because I would not have the courage and the reserve to do like you and say nothing. O Hadji, the reason I sometimes try to get you to say things, to say that you would miss me and that sort of thing, is that I long for weapons to fortify myself with; and when you do say things, I treasure them up and in moments of temptation I say them over to myself and think, "There, he *does* mind, he *would* mind, you *are* essential to him . . . It is worthwhile making yourself unhappy if it is to keep him happy," and so on, but then when you say things like that you don't miss me in Paris, and that scandal matters, I think, "Well, if it is only on account of scandal and convenience and above all *because I am his wife* and permanent and legitimate—if it isn't more personal than that, is it worthwhile my breaking my heart to give him, not positive happiness, but mere negative contentment?"

So I fish, and fish, and fish, and sometimes I catch a lovely little silver trout, but never the great salmon that lashes and fights and *convinces* me that it is fighting for its life.

You see, I know you can do anything with me; you can touch

my heart like no one, no one, no one (the nearest is Ben), and I try to *make* you fight for yourself, but you never will; you just say, "Darling Mar!" and leave me to invent my own conviction out of your silence.

And O Hadji, what you don't realise is that I am very weak, and that my life for the past year almost has been one resistance of bitter temptation; and that it is simply and solely love of you which has kept me. You are good and sweet and lovable, and you are the person I loved in the best and simplest way; but there is lots that is neither good or simple in me, and it is that part which is so tempted. And I *have* struggled, I *have* stayed; I tore myself away and came to Paris in June last year; you know I have. And it is only, only, only out of love for you, nothing else would have weighed with me the weight of a hair, so you see how strong a temptation it must be, to sweep everything aside, and you see also how strong my love for you must be.

My darling, my darling, I shall love you till I die, I *know* I shall.

HAROLD TO VITA   *Hotel Alexander III, Paris*

3 February 1920

My darling Mar,

I have just got your letter—my dearest one—and I am so moved by it, my darling. There are so many things that are difficult to explain but there is first one thing I want to clear up.

When did I say I didn't "miss" you in Paris? Darling, I miss you all the time—you must have misunderstood me. I suppose I said that I didn't miss you in Paris as much as in London, or England, but if I said that, it is only a question of relativity. I mean I simply couldn't *live* in England without you—it would be one big pang like the journey down to Dover on Sunday. In Paris it's rather like as if I were a soldier and said I didn't miss you in the trenches. It would be quite true—but it wouldn't mean that I didn't *want* you. I *want* you all the time and wherever I may be—and if I felt I was not to see you again, I can't contemplate what my attitude would be.

It would be despair like one can't imagine it—a sort of winter night (Sunday) at Aberdeen, and me in the streets alone with only a Temperance Hotel to sleep in.

Then about my general attitude. You see, what appeal can I make except that of love? I *can't* appeal to your pity—and it would be doing that to let you see what I feared and suffered. It would be ridiculous to appeal to your sense of duty etc.—that's all rubbish. So what is there left but to appeal to love—my love for you and yours for me? And how can *that* appeal be anything but inarticulate? How can I formulate in words how I love you? One has only the current coin of the English language—such used and battered currency—of course my love is dumb in that way. But you must feel it and see it—and all you have done and sacrificed shows that you have felt it.

I know that you think sometimes that if you left me I should recover in a year or two and not be unhappy. I think you are so wrong there. You see, you would have ruined my life—I mean my inside life—and all the joys you had given me would be stinking corpses. I should mind that acutely and permanently. It would poison my heart and ruin my character. You know it would.

Then I should never love any one else. I see that quite clearly. So I would be so lonely, so terribly lonely—think of Edward Johnson [Sevenoaks widower]—it would be worse than that, as even my memories would be painful.

Darling, I hate the thought of your feeling frightened. Perhaps I have thought you stronger than you are. You see, your excessiveness and your ruthlessness give the impression of strength. I am frightened myself at your being alone over there [Long Barn]. Can't you come here? My darling, I feel that if we are together it may be easier for you. *Can't* you come—I shall *choyer* [cherish] you so, my sweet, and I shan't be too busy to have to leave you alone all day.

It *is* bloody being here—with you over there and unhappy.

You know, Ben is like me in that way. I mean, his never mentioning the pantomime. I simply *can't* talk about inside things which go deep—the words won't come out, or come out different. I know I am a fool and I make up things to say and then I can't say them. It is my own particular looniness.

But darling, how I love and want you: oh my darling, I think of you every five minutes, and what a stab those thoughts would be if you were a beast to me! Even so I can't conceive of you hurting me deliberately.

What a hopeless letter!

Hadji

HAROLD TO VITA

4 February 1920

League of Nations, Paris

My dearest, I thought of you so much last night. I am so worried about you. You are all wrong in thinking that I look upon you as my *légitime.* You are not a person with whom one can associate law, order, duty—or any of the conventional ties of life. I never think of you in that way, not even from the babies' point of view. I just look on you as the person I love best in the world and without whom life would lose all its light and meaning. My darling, I do hope you can come over here—it would be bloody for you in a way, but I do so want to have you with me and you can write. The [Hotel] Alexander III is quite comfy, and very clean. I don't want to be here long—it is terribly dull if one hasn't got a lot of work, or doesn't plunge into debauchery.

VITA TO HAROLD

7 February 1920

Saracen's Hotel, Lincoln

I am not fit to consort and remain with ordinary nice people. I *hate* myself, as I have told you a thousand times over. I wish I was dead, and that you hated me and didn't care what became of me.

Forgive me for not having written before. Really it is because some latent honesty within me will not allow me to write when the future is uncertain and when I know that any day I may cross the

Channel on that desperate voyage.[1] Oh my sweet, simple, *clean* Hadji, how much I love you and look enviously at you from a long way off.

VITA TO HAROLD   *Dover*

[9 February 1920]

Hadji, since I wrote to you this afternoon things have happened. I went out to send some telegrams and to post my letter, and then I was standing looking at the sea when I saw Denys [Trefusis] coming towards me. He asked me where Violet was.[2] I said I had promised not to tell him. He said he would find out, or stay with me till I left Dover and come wherever I went because he knew I would join her sooner or later. So I told him, as it seemed useless to conceal it. So he and I are going there [Amiens] tomorrow, and he is going to ask her whether she will go back to him. I shall try my utmost to make her, O God, O God, how miserable and frightened I am—and if she refuses, he says he will never have anything to do with her again. I do not for a moment think she will consent, as I urged her *so* much this morning and she refused so positively; she said she would never live with him even if I did not exist. I will try to make her, I will, I will, I will; I will only see her in front of Denys, and he shall see that I will try.

If she consents, and goes with him, I shall come to you. I am trying to be good, Hadji. I want so dreadfully to be with her, and I cannot *bear* to think of her being with him, but I shall try to make her. We are going to France. I nearly had a fit when I saw him. I can't help seeing the ludicrous side of this journey with him—will we go in the same railway-carriage or what? The whole thing is so unreal; everything is unreal except the pain of it. He has spent all the afternoon and most of the evening walking up and down my room in this filthy little

---

1. Vita's affair was approaching its climax. She had gone to Lincoln with Violet ostensibly to tour the Fens for her new novel, but in fact to plan their elopement. Harold, in Paris, did not know that Violet was with her.
2. Violet had crossed the Channel earlier that day, and Vita was to follow her on the 10th. They were to meet in Amiens. By this time, each had pledged to the other that they would abandon their families and spend the rest of their lives together.

hotel. I do not believe she will go back to him, and he says he will have nothing more to do with her if she won't. Hadji, it is the most extraordinary situation I have ever been in; I think you would think so too if you were me.

But the point is that if, after all his arguments and all my persuasion, she still refuses, he will go away leaving her for good. And she *will* refuse, I am almost sure she will refuse.

Hadji, I will try, I swear I will try, both for your sake and a little bit for his as I think he is too fine a person to be broken, but of course it is for you really. I *will* try, I feel strong, I did this morning and I can keep it up.

Poor Denys, he is really a very splendid person, though I know you think he is mad.

O darling, there's such an awful wind and the sea is so dreadfully rough.

How terrified she will be when she sees me arrive with him.

How worried you will be by all this. I am thankful you are not in the middle of it, as things always seem a little less vivid when one isn't there.

O darling, it's awfully lonely here.

I must write to B.M. now and Dada.[3]

Your Mar

---

3. No more is revealed in their correspondence, but the sequel is clear from Vita's and her mother's diaries, and Vita's narrative published in *Portrait of a Marriage*. Vita and Denys did cross the Channel together the next day, and found Violet unexpectedly in Calais. All three took the train to Amiens, where Denys abandoned his wife, giving up hope. But on 14 February he and Harold flew to Amiens and persuaded the two women to part. Eventually Vita and Harold returned to England, and Violet and Denys to the South of France.

Vita and Violet continued to see each other, and even travel abroad together, for another year, but the confrontation at Amiens had defused their affair, and Vita's marriage was never again in danger. She and Harold had agreed that each could enjoy sexual independence of the other, and in 1923 she had her only affair with a man, the writer Geoffrey Scott, which ended more easily for her than for Scott, for he was divorced by his wife, while Vita abandoned him for the most important lover of her life, Virginia Woolf, whom she had first met in December 1922. This was the period when Harold, in the intervals of making a brilliant reputation as a diplomatist (notably on Lord Curzon's staff at the Lausanne Conference of 1923), had begun to write his first books—biographies of Paul Verlaine, Tennyson, and Byron, and his novel Sweet Waters—*while Vita was writing fiction, poetry (she began* The Land *in 1923), and the history of her family,* Knole and the Sackvilles. *At Long Barn, and in London and Paris, both were enjoying a brilliant social life.*

VITA TO HAROLD   *Long Barn*

21 July [1920]

I got such a triumphant letter from you today about your [Austrian] treaty: you *are* brilliant and successful and clever and all that, damn you—and P.V.[1] is so good—it's not fair, whereas I am nothing

---

1. Harold's biography of the French poet Paul Verlaine, published by Constables in 1921. It was his first book.

but a muddling failure, damn you again. It will be envy and not infidelity that splits up our little ménage.

Your friend [Denys Trefusis] and Violet are separating completely, and I have much to tell you. She is going abroad almost at once. I have refused to go.

HAROLD TO VITA   *Foreign Office*

8 February 1921

My own darling silly,

I telegraphed to you twice—to Hyères[1] and to Cannes, begging you to fix a definite date for your return. This morning I get a reply to the effect that you "want to stay on a bit"—and ending in some rigmarole about a housemaid. But darling, that wasn't in the least a reply to my question. I never asked whether or not you wanted to stay on a bit (I took that for granted). What I asked was the length of the bit you wanted to stay on. To that I shall get no reply. Why? Because you are more selfish than Agrippina[2] in her worst moments, and because you are more optimistic than the Virgin Mary at her most light-hearted, and more weak than some polypus floating and undulating in a pond. You see, (a) you refuse obstinately to look at my side of the case. If you think of it at all, you evoke a picture of me bending by day over new maps of the Balkans; guiding the hands of Prime Ministers and statesmen towards a saner and better world: occupied, adulated, content. By night your picture shows me radiant in immaculate clothes, bandying the bouquet of wit with the bouquet of Veuve Cliquot—and returning at last ambrosial and refreshed to my warm and honourable bed. On Sundays you picture me relaxed and paternal, playing with my children among the tapestries of your ancestral home, or directing with gay and measured eye the structural alterations on my own estate.

Such is the picture you draw of me, and if, at moments, it seems

1. Where Vita had been staying with Violet since mid-January.
2. Mother of the Emperor Nero.

a little unconvincing, you quickly switch off the light with a "Poor little Hadji, I'll be so nice to him when I get back. I'll make it up."

(b) As regards yourself there is, first, the abiding squalor of dates. What was Saturday February 28th to Hernando de Soto[3]—or what was Hernando de Soto to Saturday February 28th? But secondly, and more important, is the thought that a date means an obligation, and an obligation a scene. Besides, it is throwing away a very useful stick wherewith to stir the troubled waters of your present life. You see, when the fur begins to fly it is splendid to be able to say, "Well really, Fatushka (or whatever it is),[4] I shall leave you tomorrow"—and then one has a reconciliation and it's all quite delightful. But if there are dates in front of one, one's departure becomes a mere fact, and not a threat which one can wave as a red flag at dramatic moments. And finally there is the thought, that little friendly thought of yours, "Oh something will turn up."

But on this occasion it isn't going to work. You are to be back in England on Friday, Feb. 25. On Saturday we shall go down together to the cottage. So please take your tickets at once. And please also realise that this is definite. I shall be more angry than I have ever been if you do not come back on that date. Don't misunderstand me: I shall really cut adrift if you don't. It is a generous date: it is longer than you promised: but it is a *fixed* date and you must keep to it.[5] If it is inconvenient to you, *tell me at once* and I will alter it. Otherwise it must be accepted.

I honestly believe you think that to write to me is 'indecent'. I know that the real reason is (a) V. doesn't let you write, (b) if you do write it makes you think of me and that produces a guilty feeling. But tell me this: if it is indecent of you to write to me when you are with V., isn't it far more indecent to write to V. when you are with me? And telegraph, and telephone, and meet in hotels, and churches, and galleries—and even at Hildenborough Station. How grotesque you are, darling!

Don't think I blame you. I love you too much for that. I know

---

3. The Spanish explorer who marched from Florida to beyond the Mississippi, 1539–41.
4. Vita called Violet "Lushka."
5. Vita returned to England on 9 March 1921, her 29th birthday.

that when you fall into V.'s hands your will becomes like a jelly-fish addicted to cocaine. All I ask is *please* don't make excuses. They don't take me in. I know that they are a little cold cream for your sore conscience. But keep them for yourself. Don't give them to me. They only sadden me the more, and *telegraph* when you have got tickets.

God bless you, my looney.

H.

HAROLD TO VITA   *Sussex Sq., Brighton*

18 September 1921

After all, it's no use writing novels which are only the observations of life. Journalism and the movies will do that for us. The point is to write books which are the explanation of life—and that is where you come in and I go out.

There is a light high up in the house opposite, and the spire of the church against dark wind-scudding clouds. The babies are asleep in their little beds. There are bath salts waiting for me. And there are you out there somewhere[1]—who will always love and stimulate, God bless you, and always, oh God bless you, understand.

HAROLD TO VITA   *53 Cadogan Gardens,*
                                                London S.W.3
16 November 1922

This is just a little scribble to reach you when you come back to Long Barn[2]—so that when you arrive you won't feel lonely or deserted, but will feel warm and so terribly loved and protected by our little mud pie [Long Barn], which we both love so childishly and

---

1. Vita was on a tour of Italy with Dorothy and Lord Gerald Wellesley.
2. Harold left for the Lausanne Conference the next day and did not return to London until February 1923.

which for both of us is the place where we have been so happy, darling. I don't think we could ever leave the cottage: there is not one crook in the wall, or one stain in the carpet, which does not mean something to you and me which it could never mean to strangers: something which has been built up gradually—little cell by cell, as Mr [Walter] Pater would have said—and which means you to me, dearest, and me, dearest, to you.

And with it all a sense of permanence so that as you sit in your room tonight I shall think of you there, I dashing through the Ile de France in a train. And I shall think of the Rodin, and the blue [Egyptian porcelain] crocodile and the figure of St Barbara—and the London *Mercury* [magazine] upon the stool. And it will be for both of us as if I were there, and love still hangs, as well as smoke, about the room.

It is beastly going away—but I think of £1,500 [salary] and liberty at the end of it, and next summer, and Tennyson[3] coming out and the revisions you will be sending me of the Knole book.[4] We are always stirred and excited by the same thing—and oh my sweet we *do* love and understand each other so absolutely that being parted is really only like standing back from the picture to see it better.

Darling, you musn't be miz, will you—and you will make Chalk Stone[5] the best book you have done.

And please don't run away with anybody without giving me time to get my aeroplane ready.

VITA TO HAROLD   *Long Barn*

25 November [1922]

The garden is all dug over, and I have been so unslops; nearly everything is done. The little devil polyantha are replaced by pink

---

3. Harold's *Tennyson* was published on 15 March 1923.
4. *Knole and the Sackvilles* in November 1922.
5. This was Vita's next novel, *Grey Wethers*. It received favorable reviews, but later in life she so much disliked her early novels that she mentioned only *Heritage* in her *Who's Who* entry.

roses; the tennis court is surrounded by roses; there are new archways with Guirlande up near the chicken run; the lilacs are moved; the roses are weeded out in the little enclosed gardens; the bed under the big-room window is dug up and empty waiting for the roses to come; next week there will be hedges planted down by the right of way and up above the tennis court; there are new Guirlande roses by the entrance; masses of new orange lilies in my border; lots of manure or leaf-mould; a new strawberry bed; new roses in the oil-jars; no more Dorothy Perkins; Irish yews ordered for the top of the steps, both flights; so there really remain only the poplars to move now. Don't you long for the spring?

HAROLD TO VITA   *Lausanne [Switzerland]*

25 November 1922

Curzon's valet got drunk and went down to the hotel ballroom where people were dancing, and danced with the lovely ladies of Lausanne. With the result that he was sacked. In revenge he hid the Marquis's trousers, and the latter appeared in Allen's [Leeper] room in his dressing-gown. It was some time before they were recovered.[1]

HAROLD TO VITA   *Lausanne*

6 December 1922

I was a little fussed by hearing in one of your letters that Violet was coming to London. I can't help worrying over that a bit. I can't help being afraid that she will bother you to see her and then mesmerize you, and that then it will all begin again. You see, now that you have finished chalk-stones [*Grey Wethers*] and are going up to London,

---

1. This scene was described in the most famous chapter of Harold's most famous book, *Some People.* There he named the valet "Arketall." His real name was Chippendale.

you will be at a loose end and *so* available. And you will imagine that it will be quite safe to see her, and it *won't* be safe, and she will get hold of you again. She is so absolutely unscrupulous, my darling: and you, my darling, are so gullible and so weak. *Promise* me that you will be careful, and that if you get into a muddle you will jump into a train and come out here before it gets bad again.

Not that I care in the least how you behave: that's your business. It's simply that I don't want us both to be drawn into that vortex of unhappiness which so nearly overwhelmed us. So you will *promise,* darling, to be careful and not to go and get mesmerized; or take drugs; or go into smallpox areas; or eat too many sweets between meals? My darling—it is rather a fuss for me to have you there in London with that panther sneaking about waiting to pounce upon you.

I love you. I also love Lady Curzon. So if you go to Amiens with V. I shan't get into an aeroplane *this* time: not I: I shall get into a dinghy and row across to Evian with Lady C.

I wrote a poem today:

The expert attached to Lord Curzon
Is a strangely inferior person,
   When the Marquis rebuts
   His opinions, he puts
An expression of boredom—or worse—on.

VITA TO HAROLD   *Long Barn*

8 December [1922]

I have just come home from London and found a poor little worried letter from you about Violet, and have instantly sent you a telegram to set your mind at rest; I curse myself for having told you she was coming to London, and so having given you even a moment's anxiety.

Darling, my own darling, *not for a million pounds would I have anything* to do with V. again; I hate her for all the misery she brought upon us; so there. She did ring me up, (only I *beg* you not to say so to anyone), and I made Dots [Dorothy Wellesley] stay in the room as a witness, while I told her that nothing would tempt me to see her, and that she was utterly indifferent to me; which is true. You can ask Dots if you like. She has not tried to ring me up since, and I don't think she will again, after what she got from me! As a matter of fact, she is going back to Paris any day. But *don't worry,* oh don't, my little boy; word of honour, padlock, don't. I wish I could convince you.

And above all, I would *never* have anything more to do with her; the boredom of it . . . and the lies . . . and the rows . . . oh no, no, NO. Even if you didn't exist, you whom I love so fundamentally and deeply and incurably.

Oh yes, I know you will say, "But you loved me *then,* and yet you did." It's quite true, I did love you, and I always loved you all through those wretched years, but you know what infatuation is, and I was mad.

HAROLD TO VITA   *Lausanne*

2 January 1923

I went yesterday to Montreux and then changed and went in a funny funicular to a place called Gstaadt where we arrived at 7.30. I read Byron all the time.[1] We were met by a big sleigh with bells and went up to the Hotel. There was a dinner and a fancy dress ball afterwards, at both of which the school-boys whom your friend Neville Lytton[2] sends over to Switzerland all got drunk and noisy. I was rather bored and felt out of it. Next morning I skied. I don't think I have ever fallen about so much or so often. I rolled over and over like a rabbit. It was great fun. I was very careful. I was divided between trying to show off to the other members of the delegation and trying not to be chanticleer to my own sweet. The delegation won in the end. It was because there was a jump. One goes down the hill and then there

---

1. Harold had started researching for his book *Byron: The Last Journey.*
2. Later (1947) the 3rd Earl of Lytton, a portrait and landscape painter.

is a little nick in it and one goes right up in the air and then one falls down and rolls to the bottom. It is great fun.

By luncheon time I was dripping with heat and snow like a *bombe surprise*—and very excited. I started to go back to the hotel. I thought I should go alone just to surprise them. So I got into a little path and went on and on till suddenly I came across the railway line or rather the funicular. At a bound I had jumped it and was dashing down the slope beyond. The houses of the village rushed up to meet me: it was like coming down in an aeroplane: I thought how right you had been to warn me against winter sports: and where I had put my Will: and whether I had been good enough to Mummy: and then just as my whole past life began to rise before me, I saw that a barbed wire fence was also rising to meet me. I flung myself on my back: there was a shower of snow and skis and Hadji—and I came up crash against one of the supports of the fence.

Got up and shook myself. Very carefully felt myself all over. Limped along to the village street. The hotel was about half a mile above me. It was one-thirty. Wet, frightened, bruised and hungry I limped up the hill carrying my skis with me. It was as if Christ had been asked to carry his cross back from Calvary or like Mr Oates[3] going off to die at the South Pole.

HAROLD TO VITA [TELEGRAM]   *Lausanne*

9 January 1923

Letter just received. Delighted to expect you at Lausanne on Friday morning. Don't fail as Marquis is counting on you to help him at huge official dinner on Saturday. Lady Curzon comes today. I haven't written lately in view of your arrival. Oh God I long to see you, so bring pretty clothes and jewels. Keeping very snobbish about you and want to show you off. Isn't this an extravagant sort of telegram to send. Hadji.[4]

---

3. Lawrence Oates, who sacrificed his life in an attempt to save his comrades on Scott's expedition to the Antarctic, 1911–12.
4. Vita arrived in Lausanne as arranged, and stayed nine days.

VITA TO HAROLD   *182 Ebury St., S.W.1*

10 January [1923]

Tomorrow I dine with my darling Mrs. Woolf[1] at Richmond, "a picnic more than a dinner, as the press has overflowed both into the dining-room and into the larder." I love Mrs. Woolf with a sick passion. So will you. In fact I don't think I will let you know her.

VITA TO HAROLD   *Long Barn*

12 January [1923]

I dined alone with Virginia Woolf last night. Oh dear, how much I love that woman. Mrs [Julia] Cameron was her great-aunt, and she has lots of Mrs C's photographs, so I suppose I will have to let you meet her after all. She says Mrs C used to say to Tennyson, "Alfred, I brought my friends to see a lion, but they have only seen a bear." And she used to cut his hair.

HAROLD TO VITA   *Lausanne*

24 January 1923

I am so angry, that I am not in a fit state to write. I don't remember having been so angry in my life. It is about the Turks. They had the impudence to say that they must be allowed to dig up our graves at Gallipoli and put them all in one cemetery. I simply saw red. I told them that it was incredible that a beaten country should raise such a question. Then they climbed down, but they did not climb down far enough and I refused to go on discussing. Really they are quite, quite mad—and if they want war they will get it. I feel I won't speak to them again. I told them that the British Empire would never NEVER evacuate Gallipoli until our graves were safeguarded.

---

1. Vita had first met Virginia Woolf on 14 December 1922, dining with Clive Bell, who until then had been the Nicolsons' only link with Bloomsbury. Virginia and Leonard Woolf were then living at Hogarth House, Richmond, and it was there that they installed their printing press and published their first books under the imprint "The Hogarth Press."

HAROLD TO VITA   *Lausanne*

1 February 1923

I really think now we shall leave on Sunday *and with a Treaty*. I do really. Of course it is *entirely* the Marquis [Curzon] absolutely entirely. When I thought he was wrong, he was right, and when I thought he was right, he was much righter than I thought. I give him 100 marks out of 100 and I am so proud of him. So *awfully* proud. He is a great man and one day England will know it.

But you see Britannia *has* ruled here. Entirely against the Turks, against treacherous allies, against a weak-kneed cabinet, against a rotten public opinion—and Curzon has *won*. Thank God.

All this is after an interview with Ismet[1] when he collapsed in spite of Poincaré telling him not to collapse. And it was just due to the Marquis sitting there solid and *grand seigneur* and amused and brutal.

HAROLD TO VITA   *Foreign Office*

24 May 1923

My poppet,
They have mended my typewriter, and as I must try to see if it works, I shall write to you.
It does work.
I am rather worried about your speech tomorrow,[2] and the feeling that you will go there in your dear opty [optimistic] way, saying, "Oh No, they won't expect a speech from little me." And then suddenly when you are talking about water-wagtails to Lord Grey of Fallodon, you will be startled to hear a man, with a very grave face and a very distinct voice, say: "YOUR ROYAL HIGHNESS, YOUR EXCELLENCIES, MY LORD DUKE, MY LORDS, LADIES AND GENTLEMEN, PRAY SILENCE PLEASE FOR Miss V.

---

1. Ismet Pasha, the leader of the Turkish Delegation at Lausanne. Harold described the Conference in great detail in his *Curzon, The Last Phase* (1934).
2. At the English Association's annual dinner at the Trocadero Restaurant, London. Lord Grey, the former Foreign Secretary, was in the Chair, and Vita and the Spanish Ambassador responded for the guests.

Sackville-West." Then you will get up and feel very tall suddenly, and then very small suddenly, and in a voice like the bleat of some very distant lamb upon the mountain-side, you will begin, "YOUR ROYAL EXCELLENCY, HIGHNESS, MY DORD LUKE, MY LADIES, MY GENTLEMEN, PRAY SILENCE PLEASE . . . PLEASE . . . NO I mean . . . unaccustomed as I am to public speaking, yet I cannot restrain myself from thinking what I say about the Englosh assiciation, no I mean the Englash associotion, no I mean— well you know what I mean. Thank you very much. I HAVE ALWAYS THOUGHT . . . I HAVE ALWAYS THOUGHT . . . I have always thought . . . I HAVE ALWAYS THOUGHT . . . I have always thought . . . AND I THINK Today . . . today that that . . . AND I SHALL ALWAYS THINK . . . always . . . always . . . think . . . I think today, I have always thought and I shall always think . . . That . . . THAT . . . THAT . . . the English Association is the most english association that England has ever associated with. My Dord Luke, my excellent royal, my gentlemen, thank you very much. That's all I have to say. Thank you very much . . . great honour, unexpected pleasure . . . unaccustomed as I am. The heir to all the ages . . . the heritage of unfulfilled renown . . . the sallenge to Sirius . . . Orchyard . . . Sorry . . . Please may I sit down."

That sort of thing won't do at all. You must have something ready and learn it by heart. And have a little hot rumpled bit of paper with notes on it to remind you how your sentences begin.

Oh my sweet.

Hadji

HAROLD TO VITA   *Marlborough Club, S.W.1*

15 June 1923

They have shot poor old Stambolisky.[1] I don't think you know him. He was like a great bison with little red furtive eyes and a great massive frame. His hands were like large dimpled hams, and he painted

---

1. Alexander Stambolisky (1879–1923), the Bulgarian Prime Minister, who had represented his country at the Lausanne Conference. He was assassinated on 12 June after the fall of his Government.

his face, and roared like a bull and all his buttons came undone. He was a fine man, in a capricious way, and I can't help being sorry. He disliked me intensely—so that I am not speaking from personal prejudice. I hate the idea of someone whom I knew and abused and worked with and rather liked, lying in some dusty roadway with his tongue cut and his hair clotted with blood.

What swine the Balkans are! My pig farm. But how glad I am that they are my own speciality.

HAROLD TO VITA   *The Royal Automobile Club,*
                                  London S.W.1
2 September 1923

At noon the Embassy telephoned to say that the Marquis had left Paris. At six they telephoned to say he had arrived at Dover. Tyrrell,[1] Allen [Leeper] and I went to Victoria to meet him. The train was an hour late. We went to dine at the station buffet and returned to the platform. There was a large crowd and mounted police. The posters had got "The new War" on them, and "Lord Curzon's hurried return."[2]

There was a large space railed off for his arrival and a crowd of police, reporters, photographers and detectives. The white faces of the crowd bobbed beyond the barrier under the arc-lights. Slowly the train came in and his saloon drew up opposite the enclosure. First came a procession of red boxes and the green baize foot-rest. Then slowly and majestically came the Marquis. The reporters got out their note-books. The photographers set flame to their magnesium. The detectives detected: the police policed. The crowd crowded.

"Where is Nicolson?" said the Marquis, but the rest was lost in a burst of cheering from the crowd. He walked across and "entered his waiting motor."

"Nicolson?" he exclaimed again. I came to him, and leant into the motor. The crowd peered. The detectives kept them back. The report-

---

1. William Tyrrell, Assistant Undersecretary at the Foreign Office, and Curzon's senior civil servant at Lausanne.
2. The crisis had been caused by Mussolini's sudden seizure of Corfu after a dispute with Greece. Curzon, the Foreign Secretary, was ill with phlebitis, and rapidly returned from his holiday in France to London.

ers again took out their note-books. I pulled myself together for the instructions which were to settle the fate of Europe.

"I have been reading *Grey Wethers* [Vita's novel]," said the Marquis—"a magnificent book. The descriptions of the downs are as fine as any in the language. Such power! Such power! Not a pleasant book of course! But what English!"

He was still muttering "What English" as he drove off with Tyrrell. The latter, as he told me afterwards, was longing to ask what Poincaré had said—but no! He was given your literary biography all the way to Carlton House Terrace. "Poincaré?" pleaded Tyrrell as they arrived. "Oh, we talked about Rénan—goodnight Tyrrell."

HAROLD TO VITA   *Athens*

5 October 1923

Poppet,

I worked all yesterday like a little lamb whose fleece was white as snow, which was more than Byron's was, poor man. Atchley is really immensely useful and helps me a great deal. Suggesting there, correcting there. It was worthwhile coming here if only for him.[1] In the evening I had to go out to Kephisia bump bump bump along a dusty pepper-lined road under the stars: the goats, now and then, were frightened of the motor lamps. But Charles Bentinck [Chargé d'Affaires at the Legation] lives there and he begged me to go and dine and sleep. He has got a Villa with oleanders and a gramophone and a shower bath which sighs at one when one pulls the handle because the water has run out. So does the other thing: I was never an expert at pulling plugs but this one just said "fancy that" in a deep bass voice and nothing more. There was a japanned tin pail to help one out with water in it, and a horrid little bristly brown brush. I had a mosquito net. I don't like Kephisia. There is not even a view, and I was glad to get back to my violet-crowned Athens this evening. And I love this place. It beats Rome hollow.

---

1. Harold had gone to Greece to research for his book *Byron: The Last Journey*. S. C. Atchley had been attached as a translator to the British Legation, Athens, since 1909.

Today I went over the Acropolis alone with Wace[2] who is head of the English School at Athens. I am not in principle a good sightseer, but I remained there three hours without noticing and I asked intelligent questions. I didn't ask questions about Corinthian as I doubted whether I could render them very intelligent. Then we lunched together, and afterwards Atchley showed me the bits of Athens that remained from the time when Byron knew it. Just a little cluster of cottages round the Acropolis hill and the smell of drains. And I have got to go to Kephisia again tonight. DAMN. I go to Missolonghi[3] on Tuesday and come back here on Friday.

HAROLD TO VITA   *Garrick Club, London W.C.2*

12 February 1924

I had the most extraordinary experience here tonight, which I must record at once unless it be, or to prevent it being, disbelieved afterwards. It was this.

I dined at the Marlborough [Club]. It was dark and dull. I talked to Admiral Pakenham who is fat and dreary. I couldn't bear it. I came here. I spoke to Admiral Hall who asked me to stand as a Unionist (Good God! but why not?) candidate. Then he went away. I had some beer. I said I would have light beer and not heavy beer. This point is important. They brought me Bass.

Then I went to the lavatory. And beyond the lavatory is the little room in which they keep the sofa which was in Byron's room at Missolonghi. A sudden temptation seized me. The room was quite dark—lit only by the coke embers of a very economical fire. The lights were unlit. I knew where the sofa stood. I threaded my way between the few leather chairs which separated me from it. I bumped a bit, but still I threaded. And then I got there. I lay back and tried to make my mind a blank. I thought of sheep going through a gate: No! that was something else: I thought of nothing: I tried to make my mind as blank as possible. I thought of things like Ochs [Herbert Asquith], and clean

2. Alan Wace, the archaeologist. He was Director of the British School, 1914–23.
3. Where Byron died in 1824.

water, and Reggie Cooper, and your friend Mrs Pirie [Irene Hogarth].
Only by this means could I attain the necessary anaesthesia. I clasped
the wooden parts of the sofa. The fluffy parts might be new: but the
wooden parts were Byron, Missolonghi, Missolonghi, Byron, Byron,
Missolonghi, Missolonghi, Byron. I repeated the words, since that (I
believe) is the psychic thing to do.

Well, nothing happened. I tried again. I thought back on all the
last pages of my book, I thought myself INTO Byron. And then
gradually a sort of strange, unknown, feeling came over me. Really
it was very uncanny. The room was very dark. It was absurd, but
something white and phosphorescent began to glimmer opposite
against the curtains. I wasn't in the least bit taken in. I *knew* it was
imagination. But NO! the thing took shape. It really did: it emerged
quite definitely, darling, as a FACE.

It was a face, a white magnolia face, that looked at me across the
room. You *know* that I don't make things up: and I *swear* to you that
at that moment I saw the face of Byron looking at me. I wasn't in the
least frightened. I just sat and watched it. It didn't disappear. It got
clearer and clearer. There was a sort of drapery (or was it protoplasm?)
round the shoulders.

Then I got frightened and dashed to the electric light switch. I
turned on the light. There was a bust against the curtains, with a brass
plate underneath:—

> WINIFRED EMERY
> BY ALBERT TOFT
> Presented by Cyril Maude

HAROLD TO VITA   *Foreign Office*

4 December 1924

I have been worrying all day about Violet.[1] I couldn't bear it in
the end, and sent you a silly telegram. I hope you weren't cross. But

---

1. Vita was going to dine with friends in Paris, and Violet Trefusis was to be another guest.

my darling, I do so dread that woman. Her very name brings back all
the aching unhappiness of those months: the doubt, the mortification,
and the loneliness. I think she is the only person of whom I am
frightened—and I have an almost superstitious belief in her capacity
for causing distraction and wretchedness. Of course I know that it's
all over now, but what I dread is your dear sweet optiness—just, "Oh
but it's quite safe—and rather fun"—and then she will mesmerize you
and I shall get a telegram to say you are staying on in Paris. If I *do,*
I shall fly over at once—I'm not going to trust to luck this time.

Oh my darling—do please be very careful and take no risks. You
don't know how anxious I am.

I lunched with Mrs [Margot] Asquith. What a splendid woman
she is! I am really fond of her. It was a nice luncheon and I sat next
to her and she told me stories about Kitchener. But all the time I was
thinking of that basilisk [reptile] over there and my poor sweet opty
at No. 53 rue de Varenne.[2]

Oh how glad I shall be to hear you are coming back!

---

2. The house of Walter Berry, their host.

*Harold was appointed Counsellor (and Chargé d'Affaires be-
tween two Ministers) at the British Legation, Teheran. Vita
did not accompany him, but twice made the long and hazard-
ous journey to Persia to stay with him for a couple of months. Her
first visit was from January to May 1926, when she attended and
helped organize the Shah's coronation (which she described in her
book* Passenger to Teheran*), and the second from February to May
1927, which ended with an arduous trek across the Bakhtiari Mountains with Harold. While he was in Persia, Harold occupied his
leisure with writing* Some People, *and Vita at home and in London
developed her friendship with Virginia Woolf into an intimacy. She
was writing* The Land *and completed it in Persia. She and Harold
wrote to each other every day, posting their letters in a single
envelope to catch the fortnightly diplomatic bag.*

VITA TO HAROLD   *Long Barn*

5 November [1925]

It's a ¼ to 9—you must be thinking of arriving at Trieste. You
have gone over that strange calcined Carso country which I thought
so dramatic, only I saw it in full-moon light, and you will have had
no moon. Do you remember a moon-landscape walk we had at
Schluderbach[1] after dinner? how lovely it was? How happy we have
been, whenever we have got away together like that, and we had a

---

1. Now Carbonin in the Italian Dolomites, where Harold and Vita went on a walking tour
   in July 1924.

bare wooden room under the three peaks and there was a storm—no I'm muddling it: the storm was at Tre Croci.[2] Oh Hadji! . . . shall we ever do those things again? Everything that we have done together comes back to me with such poignancy: I am dreadfully lonely tonight, I don't mind telling you so, because it will all be so safely distant by the time you can read this and know about it: I thought I would be able to work, but the only relief I can find is in writing to you. I have already written you one long letter this evening. Now I have had my dinner, or rather Pippin [her spaniel] has had most of my dinner, and it is dark and the house is silent, and the book of Elizabethan lyrics which I have been trying to read seems to be all about love—(blast it)—so I threw it across the room in anger because it made things worse. I feel all at sea, Hadji; I cannot get a hold upon myself; but of course I shall before very long. If it was just your going away, I think I could cope with it; but you see it will be three weeks before I know you are safe.

HAROLD TO VITA

In the Adriatic
Piroscafo Helouan

6 November 1925

Oh my dear, how I wish you were with me—you know how I love the sea, and Greece, and I shall get both. But it all seems rather meaningless without my own darling. I am all right during the day. But when night falls and the electric lights come out, and the sea is something realised only by its sound, then a wave of home-sickness comes over me and I walk up and down the deck thinking, "Viti, Viti, Viti." I have not had the spirit yet to go on with MY NEW BOOK [*Some People*]. I have felt upset and jaundiced by being so unhappy. But I have taken some camomile and should regain my buoyancy tomorrow. I shall take a lot of exercise, and I hope that my intelligence, which at present is hiding hurt and muffled in a hole, will come back to me. So far I just feel bruised and stupid and terribly tired.

---

2. Between Cortina and Misurina.

VITA TO HAROLD *Long Barn*

16 November [1925]

An enormous excitement that I found when I got home was that the Encyclopaedia had come[1]—Oh darling it is going to be quite invaluable to me. So far I have only *durch-blättered* [skipped through] it, but I have seen quite enough to know that the georgics will swell in volume and in information. It looks blue and impressive in my shelves. I flung out the works of Corneille to make room for it. You were a perfect angel to have ordered it for me. I shall never be able to tell you how touched I was. I'm really going to settle down to work now. I wonder what your new book is? Oh Hadji . . . I just go stupid with missing you and wanting you.

HAROLD TO VITA *Kermanshah [Persia]*

24 November 1925

At 9.30 p.m. we hooted out of Jerusalem.[2] One drops five thousand feet down to the Jordan. It is a lovely road, but rather hair-pinned. One could see the lights of the car in front lighting up the rocky sides of the gorge, and twisting in and out down the mountain. It got warmer and warmer and then suddenly the sound of frog-croaking and the lights of a guard house by a steel bridge. We had reached the Jordan, and bumped across from Palestine into Transjordania. From there on, the road was bad and it was past midnight before we came to the poplars and running water of Amman. Beyond the town is a large enclosure shut in with barbed wire, full of lorries and motors and bell-tents. In one tent we had supper. In the other, we slept four of us on camp beds. It was there, by the light of the flickering candle, that I opened your birthday letter, my saint. The trucks on the Hedjaz

1. A four-volume Encyclopaedia of Agriculture, which Harold had ordered for Vita to help her with the technical information for her poem *The Land,* which she first called "The Georgics."
2. In 1925 travel to Bagdad and onwards to Teheran was by motor convoy from Jerusalem across the desert.

railway above me clinked and clanked all night, and all night the dogs barked.

At 5.0 a.m. a face opened the flap of our tent. "Passengers for Bagdad get ready please." With grunts and snorts we undid ourselves, had some hot tea, and climbed back into our cars while the dawn was breaking. There was a large sort of charabanc which held six people. I and an employee of the Anglo-Persian [Oil Company] were on the back seat of a Cadillac touring car, having the chauffeur and a spare chauffeur in front. A convoy going the other way had come in early in the night and as we jerked out of the wire enclosure there was much private soldier badinage and witticisms. From Amman one gets almost at once into the open country. Wide sad downs like the short cut above Rottingdean. Then ten miles or so of shale. Then ten miles of bumpy little sand hussocks, over which we swayed and lurched. Then the rising sun and the distant silhouettes of Volcanic mountains—small Vesuvius formations and table-mountains. Then forty miles of lava boulders, bump, bump, bump, then twenty miles of mud flats and puddles, then shale again. Luncheon (turkey, hard boiled eggs, tea) on a rug in the burning sun. Then start again. Flying for two hundred miles over a hard tennis court at 60 miles an hour. Then five more hours of jerking over bad country, an amazing sunset, Jupiter and Venus in conjunction doing a double evening star, and then complete darkness with the head-lights straining in front of us. We had done 400 miles and passed only one human being, and he was dead—a dead man by the roadside with his guts disarranged by vultures. On and on through the night until suddenly we pulled up with a jerk in front of an extraordinary jumble of white wood and aluminium, looking like some vast and expensive toy which had been smashed in the post. It was a wrecked aeroplane de luxe, and we lit a fire from the wreckage and had supper. Then on again after supper through the dark. I blessed my cushions and slept well enough. Woke to feel cold and found we had stopped. An armoured car detachment was encamped there. They gave us whisky and there was more badinage. A wonderful sunrise and by ten o'clock we were at Ramadi the air-station. Here we had breakfast. Left at noon and flew at 70 miles an hour across another hard tennis court, till we reached the Euphrates. Then another two hours sprint and by 3.0 p.m. we were crossing the bridge at Bagdad.

Washed, shaved, I went off to The High Commissioner. A telegram from my darling and letters from Loraine. Dashed in to see Gertrude Bell.[3] She was charming. Then dinner and off to the station. A reserved carriage or rather saloon with a bathroom. Slept like a top and woke up at 7.0 a.m. at Khamkin. Foul little motor for me. A dreadfully protracted fuss over passports, customs etc. and off at nine. A beastly road to the Persian frontier—bump, bump, bump. Then a grand house and some barbed wire, and a darling Persian official who gave me cigarettes in handfuls and delicious tea. Then off again, very uncomfortable—no room at all in the car for my feet. All my luggage in a motor long behind. Three people at the back (two Imperial Bank people and myself) and in front the driver (Irish) and the Legation orderly. The road was good enough—but the car was so rotten that we crawled and crawled. We should have got here by 5.0 p.m. but by then we were 100 miles away and it was dark and bitterly cold. On and on very slowly, till suddenly *crash* and we collapsed into a hole in the road. We all climbed out, extricated the car, and found that the front axle was bent and the exhaust pipe broken. Very slowly we limped onwards—getting here at 10 p.m., five hours late.

The Consul and his wife did their best. But they have no spare room and I slept on a camp bed in their drawing-room, too small for me, hard, and incredibly cold. My one consolation was your dear letter.

This morning we were to start at nine. I waited and waited till 12.0 and then sent a message to see what had happened. The car was too badly broken to continue. So I shall have to stay here another day and have another day in that beastly refrigerator. You can imagine how furious this makes me. If the car had been even averagely good I should have got through easily. The road itself is excellent—just as good as the road from the village to Sevenoaks.

Of course I expect that people here get used to never knowing when one starts and when one arrives. But to me this hanging about is really maddening—and destroys the pleasure I should get from the amazing beauty of the scenery.

---

3. The traveler and writer. She was then Oriental Secretary to Sir Percy Cox, British Commissioner in Iraq, and Director of Antiquities.

HAROLD TO VITA   *Teheran*

28 November 1925

The Chancery is exactly like all other chanceries—even to the smell of sealing-wax and mail-bags. The staff is enormous (soldiers, archivists, interpreters, dragomen)—but the only two diplomatic members proper are Warner and Jebb.[1] The former erudite, slightly uncouth, efficient, rather attractive. The latter of great beauty (half Hugh Thomas and half Lady Curzon) and possessing a gentle charm. Rather shy at first.

HAROLD TO VITA   *Teheran*

3 December 1925

This morning early I dressed in my tail-coat and was taken by Percy [Loraine] to see the Foreign Minister. The Foreign Office is rather a jolly old building with a courtyard and a fountain and the most heavenly picture running right across the top of the staircase. A life-size (or over-life-size) fresco of a Foreign Ambassador being received by Fat Ali-Shah.

Then we went into a little room with a wallpaper of yellow chrysanthemums and red damask curtains. And there were little red arm-chairs with tockles [lamps] and cigarettes: they brought us tea. The minister is a copper-coloured man, or rather bronze-coloured, and after a long discussion about my nativity,[2] we settled down to business, which meant just silence and sighs. I see that this is no place for impiness [impatience], and that I must realise that what took 5 minutes at home must take two hours here. So we smoked and drank tea and talked at very distant intervals about the weather, and then the M.F.A. [Minister for Foreign Affairs] fished in his frock coat and brought out a tiny bit of paper which the interpreter translated and which was all

---

1. Christopher Warner and Gladwyn Jebb, respectively Second and Third Secretaries.
2. Harold was born on 21 November 1886 in the Legation Compound in Teheran, where his father was Secretary.

about a river I had never heard of and the iniquitous treatment ac-
corded to that river by the Government of Iraq. And so by easy
flatulent stages one passed on to more serious business.

VITA TO HAROLD   *Long Barn*

8 December 1925

I am reading Proust, and dislike his mentality more and more. I
get the sense of that flabby, diseased, asthmatic man, all frowsty in bed
till evening, and preoccupied with such contemptible things—nothing
but women and snobbery. It makes me angry that he should write so
exceedingly well, having nothing worthwhile to write about.

HAROLD TO VITA   *Teheran*

10 December 1925

In the afternoon I went to see Reza Khan [the Shah of Persia]. He
lives in a little white villa in a garden. We went in by the street door,
as the garden-door was crowded with guards and lancers. We were
shown into a little white room with a huge fire and atrocious Louis
XVI furniture. The room gave on to a sort of balcony or loggia and
we hadn't been there long before the windows were darkened by an
immense figure passing in front of them. The end-windows opened and
he came in. He was in Khaki uniform with a peaked Khaki hat—
slashed at the corners. He hadn't shaved very well and glowered out
of the corner of his eye at us. He was quite alone. He is about
six-foot-three and inclined to corpulence. He has fat red hands like
Gerry [Wellesley]. He has bad teeth, fine eyes and chin, and a determined nose. A clipped greyish moustache. But he looked cross and
tired and dirty. Then he sat down.

I told him of the interest he aroused in England and how we hoped
he would make a nice good kind Shah. He was pleased by these
assertions, and relaxed. He gave us cigarettes and cakes and tea. Sud-

denly he took his hat off—disclosing a tiny little shaven head like a Russian Cossack. He looked more of a scallywag than ever. But then gradually he began to talk quite calmly about becoming Shah, and his arrangements for his coronation, and how cross everyone was, and how he had felt his collar too tight at the opening ceremony, and how Farman Farma[1] had been photographed sitting on the steps. And then he laughed a sort of non-commissioned officer laugh—and asked me how old I was. He wouldn't believe it when I told him[2] and said evidently I had had no troubles in love or politics. I thought of my darling digging away over there at our mud-pie. Then he laughed a great deal—and for the rest of the interview was simple and jolly and with a certain force and dignity. But I am not so sure about him. I haven't seen enough Persians yet to compare him with. Anyhow he was very cordial and told me to come and see him as often as I liked when he was Shah. He adores Percy[3]—and Percy is rather pleased with himself (and with justice) at having backed a winner from the start— and *such* a winner.

VITA TO HAROLD   *Long Barn*

17 December [1925]

Well, I took my letters for you to the [Foreign] office, and I took my box of rosemary, and I sent off my puppy from Waterloo to Winchester, and I fetched Virginia, and brought her down here.[4] She is an exquisite companion, and I love her dearly. She has to stay in bed till luncheon, as she is still far from well, and she has lots of writing to do. Leonard [Woolf] is coming on Saturday—(oh dear, how meaningless all these Saturdays and so on must be to you at that distance. The only thing is to go on writing, day by day and to allow you to

---

1. A Qajar prince of the old regime.
2. Harold was just thirty-nine.
3. Sir Percy Loraine had been Minister in Teheran for four years and, although a somewhat conventional and ponderous British diplomatist, he had won the confidence of Reza Khan who regularly consulted him even on domestic affairs.
4. It was on this visit that Vita's love affair with Virginia Woolf began.

fill in the dates from your imagination,—just living my life from day to day and let you re-live it at a month's remove.)

Oh, the doves are cooing. It is midnight. The doves cooing *always* make me think of you because you love them, and they are so much the cottage.

Please don't think that

(a) I shall fall in love with Virginia

(b) Virginia will fall in love with me

(c) Leonard   "   "   "   "   "   "

(d) I shall fall   "   "   "   Leonard

because it is not so. Only I know my silly Hadji will say to himself, *"Allons, bon!"* when he hears V. is staying here, and *"Ca y est,"* and so on.

Loud coo from the doves.

I miss my puppy, which was the nicest I ever had.

I am missing you dreadfully. That is why I am writing to you last thing at night. I am missing you specially because Virginia was so very sweet about you, and so understanding.

Oh darling, I do love you SO AWFULLY. It doesn't get any better as time goes on. I hoped it would. But it doesn't.

VITA TO HAROLD   *Brighton*

26 December [1925]

I lunched at Charleston[1]—very plain living and high thinking. I like Virginia's sister [Vanessa] awfully. There were two huge, shaggy, rather attractive boys [Julian and Quentin Bell] who call their father and mother Clive and Nessa. There was Clive, and Virginia and Leonard. Virginia discoursed about the Georgics [*The Land*] till I was shy. She does this to everyone, I find—a good preliminary advertisement! I drove them over the Downs. So lovely in the mist, and I longed for Hadji. Virginia *loves* your mar. She really does. It is a soul-friendship. Very good for me; and good for her too.

---

1. The farmhouse under the Downs near Lewes, Sussex, which Vanessa Bell and Duncan Grant had made their home.

I find that not one person in six knows where Persia is. Vanessa could say only that it was "not in America." Oh my dear, they do live in such squalor! How luxurious they must think the mars.

VITA TO HAROLD   *Long Barn*

29 December 1925

Geoffrey [Scott] rang me up suddenly this evening in a state of hysteria (or so it sounded), and said could he see me tomorrow. I said I was sorry, I was too busy. He said, "I want to say goodbye to you." I said, "Why, are you going to Mexico after all?" He said, "No, I mean I want to see you for the last time, but of course if you are too busy to accord me a quarter of an hour, it doesn't matter: I'll say goodbye here and now"; and slammed down the receiver. So I don't know what the position is. He has been furious ever since you left because I wouldn't see him, or scarcely. Really, Hadji, I should be relieved, except that I would rather have remained good friends with him if possible. But he minds too much for that. I don't know why I bore you with this. It must all seem very remote. And indeed it seems very remote to me. I am too concentrated on you—little pig. And you have gone away.[1]

HAROLD TO VITA   *Teheran*

8 January 1926

I am not really bothered about Virginia and think you are probably very good for each other. I only feel that you have not got *la main heureuse* in dealing with married couples. And how dare you say you won't tell me what she said about the Georgics—when you know that is such an excitement to me? Don't get them put into print until I have

---

1. Vita felt guilty about her abandonment of Geoffrey Scott, the writer, because she had smashed his marriage by their brief affair. He went to live in New York, where he died in 1929, aged forty-six.

seen them, and you have been able to put in some purple passages from the East. (Like the Lebanon honey, and the Tuscan wine.) Oh dear, what fun we shall have sitting there in our beastly little room reading them over again! Have you yet coped with the vast problem of who is to publish them?[1]

HAROLD TO VITA   *Teheran*

15 January 1926

The Military Attaché is called Fraser. His wife is called Mrs Fraser. She is rather a jolly woman really and you will like her. Only she came in here today to see whether she would buy any of Monson's[2] things, and on the Po-stand she saw that piccy of you holding Benzie [Ben] when he was in his christening clothes. She looked at it for a long time and then she said: "I like that woman; she knows how to hold a baby." And oh my sweet I thought of what a ridiculous piccy that was of you—so I have drawn one of what that phrase awoke in me. I always make you look like Venetia Montague in my piccies—I must try another:—

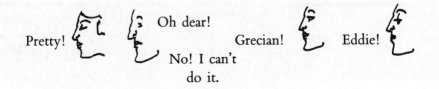

Pretty!   Oh dear! No! I can't do it.   Grecian!   Eddie!

---

1. *The Land* was published by Heinemann, to whom Vita was bound by contract, not (as she would have preferred) by the Woolfs' Hogarth Press.
2. Edmund Monson, Harold's predecessor as Counsellor.

HAROLD TO VITA   *Teheran*

3 May 1926

When you get this it will be at Brighton[1] and we shall both have
a great iron chunk of misery behind us. Dearest one—what an odd
thing it all is: the whole centres of us both aching for each other and
then going off in opposite directions. Oh my dear—I do hope that
when you read these words we shall both be happy again or at least
not unhappy. I know now that I can't really be happy without you
being there, or being imminent. These months will be waste months
in my life—arid thirsty deserts. That's why I turn to the thought of
work as my only solace. I feel quite ill this evening with it all. And
the sun setting among the planes looks as if it were doing it in some
different way—like when one has cotton-wool in one's ears.

HAROLD TO VITA   *Teheran*

12 May 1926

Tray is writing his article about alternatives to chastity.[2] It is very
good—perfectly simple and closely reasoned. He concludes (having
watched the Mars and knowing how much they love each other) that
the best life is marriage plus liaisons. Or rather his argument is:—
  (1) Passion, i.e. being 'in love', can only last a certain number of
      years.
  (2) After that both sides instinctively search for variety.
  (3) If the doctrine of fidelity is too rigid, then they both have a
      sense of confinement and frustration, and irritation results.
  (4) But if there is mutual physical freedom, this sense of bondage
      does not arise: good relations are maintained—and from this
      emerges community of life, and *'love'* (with a big L)—which
      is something quite different from passion, and far deeper than

---

1. Vita was about to leave Teheran after her first visit to Harold. She traveled to the Caspian,
   thence to Baku-Moscow-Berlin-Holland.
2. "Tray" was Raymond Mortimer, who remained Harold's guest in Teheran after Vita's
   departure. His article was a pamphlet about liberal attitudes to sex, but Leonard Woolf
   thought it too frank for publication.

affection. He says that only really fine characters and deter-
minedly intellectual people can attain to this. But that the
confusion of 'love' and 'in love'—and the idea that "Love
equals merely affection"—leads to great confusion. There is
something in all this, but I expect there is a snag somewhere.
You see, our love is something which only two people in the
world can understand. The first and dearest of these two people
is Viti. The second, poor man,

is your own
Hadji

VITA TO HAROLD   *[In the train Moscow–Warsaw]*

13 May 1926

Now I will tell you what my impression of Russia was. It was one
of terror. Everyone seems to go in fear of being overheard; everyone
looks furtive and afraid. All the people at that dinner-party at the
[British] Mission [in Moscow] said to me, one after the other, and not
in reply to any prompting on my part, "You see, it is so dreadful living
here. One never knows who will disappear next." There are arrests
nearly every day. If they cannot or will not bring a political accusation
against someone they want to catch, they cause false money to be
slipped into his pockets and then arrest him on that charge. The
Russians hardly dare to consort with foreigners. Of course the obvious
thing to say is that one is 'suggested' into these impressions, but truly
I believe I should have felt the same even had I known nothing about
the state of the country. Baku was quite different—quite gay and
lively—but Moscow is terrible. One sees people sitting or standing at
the street corners in attitudes of despair; and yet they say it is better
than it was a year or two years ago.

Dear me, I hope they won't open this letter! I shall post it from
Warsaw if I can get a stamp, otherwise it will have to wait till I reach
Germany. Oh my darling, what a long way it is, to go half across the
world like this! country after country unrolling itself, frontier after
frontier—and all so ugly.

Polish frontier. Here is a pretty kettle of fish! There is a revolution in Poland, and no trains can go through Warsaw. So we have to be sent round—some people say by Cracow and Prague, others say by Königsberg. The officials seem to be extremely vague. I hope there won't be an accident, that's all. In any case I fear it will mean a great deal of delay. How I wish now that I had gone by Riga. The train has started. It consists of only two carriages, and we are apparently making for a place called Bialystok. Anyway I am seeing the world. There are two nice Germans in my carriage. I find the way to talk really lovely Persian is to try to talk German. I feel rather a waif, and wonder where I shall sleep tonight—if anywhere.

Saturday, May 15th Königsberg station, between 2 trains.

My precious Hadji, well, anyway I am in Germany, having escaped from Poland on a railway engine, so with any luck I may get home before long. It's been one of the most absurd experiences I ever had; I wish I could reproduce it all for you, and above all, oh above all, I wish you had been there. If I had had anyone to laugh with, it would have been the best possible joke. Now I'll go back to yesterday.

The train pulled up with a jerk at Bialystok, which is a little junction somewhere in Poland, and there it became necessary to devise a plan of campaign. There were a great many soldiers, and everybody in a fluster, and no news from Warsaw as the telephones were all cut and no train had come down the line from Warsaw that day. All that the officials would promise was to take us (in the Russian train) to a station ten miles from Warsaw; after that they would guarantee nothing.

So, with ten other people, we made up a party determined to get to the nearest German frontier. (I am now no longer at Königsberg, but in Berlin. It's a muddling life. Here, after the infinite squalor of the last few days, I sit at the Kaiserhof, having ordered the best dinner and the best wine from a crowd of obsequious waiters. But I anticipate.) Behold me, then, at Bialystok, ejected with my little packages into the middle of revolutionary Poland, in company with 7 Germans (commercial travellers I should think), a Russian, and two Austrians— one of them a young woman with cropped golden hair, no better than she should be, and the other her? husband. Anyhow we all went and ate Wienerschnitzel very merrily in the station buffet, not knowing when we should get our next meal. And then the little train came in, and we launched off, meandering about Poland, seeing troops in occupation of every station, and finally after dark we came to Grajewo, which is the German frontier. A tiny place, with a shed for a customs house. There were, it seemed, no more trains that night, and very doubtful whether there would be any at all next day. So, being determined to get out of Poland at all costs, we got the promise of our engine to take us across the frontier. But it was not available till after midnight. How, then, to spend the hours from 8 to 12 at Grajewo? a charming village doubtless, but not offering much resource. Stay! there was 'ein Kino'. We made for it, through the quiet village streets under the new, sickle moon.

But Kinos, apparently, are as popular in Grajewo as elsewhere, and it was full. So we set out to return, sadly, to the station, with four hours to put away. I confess that I was by then so tired that I could have gone to sleep on a table. However, on the way we passed some little shack which flaunted the word 'Restaurant' in the fan-light over its door. We went in. We were shown into a little narrow room with a coloured lithograph of Millais' Angelus and a coloured print of a Russian sleigh stopped by wolves in the snow; also ibex horns, a falcon, and other trophies. Next door, some Polish officers were drinking at a little table. It was all very Slav. We sat, the ten of us, at a long narrow table, like the Last Supper. We were all tired and gloomy. Then a bottle of vodka appeared as though by magic. Tongues were loosed. (Not mine; I was tired beyond vodka, but vastly amused in a quiet detached way.) One of the Germans leant across the table and suddenly said to me, "I have travelled Singer's sewing machines one hundred thousand kilometers over Manchuria." And indeed his luggage was plastered with Chinese labels. The golden-haired Austrian woman, who had been asleep on her arms on the table, woke up and drank six glasses of vodka straight off, and began to dance while one of the Polish officers crashed out a czarda of sorts on a crazy cottage piano. The atmosphere became thicker every minute with Slav-icism and cigarette smoke. Every language fluttered across the room—Russian, Polish, German, English, Chinese. Everybody wanted to show off. The traveller in Singer's sewing machines beat a spoon on the table and shouted, *"Ich Komm aus China."* They asked me what *Guten tag* was in Persian, and the familiar *Salaam aleikem* echoed in unfamiliar voices. They poured the vodka generously, and all got very drunk. Somebody played the Blue Danube on the cottage piano. The two Austrians made love openly. Then they all swayed swinging into the village street, irrupting noisily into that sleeping place under the stars and the young moon. And there was our engine puffing in the station. Passports; luggage. We clambered in, and puffed away, down the shining silent line. They burst into *"Deutschland über alles";* then looked suddenly at me and said they hoped I didn't mind. The conquering race said it didn't mind at all. And so we came into Germany.

The place we slept at was called Prosten, I think; another little sleeping village. We reached it at 1 o'clock. I was *dead;* and fell asleep in a strange little room. At 4 I had to get up again. We caught another train, and after several changes arrived at Königsberg, where I went on with this letter. Then another train, and finally Berlin. I went to the Embassy; but as it was then after 8, everyone had gone. So I came to the Kaiserhof, where I have now dined extremely well, and in a quarter of an hour must catch the train to Flushing.

I have telegraphed to you, my darling, as you will have heard of the Polish business, and may perhaps be worried if you realise that just on that day I was due at Warsaw. I still feel slightly bewildered. I fear this letter will give you no idea of the fantasy of this journey, but it has been written so disjointedly; you won't be able to follow my movements at all! I can scarcely follow them myself, as I re-read it. I have no wagon-lit, of course, and shall have to sit up all night. I think I must have a constitution of iron, as I am not really very tired. The Kaiserhof has a really Ritz-ian atmosphere, which forms an odd contrast with that little restaurant at Grajewo, where I was only 24 hours ago.

I am due in London at 8.30 tomorrow night, and have wired to Dotz [Dorothy Wellesley] to meet me. But as it is Sunday tomorrow, she probably won't get the telegram.

Oh my darling. There is a pot of pink azaleas on my little solitary table. One of the Germans has just rung me up to know if I am all right. Their niceness and efficiency was beyond praise. Also they lent me money, as of course I couldn't use my ticket, and had only £10 with me. I hope I can recover my ticket money. Or is it the King's Enemies?

Please tell me if you get this letter. Goodbye my beloved; you can see that my thoughts are always of you, from the way I start writing to you whenever I have 10 minutes. Though I admit it produces a tiresome disjointed result.

VITA TO HAROLD   *Long Barn*

22 May [1926]

The garden is lovely; the wood-garden especially is a dream. Everything is so tidy; everything looks so healthy. I will tell you in detail, now that I have had time to go round.

The limes are alive. Your new poplar-walk is alive. The wood is a blaze of primulas, anemones, tulips, azaleas, irises, polyanthus. The horse-chestnut is alive. The apple garden is a mass of lupins and irises. The walls are still rather bare, but everything doing well. The turf is perfect. The new, lower lawn is almost the nicest thing of all—so smooth and green and level. All the edges are straight and tidy. The top of the wall is better than I have ever seen it. The roses are beautifully pruned; the lilac is smothered in blossom. Your honeysuckle by the big room door also. Your Hugh Dickson [rose] under your bedroom window is up to the roof, and covered with buds. The tennis court is a disaster. The new orchard is a tig [triumph]. The greenhouse is full of tidy boxes, with seeds. The hedges are all alive and shooting. There is not a weed to be seen. The doves are alive. There are seven grey puppies and four yellow kittens. Four yews in the new garden are dead, but the rest flourishing, and not really too silly. The new box trees are all alive. I shall take lots and lots of photographs for you tomorrow; I have got two films.

I have got my proofs [of *The Land*], and will send you a set by this bag.

I should be so happy if only you were here; but, my darling, there is no happiness for me without you, none, none, none. I can only think of when I shall bring you here next year. That thought is the one thing which makes me able to enjoy the garden now.

H A R O L D   T O   V I T A   *Teheran*

31 May 1926

I went to tea with the Shah. It took place at his summer Palace near Pashkolé. There was a huge long gravel path along the terrace and at the end of it I saw the Shah. But at the beginning of it, out of sheer

nervousness, my bootlaces came undone—all four of them. Now why does this always happen when I go to see the Shah? I had known it would happen and had tried on my button boots instead. But three of the buttons had come off, so I put on my Oxford shoes instead and tied the knots as no knots have ever been tied before. On getting out of the motor I glanced at the knots:—there they were, firm and tidy. But when they saw that long vista of garden path, a hundred yards of garden path, they got nervous and untied themselves. I knew that the Minister was watching from beside the Samovar. It was a trying ordeal. I said, *"Hoda hafiz i alahazret,"* which means "Goodbye your Majesty"—but I said it so humbly that I don't think he could have borne me much resentment. Then I went and stood beside the Samovar and watched the other guests arriving.

VITA TO HAROLD *Long Barn*

31 May [1926]

Tray's theory[1] is all very well so far as it goes. But he leaves out the stipulation that the two people who are to achieve this odd spirito-mystico-practical unity must start with special temperaments. I.e. it is all very well to say the ideal is "marriage with liaisons." But if you were in love with another woman, or I with another man, we should both or either of us be finding a natural sexual fulfilment which would inevitably rob our own relationship of something. As it is, the liaisons which you and I contract are something perfectly apart from the more natural and normal attitude we have towards each other, and therefore don't interfere. But it would be dangerous for ordinary people. Besides, you cannot make laws about emotional relationships: either you love, or else you don't love, and that's that.

VITA TO HAROLD *Long Barn*

12 June 1926

The Woolfs are not coming today after all, because Virginia has started one of her attacks of headache again, but I am going to Rodmell[2] tomorrow for two nights; Leonard will be away and she doesn't want to be alone. Your cabbage doesn't want to go much, thank you, and would rather stay here. I have come to the conclusion that I should like to be very eccentric and distinguished, and never see anybody except devout pilgrims who rang the front door bell (which doesn't ring), and remained for an hour talking about poetry, and then went away again. But the eccentricity is easier to acquire than the distinction. The eccentricity, indeed, is native. I am quite alarmed at the rapidity of its growth; that I don't want to see even Virginia as a dreadful symptom, for not only am I very fond of her, but she is the best company in the world, and the most stimulating.

---

1. For Raymond Mortimer's views on marriage see pp. 138–139.
2. Monk's House, Rodmell, near Lewes, Sussex, the Woolfs' country cottage.

VITA TO HAROLD   *Monk's House, Rodmell, Sussex*

Monday, 13 June [1926]

My own darling Hadji,

I am, as you see, staying with Virginia. She is sitting opposite, embroidering a rose, a black lace fan, a box of matches, and four playing cards, on a mauve canvas background, from a design by her sister, and from time to time she says, "You have written enough, let us now talk about copulation," so if this letter is disjointed it is her fault and not mine. I arrived yesterday. They have put in a bathroom and a b.s. place [lavatory] on the proceeds of *Mrs Dalloway*. [1] They both run upstairs every now and then and pull the plug just for the sheer fun of it, and come down and say, "It worked very well that time—did you hear?" rather as the mars might do if their standard of luxury were lower than it is. Leonard had to go back to London last night, so I remain alone with Virginia. There is a woman from the village who washes up, but otherwise we boil an egg and make coffee, and I have brought 2 bottles of Allella [a light Spanish wine] and a box of cherries, and that's all. Darling, you would love the country round here: water-meadows and green tracks, Downs and buttercups, plover and larks, ricks and a river. One day we must walk along the Downs in the opposite direction. I mean, away from Chanctonbury,— oh my dear, I wish it was next summer!

Later

I went over to Rottingdean to see Enid [2]; Virginia sat in a tea shop and ate Sally Lunns [buns] meanwhile. Enid is very bovine and lactiferous, but very happy. Then I took Virginia to White Lodge [3] (B.M. being in London), where she was rivetted with amusement. She 'got' B.M. in the twinkling of an eye of course, and made a number of illuminating observations which I had never thought of. I can't write this letter properly, because V. who is an outrageous woman keeps on getting up and reading it over my shoulder. She says you are to give up diplomacy and find a job from £600 a year onwards.

---

1. Virginia Woolf's novel had been published in May 1925, and was a best-seller.
2. Enid Bagnold, the novelist, who was married to Sir Roderick Jones, head of Reuters.
3. Lady Sackville's house between Rottingdean and Brighton.

VITA TO HAROLD   *182 Ebury Street*

16 June 1926

I dined with Virginia and Leonard in one of their Bloomsbury pot-houses; and then went on alone with her to the ballet. She had got on a new dress. It was very odd indeed, orange and black, with a hat to match—a sort of top-hat made of straw with two orange feathers like Mercury's wings—but although odd it was curiously becoming, and pleased Virginia because there could be absolutely no doubt as to which was the front and which the back. We had press tickets, and sat in the dress circle. Virginia made up stories about everyone in the audience, but not so audibly as B.M. The ballet was Carnival, Pulcinella (a new one—not very good), and Igor.

We came out into the misty Haymarket. Virginia was shivering, I thought she was cold; but no, it was excitement. I couldn't get her away from the theatre at all, and we strolled up and down, with the dark blue sky overhead, and groups of well-dressed people talking, and it was all very like Mrs Dalloway; and then, to complete the likeness, we saw a dwarf on crutches, under a street lamp, with locomotorataxy. That frightened Virginia, so we went to the Eiffel Tower [restaurant], and drank coffee, and were joined by Viola Tree[1] and the fashion editress of Vogue.

HAROLD TO VITA   *Teheran*

26 June 1926

Don't think, dearest, that I'm unhappy. Only sort of suspended neutral feeling. You see this sort of life is really what I like best: Work, riding, hot weather, reading, writing, bathing. But it seems to have no point without you. I get through the days quickly, contentedly, mechanically—but it is only when something like Tray coming back jerks me into being myself again and not a machine that I realise how automatic and perfunctory is my general existence.

---

1. Author of *Castles in the Air*, published by the Hogarth Press in April 1926.

V I T A   T O   H A R O L D   *Long Barn*

28 June 1926

The Laureate[1] breakfasts at 8.30. I was brought early tea, which Hadji would have liked, but which I scorned; rose and dressed. I descended. The Laureate was playing the clavichord which his admir-ers—me amongst them—had presented to him on his 80th birthday. I peeped through the curtains; he was dressed in his evening shirt of the previous evening, a tweed Norfolk jacket, and grey flannel trousers. There he was, tinkling away at Handel. I crept away unobserved, on my crepe soles. I went and got the motor out of the garage and brought it round to the front door. By then Mrs Bridges had appeared. There were eggs and bacon for breakfast. After breakfast the Laureate said, did I still want to consult the Oxford Dictionary? I said I did. He took me into his library, and left me there sitting on the floor. I had my proofs [of *The Land*]; and verified my odd words to my satisfaction. Presently the Laureate returned, his spectacles pushed up on to his forehead, very indignant. "It is perfect nonsense," he said, "the way these people *will* edit Chaucer." He sat down on the floor beside me, and helped me to look up 'droil'. "What's this?" he said, taking up my proofs. I simpered. He took them out into the garden, spread a rug very carefully on the grass, and began to read. I fled upstairs and packed. After an hour I re-appeared. The Laureate was still reading. He got up and came towards me. "Have you," he began, "read Virgil a great deal?" I said no, I didn't know Latin; had, however, read the Georgics in a translation. "But how," he said, staring at me very hard with a fierce blue eye, "but how, then, have you got this Virgilian *bite?* eh?" I quailed. "It's VERY GOOD," he said, still staring at me, "I'm VERY PLEASED—very pleased indeed—you've got your feet on the ground—nothing woolly there—not a woman's writing at all—damn good—I congratulate you." I said, I, too, was pleased that he should think so. "Send it me," he boomed, "when it comes out." Mrs Bridges appeared. "Good STUFF," he said to her, striking the pages angrily with his hand, and looking at me meanwhile as though

---

1. Robert Bridges, the Poet Laureate, at whose house near Oxford Vita had been staying the night.

I had committed a crime. I was overcome with confusion, and to cover it up said should I photograph them both for their daughter? The Laureate posed happily amongst his pinks. Suddenly he grabbed his wife by the wrist. "Do you think," he whispered, "that she would photograph THE CURTAIN?" They both looked apprehensively at me. Of course, I said; fetch the curtain! They fetched it—at a run. They hung the curtain, a Jacobean crewel-work affair, over a dry-wall, standing themselves at the top and each holding a corner. I solemnly photographed them and it; pray God it may come out. Then I rescued my proofs, and climbed into the motor; they urged me to come again. They opened the gate for me, and stood there waving.

I went down into Oxford,—a lovely morning,—out to Summer-fields[2] and there were the babies in grey flannels with Eton collars. They took me into chapel, and between the two of them I worshipped God. They were very serious, and sang loudly, if out of tune. I shared Nigel's hymn book. Then we came out,—"Oh Mummy, didn't you think it was a lovely service?" They changed their collars for soft ones, and we started off. All the way Ben taught Nigel Latin.

VITA TO HAROLD   *Long Barn*

28 June 1926

No, I am in no muddles [love affairs]. Pat[3] writes, occasionally, but I don't answer. Geoffrey [Scott] writes, but I have refused to see him, and he has accepted that. He now writes me sentimental letters about "Remember what I was once . . .," and hints darkly at troubles with Dorothy.[4] Dorothy I have not seen. Louise, no muddles (either Genoux or Loraine[5]), Vera,[6] no muddles. Lady Hillingdon, no muddles; don't know her; don't want to. Violet [Trefusis], no muddles; don't even know where she is; don't want to get into touch, thank you.

2. More correctly written, Summer Fields, the preparatory school on the outskirts of Oxford.
3. Margaret ("Pat") Dansey, who had been Violet Trefusis' most intimate friend.
4. Dorothy Warren, who had been simultaneously in love with Geoffrey Scott and Vita.
5. Louise Genoux was Vita's French maid; Louise Loraine, the wife of Sir Percy.
6. Vera Cardinal, who farmed the land at Long Barn.

Virginia [Woolf]—not a muddle exactly; she is a busy and sensible woman. But she does love me, and I did sleep with her at Rodmell. That does not constitute a muddle though.[7]

HAROLD TO VITA   *Teheran*

1 July 1926

Well I have had my party.[8] There were 36 people. I sat one end of the table and Percy [Loraine] the other end. The whole staff was there, plus the heads of the colony. There was a balalalalalalaika orchestra on the lawn and a great number of little miffy chinese lanterns. We had soup, trout, cutlets in aspic, turkey and an apricot ice. My wine had arrived two days before. I made a nice English-public-schoolboy sort of speech. Percy replied very slowly and with some emotion. I was rather pleased with my speech and when it was all over I went up to Tray [Raymond Mortimer] and said, "Well how did it go?"—expecting praise. He said it had made him almost sick. He was really angry about it. Funny Tray. Because really the speech was quite moderate and devoid of undue sob-stuff. But I admit that it was rather an Empire builder's speech and aroused Tray's anti-virility complex. Also I think he thought it rather shaming: he said it had irritated him as much as I would be irritated if I saw him dressed up as a woman at some Paris dancing-hall. I think this really was his attitude, and he is right in feeling that I loathe the *tapette* [gay] side of him as much as he hates the Kipling side in me.

Well, feeling rather crushed by this attack, I led the way to the second part of my party—which took place in my own house. It really looked rather well, and there was another band there and a good buffet and heaps of drink. It really *was* a success; people danced and drank and enjoyed themselves. It went on till 2.0 a.m. Oh my Viti, how I missed you! The Minister was impressed, I think—and I have at a stroke removed all criticism of my not entertaining. Also whatever

7. Harold replied (7 July): "Oh my dear, I do hope that Virginia is not going to be a muddle. It is like smoking over a petrol tank."

8. For the British colony in honor of the Minister, Sir Percy Loraine, who was leaving Teheran the next day. Harold remained in charge of the Legation.

Vita in 1910,
the year when
she first met Harold.

Harold in 1911,
as a junior official
in the Foreign Office.

*Lord and Lady Sackville, Vita's parents, in 1913, setting out for the courts
to defend themselves in the famous Scott case.*

*Vita on her way to give evidence
in the Scott case, accompanied
by Harold (left), Rosamund
Grosvenor, and her father,
Lord Sackville.*

*Vita and Harold are married in
the chapel at Knole on
1 October 1913.*

Vita at about the time of her elopement with Violet Trefusis (1920).

Violet Keppel (Trefusis) in the early 1920s.

In Persia, 1926. Vita and Harold are in the front row, with Raymond Mortimer (left) and Gladwyn Jebb behind.

*Virginia and Leonard Woolf, in a photograph taken by Vita at their
country cottage, Monk's House, Rodmell, Sussex, in 1926.*

Vita at Long Barn in 1928, photographed by Leonard Woolf for Orlando.

Her sitting room at Long Barn, where she wrote The Land *and* The Edwardians.

The Nicolson family at Long Barn in 1927, when Harold was on leave from his diplomatic post in Berlin. Left to right, Ben, Harold, Nigel, Vita.

Tray may say, I think the colony were impressed by my noble uplifting patriotic sturdy homily. Perhaps it *was* a little revivalist in tone—Yes? No?

VITA TO HAROLD   *Long Barn*

1 July 1926

My own Hadji,

I seem to be drawn into doing a lot of things these days, which I don't really want to do, and really only want to be here by myself quietly; but I suppose they do amuse me, and I suppose they are good for me in that they do prevent me from becoming a complete cabbage.

Well, you see, I went to the Sitwells' show[1] with Virginia [Woolf]. We dined first at the Eiffel Tower, and talked about literature. So absorbing a subject was it, that we were very late for the Sitwell party. We had one complimentary ticket, and one promise from Edith (Sitwell) that we would be admitted on mention of our names. We mentioned our names, and were ushered to a back seat where even the megaphone failed to reach us. Virginia was not satisfied with this, nor was I. We began pushing. There were some empty seats, and to these in the interval we elbowed our way. Virginia made me go first, much as the German troops pushed the Belgian civilians before them during the war. So I bore the brunt and got all the blame; encountered Sachie [Sacheverell Sitwell]: "Oh, Sachie, you know Mrs Woolf, don't you?" *I* wasn't going to be made wholly responsible. Finally we were ensconced, under the wing of Sachie, in good prominent places. The audience was the best part of the show. Long-haired young men, short-haired young women; you never saw such a collection. And Augustus John's picture-show hanging on the walls. There was a sort of embryo Ottoline [Morrell] in an 1840 dress with a train, and a young man with hair like Struwel-Peter [shock-headed Peter], and an obscene red lily in his buttonhole,—a red plate of a lily, with

---

1. A performance of *Façade* at The Chenil Galleries in Chelsea. The poem was by Edith Sitwell, the music by William Walton. The words were spoken from behind a screen through megaphones.

a pink penis sticking out of it—you must have seen them at Knole—
that was a sample of the audience. Now and then Osbert's [Sitwell]
voice said down a subsidiary megaphone, "Ladies and gentlemen, I do
like to be beside the seaside," and then to the crash of gongs and
cymbals the poem began. But nobody knew when they (the poems)
were meant to come to an end; therefore the applause always came in
the wrong place, either too soon or too late; either the poem came to
an end unexpectedly and was received in complete silence because the
audience expected it to continue, or else there was a deafening applause
in the middle, where the reader had merely paused for breath. Anyhow
it was a great success; and one clap from a vague pair of hands was
enough to make Osbert's megaphone say, "Ladies and gentlemen, with
your permission we will now repeat that number," and duly repeated
it was. But you know, Hadji, I am quite sure that in 50 years from
now no one will ever have heard of those frauds the Sitwells, any more
than they will have heard of George Robey.[2]

I saw everyone I had ever known. I was quite impressed by the
number of people I knew. Then when I had dragged Virginia away—
but she gets drunk on crowds as you and I do on champagne—we went
back to Bloomsbury. On the way, through one of those dark squares,
we overtook Mrs Bell [Vanessa, Virginia's sister]. We stopped. Virginia hailed, "Nessa! Nessa!" She loomed up vaguely, and said, "Duncan [Grant, the painter] is in the public house." We drove on. Presently
we overtook Duncan, hatless, and very carefully carrying one hard-
boiled egg. We drove on to Clive's [Bell]. There were Leonard
[Woolf] and [Maynard] Keynes. Presently came in Mrs Bell and
Duncan. Clive produced vermouth and more eggs. The conversation
became personal and squalid. I was amused. At half past twelve Clive
and I departed for Argyll House.[3] There I met Dada [Lord Sackville],
very fish-out-of-water. There was an immense party, with everyone
you have ever heard of, from Mr Balfour (Arthur, not Ronnie) to
Mary Pickford and Douglas Fairbanks. Really a triumph for Sibyl
[Colefax]. Mr Balfour was sitting on the floor. Very convivial altogether. I had supper with Desmond [MacCarthy, literary critic]. Then
there was Ruth Draper [the actress]—oh my darling, does it make you

2. The comic actor (1869–1954).
3. In the King's Road, Chelsea, the home of Sir Arthur and Lady Colefax, the London hostess.

long for London? or merely feel superior? Anyhow it was great fun: and the garden was illuminated, but not so nice as the Gulistan and no fireworks. And I lost no emerald.

HAROLD TO VITA   *Gulahek, Teheran*

10 July 1926

I have got two Virgins staying with me. They came in a Ford car from Isfahan. The smaller one is called Miss Richardson. She has an inquisitive little face like a ferret. She has lovely deep copper hair—all oily and smooth like women should. But like women should *not,* she has bobbed it, after the manner of the Sassanid dynasty, so that it looks like a hay-field which has been nibbled at by a small pair of blunt nail-scissors. The other is called Miss Winifred Eardley, known to her friends (of whom Miss Richardson is one) as Winnie. She has either got very acute indigestion or else an inferiority complex. Anyhow she sniffs.

Now, how comes it that I, who loathe women in general and virgins in particular, should for three whole weeks have to entertain these types? How comes it that I who am rendered rather ill by the thought of the church, who don't like missionaries, and who hates society, should entertain these vestals of the Church Missionary Society? Will you please explain all this to me? Like Wordsworth, I "wonder at myself like men dismayed."[1] I suppose it is the white man's burden. And the maddening thing is that Trott,[2] who rather likes them, being a white man all through, gets all the credit. And that I, who am bored stiff and have to make an effort to be polite, am just thought an amiable pagan. And last night Trott's motor broke down and I had them alone for dinner: and I had toothache. And they said, or rather Miss Richardson said, "This is heavenly—one might be anywhere but in Persia." She said it in a wistful way, poor little bitch, gazing at *The Field* spread out on the table under a lamp with a red silk fringe to it. One could see the poor little sparrow-mind fluttering

---

1. The quotation should be, "We wonder at ourselves like men betrayed." Wordsworth, *The Borderers.*
2. Alan Trott, one of the consular officials at the Legation.

back to the rectory drawing-room. "Too Too Too," went the owls: the fountain splashed on the blue tiles: the durbar tent bulked billowly against the white hot stars; and yet that effect of red light on *The Field* took her away back to the Eversley [Surrey] Rectory. I was touched by this, and went to bed with that evening-service feeling, trying to feel more hospitable about them—had I put Bromo for them? Would they like a book?

But really I don't mind much. I see, as I write, a flash of white muslin going towards the tent. "Winnie!—breakfast's ready—there's honey." "Coming, dear!" Oh England—my England—how I *love* you. That's why I don't mind having them.

VITA TO HAROLD   *Long Barn*

27 July 1926

Virginia [Woolf] was very charming and amusing. She had been to see old [Thomas] Hardy, and had come back impressed by the Great. "I felt, here's a great man, and I'm only so damned clever." She says he talked about his writing in a sort of puzzled way, as though he had done it all in the dark, and as though his life was really important only in so far as it affected his tea and his dog. He told her he had had to write all his novels as serial stories: that was why there were so many moments of crisis, because each instalment had to end on an exciting note. But I can't, myself, see many crises in that slow broad stream. She says he is a simple, ugly, insignificant little old man, and almost illiterate; also that literature, as such, has no interest or importance for him at all.

Well, then, today I took her over to Rodmell, which was nice of me, and Clive and Leonard arrived from London with one of Clive's shaggy sons [Quentin Bell], and there was a thunderstorm. On the way back I went to see Plankino who was working on the woodcuts for *The Land*. [1] Then I dined with Dada alone [at Knole] and now am not awake at all. Besides, I talked to V. till dreadfully late last night. I gave

---

1. George Plank, the American artist who worked mostly in England and was an intimate friend of Lady Sackville.

Leonard one of Pippin's [spaniel] puppies. He *was* pleased, he adores dogs.

Goodnight, my sweet, my darling. I told V. how much we loved each other. Oh yes, and I gave her Tray's essay on chastity. She is pleased with it. Why don't you write a Hogarth Essay? She would like you to. Oh darling, she is so funny, she does make me laugh! And *so* sane, when not mad. And *so* how [pathetic], about going mad again. What a nightmare it must be.

HAROLD TO VITA *Teheran*

1 August 1926

My darling,

The Bishop *in* Persia came to dinner. He said, "I should like to give you a little service while here. I generally celebrate all the Legation when I come." That word 'celebrate' should have warned me—but I am (in spite of the *Golden Bough* [1]) obtuse to ritual. I said, "Oh that would be delightful." So he came. It was rather fun arranging a church for him. We did it on the wide veranda upstairs. The Warren Hastings arches looked like some Saxon church once the chairs had been arrayed with an aisle between them. There were cushions to kneel on—and flowers and a table covered with an Italian brockade (I mean brocade) as an altar. A screen arranged behind the altar gave the appearance of a triptych. I had put candles on the altar, but Trott, being low church, made me take them away. It looked terribly naked and grim so I borrowed a bible and put beside it a copy of *Vogue* and *Gentlemen Prefer Blondes*. Trott objected to these also, so they were taken away. The bible remained: rectangular, English, misleading.

I had written to the Bishop asking (a) whether he would mind if I didn't communicate (the word reminded me of my book on Swinburne) myself. (b) Whether he wanted any wine or stuff. He replied to both in the negative.

---

1. *The Golden Bough* by Sir James Frazer, published in twelve volumes, 1890–1915, a study of mankind's magical and religious thought.

The service was fixed for 11.30. A Persian had come to see me at 9.45 and was of course still there. I had to get rid of him. I went upstairs and on the staircase I met Gladwyn [Jebb] suitably arrayed in black. He said that the Bishop wanted (a) wine (b) bread (c) a napkin (d) a champagne glass. I shouted *"Biar!"* Taqhis appeared and I told him what was required. He got terribly fussed and disappeared flopping in his slippers. It was then 11.45. Finally Taqhis emerged with 15 glasses on a tray and a bottle of champagne. Also some toast. This had to be coped with, and by 12.0 we were ready. The congregation consisted of nine people. I sat in front. Henry [Harold's dog] yelled pitiably from the room where I had shut him up. The Bishop preached a sermon about how even as when we shed our nice fleecy great-coats when the referee whistled and appeared in shorts, so also when Christ whistled should we cast off the vanities of this world and engage in the strife. As always when I hear sermons I wanted to contradict. I wanted to point out (1) that we only take off our greatcoats because, so I am told, it is irksome to play football thus encumbered; (2) that the motion of the said game produces a circular warmth which compensates for the nice fleecy greatcoat; (3) that, therefore, once you decide to play football there is no apparent virtue in doing so without a greatcoat; and above all (4) that any decent religion, as Christ, being a man of sense, kept on pointing out, allowed one to exploit the flesh as well as the spirit. (5) that people who went about in shorts were either (a) exhibitionists (b) eccentrics or (c) liable to get pneumonia. (6) that if some people went about in shorts . . .

Well, well, we can leave it at that. Then came the communion service. Never have I heard such lovely prose! "We do not presume to come to this thy table." It wasn't his table, it was mine. And none of them knew that Barbara,[2] hidden by the Italian brocade, was chuckling underneath. Anyhow, Mrs Durie, Warner, Humphrey [officials of the Legation] all went up and became Christophagists. They returned to their places in an aroma of sanctity and Messrs Berry Bros' port. Then they all went away.

I went and read the Greek Anthology before luncheon. I am glad that the Christian religion is on the decline.

---

2. See p. 19, note 1.

8 August 1926

Here is a story—a true story—which will amuse you. You know
that after the war we occupied northern Persia and even extended our
operations against the Bolsheviks. In this way a British detachment
under a Colonel Thompson occupied Baku where the White Russians
flocked to meet him. In the harbour of Baku was the Russian Caspian
fleet who had surrendered at the first appearance of Col. Thompson
and who declared themselves to be White Russians. They were thus
regarded as allies and left where they were. It slowly dawned on them
however that Col. Thompson had only 500 British troops in Baku and
that there was no need for them to have surrendered at all. So one
morning Col. Thompson woke up to find that the fleet had gone
Bolshy, had left its moorings, and had taken up a position a mile out
at sea where his field guns could not reach them but from where their
heavy guns could blow Baku to bits. From this position of incontesta-
ble advantage the fleet gave Thompson two hours to surrender failing
which they would bombard the town.

Thompson called a council of war. He had a captain and a lieuten-
ant and the man who looked after the motor boats. There were two
motor boats and they each had one torpedo. It was decided that the
faster of the two motor boats should take the two torpedos and attack
the Russian fleet. The torpedos were the very latest sort from White-
heads and nobody knew quite how to work them. Anyhow they
started off and circling round the biggest of the Russian gun-boats they
discharged the first torpedo. It went straight at the gun-boat and then
dived elegantly right underneath it coming up the other side. The
motor boat dashed back under fire to within signalling distance and
informed Thompson that they had fired the first torpedo and missed.
"Fire the other," he replied, "and don't miss." So they went back, again
circled round the flag-ship, and fiddling carefully with the mechanism
sent off the other and only remaining torpedo. Its behaviour was
identical with that of its predecessor. It made a bee-line on the surface
of the water towards the flag-ship and when twenty yards away, kicked
up its tail and dived neatly underneath. The motor boat dashed back
to the harbour. It was slowly followed by the whole Caspian fleet

flying the White flag. They surrendered to a man. It was only when the crews had been locked up in barracks and British platoons had occupied the several warships that Col. Thompson disclosed to the Russian admiral that those two torpedos were the only two we possessed—and that they had been fired in earnest and not as a warning of worse to come. A few days later the Russian ships were towed out and blown up at sea.

So we did sometimes have luck on our side.

VITA TO HAROLD   *Long Barn*

17 August 1926

You have never understood about Violet [Trefusis] (a) that it was a madness of which I should never again be capable—a thing like that happens once, and burns out the capacity for such a feeling; (b) that you could at any moment have reclaimed me, but for some extraordinary reason you wouldn't. I used to beg you to; I *wanted* to be rescued, and you wouldn't hold out a hand. I think it was a mixture of pride and mistaken wisdom on your part. I know you thought that if you tried to hold me, I should go altogether. But in this you were wrong, because I never lost sight of how you were the person I loved in the sense of loving for life. Only I suppose you either didn't believe this, or else you wouldn't take the risk.

But anyway that is a thing of the past, and not worth going over, and only the present remains.

Darling, there is no muddle at all, anywhere! I keep on telling you so. PADLOCK! And padlock I would tell you if there was. You mention Virginia: it is simply laughable. I love Virginia, as who wouldn't? but really, my sweet, one's love for Virginia is a very different thing: a mental thing, a spiritual thing if you like, an intellectual thing, and she inspires a feeling of tenderness which I suppose is because of her funny mixture of hardness and softness—the hardness of her mind, and her terror of going mad again. She makes me feel protective. Also she loves me, which flatters and pleases me. Also—since I am embarked on telling you about Virginia, but this is all absolutely padlock private—I am scared to death of arousing physical feelings in her, because of the madness. I don't know what effect it would have, you see; and that is a fire with which I have no wish to play. No, thank you. I have too much real affection and respect. Also she has never lived with anyone but Leonard, which was a terrible failure, and was abandoned quite soon. So all that remains is an unknown quantity, and I have got too many dogs not to let them lie where they *are* asleep. Besides, *ça ne me dit rien;* and *ça lui dit trop,* where I am concerned; and I don't want to get landed in an affair which might get beyond my control before I knew where I was. So you see I am sagacious—though probably I would be less sagacious if I were more tempted, which is at least frank! But, darling, Virginia is *not* the sort of person one thinks of in that way; there is something incongruous and almost indecent in the idea . . . I *have* gone to bed with her (twice), but that's all; and I told you that before, I think. Now you know all about it, and I hope I haven't shocked you.

Oh, darling, send away Iago, or I shall think you don't even begin to realise how absolutely I love you. It *is* a little hard, to have Iago thrown at me, when all the time I am miserable about not being with you. Don't you know, you silly, that the whole of this summer is as meaningless to me as it is to you? I, also, am only half alive.

Please make a comment on all this, and say you understand. But don't say you understand unless you really do. My darling, you are the one and only person for me in the world; do take that in once and for all, you little dunderhead. Really it makes me cross, when I am eating out my heart for you; and it makes me cry.

HAROLD TO VITA   *Teheran*

30 August 1926

I had a nice day yesterday lying out under the trees in a deck-chair reading Bertie Russell's *On Education* [published 1926]. A good firm book. I don't think we have made any mistakes [with their own children]. Most of what he advises we have done instinctively. There is one point however which he makes much of, that one should never show fear in front of children. As a matter of fact you are particularly good at that and try to restrain your panics. But I think he is right in preaching that principle. He also believes in allowing children to absorb sex facts naturally and in letting them see grown-ups naked. I daresay he is right, but my incest complex is too strong for me. Of course I think one may be optimistic about one's own children. Both Ben and Niggs [Nigel] seem perfectly clear and open with no knots now. And I really think they are. He also says one should not expect any response in affection at least until the age of puberty. But we were never morbid on that score—and I think they both love us very warmly and intelligently. In fact the book cheered me a great deal since so many of our principles (i.e. never telling them a lie or breaking a promise) are cardinal with him. You see, I think what guided us was your instinct to treat them as potential men and never as pretty little kittens. We have probably formed their characters much more than we imagine.

Oh my darling, it makes me homesick to write of us four.

HAROLD TO VITA   *Teheran*

7 September 1926

My last letter was written at Pelur. I sat there scribbling to my darling under the tent and with a blanket over my knee. I had just finished when I saw Gladwyn [Jebb] coming down the path with a rifle slung over his shoulder—gaunt and slightly bearded. I was so delighted to see him as I was getting rather bored with Patrick Hepburn.[1] I do hope Ben isn't *too* good looking. Hepburn is really amazingly beautiful, but it gives him the self-consciousness of a professional beauty. Which is tiresome. He is not in the least b.s. [homosexual] but he has got so used to being made-up-to that he rather expects it. Gladwyn and I teased him dreadfully. We said he was like Mrs Langtry [mistress of Edward VII]. Apart from his looks he is a rather soft and colourless

---

1. Patrick Buchan-Hepburn, then aged twenty-five, was attached to the British Embassy in Constantinople and on temporary secondment to the Teheran Legation. After a distinguished career in politics he was created Lord Hailes and became Governor General of the British Caribbean Islands.

youth with a lack of vitality and a great many rectory corners in his mind. One has the impression of his having been a mother's darling, and he has a lot of undigested ideas about having to keep up one's position: "Of course I like some of those clever people but it's a bad thing to see too much of them." He is not exactly a fool—but a youth who is at moments coyly skittish. Thus he is beginning (oh so slightly) to get on my nerves, and I regret the time when he lay there as a beautiful corpse.[2]

All these reflections are provoked by thinking how glad, that grey Scotch morning, I was to see Gladwyn. He makes Hepburn, poor boy, look merely a little (or rather a huge) fancy piece. He makes him look terribly bedint—which is odd in a descendant of Bothwell.[3] Poor Patrick, I fear he is the "charming boy" and will become less so each year. But the contrast between him and Gladwyn was very striking: Gladwyn so absolutely real: Patrick so beautiful and so second-hand. Oh I *do* hope Benzie won't be like that.

Mar will smile at all this and think it is merely because Patrick was so stand-offish and that Hadji was re-buffed. Not so. Don't like sleeping with Archdeacons' daughters and didn't want to in the least, the moment the Deanery began to obtrude with his retreating fever. But it shows one how bloody critical we all are, and how we really don't like people who have no personality inside. Poor Patrick!

VITA TO HAROLD   *Long Barn*

26 September 1926

It is really autumn now. A week ago the thermometer was at 83 and this morning there is frost on the ground! But such lovely days, with that lovely light over the ridge at sunset. I don't dislike it, only my nose and knees are cold when I wake up. I am busy taking the garden to pieces, pulling out the dead annuals, cutting down the dead stalks. And everything I plant now in their places is for you. This makes me incredibly happy, because you will like it, and "I can't be

2. He had become very ill on first arriving in Persia, and Harold looked after him.
3. Mary Queen of Scots' third husband, from whom the Hepburns claimed descent.

happy unless you're happy too." I am planting more azaleas in the wood, more scarlet anemones, a row of plum-trees in the new orchard, lots more roses in the top garden, turning one of the Michaelmas daisy beds up there into a big bed of *Moysii,* and putting 100 Madonna lilies into the border where it runs along the tennis-court wire. Also replacing some roses on the Calvary, and making a honeysuckle arch into the apple garden, where that crazy little gate used to be. Planting 100 more *iris sirilica* round the pond. It is all great fun and I love it. Barnes [the gardener] is as keen as I am, and keeps on saying, "I must do this and that before Mr Nicolson comes back." Yet he never prepares horrors as a surprise for me—like Goacher, who while Dotz [Wellesley] was away, filled six tubs with scarlet geraniums and set them all round the house.

Then I come in and work—i.e. do my lecture—and Pippin [spaniel] snores, and I have a fire. If only you were locked away into your little room it would be the perfect life. Oh darling, if you are an aubergine, I am a cabbage. I drink nothing at all, eat very little, and feel extremely well. So now you know all about it, and I only wish it could last longer, but I have the threat of poor dear B.M. coming to stay here. However, that is not yet certain.

You know, Hadji, I think I can analyse why I have this obsession about being here alone. It is because (a) I put myself together again and become a unity instead of a patchwork, and (b) I know I go soft when I am with people, idle my time away, talk too much, eat and drink too much. What I really like is a severe life, but have too weak a character to withstand the dissipations of company! I never spoke a truer word than

> the heart, the very heart of me
> That plays and strays, a truant in strange lands,
> Always returns and finds its inward peace,
> Its swing of truth, its measure of restraint,
> Here among meadows, orchards, lanes, and shaws.[1]

Forgive me quoting myself, but it puts the matter in a nutshell. And that is why it is so odd and wrong that you should not be here, because you are so intrinsic a part of the inward peace.

---

1. From Vita's poem *Orchard and Vineyard* (1921).

Darling, do you know what I did last night after writing to you? I meant to finish my lecture, but fell to reading the Georgics (mine, not Virgil's) [*The Land*], and really I thought they were rather good.

HAROLD TO VITA   *Teheran*

1 October 1926

I have just typed out a telegram to you. First, many many happy returns to us of this lucky day.[1] (Oh dearest—I have thought and thought about it all. How mar we were! Rather sweet really and how. My angel, we *have* grown close together since then. Little weedy saplings we were then. We are oaks today.)

Well then the second part of my telegram was about your Persian book,[2] and as it is rather about that than about what happened 13 years ago that you want to hear, I shall now drop the sob-stuff.

Well, *en somme* I think the Persian Book *absolutely first class*—infinitely better than I had expected.

What is really interesting about it—or what is *arresting*, rather, and so original—is that one feels all through that there is an interesting mind trying to mould all these pictures into shape. It is all the difference between looking at coins or cameos in a museum, or being shown them by some sort of Roger Fry who explains the point. I don't quite know how you have achieved this effect, but it is very striking: it makes the book wholly different from other travel books: it gives it a psychological interest far above the Cook's tourist part. The tone, of course, is set by the Introduction: but where Mar has been so tremendously clever is that she never diverges for one instant from the same key. The book is the same colour throughout; it leaves the same colour-tone in the mind.

It is this which gives it its continuity. (I read it through at a sitting—but that of course is not a good test in one Mar about the other's book.) One gets the dominant impression of a very real and

---

1. Their wedding anniversary.
2. Vita's *Passenger to Teheran,* about her first journey to Persia, earlier in 1926.

sincere person accepting nothing second-hand and feeling everything. One feels that all those emphatic landscapes have been given a personal interpretation. It makes all the other travel books I have read look just like coloured picture-post-cards.

"The wise traveller is he who is perpetually surprised." Oh my sweet—you have got something of the essential Vita into this book. Rather an alarming Vita. But so aloof and independent and real. One thing which I particularly relish is your rapid fore-shortening. India in one page—five pages to little Dilijan![3] *That's* the way to do it!

I won't talk about the beauty of the style—or the real conviction carried by the description—because that I expected. I let Colonel Haworth read a bit of it. "By God!" he said, "this is the first book I've read on Persia which gives one the slightest idea what it's like." All *that* part is excellent—but I expected that.

No—it's just the writer's personality which makes it such a good book. I think it is lucky you had to write it in a rush: it has helped to produce that smooth uniform surface which is so effective.

Of course there are things which I shall never forgive. NEVER. Poor Hadji—in his mind remains for ever that night when he waited under the moon, listening to the dogs barking, straining his ears for the sound of a motor.[4] She acted well: she pretended to be pleased to see him: But No!! It is clear now. It was all put on. She was, in fact, "Sorry when she saw the lights of Kermanshah."

Well, well: one gets used to such wounds I suppose.

It is a pity also that she should have called the Ali Kapi the Ali Carpi—thinking of Capri I suppose. Or that she should have said Chel Setum, when she meant Chebel Sirtoon, or that, when once she breaks into Persian, she should say it wrong. Also there is no Isphahan gate—it is called the Gate of Shah Abdul Azim. And oh! *Viti*—"Say something in Persian," they demanded, and I repeated a verse from Hafiz!"—oh Vits! Vits! But I will cease Ali carping: this is nothing

---

3. A village on the road to Isfahan, where they had spent the night.
4. It was at Kermanshah, western Persia, where Harold awaited Vita's arrival in the car from Bagdad. Vita in her reply explained that her apparent indifference was a joke.

to carp about. It is a splendid lovely book; it has given me such an up on life.

Your Hadji

VITA TO HAROLD *Long Barn*

2 October 1926

Ronnie [Balfour] and I were climbing over the gate into the orchard, when we heard Dottie [Wellesley] call out, "Look at that aeroplane!" We looked up, and saw a huge machine just overhead, with a long blood-red plume of fire streaming from it. It swerved away as though it were making for Penshurst; Ronnie and I stared at one another, appalled; after a minute we heard the engines stop; after another minute (though it seemed an eternity) we heard the crash. Of course we thought it had come down quite close, and ran for all we were worth; then we saw a column of black smoke rising up out of the Westwood trees. Well, we rushed across the fields, and there was the ruin in a field, still blazing, an appalling sight. You will read about it in the papers, of course. There was absolutely nothing left of that machine but a blackened circle of grass, some twisted iron, some fluttering coloured silks, and seven sinister heaps covered over with sacking. They had got the bodies out with hay-rakes—just charred stumps, and the same smell as at Potter's Bar when we went to see the Zeppelin [crash]. The most poignant thing of all were the clothes, they had been in the luggage and consequently had not had time to burn; they lay strewn all round the wreck, pathetic frivolous things, bright silks and bits of fur, intended to adorn those charred remains.

There was of course nothing to be done, and we walked home. Plankino [George Plank] nearly fainted when we got back, and we had to pour brandy down his throat.

Now this morning the papers are full of the Weald names: Westwood, Geffers, Marchant, Ketney—it will look so strange to you when you read it. I am *thankful* the thing did not fall in one of our fields, though I can't think why it didn't, as in the end it turned upside down and fell like a stone. I shall never forget that blazing thing flying over the trees of our orchard and staggering away to its death. Glad the babies weren't here.

VITA TO HAROLD   *182 Ebury Street, London*

12 October 1926

I hear from Dotz [Dorothy Wellesley] that all my Persian bulbs (irises and tulips) which I left in her greenhouse are coming up. This excites me to madness. If you see any exciting vegetation, dig it up and send it *now,* while it is dormant. Some of the wild broom? Sage? Lavender? Oh please, Hadji, some of the lavender with the big pink flowers. But wrap it in something damp (moss, tissue-paper) and put it in a biscuit tin.

VITA TO HAROLD   *66 Mount Street, London*

26 October 1926

Ouf! I breathe again. Lecture over.[1] Did you think of me? I hope so. I thought of you thinking of me, even as I stood terrified and with tremulous voice before the audience in the R.S.L. room. People I knew in said audience: [Sir Edmund] Gosse [the literary critic] (in the chair), John Drinkwater, Philip Guedella, Dotz, Irene (Cooper-Willis), George Plank, your mummy, Eric!! Katherine[2]!!!! And, in the back row, grinning at me, ironical, *émue,* Virginia [Woolf]. Others were strangers. A sea of faces—Gosse speaking—the sensation of being on one's feet—"Ladies and gentlemen . . ."

Then the sensation of speaking, speaking, speaking . . . The blessèd sensation of coming to an end. Applause. The refuge of sitting down again. Then Gosse . . . Silly old ass. Silly little arch bows towards me. *The Land* flattened open on the desk before him. "A poem of which

---

1. Her lecture was on *Tradition in English Poetry* to the Royal Society of Literature.
2. Eric was Harold's older brother, later 3rd Lord Carnock, and Katherine his wife.

neither Tennyson nor Wordsworth need have been ashamed." "This truly Virgilian solidity . . ." "This most important contribution to English literature . . ." Silly ass, silly soapy old ass. Gosse intoning my lines. I shrank behind my desk. I escaped at last with Virginia who put me properly in my place in the mists of Bloomsbury Square. She wants to print my paper as a Hogarth Essay.

I love you endlessly. I feel bruised and raped; an odd feeling. As though I had been stripped publicly naked. Yet I suppose I ought to be pleased. I shall write to you tomorrow from home, where I am myself.

You are the only reality. Oh darling, darling . . .

HAROLD TO VITA   *Teheran*

7 November 1926

Dearest—you don't know what *The Land* means to me! I read it incessantly—it has become a real wide undertone to my life. I forget absolutely that it is by you: it is such a lovely thing, darling, so beautiful a thing. It gives one a sense of permanence. It seems infinitely better each time one reads it. I keep on coming with surprise on lines I hadn't noticed:

"How delicate in spring they be / That mobled blossom and that wimpled tree."
or:
"Some concord of creation that the mind / Only in perilous balance apprehends."
or: "She being beautiful, and Leah but tender-eyed."
Lines which one could instance as the very stuff of poetry—lines which are memorable as catching a swallow-wing of thought which would have been lost by the trudge of prose. Oh my dear, if there was ever a work of art about which I felt *certain* it is this. So certain, that, except for fun, I don't care what other people say. So certain that I feel shy about it, like I feel shy about all my profounder feelings. My darling—it is so absurd—but I feel *grateful* to you for it. I don't mean to exaggerate, but it has added a pleasure to life. It is so firm, reliable.

It never lets one down. Dearest, the fact that it is by you (a fact which is too incredible to be realised) really does not weigh with me. But I know that the side of you which wrote that poem is detached from all mundane things—that it is above all exterior connections. You will get outside it in the same way some day. You will think, "Did I really write that?"

Of course naturally I want it to be a public success. But intrinsically I don't care. I simply know that it *is* a part of English literature, whereas all the other stuff is just like *Vogue* or the *Daily Mail*. Funny Mar![1]

VITA TO HAROLD   *Long Barn*

7 November 1926

It is such a lovely day, so warm that we (Leonard, Virginia, and I) have been sitting in the sun by the big-room door all morning. The woods are golden, the distance deep blue—a blue and brown day. The garden looks incredibly neat; all sharp edges to turf and hedges everywhere, dug borders, black earth. It was fun waking up this morning and seeing what had been done during the past week. Such a nice dinner last night, with Eddy [Sackville-West] and Desmond [MacCarthy], the latter at his most amusing. But I agree with Virginia: he is really too mild. It is becoming too much of a stunt. Too negative. But very charming and amusing he is all the same.

Leonard is perfectly happy with a crowd of puppies. He has brought his own, and she and her sister are tearing madly up and down the lawn. The three elk [hound] babies try tentatively to join in. Leonard is a funny grim solitary creature. Virginia an angel of wit and intelligence. Leonard goes back to London this evening and she stays on with me till tomorrow, which I enjoy more than anything, as she then never stops talking, and I feel as though the edge of my mind were being held against a grindstone. Hadji not worry, though. It is all right.

---

1. *The Land* was awarded The Hawthornden Prize in 1927.

Later. We went to tea with Eddy at Knole, and then took Leonard to the station. A young moon, which Hadji must be seeing through the planes, oh dear. I think today has been one of the most beautiful days I ever remember; our Weald was looking its best, and such a sunset burnishing the brown trees. It made me absolutely long for you to be there.

VITA TO HAROLD   *Long Barn*

9 November 1926

Oh dear, Virginia . . . You see, Hadji, she is very very fond of me, and she says she was so unhappy when I went to Persia that it startled and terrified her. I don't think she is accustomed to emotional storms, she lives too much in the intellect and imagination. Most human beings take emotional storms as a matter of course. Fortunately she is the sensible sort of person who pulls themselves together and says, "This is absurd." So I don't really worry. (Rather proud, really, of having caught such a big silver fish.) I look on my friendship with her as a treasure and a privilege. I shan't ever fall in love with her, *padlock*, but I am absolutely devoted to her and if she died I should mind quite, quite dreadfully. Or went mad again.

HAROLD TO VITA   *Teheran*

10 November 1926

My own darling Viti,

Sweetest, it's rather awful but I don't think I like Mrs Clive[1] at all, at all. It's so bedint not to like one's chief's wife (like the wife of the Colonel being snuffy about the wife of the brigadier), that I don't say so to anyone else—and Mar [must] not repeat it. Besides I may

---

1. Robert Clive had come to Teheran as British Minister on 5 November. His wife was Magdalen, daughter of Lord Muir Mackenzie.

change my mind. It is far better to start disliking someone than to start liking them—that is, when one has *got* to have close relations over a long period. I will scarcely get to *dislike* Mrs C. more and I may get to like her more. Whereas the reverse process would be a diminuendo.

But in the first place I think her affected. Now what on earth do we mean when we say 'affected'? Clive Bell I suppose is affected, and Raymond [Mortimer], and Virginia, and Vita and Harold. So all one means is that her mechanical habits (whether mental, moral, aesthetic, or merely laryngeal) are not the sort of habits I like. One means also that the mechanism is a little too obvious. That certain habits of attitude occur with too regular a precision. Now she has a form of affectation which irritates me particularly and which I have met before in women of birth, education and ill-health. It is a trick (1) of pinning situations to a phrase, (2) and of doing so in an off-hand way, with a sort of flicking gesture—to show how easily such apothegms come to one, that they are but the hors d'oeuvres of the banquet of one's soul. The victim of this habit thinks, I suppose, that it gives to situations and their own comments thereon a light and amusing effect. Thus I say I must be going off to the chancery—"Robot!" she says. The catch-words of the day are applied by her to the incidents of daily life, but they are the catch-words of a world I don't like at all, the world that lives in Hans Place, and dines at Prince's Restaurant, and goes to the best plays, and reads *Punch,* and has relations in all the countries, and simply revels in the Army and Navy Stores.

Then her meanness is simply terrifying. He may be just as stingy as she is, but he hides it better. She has no shame at all. Following [was the] dialogue yesterday while I was in his study going through tele-grams. Enter *Mrs Clive:* "Daddy, sorry to interrupt you two important people (oh yes I know I'm a bore) but just fancy, one has to pay 1 Rial 25 for the most rotten little note-book here. Isn't there some rough government paper on which Mimi [her daughter, aged 15] can do her lessons?" *Clive:* "But after all, I Rial 25 is only just sixpence." *Mrs Clive:* "But my dear man, you should see the note-books. Why at the Stores one could get something far better for 5d. Of course I sent Mimi back to the shop to return them . . ."

And then her voice is dreadful. A sort of brave whine—courage struggling against ill health: a sort of plaintive tolerance, superior

No. 185.   November 10.1926
                                              Wednesday

My own darling Vita,

            Sweetest its rather awful but I
don't think I like Mrs Clive at all at all.
Its so tedious not to like one's chief's
wife (like the wife of the Colonel being
snuffy about the wife of the Brigadier)
that I don't say so to anyone else —
& man not repeat it. Besides I may change
my mind. It is far better to start
disliking someone than to start liking
them — that is when one has got to
have close relations over a long period.
I am scarcely ever to dislike Mrs C. more
& I man get to like her more. Whereas
the reverse process would be a diminuendo.

            But in the first place I think
her affected. Now what on Earth do we
mean when we say "affected"? Clive &
Saffron is affected, and Raymond, and
Virginia, & Vita, Harold. So all one
means is that her mechanical habits

education tolerating a world of fools—("one must keep one's sense of humour . . .").

He is amiable and not a bit pompous—but I fear a light-weight.

Oh Viti Viti—I fear the Mars are not easily satisfied. Of course it is an impossible position being forced to live in subservient intimacy with people unlike oneself. The only basis for such a relationship must be one of blind admiration.

VITA TO HAROLD   *66 Mount St., London*

15 November 1926

After breakfast I was caught by the old man,[1] who glowered at me from under his eyebrows and said didn't I want to know his opinion of my poem? I wasn't at all sure that I did. I wanted to write to Hadji, I wanted to put on my fur coat, I wanted to say goodbye, Dr. Bridges—however I sat down meekly, as near as possible to the bit of smouldering peat which did duty as the fire, and composed myself in an attitude of proper respect, a nice blending of (1) Little Lord Fauntleroy, (2) the younger generation, (3) the young Swinburne at the feet of Victor Hugo. I was then treated for two hours to a lecture on English prosody. Chaucer, elision, syllabic verse, the diatonic scale, Shakespeare, Milton, the iniquity of daring to exist at all—all this was thundered at me in true Tennysonian manner. I huddled myself together, getting smaller and smaller, longing for a coat-collar, an umbrella, anything to creep behind and hide.

HAROLD TO VITA   *Teheran*

19 November 1926

I went to Clive's opening reception for the Persians. In the middle of it all Mrs Elgood came and told me that they had thrown Henry's

---

1. Robert Bridges, the poet laureate, with whom Vita had again been staying the night at his house on Boars Hill, outside Oxford.

body on to the dust-heap outside the Russian Embassy.[1] I don't think I have ever been quite so angry in my life. I absolutely saw red. I left the Legation and dashed across to my house. I quite unconsciously seized the two sticks you used for your ankle and called for Bogber. He must have thought his last hour had come—seeing me standing there in a frock-coat transfigured with rage and waving two sticks in my hand. He got as white as a sheet and dodged behind the table. I spoke to him in Persian at first. He said, of course, that it was the fault of the Dispensary people. He had told the latter exactly what to do, but had had to come back here because of his work. I then stopped talking Persian and spoke to him in English. I then sent him out with lanterns and a man to rescue that poor little corpse and bury it decently.

It is things like this that really exhaust me—I felt as if I had been beaten all over—like you, my sweet, after a scene with B.M. It is things like this also that show one what savages these people really are. I walked back to the reception, and looked at all those polite frock-coated people with a feeling of loathing.

VITA TO HAROLD   *Long Barn*

20 November 1926

I got a letter from Virginia, which contains one of her devilish, shrewd, psychological pounces—so true that I'll transcribe it for you:

"You'll be tired of me one of these days (I'm so much older), so I have to take my little precautions. That's why you say I put the emphasis on 'recording' rather than feeling. And isn't there something obscure in you? something that doesn't vibrate? It may be purposely—you don't let it, but I see it with other people, as well as with me: something reserved, muted. It's in your writing too, by the by. The thing I call central transparency sometimes fails you there too. I will lecture you at Long Barn."

Damn the woman, she has put her finger on it. There *is* something muted. What is it, Hadji? Something that doesn't vibrate, something that doesn't come alive. I brood and brood; feel that I grope in a dark

---

1. Harold had been obliged to have his dog put down when Henry developed incurable sores.

tunnel, persuaded that somewhere there is light, but never can find the way to emerge. It makes everything I do (i.e. write) a little unreal; gives the effect of having been done from the outside. It is the thing which spoils me as a writer; destroys me as a poet. But how did V. discover it? I have never owned it to anybody, scarcely even to myself. It is what spoils my human relationships too, but that I mind less.

She ends up her letter by saying, "Do you know this interesting fact: I found myself thinking with intense curiosity about death. Yet if I'm persuaded of anything it is of mortality. Then why this sense that death is going to be a great excitement?—something positive, active?"

There is no doubt about it, Hadji: that as one grows older one thinks more: Virginia worries, you worry, I worry.

Oh dear, what a solemn mar—that's what comes of living alone in the rain and reading Wordsworth. Yet I would rather do this, and become introspective, than rattle about London, while people's voices become more and more devoid of meaning.

VITA TO HAROLD   *Long Barn*

23 November 1926

Sibyl Colefax told Virginia you had the most delicious nature she had ever known. There now! I always told you she was an intelligent woman. V. was impressed at Sibyl corroborating what *I* had told her. I'm a little bothered about Virginia, but fortunately she is a sensible and busy person, and doesn't luxuriate in vain repinings. She is an absolute angel to me, and the value of her friendship is not to be measured in gold. Oh my dear, *what* intelligence! it is amazing—what perception, sensitiveness in the best sense, imagination, poetry, culture; everything so utterly un-shoddy and real. I long for you two to know each other better. I hope to God she won't be too unhappy when I go away; she told me that last year she was terrified by her own unhappiness and I fear this will be worse. Darling, this all sounds very conceited, but I don't mean it like that, and it is *padlock* anyway. She is very much on the crest of the wave, which pleases her vanity, but so *how* always: "I want you to be proud of me." I think she's coming here for the weekend as Leonard has to go away—or perhaps weekend after next.

Oh my darling, how well I know that feeling about "how can a fountain-pen express my ache for you?" I simply cling to the idea that the time is going by. But I cannot believe that next summer will ever come, it is too good to be possible.

VITA TO HAROLD　　　　　　　　　　　*Long Barn*

30 November 1926

I'm alone. It is very cold and wet. I have got Virginia coming for the weekend. Darling, I know Virginia will die, and it will be too awful. (I don't mean *here,* over the weekend; but just die young.) I went to Tavistock Sq. yesterday, and she sat in the dusk in the light of the fire, and I sat on the floor as I always do, and she rumpled my hair as she always does, and she talked about literature and Mrs Dalloway and Sir Henry Taylor, and said you would resent her next summer. But I said no, you wouldn't. Oh Hadji, she *is* such an angel; I really adore her. Not 'in love' but just love—devotion. I don't know whether it annoys you that I should write so often about her? One has to be so careful at this distance; but really Hadji shouldn't be annoyed, because her friendship does enrich me so, and she is so completely un-silly. I absolutely long for you to know her better. I don't think I have ever loved anybody so much, in the way of friendship; in fact, of course I haven't. She knows the mars adore each other; I've told her so, and so has Tray. Oh my sweet, they do, don't they? God, how I want to *talk* to you; just talk and talk and talk. Yes, 'the time' is a real personal thing—like a snowman that dwindles very, very slowly. But still dwindles.

HAROLD TO VITA　　　　　　　　　　　*Teheran*

3 December 1926

You *do* promise to tell me if there is a muddle with Virginia! I am so worried about that. It is *such* a powder magazine. I am far more worried for Virginia and Leonard's sake than for ours. I *know* that for each of us the magnetic north is the other—and that though the needle may flicker and even get stuck at other points—it will come back to the pole sooner or later. But what dangers for them![1] You see, I have every confidence in your wisdom except where these sort of things are concerned, when you wrap your wisdom in a hood of optimism and only take it out when things are too far gone for mending.

HAROLD TO VITA   *Teheran*

17 December 1926

No my sweet—it doesn't annoy me that you should talk so much about Virginia. From your point of view I know that the friendship can only be enriching. I am of course a little anxious about it from her point of view as I can't help feeling that her stability and poise is based on a rather precarious foundation. I mean it would be rather awful if your coming out here made her ill. That is my main consideration. Attached to it, like a little ivy growing at the foot of a castle, is the feeling that she will make me seem dull to you. Not jealousy, darling—only an instinctive movement of self-defence. But my dominant idea is one of pleasure that the rich ores in your nature should be brought to light—I *know* that it does you moral and mental good to be with her and be loved by her, and that is all that matters. I think you are very akin—the marriage of true minds to which I will not allow myself (even to myself or to you which is the same thing) to admit impediment.[2]

And as for *my* relations with Virginia—I shall never forget how she was kind to me when I was smarting from Lytton's rudeness.[3] There was no reason why she should have been nice about it except that she saw I was flustered and in real pain. So at the bottom of my

---

1. He was, of course, fearing that their love affair might trigger a new attack of insanity in Virginia Woolf.
2. "Let me not to the marriage of true minds / Admit impediments." Shakespeare, Sonnet 116.
3. Lytton Strachey had been disdainful to Harold at their first meeting at a Bloomsbury party on 15 March 1923, the day when Harold's *Tennyson* was published.

terror of her glimmers a little white stone of gratitude. Which can only be increased by her loving you.

VITA TO HAROLD   *Long Barn*

17 December 1926

I have read so much of the 19th century lately that I can scarcely restrain myself from writing in that manner—whether in prose or poetry—and the more I read, the more I am convinced that I was born out of season: I should have lived in an age when seriousness and noble thoughts found an echo. Not that I like it; and I dislike it the more, now that I recognise in myself the natural tendency to precisely such earnest bombast; so, as we dislike in others what we mistrust in ourselves, I annotate my Wordsworth with angry comments and throw my Arnold across the room. I have now taken to Jane Austen, but although the genius of Proust forces me to tolerate a fiction founded upon snobbery, materialism and hypocrisy, her mere sly pokes of humour cannot persuade me to the same enjoyment—*I can't do with it;* she seems to me only a degree removed from Galsworthy. I agree with Charlotte Brontë about her.[1]

In fact, I don't know what I want from literature; I don't hold with the dunghill despair of Eliot; I don't like the hearty Victorianism of God's-in-his-heaven, all's-right-with-the-world; I, even *I*, can't stomach the self-righteous sententiousness of Wordsworth (although I think *Tintern Abbey* one of the finest poems in the language, and some of his sonnets the same). The 18th century is out of the question. There remain only the metaphysicians (who are obviously limited) and the Elizabethans. I'm not sure that they don't have it every time, with their *awakeness* and virility—yet even they had their affectations: the Italian tragedy, and all that. There seems to be no escape from affectations, of one sort or another, in literature; perhaps inevitably; every one

---

1. In a letter to G. H. Lewes of 12 January 1848 Charlotte Brontë wrote of *Pride and Prejudice:* "What did I find? An accurate daguerreotyped portrait of a commonplace face; a carefully fenced, highly cultivated garden, with neat borders and delicate flowers; but no glance of a bright, vivid physiognomy, no open country, no fresh air, no blue hill, no bonny beck."

seems conscious of a mission, whether to introduce new concepts (as Donne and Herbert and Vaughan and Co) or to redeem the language from a conventional groove (as Coleridge and Wordsworth), or again as Eliot and his kin. All a question of reaction; never a question of approaching LIFE, through the medium of poetry, with a true personal attitude—save in people like Blake, who rapidly become such cranks as to become bores. Yet what should poetry express, but an attitude towards life? Fresh, thought-out at first hand, uncoloured by fashion (least of all!) or by what has gone before? But a damned difficult thing to do. (I mean *major* poetry of course; the Herricks and Sedleys always have their place—a different one.) All this comes of reading *Mansfield Park;* I try her [Jane Austen] periodically, and always with the same result—*I am sure* she is for the Desmonds [MacCarthy] and Eddie Marshes, and such littérateurs.

Tired out now with temper and going to bed—this is the third letter I have written you today. I wish I understood what life and literature was all about.

Your own puzzled
Mar

PS. It usually seems to me that serenity is the only thing worth aiming at, yet what is the Eliot school but the opposite facet of the same conviction (the sour grapes sides of it), and then one knows all the time how false one's serenity is—how instantly it would be shattered by the touch of personal tragedy. What *is* it all about?

VITA TO HAROLD — *Long Barn*

21 December 1926

My own, *nothing* is wrong. PADLOCK. What 'reservations' or 'half truths' have you detected in my letters? There have been none, I have told you everything day by day exactly as it has happened. I swear to tell you at the first sign of "muddle with Virginia." My dearest, how can you speak of reservations and half truths when I have told you all about that business? Even that I *did* sleep with her, which I need never have told you—but that I wanted you to know everything that happened to me while you were away. (If you had been at home I might not have told you.) There is nothing I will not tell you, that you want to know. I am absolutely devoted to her, but not in love. So there. Oh my darling, has all my wretchedness at being separated from you then failed to convince you of my absolute love for you? It can't, it can't; you *must* know. It was only that you had 'flu, wasn't it? Oh darling, I get frantic when I think of you having even a moment's anxiety.

VITA TO HAROLD   *Knole*

26 December 1926

Ben is in bed in Cranmer's dressing-room—your room!—and I am in bed in Cranmer's bedroom, and we have the door open between us, so that we can talk. I can hear him saying to himself, "The mild continuous epic of the soil,"[1] like somebody rolling a sweet round and round his tongue. Niggs [Nigel] is the same little clown, a born comic. He has got his bicycle, and is as happy as a king. He is infinitely *serviable,* unselfish, and affectionate. Also sturdy, practical, resourceful, independent, humorous. I see *no* flaw in him, as a character; everybody loves him. I have had to institute scrubbage, as never was there such a little guttersnipe. Otherwise he is perfect; not an intellectual, but we shall have enough to spare of that in Ben. My darling, we are very, very lucky in those two boys. They will, respectively, satisfy all that we could wish for: Ben our highbrowness, Niggs our human needs. Or, at least, so I read them. Ben may be selfish to us, though I think we are both intelligent enough to cope with that; Niggs may be conventional and English but, again, we are intelligent enough to cope with that. It remains, that we are very lucky in them, and that they are very lucky in us. What I really do look forward to is having them next summer, as Ben will be just at the age then when you will be most valuable to him, and your influence most important.

---

1. From Vita's own poem *The Land.*

Eddy [Sackville-West] wandered in and interrupted, but I have decided that I am fond of Eddy, so I don't mind. He is gone now, and I have had my luncheon, and presently I suppose I must get up—I should like to stay in bed today, but it is not fair on Dada, whose Olive [Rubens] has got boils.

What is the point, in our enlightened world, of *marriage?* You see, if the mars had just lived together, they would be living together still, just as happily, and it would make no difference to their passion for their garden, or to their interest in their mars. The whole system of marriage is wrong. It ought, at least, to be optional; and no stigma if you prefer a less claustrophobic form of contract. For it *is* claustrophobic. It is only very, very intelligent people like us who are able to rise superior; and I have a suspicion, my darling, that even *our* intelligence (about which there seems to be a good deal in this letter), wouldn't have sufficed if our temperamental weaknesses didn't happen to dovetail as well as they do, e.g. my impatience of restraint and Hadji's constitutional dislike of scenes. In fact, our common determination for personal liberty: to have it ourselves, and to allow it to each other. (There is no *arrière-pensée* about all this; just thinking aloud, and just a smug satisfaction with the way we have solved the problem.)

But of course the real secret is that we love each other—one always comes back to these simple human things in the end, and 'intelligence' goes on the scrap-heap.

HAROLD TO VITA   *Teheran*

31 December 1926

Darling, I don't like rhododendrons—I am sorry. I don't mind them in a big place round a big lake. But I think they are as out of place at our cottage as a billiard-table would be. To me it is exactly the same. Then I don't like putting in big things (as distinct from small flowers) which are not indigenous: I am opposed to specimen trees. You see, I think our stunt at Long Barn is to keep the Kentish farm background, and on that background to embroider as much as

we like. But rhododendrons would spoil the background. I feel sure
you agree really—only you think, "He doesn't understand that the
pond garden has to be backed and enclosed by something large and
bushy and dark." But I do understand this, and I agree that if rhododendrons were natives to Kent they would be exactly and absolutely
what we want. But they are *not* natives and we should spoil our
lovely Kentish atmosphere. I'm sure I am right. But what then can
we have? Well, cob nuts, and hazel, banked right at the back, with
holly as a background to them—and in front some syringa and
flowering shrubs. Yes, I know it's difficult. Shrubbery is a great
problem if one is to avoid the suburban. But it's not a problem
which can be solved by rosie-dendrons. I don't mind holly so long
as it's not variegated. But be clever and think of all the indigenous
things and get an idea of derivatives. What about more flowering
peaches against a background of holly? I think that the pond garden
wants a great deal of dark background. In fact I think the nuttery
should be made with a plantation of dark trees. One wants the pond
to look like a clearing in a wood: not like a piece of water in a rock
garden.

HAROLD TO VITA   *Teheran*

7 January 1927

Such a marvellous day yesterday. An absolute stillness. It is so odd
that cloudless days should differ so much from each other. I think this
place is so excellent for training the observation. There is the vast
uniformity in space and even time: the feeling that it will all be the
same colour and contours right away to China: the feeling that it was
the same colour and contour five thousand years ago: that is the first
background. The second background is the climate. The fact that one
really does get about 300 days in the year which are absolutely cloudless—and thus in appearance absolutely the same. The fact that there
are no breezes in Persia—rare gales only, howling against an absolute
stillness. All this produces a monochromatic background against which
little changes—the sound of a dry leaf pattering on a tin roof, the trail

of smoke against the umber plain, take a far intenser significance. I think it is this which has made me so sensitive to nature-sounds. Persia in effect is a great stillness: that really is its charm. And darling, how immense that charm is! Now that my happiness has come back to me I savour it with joy. I ride out over the hills and look back on that amazing design of plain and mountain. And I shout—so that Bay Rum [Harold's new horse] pricks his ears—"Viti!—Viti!"

VITA TO HAROLD   *Long Barn*

22 July 1927

My own precious Hadji

It seems so funny to be writing to you again,[1] and the pot pourri is such an awful coffee cup [reminder].

I have lots to tell you:

I went to lunch with the priest. Talk about Clive [Bell] having a Restoration appearance! it is nothing to the Rev. Summers.[2] Dressed in black, hung with amethyst crosses and bits of jet, black suéde shoes, fat white hands, a fat dimpled face, oiled black curls, very carefully disposed—he is just like a Lely. He gave me a very good lunch and lots of information, then when I asked him to tell me the way, he said he would come to the end of the street, and put on a top-hat with a curly brim, and black silk gloves. You never saw such an old sod in all your life.

Then I went and met Virginia, who had come down with Leonard to Richmond Park where V. was to have a driving lesson. Leonard and I watched her start. The motor made little pounces and stopped dead. At one moment it ran backwards. At last she sailed off, and Leonard and I and Pinker [dog] went for a walk at 5 miles an hour. Every five minutes Leonard would say, "I suppose Virginia will be all

1. Harold and Vita, having walked across the Bakhtiari Mountains to the Persian Gulf, returned to England together on 5 May. On 21 July Harold went to Paris with Raymond Mortimer for a week's holiday.

2. Rev. Alphonsus Summers, the expert on Restoration plays. Vita visited him in connection with her book on Aphra Behn published in 1927. He lived on The Green, Richmond.

right." We walked round a plantation and he told me how once he had walked there with Desmond [MacCarthy] on a moonlight night, and the night got mistier and Desmond got more and more romantic, and was pouring out all the secrets of his heart, when they came to a clearing in the midst of the plantation, and there, gleaming in the moonlight, was a white, solitary, enormous chamber-pot.

Well, then we got back to the trysting place and there was Virginia taking an intelligent interest in the works of the car. So Leonard drove off back to London, and V. and I went to Kew (in *my* car), and walked about and sat there till 6.30—and then came back to London and tried to go and see Ruth Draper but there were no seats, so we dined at the Petit Riche and had a lot of Chianti and went back to Tavistock [Square] and sat in the basement and talked more.

HAROLD TO VITA *Long Barn*

12 September 1927

My own own darling Viti,

Dearest—isn't it absurd that after all these years of marriage and all these delicious months of constant companionship I should feel a wrench, a cleavage, a real gulf and gap—just because you go away for one night? The afternoon is all still grey and purple: there is a faint sun: the poplars stand straight and unwanted: the house seems empty and broods on its little untidy self. My dear, my dear, what *would* happen to me if you really went away? Such desolation. I couldn't survive it. I wonder what I should do and from what part of myself I could dig up the stores of courage required. Has one reserves of fortitude? I feel that my present stock of it would be but as a tea-cup capacity compared to all the tanks and cylinders of Abadan. And he was cross to her about the Income Tax! And it *is* such a lovely soft and silent day here, whereas at Brighton there will be a wind, and hard colours, and the feeling of cement against shingle, and shingle against a cold and noisy sea.

Your own
Hadji

HAROLD TO VITA *Long Barn*

23 October 1927

Viti—I am sitting in my rabbit hutch and you are in reach of me. But when you read this I shall have no dear neighbour.[1] Little one, be not angry with me for being so obstinate and selfish. It *is* Othello's occupation [diplomacy]—and however much it may depress and irritate me, I feel that without it I would become *not* a cup of tea but a large jug of tepid milk.

Darling, do you remember saying once that you had never established an absolutely satisfactory relation with anyone—not even with me? That was years ago. I don't think you would say that now. I feel that our love and confidence is absolute. I mean in the technical sense of absolute: it is relative to nothing but itself: it is untouched by circumstances, emotions: it is certainly untouched by age. Darling— isn't this a great comfort? *Cosa bella mortal passa: ma non d'arte.*[2] I feel that our love is something as detached from circumstance as the beauty of a work of art. This gives one security in all this transience. If one of us died, this love would live, although in agony. Our love will only die with both of us.

---

1. He was about to leave home for Berlin.
2. "Human beauty fades: but art never."

H arold remained in Berlin for the next two years as Counsellor in the British Embassy and Chargé d'Affaires between two Ambassadors. Vita visited him there quite frequently, hating Berlin and its diplomacy, and it was partly because of her unhappiness at their recurrent separations that he took the decision, after much self-questioning, to resign from the Foreign Service at the end of 1929. Vita at Long Barn was busy writing poetry and her book on Andrew Marvell, and took to regular broadcasting for her new friend Hilda Matheson, the BBC's Director of Talks. Her love affair with Virginia Woolf culminated in 1928 with the publication of Orlando, Virginia's mock-biography of Vita. Harold in Berlin wrote the life of his father, Lord Carnock, who died in 1928, the same year when Vita's father, Lord Sackville, also died, at Knole.

3 November 1927

I love foreign politics and I get them here in a really enthralling form. If I chucked them merely for emotional reasons I should feel a worm—unworthy of what is one of the few serious and virile sides to my nature. "Yes," you say, "that's all very well—but what about me?" I know, my saint, and I am bothered by that consideration. But somewhere right deep down in you you must realise that Hadji's willingness to do hard drudging work merely because it is interesting is a very respectable form of looniness. It should give you, somewhere, somewhere deep down, a twiddle of respect. Doesn't it? So bear with me, my sweet. I won't undergo anything *intolerable* for this idea: but Berlin is not *intolerable* and I can't pretend that it is.

VITA TO HAROLD   *Long Barn*

4 November 1927

Well, I've got home, you see, and there were two letters waiting
for me from Hadji—also an array of photographs of the perfect
diplomatist. Oh my darling! I *don't* like perfect diplomatists, no I
don't. I like Hadji's soft collars—and his laughing eyes—not that
white cardboard round his neck and that severe expression. Oh my
darling, where have you gone? and what become? Where's my own
neighbour with his tousled head?

HAROLD TO VITA   *Berlin*

7 November 1927

My angel,

I had Noel Coward[1] to luncheon yesterday. Then we went on to
a review at the big Music Hall here. It was rather an odd thing to do
but Coward has little time and is anxious to pick up something original
for the review which he is himself producing in London [*This Year
of Grace*]. I must say, he *is* rather remarkable. Completely self-educat-
ed—and producing a review in which he acts, sings and dances himself
and of which he has written the plots, the words and the music. When
you add to this the fact that he also writes excellent social satire, one
can't help treating him with respect. He is a bounder of course—but
I really don't mind that when combined with real talent and energy.

We left at about 4.30, and went to a party at Mrs Albert's. Mrs
A. is the American wife of Dr Albert who was the man who invented
poison gas. They are very rich and have a large house with damask,
Dutch pictures, tapestry and very heavy Italian furniture. Mrs Albert
turned to me: "I didn't see you in church today, Mr Nicolson."
"No—I hate church." "But the Bishop was there." "I loathe Bishops."
Complete consternation on the part of Mrs Albert. Change of subject:

---

1. Noel Coward, who was then only twenty-seven, had just achieved his first major success
   with *The Vortex* and *Hay Fever*.

"Don't you play bridge Mr Nicolson?" "No—not on Sunday afternoons." Whereat Mrs Albert became so puzzled that she gave me up and returned to the subject of servants. Never, *never* will I set foot in that house again.

VITA TO HAROLD   *Long Barn*

7 November 1927

Roy[1] returned from London after two nights of debauch, and is now very ill. I have sent for the doctor. Mary, poor child, looks like death. He has been drinking, and sleeping with Dorothy Warren. Keep this to yourself. I think he is absolutely crazy. I feel most frightfully sorry for Mary. He went for her last night with a knife. But I suppose that after he has got over the effects of drink he will quiet down.

VITA TO HAROLD   *Long Barn*

10 November 1927

Roy, after a series of incredible scenes and rows, in which he has alternately threatened to commit suicide or disappear to S. Africa, and invited Mary to commit suicide with him, offering his razor for the purpose, has recovered his senses. Fortunately I have a calming effect on him, and he now rushes down here instead of venting it all on Mary. It is very odd altogether. I have the strangest conversations with him, which always end in expressions of mutual respect, and he goes home beaming. But really he is a strange creature—weak and violent. I got quite alarmed at first, as I didn't want him to drown himself in our pond or anything like that, but I soon saw that he was quite incapable of action, and indeed he admits it himself. His two days of orgy in

---

1. Roy Campbell, the South African poet, to whom Vita had lent the gardener's cottage at Long Barn. She had fallen in love with his wife, Mary, and Roy had found out, both facts that Vita conceals from Harold.

London thoroughly upset him, and he came home in frenzy and despair. He's all right now.

9 December 1927

I lunched yesterday with the Military Attaché to meet the four Chiefs of the German Military Staff. It was a curious experience. They came in uniform and clicked their heels and were very polite and stiff. The military attaché (Colonel Sandilands) is an absolute peach. He *is* Colonel Bramble.[1] I am sure of it. You must get him to tell you the story of the Calais rebellion. It is too marvellous. You see, in 1919 some troops—about 5,000—declared a Soviet at Calais, arrested their officers and captured the whole camp. Sandilands was sent "to deal with the situation." He went there. "Well you see—er—it was—er er—difficult to know what to do. So I—er—just—er—told them to bugger off." "And what did they do?" "Oh—er—well, they did bugger off." He is a gem.

I went in the evening to tea with Frau [Lalli] Horstmann. Her husband is head of the English section of the Foreign Office. He is a rich Jew and their home is the only 'fashionable' centre in Berlin. She, *mirabile dictu,* is some relation of Maud Cunard.[2] He is a fat, vulgar, lecherous, self-indulgent scoundrel—with a faint dash about him of something adventurous which prevents one from really disliking him. She is a dark, clever little woman who "likes books and things" and has a "small circle." The small circle seems to centre round Mario Pansa,[3] but all the same it *is* the most interesting house here and one feels less provincial there than in other places.

She was alone and we had a heart to heart. She told me that Princess Lichnowski[4] is acutely miserable and that he ill-treats her. The

---

1. In André Maurois's *Les Silences du Colonel Bramble,* sketches of a British officers' mess.
2. The American-born London hostess.
3. Formerly Mussolini's private secretary, he was then on the staff of the Italian Embassy in Berlin.
4. The wife of the German Ambassador in London at the outbreak of the First World War.

Princess is always falling desperately in love with people who are frightened by her passion and run away. I think myself that she would have found greater happiness had she been b.s. [lesbian] and not fallen in love with men, who don't like amorous tigresses. She also told me that the Princess had been really plain as a young woman and that her beauty has only come to her at 48. That in itself is rather tragic.

HAROLD TO VITA   *Berlin*

27 December 1927

A few nights ago there was a large subscription dance at the Central Hotel in aid of the British Relief Fund. A feature of this dance was the Tombola organised by Lady McFadyean.[1] Several English firms had provided prizes, and there were 500 tickets of 1 mark each, and about 300 prizes. As everybody took at least ten tickets they each got at least two prizes. The prizes had already been arranged by Lady McFadyean all in their right order and numbered to correspond with the tickets. She had arranged a sort of counter, and behind it she stood, backed by mountains of prizes—pyramids of cocoa-tins, obelisks of Pears soap tablets, huge triumphal arches of pineapple in tins. Everybody clustered round to get their presents and a hundred outstretched arms waved tickets at the firm but harassed face of Lady McFadyean.

It was then that, most unwisely, I offered to help. I leant across and said, "Lady McFadyean, can I come and help you?" Fool that she was, she said "Yes." Fool that I was I climbed in under the counter. The first thing that fell was a pile of those little soap-tablets which one puts in guests' bed-rooms. Each tablet had been numbered separately and the whole had that afternoon been arranged by Lady McFadyean in a neat sort of façade, a pyramid, a slightly baroque façade. This, I fear, crumbled at my approach, and as I stooped to pick them up I banged Lady McFadyean's bottom with my own. "Oh *do* be careful, Mr Nicolson, you know it's a tight fit behind here." It was. I got very

---

1. The wife of Sir Andrew McFadyean, the British Representative on the Reparations Commission in Berlin.

hot rearranging the soap, but when it was finished, I took a ticket from one of the outstretched hands. No. 406 it was.

Now the 400's were up Lady McFadyean's end of the counter, and to get to them I would have to push past her. I pushed. She said, "Easy on," and picked up a covey of candle-shades which she (or perhaps I) had noticeably disarranged. Now 432 was there all right and a little to the left of it was 389. Between them shivered a high and slender tower of Three Castle cigarettes. Each diminutive packet had a separate number, and 406, of course, was near the base of the pile. I thought I could jerk or flick it out without really disturbing the rest of the structure. But I thought wrong. It took me a good time picking them up again, and when I had finished I realised that once again I must push past Lady McFadyean to present this guerdon to the holder of No. 406—to the man who, earlier in the evening, had handed me his ticket. So much, however, had passed since then, that I had forgotten what the man looked like. I pushed oh so gingerly behind Lady McFadyean—and got back to my point of departure. I held the packet of Gold Flake (it must have contained at least six cigarettes) high in the air and asked if anyone claimed it. No one did. Obviously that was the wrong method.

The thing to do was to choose an object first and then ask who had the number. Now the best object was a receiving set presented by the Marconiphone Company. There it was on the top shelf behind me—in the place of honour behind two pyramids of pineapple tins. Its number was 387. I memorised the number carefully and then turned with engaging brightness to the crowd which by then was becoming a little out of hand. "Who," I cried, "has No 387?" *"Wer,"* I translated, *"hat den drei hundert sieben und achtzig gewählt?"* A short little man began to wave frantic fat fingers from the back. "Please, please . . ." I said to the front ranks, indicating that the man at the back should be allowed to step forward. He stepped. I then turned to get the receiving set. It was a nice square box with two dials in front. All I had to do was to lift it down from the shelf, turn round, and hand it with a certain style to the recipient. Such actions are only graceful if done in a single motion, as it were; if done, as it were, with swift ease. I turned. I grasped the box. I turned rapidly again, holding the box in both hands, smiling generously on the lucky recipient. I felt a slight tug as I did so and then followed a noise like a bombardment.

I was struck in several places by tins of pineapple: tins of pineapple leapt the counter and rolled out into the ball-room: tins of pineapple fell battering down on the lowering form of Lady McFadyean. You see, some ass had attached two ear-pieces to the receiving set by a long flex at each end, and some greater ass had draped the flexes and ear-pieces behind the pyramids of pineapple. Now an ear-piece is a prehensile object—and my particular two gripped the pineapples in what was, in fact, a grip of death.

I apologised to Lady McFadyean. I crept under the counter again, and mingled hot and bruised with the crowd.

VITA TO HAROLD   *Knole*

18 January 1928

I went down to Long Barn today and was telephoned almost immediately by one of the nurses, as Dada's temperature had risen and they were alarmed. I came back at once, and have sent for Horder.[1] He is *very bad,* and I am terrified. Horder should be here in an hour or so—God grant that he may be in time. Hadji, I feel really desperate. He (Dada I mean) is under morphia now and asleep—I found both Sichel and Burnett [Sevenoaks doctors] here—Sichel says his condition is critical. Hadji, I would mind so dreadfully if he died. Oh I *wish* you were here. He mustn't die. I feel Horder can save him if anybody can, but beyond sending for Horder I feel absolutely helpless. It is so awful to see anybody ill like that, and to be able to do nothing for them. One *feels* so strongly that one thinks one ought to be able to perform a miracle, but one cannot. Oh I do wish you were here—so sane as you always are, bless you my own Hadji, you must never, never get ill. I do long for you now—but I expect Horder is the better substitute, a more practical substitute, I mean. We have got a lung specialist coming too. I have not telegraphed to you yet today as I simply don't know what to say.[2]

---

1. Sir Thomas Horder (later Lord Horder), who was the senior physician in St. Bartholomew's Hospital, and doctor to several members of the Royal Family.
2. Lord Sackville died at Knole, of pericarditis, on 28 January 1928.

HAROLD TO VITA   *Berlin*

11 February 1928

Sinclair Lewis[1] is an odd red-faced noisy young man, who called me Harold from the start, and wouldn't leave me. He insisted on me going to a bar with him and then he insisted on coming back to dinner with me. He talked the whole time and drank and drank. At 9.30 he remembered that he had got to take his fiancée to a ball, and off he went dragging me with him as he said he was too tight to dress. He then spoke of Anglo-American relations. What could be done? Were we drifting into war? Good God!—what was there to do? Would I write a joint letter with him to the Evening Standard? And yet what could we say? Perhaps it would be better to leave it alone? And yet he did so love England. No wonder we hated America. And would I come round with him to Edith Thompson's?[2] She might be annoyed at his being so late. And of course I wasn't ill—why, he could feel my pulse. Yes, I must come. And oh yes he was sleeping with Edith tonight and must take his pyjamas round. And would I telephone for a taxi? And did he look very tight? Because Edith minded.

I went to see Edith. She was a nice wise woman with charm and good sense, and I packed them off together to a ball and went to bed.

HAROLD TO VITA   *Berlin*

14 April 1928

I went to the Puccini Abend at the Staats Oper. It really was very good. I enjoyed it hugely. In the intervals Ivor[3] and I ate more and more sausages. I like him so much. He is completely un-spoilt by his success and absolutely *thrilling* about his life. He has contracts which will bring him in £35,000 by November year. He calculates that if his health lasts he should be able to make about £500,000 before he is

1. Sinclair Lewis (1885–1951), the American novelist, whose *Main Street* (1920) had been an immense success. He was awarded the Nobel Prize for Literature in 1930.
2. In fact she was Dorothy Thompson, the American journalist, whom Lewis married as his second wife in 1928, and divorced in 1942.
3. Ivor Novello, the Welsh-born composer, actor, dramatist, and film star, then aged thirty-five.

forty. He is rather appalled by this—and is very sensible about it. Says it makes one feel such a fool to be worth so much money solely because of one's profile. He suffers dreadfully from the worship of flappers. Every day there are two or three of them who wait outside his house just to see him. There were twelve of them at the station to see him off! All this must be terribly bad for a person—and he is himself terrified of becoming fatuous about it.

VITA TO HAROLD   *Long Barn*

18 April 1928

This morning I went down to Pemberton's [solicitors], and was doing my business with him, when a messenger came in to say B.M. was downstairs and wanted to see me. Well, I went down to the waiting-room, and there was B.M. in a towering rage—"I wish to see you in Mr Pemberton's presence." I said I would call him. "Give me your pearls!" screamed B.M., "twelve of them belong to me, and I wish to see how many you have changed, you thief." Then young Pemberton came down. He went to shake hands with her, and she put both hands behind her back. Then the scene began in real earnest. Darling, never, *never* have I heard such floods of the vilest abuse, aimed at both Pemberton and me. She was like a mad woman, screaming Thief and Liar, and shaking her fist at me till I thought she was going to hit me. It was quite impossible for either P. or me to speak, and equally impossible to make out what it was all about—the jewels, mostly. In the middle, the Commissioner for Oaths arrived, before whom I was to sign the papers—I cannot begin to tell you all the dreadful things B.M. said, none of them with even the elements of truth or reason in them. Then she started abusing Dada, at which I simply walked out of the room, and went upstairs with young P. and the Commissioner and signed the papers. B.M. followed, and broke into old P.'s room, where he was engaged with a client, and started calling him names too. Finally she went away, after a very long scene, but Bull [Lady Sackville's secretary] came up in a minute and said she wanted me to go with her to a jeweller to get her 12 pearls cut out of my necklace. I refused to do this but said I would cut them out myself in her presence. So I went down to the street where she was in the car, and cut them out. She then started off worse than ever. Said I was to return to her all the jewels she had ever given me, and the Isfahan rug—that I was to bring them up to London next day and send them to her room at the Savoy by a waiter, and that I should "wait outside her door like a servant while she looked over them to see how much I had stolen from her while she was ill." I said that I would do nothing of the sort, but that as I had no wish to keep anything she did not want me to have I would take them over to Brighton and give them to Bull—but that I would not see her to be insulted again. She screamed that she hated me, and wished I would die—wished, indeed, that I might be run over and killed that day—in fact there is no end to the horrors she shrieked at me through the window. She then began abusing you—at which I hailed a passing taxi and drove off. All this lasted from 12.30 to 2.15.

Darling, I fear that all this gives you but a faint idea of the scene. It was really dreadful. But apart from that, there are two important points which I have left to the end, (1) that she refuses to pay my allowance any longer,[1] and (2) that she wants everything sent back from Berlin [furniture lent for Harold's flat]. Now these are two very serious things. As to the allowance, of course legally we can insist on it—as she knows, and she dares us to do so—but I have a strong disinclination to accept a penny, except enough to cover the boys' education. As to the things from Berlin, this is more serious, and I propose to ignore the suggestion until she raises it again. She may forget about it, or she may be ashamed when she thinks everything over. Anyhow I shall take no steps for the moment. But heaven help us if she adheres to it!

When I finally escaped, I went to meet that little angel Tray [Raymond Mortimer], with whom I was lunching anyhow and to whom I had telephoned, and we went into a restaurant and he poured half a bottle of champagne down my throat—bless him.[2]

---

1. Lady Sackville owed Vita £2,400 a year as her marriage settlement.
2. Harold replied to this letter: "You must refuse to see her again under any circumstances. You must not expose yourself to such a scene again. If she comes to Long Barn, you must tell Louise to say you are out—and then you must bolt out of the back door and take to the woods."

HAROLD TO VITA   *Berlin*

16 May 1928

It must have been simply awful for you going to Knole. My poor sweet—it *is* beastly about Anne[1]: and I feel for Eddy almost as much as I feel for you. It wouldn't be so ghastly if Charlie had died first and if Eddy was now the owner. But it ought, it ought, to belong to you my sweet. *Personally* I am glad it doesn't, as it would be a bore for Hadji who doesn't like being a Prince Consort, and who loves his mud-pie. But Mar would love it—bless her dear heart—and Hadji would be allowed to build a little cement cottage for himself at the Mast-head [in Knole Park]. But best of all would be if Lionel [Sackville] had not died. What a shock and a blow that was! I feel it acutely even now. The tissues of my mind are bruised all round that part.

Cyril Connolly[2] came yesterday. Like the young Beethoven with spots—and a good brow, and an unreliable voice. And he flattered your husband. He sat there toying with a fork and my vanity, turning them over together in his stubby little hands. He tells fortunes. Palmistry. But the main point of him is that he thinks *Some People* an important work. IMPORTANT!! And it was just scribbled down as a joke.

VITA TO HAROLD   *Long Barn*

16 May 1928

My own Hadji

I allowed myself a torture-treat tonight: I went up to Knole after dark and wandered about the garden. I have a master-key, so could get in without being seen. It was a very queer and poignant experience; so queer, and so poignant, that I should almost have fainted had I met anybody. I mean, I had the sensation of having the place so completely

---

1. Vita's father was succeeded as 4th Lord Sackville by his brother Charles, who had married Anne Bigelow, an American, in 1924. Eddy Sackville-West, who was to become the 5th Lord Sackville in 1962, was Charles's only son.
2. The author and literary critic (1903–74).

to myself, that I might have been the only person alive in the world—
and not the world of today, mark you, but the world of at least 300
years ago. I might have been the ghost of Lady Anne Clifford.

VITA TO HAROLD   *Long Barn*

24 June 1928

Robert Harris read [on BBC radio] the *Ode to the West Wind,* part
of *Adonais,* and the *Ode to a Nightingale,* and I sat with the tears
pouring down my face. Oh Hadji, what poetry! What pure gold of
poetry! What a heritage—*damn* T. S. Eliot, bloody American that he
is, with his 'combinations drying in the sun'. I could not have believed
that I should be so moved by anything so familiar. Those lovely, lovely
lines seem to be floating round the room still—

Then more than ever seems it rich to die,
To cease upon the midnight with no pain. . . .

I don't care what you say about Shelley; he was divine when he
wrote.

HAROLD TO VITA   *Berlin*

28 June 1928

Yesterday I lunched with President von Hindenburg. It was rather
fun. The Ambassador[1] went on ahead as he had a private audience to
hand over his letters of credence. Lady Lindsay and I followed at 1.0
p.m. In the hall we were met by Hindenburg's son, surrounded by
about six footmen and a man with a large cocked hat and a silver mace.
Escorted by these we went upstairs. There was another man with a
silver mace at the top of the stairs, and when we reached the landing
he brought his mace down crack! As if by magic *(c'est magique,
Excellence)* two huge doors flung open in front of us and there were

---

1. Sir Ronald Lindsay, who was retiring as British Ambassador in Berlin, leaving Harold in
   charge of the Embassy. In 1930 Lindsay was appointed Ambassador to the United States.

a group of figures in a great saloon. We advanced towards them. The President advanced towards us. He kissed Lady Lindsay's hand: he shook mine warmly. The Chancellor [Herman Müller] was there and the Von Schuberts [Foreign Secretary]: a ghastly silence, broken only by the distant hum of traffic, descended upon us. Suddenly the man with the mace, who alone of the party displayed any initiative, beat the floor again—and the Victor of Tannenberg [Hindenburg] advanced towards Lady Lindsay and very slowly started, with her arm in his, to go to luncheon. We followed. I sat opposite the President, and between the Chancellor's wife and the wife of the President's sort of Chamberlain man. We spoke in German. *"Was für schöne Rosen haben sie hier in Berlin!"* *"Ja—sie sind schöne Rosen."* And so on, and so on. The President is an old darling: he has a trick of raising his eyebrows and laughing like a school boy: he talks very simply, almost boyishly, but is pretty shrewd: he is wonderful for his age [81]— neither deaf nor blind. I don't wonder that they all worship him. After luncheon we all sat round a table and had coffee. This time I sat next to Hindenburg. He spoke about father [Lord Carnock], and asked where I had learnt German, and how when he was a boy, there were still many English expressions current at Hanover, and how he remembered the Embassy here before it was an Embassy, and how he had gone up in the first Zeppelin. A splendid old man, and I wish Mar had been there. She was asked.

Then a walk with Henry [spaniel]—and in the evening comes a telegram "Don't fly!" Oh my sweet, my sweet, of course I won't fly without permission. I didn't count just going up over the aerodrome as *flying*. But I do want terribly one day to do the flight Berlin-Vienna-Venice. But I promise *absolutely padlock* not to do any such thing without your permission.

VITA TO HAROLD   *Long Barn*

6 July 1928

Virginia has just gone. She was absolutely enchanting. We talked a lot about poetry and she said it doesn't matter a bit about not being modern.

Darling, really the Wolves are funnies. You see, they haven't got a garage, and it goes to Leonard's heart to pay garaging fees for the umbrella.[1] So for some time past he has been saying what a good garage Virginia's studio would make, but she didn't respond very much because she didn't want her studio taken away from her. So Leonard didn't *quite* dare to suggest taking it away altogether, but finally he said, did she think they could poke a hole in the wall which abuts on to the mews [in Tavistock Square], and get the motor in that way, if it wouldn't disturb her to work with a motor in the room? So now she and the umbrella are going to share the studio between them. A funny pair.

VITA TO HAROLD   *Long Barn*

12 July 1928

My own darling Hadji,

I was plunged into despair this morning by your letter saying you might have to stay in Berlin till 1930. I had come to count really on you getting away in the spring of next year. I see the point about staying with Rumbold[2] till he has settled down, but it can't take him two years to settle down! and from now till 1930 is two years, or nearly. I can't believe that IF Lindsay knows you want to come home, he will leave you there all that time; but I don't trust Hadji a yard about what he has said or not said to Lindsay. I really do get into despair about it; you would too, my sweet, if I went and lived in a place you loathed in pursuit of a profession you really deprecated because it took me away from what you considered to be my legitimate pursuits; and a profession moreover which (as practised abroad—*not* in London), entailed a great many obligations which you thought utterly *infra dig* [humiliating]. No, Hadji would not like it either. No, he wouldn't.

---

1. Leonard Woolf had just bought a Singer car, which he and Virginia called the umbrella.
2. Sir Horace Rumbold, who was to succeed Lindsay as British Ambassador in Berlin.

VITA TO HAROLD   *Long Barn*

26 July 1928

I have got Clive [Bell] staying here. He came last night and we
talked without stopping from 5.30 to 12.30. About life, middle age,
love, books, drugs, Mary,[1] and Virginia. He is very gloomy, and wants
Mary back, but she is in the throes of a *béguin* for some man unknown.
They have, however, met again quite recently; and it was a success. Not
as lovers, but as friends, and he hopes that some day it will come right
again. It is really rather sad that a liaison of 14 years standing can be
knocked out by a mere *béguin*. She doesn't even *like* the other man.
Clive says he has made no provision for his middle-age, and asked if
I had? My darling, I thought of our love for each other and how firm
a foundation that was. I told him occupation was the only thing. He
said that was a makeshift like everything else. I said I thought the only
occupation which one couldn't look on as a mere makeshift was
science.

And so on.

He is going this morning.

Talking of Jean Cocteau, Clive saw him recently in Paris, and says
he has taken to cocaine. He knows it will kill him in a few years, but
he is happy in the meantime, and doesn't care how much he has to
increase his dose. Clive seemed to think this a good plan. Altogether
I fear poor Clive is very low.

HAROLD TO VITA   *Berlin*

3 August 1928

At seven I had to get up in order to meet old [Sir Horace]
Rumbold. I put on my top-hat and tails, and motored in on a lovely
clear morning feeling rather cross and uncomfortable in my stiff
clothes. There is no doubt moreover that I do *not* like Ambassadors

---

1. Mary Hutchinson, wife of St John Hutchinson, the barrister. She had been the intimate
friend of T. S. Eliot and Clive Bell.

arriving when I am in charge. They had opened the special waiting rooms at the Friedrichstrasse [station]—and there was the whole staff there looking very lovely, and two representatives of the German Government. The train came in and old Rumby bundled out rather embarrassed with an attaché case in one hand and in the other a novel by Mr Galsworthy. I introduced him to the German Representatives and to the staff, while the crowd gaped and gaped and the policemen stood at the salute. Photographs were taken, and then very slowly we passed through the waiting rooms preceded by the Ober-bahnhofführer [station master] to the waiting cars. I carried the attaché case. We drove round to the Adlon [hotel] where he is staying until the Embassy is in order. We were greeted by the whole Adlon family.

Rumby was confused. "Never," he said, "have I felt so odd." You see, the last time the poor man was in Berlin was exactly fourteen years ago to the day almost—on August 4 1914—when he was Counsellor and crept out of Berlin under cavalry escort and amid the booings of a crowd. It is odd thus to return. He is a nice old bumble bee—and I am quite happy with him. But he is *not* Lindsay—no no.

VITA TO HAROLD   *Long Barn*

4 August 1928

Read Leonard's review in this week's Nation of a book called *The Well of Loneliness.* [1] I agree with all he says. It is a perfectly serious attempt to write a quite frank and completely unpornographic book about b.s.ness [lesbianism]. The pity is, that although serious and not sentimental, it is not a work of art—he says this. I have got the book and will bring it if it would interest you. Let me know. Perhaps Cyril [Connolly] or Tray have given it to you already. More than ever do I feel that a really great novel remains to be written on that subject. This is not a great novel, but it is quite a decent piece of work, and

---

1. By Radclyffe Hall. It was prosecuted for obscenity and banned until its republication in 1949.

it is a miracle that it should ever have got published by a publisher like Cape.

Heinemann refused it! They would!

HAROLD TO VITA   *Berlin*

9 August 1928

We had a long argument last night as to what was a test of intelligence. Cyril [Connolly] said that if he found a woman had *really* read through the whole of Proust he would think her intelligent. I said that was rubbish, as I felt sure that Lady Gosford had read through the whole of Proust. That I tested intelligence not by knowledge or culture but by imagination and ability to draw quick and original associations. Raymond [Mortimer] stuck up for culture: he said that one could tell by what a person had read how intelligent they were. The discussion, I felt, was about to become angry. The figure of strife stood gaunt and impatient at the next cross-road.

So I changed the subject to day-dreaming. Cyril and I both agreed that we had had day-dreams. I said I dreamt of doing brave things—of shooting ibex from a very far distance, of behaving with conspicuous courage at fires, or revolutions, or during a debate in the House of Commons. Cyril said that his day-dreams were largely stories in which he himself figured as the Sheikh Senoussi and in which, disguised in white scarfs, he captured European tourists and put them all to death with the exception of Bobby Longden,[1] who, on his side, would be grateful for this privileged treatment. Tray, for his part, said that he never day-dreamt: that he thought it "shocking" to do so—a relaxation of intellectual fibre which was worse than drugs.

Again the figure of strife loomed in the distance, so the conversation was diverted once more, from personal experience to culture. Cyril said that the difference between Bloomsbury and Chelsea culture was that the former would think the *Oedipus Rex* better than the

---

1. He was on a visit to Berlin from Magdalen College, Oxford, of which he was a Fellow. He became Master of Wellington College in 1937, and was killed by a German bomb in 1940.

Epictetus, and the latter, for their part, would prefer the *Epictetus* to the *Oedipus Rex.* Tray was a little disconcerted at this and retreated into the French XVIIth century: where he was fairly safe. I, for my part, said I must take Henry out to pee.

VITA TO HAROLD   *Long Barn*

10 August 1928

Got a pi-jaw from Hadji this morning.[1] I quite agreed about Acid X [eccentricity]: that it is impossible, and indeed undesirable to eliminate altogether, and that absorption is the only method. But your initial premise is mistaken. You think I mind the inevitable interruptions of life: I don't. They can be organised and so become no bore at all. I don't notice them. The boys are a different matter. No one, not even Hadji himself, would want to have entire charge of two children for four months of the year. I should like to see you try it; you would be screaming by the end of a week. You see, one is not permanently in the mood for children—even you wouldn't be. It is really quite reasonable on my part, Hadji, and not entirely a question of being willing to waste two months.

HAROLD TO VITA   *Berlin*

17 September 1928

I asked Ben how much he knew, and he said that Williams[2] had told him "some details." I then explained how when one came to a certain age one had new physical powers and pleasures—and that these

---

1. Harold had written to her: "Oh my love, it would be such a good thing if you could throw a little more eccentricity into your writing and a little less into your life. How I wish I could get at the fool (was it Violet?) who gave you the idea that responsibilities, instead of being stepping-stones through a marsh, were something to evade and regard with shame."
2. Dr. Cyril Williams, headmaster of Summer Fields school. Ben was fourteen and about to leave his preparatory school for Eton.

pleasures if properly controlled were the best in the world. But I kept on getting out of my depth—and I *hated* it. Anyhow I told him he must work it all out for himself, and that if he got puzzled he could always ask us, as we should always understand. I said that about masturbation he must put it off as long as he possibly could—and that then he must only do it on Saturdays. But I loathed talking to him about it. I have the incest inhibition very strong. He was very sensible and sweet, and said that he would never worry about those sort of things as he could always talk to me or you about them.

Poor boy—I don't suppose he understood much. By the way I wrote to Chute[3] just a polite letter—and saying that I should like his advice about Ben being confirmed, adding that I would prefer sooner than later. I mean, he will *have* to be confirmed and I think it would be a good thing to get that nonsense over as soon as possible. It will be a great bore for us—but we can't get out of it.

VITA TO HAROLD   *Saulieu [France]*

25 September 1928

My own darling Hadji

I am lying on the grass in a field, with Burgundy spread out before me. It is warm; it is sunny. There is a fair going on in Saulieu, where Virginia bought a green corduroy jacket for Leonard.[4] I nearly bought one for you, but I was sure you would not wear it. So I bought a blue bottle instead, with full-stops, marks of interrogation, marks of exclamation, and commas all over it.

But the point of Saulieu is not the fair, which is just a chance, but the restaurant. It is kept by a chef who was the chef for some Embassy in Berlin before the war—I have not yet found out which—and it is as good as Boulestin [Covent Garden]. Really it is. Yet Saulieu is a

---

3. The Rev. J. C. Chute was to be Ben's housemaster at Eton.
4. Vita and Virginia Woolf went to Burgundy together for a week's holiday. It was their only expedition abroad together, and the only occasion when Virginia had a holiday without Leonard.

tiny place—a mere village. Nobody seems to stay in it, but people motoring through stop for lunch.

We left Paris early this morning—got up at 6, so I am not quite awake—and drove through empty streets to the Gare de Lyons. I feel very much tempted, with the south lying so to speak just over the hill . . . and if it were not for the BBC on the 2nd [Vita's broadcast] I would go on down into Provence. I foresee that if we stay here for two days eating *canneton en croûte* and *crème double,* washed down by *Bourgogne mousseaux,* we shall get dyspepsia.

Darling, it is very nice: I feel amused and irresponsible. I can talk about life and literature to my heart's content—and it amuses me to be suddenly in the middle of Burgundy with Virginia. I like doing expeditions with you. But failing you, I could not wish for a better companion than Virginia.

Your own Mar

VITA TO HAROLD   *Long Barn*

2 October 1928

From Vézelay we went to Auxerre, where we stayed one night, and left next morning very early for Paris. Lunched in Paris, and went on to Rouen, where we were met by Ethel Sands'[1] motor and taken to Offranville. A lovely little chateau, done up, as you may imagine, with the most faultless taste. Ethel and Miss Hudson[2]; Vanessa [Bell] and Duncan [Grant]. The last two have painted a loggia for Ethel, which made me long to have one here, and I thought that when we built our summer house we would get them to decorate the inside? They have done six scenes of rustic employments—vintage, haymaking, harvest, and so on—in a manner mixed between idyllic-pastoral, romantic—and the very modern: the result is absolutely enchanting. After dinner, (a delicious dinner), Virginia read us her memoir of Old Bloomsbury.[3] She had read it to me already at Saulieu, but I loved

---

1. The American painter, who lived part of the year in London and part of it at her house in Normandy, at Auppegard near Dieppe.
2. Nan Hudson, also an American painter, and Ethel's lifelong friend.
3. She had read it to the Memoir Club in 1922, and it was first published in *Moments of Being,* ed. Jeanne Schulkind, in 1976.

hearing it again; I want you to hear it. It is very amusing, and terribly improper; the two old virgins bridled with horrified delight. I wondered whether V. was going to shirk any of it; but she didn't shirk a word. Then, as they had no room to put us up, we motored into Dieppe—passing through Sauqueville[4] on the way—and stayed at a hotel, and left by the boat next morning. It was rather rough, so I made V. drink the best part of a bottle of Burgundy with the result that she went to sleep as I had foreseen.

HAROLD TO VITA   *Berlin*

11 October 1928

Virginia is quite right about your ridiculous diffidence. It is the same part of you that makes you shy at parties, makes you creep into corners and hide there, and stay there all evening so as not to be seen. But it is absurd you being diffident about your writing since you have such a compelling literary gift. I think you are a late flowering plant in the sense that it will be your fruit which will be important rather than your blossom. But I would rather produce nectarines in September that burst in April with all the blossom of our crab-apple.

VITA TO HAROLD   *Long Barn*

11 October 1928

My own darling, I write to you in the middle of reading *Orlando,*[5] in such a turmoil of excitement and confusion that I scarcely know where (or who!) I am. It came this morning by the first post and I have been reading it ever since, and am now half-way through. Virginia sent it to me in a lovely leather binding—bless her. Oh Lord, how I wonder what *you* will think of it. It seems to me more

---

4. Where the Sackvilles came from in 1066.
5. *Orlando,* by Virginia Woolf, was published on 11 October. It was a novel in the form of a mock-biography of Vita, Virginia's longest love letter to her. Vita was not allowed to read a word of it until it was published.

brilliant, more enchanting, more rich and lavish, than anything she has done. It is like a cloak encrusted with jewels and sprinkled with rose-petals. I admit I can't see straight about it. Parts of it make me cry, parts of it make me laugh; the whole of it dazzles and bewilders me. It maddens me that you should not be here, so that we could read it simultaneously. I scarcely slept with excitement all night, and woke up feeling as though it were my birthday, or wedding day, or something unique.

Well—I don't know, it seems to me a book unique in English literature, having everything in it: romance, wit, seriousness, lightness, beauty, imagination, style; with Sir Thomas Browne and Swift for parents. I feel infinitely honoured at having been the peg on which it was hung; and very humble. Oh I do want to know what Hadji thinks.

HAROLD TO VITA   *Berlin*

27 November 1928

I have no desire whatsoever for fame, and would really be bored to feel that the people in a Harrogate Hydro knew about me in the sort of way they know about Hugh Walpole. "There's H. Nicolson," they would exclaim as a ham-faced arthritic limped through the palm-court. No thank you very much. I want *influence,* and to be esteemed by the people I like.

HAROLD TO VITA   *Berlin*

28 November 1928

I am terribly busy with my father's papers.[1] Of course it is all absolutely thrilling to me, but I can't get outside it, or estimate how

---

1. Harold's father, Lord Carnock, who had been the British Ambassador to St. Petersburg and civil head of the Foreign Office, died in London on 5 November 1928, and Harold immediately began to write his biography, which later in life he considered the best of his books.

interesting exactly it will be to others. For instance the Persian part is of real importance to the development of the book, but may seem an interlude to the casual reader. Anyhow I shall go ahead and see how things fall into shape. There is a real wealth of material—all that I want. Oh God! how I wish life were twice as long and that the days consisted of 100 hours each!

Every morning I wake up thinking how I want to write a book about Puritanism, and spend a winter in Tahiti, and learn how to fish for salmon, and go a walking tour through Patagonia, and try and get at the secret of Cézanne's landscapes (I am really wild about Cézanne just now), and do nothing for six weeks except visit the Greek islands with my darling and the boys, and build a home in the anti-Lebanon, and visit Australia, South Africa, and America, and do a fuller life of Byron, and Ludwig II, and through all this to go on being a diplomat, and having Long Barn, and seeing, every autumn, the wood-smoke drift across our dear remembered woods. And God has given me only a little handful of years—a little attaché case into which to cram the furniture of Knole. I seriously thank God, bless his heart, that these 42 years so far have not been so empty after all—love and life and literature and politics—work and old brandy, gardens and adventures, a thousand friends and one deep love, the whole essence of liberty and the whole essence of security, as if one had one's own writing table on a yacht crossing the Pacific.

All this lyricism is induced (a) by reading my father's papers and realising how much he missed; (b) by having had a good night; (c) by going to lunch with a Bishop.

HAROLD TO VITA   *Munich*

8 December 1928

My darling Viti,

Sorry to type, my dearest, but there is no ink available, and as little Mr Remington [his portable typewriter] has come down with me to Munich, he may as well write my letter for me.

I had an odd luncheon party yesterday, consisting of Emil Ludwig[1] and Mrs Ludwig, Ethel Smyth,[2] Eddy [Sackville-West], Sir Horace Rumbold and [his daughter] Constantia. Emil Ludwig is really rather a disgusting creature. Ethel arrived late in a fine to-do. Her tricorne kept on falling over her eyes in her excitement, and she screamed loud in her indignation against the Jewish republic that Ludwig and his friends had elevated in Germany. He was rather hurt by this. He said that the old gang had done nothing except land Germany into the Great European War. She said that his friends had destroyed the Old German culture. He said, "Not at all, not at all." She said yes, they had, and ("God! Harold, why do you give me cold sauce with sole, I hate cold sauce with sole"), "what about the Grand Duke of Weimar?" Ludwig said which Grand Duke? "Weimar!" said Ethel triumphantly. Ludwig asked whether she meant the Goethe one? She said, No, she meant the Ethel Smyth one, the one who had been Grand Duke at Weimar when she had been there as a girl. Ludwig said that that one had been gaga. She said that of course he had been gaga, but that at least he had cared for art, and did not think a book was a good book merely because it had sold 13,000 copies. Ludwig said that he didn't see why he should be scolded merely because the Grand Duke of Weimar hadn't sold 13,000 copies, and if it came to that the number was nearer 130,000 than 13,000. Ethel said, "The number of *what?*" He said that he had supposed (and with justice) that she had been referring to his 'Napoleon'. She said (oh woman!!) that she had not read his Napoleon and did not intend to. At which, throwing her head back with a challenging gesture of defiance, the tricorne, wobbling for a minute, fell, not *off,* but right *down* over her face, and for a moment her torrent of invective was stilled.

The Ambassador [Rumbold], who had been vaguely aware that all was not proceeding with that amity to which he is accustomed at table, asked, "Had she been in Berlin long?" She said that she had only arrived the day before and that was why she was so out of temper. The Ambassador did not know what to say to that, and just bubbled silently for a bit. Then Mrs Ludwig, a tactful woman, began to talk of the

---

1. The German author and playwright, born in 1881. He wrote biographies of Goethe, Wagner, Bismarck, Napoleon, and Christ.
2. The English composer and suffragette. She was then aged seventy.

servant problem at Lugano. By the end of which, Ethel, having swallowed three glasses of Rieslinger Auslese, was able to talk, not with calm, but with less violence. And so, almost amicably, the luncheon party drew to an end.

I took the night train down here and slept like a top, or pot, or whatever a dead sleep is.

Your own,

Hadji

VITA TO HAROLD   *Long Barn*

12 December 1928

On Monday I met Hugh and Hilda Matheson[1] at the Savoy grill at 7, where Hugh had sausages and coffee, and I had oysters and coffee. Then we adjourned to Savoy Hill, Studio No. 6. Two armchairs (very luxurious); two microphones; small table between us, with a siphon, a bottle of whiskey, two glasses, cigarettes, matches, ash-trays. Red light flickers. Silence, please. "Miss V. Sackville-West, the poet, and Mr Hugh Walpole, the novelist, will now hold a discussion on The Modern Woman. Miss V. S-W. is well-known to listeners by her talks on modern poetry; Mr Hugh Walpole is broadcasting this evening for the first time. Miss V. S-W.: Mr Hugh Walpole." And the British Isles waited breathless. Mr Hugh Walpole and Miss V. S-W. confronted each other; Miss Matheson sat on the floor,—a small, but efficient, impresario.

Mr Hugh Walpole led off. "Well, Vita, *you* begin,—it's your prerogative as a woman."

Miss V. S-W., "I don't see why you should say that, Hugh; I don't see why the prerogative should be mine any more than yours . . ."

All went swimmingly. For what seemed a long time. Then Miss V. S-W. looked at her watch. 8.30. Half the time gone. The room

---

1. Hugh Walpole, the novelist (*Rogue Herries,* etc.), and Hilda Matheson, the Talks Director of the BBC, who became Vita's most intimate friend in the years 1928–32.

began to swim. There was Hugh's nice rubicund face; there was Hilda's nice reassuring smile; but there, also, was the microphone and four million homes listening all agog to the Modern Woman. The room swam wildly. Miss V. S-W. lost all sense of what Mr Hugh Walpole was saying. She thought, "Whatever happens, I must not faint. I must not get up and rush from the room. I must not exclaim, 'I can't keep it up!' At all cost, I must not let Hugh, Hilda, and the BBC, down."

So she neither fainted (though she felt near to it), nor rushed from the room; but she did signal despairingly to Mr Hugh Walpole to go on, at all costs, to go on talking. And Mr Hugh Walpole rushed nobly into the breach. He talked; he talked. He said a million things Miss V. S-W. in calmer moments would passionately have disagreed with; but as it was, she let them all pass.

VITA TO HAROLD   *Long Barn*

13 December 1928

Women love too much; they allow love to over-ride everything else. Men don't. Or, rather, men see to it that the people who love them should submit themselves. I love you too much. You are much more important to me than anything else. That is the long and short of the matter. But, darling, I am not a good person for you to be married to—said she, avoiding the word wife. When people like you and me marry—*positive* people, when men and women ought to be positive and negative respectively, complementary elements—life resolves itself into a compromise which is truly satisfactory to neither. But I love you; I can never never never cure myself of loving you; so what is to be done? And you love foreign politics. And I love literature, and peace, and a secluded life. Oh my dear, my infinitely dear Hadji, you never ought to have married me; and I feel my inadequacy most bitterly. What good am I to you? None. What with one thing and another.

But at least I do love you, incurably, ineradicably, and most oddly. That remains, fixed. Immutable.

HAROLD TO VITA   *Cologne*

15 March 1929

After writing to you yesterday I went to see the Oberbürger-
meister. His name is Adenauer[1] and he is a rather remarkable figure
in modern Germany. There are some who say that if Parliamentarian-
ism really breaks down in Berlin they will summon Adenauer to
establish some form of fascismo. For the moment he rules Cologne
with an iron hand, and is responsible for such things as the new Rhine
Bridge and the Presse exhibition. There was some sort of fuss going
on around his room when I got there, private secretaries dashing about,
people opening doors, squinting in, then shutting them again rapidly.
I was asked to sit down while bells buzzed and people hurried in and
whispered to each other, and then hurried out again. I am to this
moment unaware what had happened, but the contrast between the
scurrying and whispering outside, and the sudden peace of his own
large study, was most effective, and this strange Mongol, sitting there
with shifty eyes in a yellow face, sitting with his back to the window,
talking very slowly and gently, pressing bells very slowly—"Would
you ask Dr Pietri to come here?"—snapping with icy politeness at the
terrified Dr Pietri when he arrived—possessed all the manner of a
Dictator. It is not a manner which I like, but it is a manner which once
seen is never forgotten. I feel I could adopt it at once. I shall try to
do so. One of the main stunts is to create an atmosphere of rush and
flurry around one and to be oneself as calm as the hollow in the centre
of a typhoon. Another stunt is to talk to one's subordinates in a very
gentle voice but with a sudden flash of a shifty eye.

He was very expansive on the subject of town planning. I told him
how impressed I had been by the garden suburbs at Frankfurt, and he
was not pleased at this, knowing that his garden suburbs were not up
to the same level. He said in the first place that the Frankfurt people
had lost a great deal of money by extravagance in garden suburbs, and
in the second place that his own aim was not to bring the town into
the country but the country into the town. It was at that stage that

---

1. Konrad Adenauer, Chancellor of the Federal Republic of Germany, 1949–63. He was Lord
   Mayor of Cologne, 1917–33, when he was dismissed by Goering and temporarily imprisoned.

he summoned the agitated Dr Pietri and told him to show me all that
there was to be seen.

HAROLD TO VITA   *In the train Munich–Berlin*

17 March 1929

I have had a health-panic this evening, and before I die I should
like to record it on paper.

As you know, for the last fortnight, I have had a cold in the head
and in the chest which I originally caught from you. Damn you, my
own adored darling Mar, to whom I can pour out all my silliness and
know that I shall provoke only a gentle smile, "Silly Hadji." Oh My
God! what a wonderful day that was when I decided to marry you
for your money.

Well you see, tonight I got a health-panic. It happened this way.
I went to call on Thomas Mann.[1] He had asked me to call on him as
he had been unable to attend my lecture, and thus very civilly he had
telephoned to ask me to tea. So I went. He was alone. He talked about
how lovely life was, and how polite they had been to him at the P.E.N.
Club, and how much he admired Mr Galsworthy. And I, being snuffly
but interested in life and death, asked him how long, generally, as a
fellow *littérateur,* it took him to get rid of his colds. He said three days
to prepare, three days suffering, and three days to get rid of it. Being
quick at *le calcul,* I made that out to be ten or even nine days, that
is five days later or longer than my own disease, I mean five days
quicker than my actual present cold. Having worked out this sum I
became alarmed. My cold was not a cold, it was PNEUMONIA—
that's what it was. SCEPTIC PNEUMONIA. I could feel the sceptici-
tis growing within me. I felt a wave of fear pass over me. There was
a large mirror on the wall opposite and in it I saw my distorted and
pallid features. Yes, I was looking very pale. That meant consumption
of the galloping variety. I talked feverishly to Thomas Mann about
the younger generation in England, and when I next glanced at the
mirror, my face was flushed. "Fever," I quaked, "fever, high fever.

---

1. The English translation of his best-known novel, *Der Zauberberg* (The Magic Mountain),
   had just been published.

Sceptic pneumonia, as I thought from the start." So then I took leave of Thomas Mann. I was sorry to leave him knowing that he was the last man I should see on earth. But I said goodnight.

HAROLD TO VITA   *Berlin*

2 April 1929

I went for a long walk with Peter Clive.[1] The latter is a good, handsome, but very dull young man. He believes in virginity. I said I believed in it too, but only for people of unexampled ugliness who never had a chance of anything else. He was silent at this, and we walked along the side of a lake in the rain while Henry [dog] cast his goggly-eyes at two ducks at the edge of the ice. The ice had broken up a little and tinkled against the edge of the lake, like sleigh-bells among the reeds. I do hope that I do not have a bad influence on young men. I should hate that. I obviously have an influence, but there is nothing that would fill me with deeper remorse if I felt that I had led them astray. I imagine that I teach them to be active, interested, happy, kind, and filled with the zest of experience. But I may really be destroying some of the scaffolding of their beliefs without putting anything in its place. Then I always want them to enjoy themselves so much, that I am bad at discouraging them from any experience even if I know it to be bad for them. But my intentions are beyond praise.

HAROLD TO VITA   *Berlin*

16 April 1929

I went to H. G. Wells's lecture in the Reichstag. One simply could not hear a word. Not a single word. It was rather a disaster. After that there was a dinner at the Adlon. Einstein presided. He looks like a child who for fun has put on a mask painted like Einstein. He is a darling. He made a little speech for Wells which I then translated. I began by saying, "I have been asked to translate Professor Einstein's speech. I

---

1. Elder son of Sir Robert Clive, Harold's Minister in Teheran.

may add that it is the first thing of his I have ever understood." They thought that a funny joke.

HAROLD TO VITA   *Berlin*

18 May 1929

Cyril [Connolly] is not perhaps the ideal guest. He is terribly untidy in an irritating way. He leaves dirty handkerchiefs in the chairs and fountain pens (my fountain pens) open in books. Moreover it is rather a bore having a person who has *nothing* of his own—not a cigarette or a stamp. In fact the poverty of this colony[1] is heart-rending. Christopher and David[2] are both absolutely bust. But I really am firm about it, and won't take them all to Pelzer's [Restaurant] to eat plover's eggs. In other ways, however, Cyril is a pleasant guest, easily amused, and interesting about things. I don't trust him a yard and I think he makes mischief. He is very thick with Violet Trefusis, and I imagine that he is very disloyal about me when with her. I rather mind that, as she is so unscrupulous and appears never to have got over the desire to revenge herself on me. But what does it all matter so long as none of these people can make trouble between you and me?

HAROLD TO VITA   *Berlin*

25 May 1929

We motored the Yorks[3] out to the golf-course for luncheon. She is really a delightful person, incredibly gay and simple. It is an absolute tragedy that she should be a royalty. Moreover she is no fool. She talked to me so intelligently about *Some People,* whereas he had clearly

---

1. Harold's flat in 24 Brücken Allee in northwest Berlin, where he put up his transient and sponging friends.
2. Christopher Sykes, the author and biographer, was then aged twenty-two and a temporary attaché at the British Embassy in Berlin; David Herbert, the son of the Earl of Pembroke, was twenty-one.
3. The Duke and Duchess of York, later King George VI and Queen Elizabeth (still later, Queen Elizabeth, the Queen Mother).

only read the Arketall story and had got it wrong. But she and Cyril Connolly are the only two people who have spoken intelligently about the 'landscape' element in *Some People*. She said, "You choose your colours so carefully—that bit about the palace at Madrid was done in grey and chalk-white; the Constantinople bits in blue and green; the desert bits in blue and orange." Of course that may be second-hand, but I don't think so—and even if I am making a mistake about her intelligence, I am making no mistake about her charm. It is quite overwhelming. He is just a snipe from the great Windsor marshes. Not bad-looking—but now and again there is that sullen, heavy-lidded, obstinate dulling of the blue eyes which is most unattractive.

VITA TO HAROLD   *Long Barn*

25 June 1929

My darling,

What is so torturing, when I leave you at these London stations[1] and drive off, is the knowledge that you are *still there*—that, for half an hour, or three quarters of an hour, I could still return and find you; come up behind you, take you by the elbow, and say, "Hadji."

I came straight home, feeling horribly desolate and sad, driving down that familiar and dreary road. I remembered Resht [Persia] and our parting there; our parting at Victoria when you left for Persia; till our life seemed made up of partings, and I wondered how long it would continue.

I got home, and all the way was strewn with coffee-cups [reminders]: specially the road through the beeches on the [Sevenoaks] common. I remembered how you had said that so long as you were alive they were there for you, and when you were dead it wouldn't matter.

Then I came round the corner onto the view—our view—and I thought how you loved it, and how simple you were really, apart from your activity; and how I loved you, for being both simple and active, in one and the same person.

Then I came home, and it was not consolation at all. You see,

---

1. Harold had been on a fortnight's home-leave from Berlin.

whenever I am unhappy for other reasons—Knole, or Dada, or B.M.,
let us say—the cottage is a real solace to me; but when it is on account
of *you* that I am unhappy (because you have gone away), it is an
additional pang—it is the same place, but a sort of mockery and
emptiness hangs about it—I almost wish that just *once* you could lose
me and then come straight back to the cottage and find it still full of
me but empty of me—then you would know what I go through after
you have gone away.

Anyhow, you will say, it is worse for you who go to a horrible
and alien city, whereas *I* stay in the place we both love so much, but
really, Hadji, it is *no* consolation to come back to a place full of
coffee-cups—there was a cardboard-box-lid full of your rose petals
still on the terrace.

You are dearer to me than anybody ever has been or ever could
be. If you died I should kill myself as soon as I had made provision
for the boys. I really mean this. I could not live if I lost you. Every
time I get you to myself you become dearer to me. I do not think one
could conceive of a love more exclusive, more tender, or more pure
than that I have for you. It is absolutely divorced from physical
love—sex—*now*. I feel it is immortal, I am superstitious about it, I
feel it is a thing which happens seldom. I suppose that everybody who
falls in love feels this about their love, and that for them it is merely
a platitude. But then when one falls in love it is all mixed up with
physical desire, which is the most misleading of all human emotions,
and most readily and convincingly wears the appearance of the real
thing. This does not enter at all into my love for you. I simply feel
that you are me and I am you—what you meant by saying that you
"became the lonely me" when we parted.

Darling, there are not many people who would write such a love
letter after nearly sixteen years of marriage, yet who would be saying
therein only one-fiftieth of what they were feeling as they wrote it.
But you know not only that it is true, every word, but that it represents
only a pale version of the real truth—I could not exaggerate, however
much I tried—I don't try. I try sometimes to tell you the truth and
then I find that I have no words at my command which could possibly
convey it to you.

Your Mar

HAROLD TO VITA   *Berlin*

7 July 1929

Cragg is the parson here, and on him fell the duty of arranging the mumbo jumbo for King George.[1] Now the whole point of that show was that it was to be identical with what was being said in London and throughout the Empire at the same time. But Cragg added and altered it. Damn him! Of course, as I take no interest in his bloody church, I cannot complain to him, but if I were the Ambassador who attends regularly, I should have made a row. The service was silly enough anyhow—just imagine that with all the prayer-book, bible and hymn book to choose from, they selected a ditty which contains the following verse:

> The Lord, ye know, is God indeed;
>   Without our aid he did us make;
> We are his flock, he doth us feed,
>   And for his sheep he doth us take.

Now lines as bad as that would be rejected by Niggs from the Summer Fields magazine. The first line is meaningless, the second indecent and singularly untrue, the third is a direct misrepresentation of social conditions, and in the last line alone is there a glimmer of irony and truth. I looked over my shoulder—row after row of English mouths singing this rubbish. It passes my comprehension how any person can be religious and an Anglican. At the end they did the Blake poem which pleased me:

> Bring me my bow of burning gold!
>   Bring me my arrows of desire!

And I do not suppose that one soul in the congregation realised that Blake's twaddle was any better than the twaddle of "All people that on earth do dwell."

Well I was cross. "O enter then his gates with praise, Approach with joy his courts unto." Now I suppose most people think that His courts UNTOOOO are some summer residence of God outside the capital. "The court moved to Untoo in the first week of May."

---

1. A service of thanksgiving for the King's recovery from a severe illness.

VITA TO HAROLD   *Long Barn*

10 July 1929

My voluntary exile from Knole is very curious. I think about it a lot. I feel exactly as though I had had for years a liaison with a beautiful woman, who never, from force of circumstances, belonged to me wholly; but who had for me a sort of half-maternal tenderness and understanding, in which I could be entirely happy. *Now* I feel as though we had been parted because (again through force of circumstances and owing to no choice of her own) she had been compelled to marry someone else and had momentarily fallen completely beneath his jurisdiction, not happy in it, but acquiescent. I look at her from far off; and if I were wilder and more ruthless towards myself, I should burst in one evening and surprise her in the midst of her new domesticity. But life has taught me not to do these things.

HAROLD TO VITA   *Berlin*

22 July 1929

My sweetest,

Tikki [his typewriter] must write this letter as it is VERY IMPORTANT and I want you to be able to read it easily and calmly. Without those efforts of decyphering, without that personal emotionalism, which I fear and hope are evoked by my beastly scribble. Bless you my sweetest Mar.

But never have I more wanted to consult you calmly than at the present moment. If you were at the cottage I should telephone although that would not be of much value since a long discussion is what I want and I cannot wait till the end of the month.

The PROBLEM is as follows:—

(1) I have spoken to you I believe of Bruce Lockhart, an attractive scamp who was our Chargé d'Affaires in Moscow and is now the Londoner of the Londoner's Diary of the *Evening Standard* of the Lord Beaverbrook.

(2) Well I have got a letter from him.

(3) In this letter he writes as follows:—

My dear Harold,

When I was in Berlin in April, you hinted that you might not stay indefinitely in the diplomatic service. I did not take you very seriously, but it may be worth while to put the following before you. Please treat what follows as very confidential and for yourself only.

Beaverbrook is looking for a man of your ability (jub-i-jub) and your knowledge (JUB-i-jub) of men and affairs, and would offer a very considerable inducement for his services. His job would be to write and edit a page like the Londoner's Diary in the *Evening Standard*.

As far as you yourself are concerned, you would do it admirably. It would bring you into close touch with politics and the politicians again. It would also leave you time to write your books and would leave the door open for a literary or a political career. And, as I have said, it would be well paid.

I have already suggested your name to Beaverbrook and he would be glad to 'capture' you. The object of this letter is to ask if you would be prepared to consider such a proposal. Please let me have your views on the subject as soon as ever you can.

Yours ever
Bruce Lockhart

Well, my poppet, obviously this is very tempting. It means London, liberty, scope, salary, freedom of time and opinion, plus a tremendous score over the Foreign Office. But I must not allow these mixed feelings to affect my judgement, and would put the thing as follows:— *Objections to accepting this offer.*

(1) Beaverbrook is not a man of very savoury reputation. I am not sure that I should like to be identified with the dirty politics of the *Evening Standard*.

(2) I do not wish to abandon my radical opinions, or to be forced to write things which I do not believe. I am prepared to provide them with facts and fancies, but I am not prepared to express views with which I do not agree.

(3) It might entail a great deal of lobbying. I am bad at that. You know how bad I am at asking people the way or the time. The job might degenerate into a constant process of accosting Cabinet Ministers and worming things out of them. A great deal of my time would be employed in talking to people whom I do not like and in suffering

fools gladly. I fear I am too 'proud' and in a way too 'upright' for this sort of work.

(4) If I ever wanted serious work in the future it would do me harm having been connected with the Beaverbrook group. My stunt is not that sort of stunt. If I ever went in for politics I should succeed only in terms of being a high-brow of unquestioned integrity. I could never succeed on the basis of brazen-faced pushing. I feel it is like playing poker when one had very little capital and does not care much for cards.

(5) I feel therefore that if I accepted I might regret it later, and regret that I had yielded to a momentary temptation which had not turned out a success and which had prejudiced my general prospects.

What I am doing therefore is (A) To write today to Lockhart saying that I should be prepared to consider the proposal, but must know what the salary will be and what the job entails. (B) To write to Leonard [Woolf] putting the above objections, but more modestly, before him and asking his advice.

What I want you to do my sweetest is to telegraph on the receipt of this letter, "Advise accept" or "Advise refuse." I do not suppose that you will be able to group your feelings under any one of these two formulas. But if, on thinking over the advantages and disadvantages, you are quite clear one way or the other, please telegraph. Consult Hilda [Matheson] but under the seal of confidence. I do not undertake of course to follow your opinion or to blame you for it in after years. But I trust your judgement enormously when you sit down and think a thing out.[1]

HAROLD TO VITA   *Berlin*

8 August 1929

Today, for all I know, may be a decisive date in my life. I feel rather wretched. Whatever happens—whether I get this [Beaverbrook] job or not, I shall feel rather gloomy. If I fail to get it, then

---

1. Vita replied, advising acceptance.

I shall feel *blamiert* [ridiculous]. If I get it, however, then I shall feel depressed at leaving diplomacy. Gloom in either case. But it may simply be liver.

I daresay that the main cause of my gloom is fuss about money. My poverty is really getting on my nerves. I mean it is awful not to have any money in the bank. Of course I have got enough to go on with and I am not in serious difficulties. But it is just the feeling of having spent so much money here and having absolutely nothing to show for it. Anyhow I funk all bills. *J'ai peur des notes comme d'une abeille.*

I heard from the Ambassador that there are five Legations to be filled—Mexico, Athens, Belgrade, Bucharest and Oslo. Now it is *quite* likely that they will offer me Athens, Belgrade or Bucharest. If they don't, then I shall have no qualms at all about resignation. But if, a week after accepting Beaverbrook's offer, I get appointed to Athens, then I admit that I shall think that fate has played me a scurvy trick. Five years in Athens, and then an Embassy. I should probably think of it in those terms. Poor Hadji—not much of a success in life. Everybody will think me quite, quite looney.

You see, my darling, supposing I hear, after I have resigned, that they really were about to offer me Athens. Supposing that, having become a hack journalist cadging interviews from people, I think of the man who got my job at Athens sailing from Aegean island to Aegean island. Supposing that when Beaverbrook has chucked me out after four years, I hear that my successor at Athens has been appointed to Rome. But perhaps I'm doing a White Queen [in *Alice in Wonderland*] and getting all my regrets over in anticipation.

VITA TO HAROLD   *Withyham, Sussex*

11 August 1929

Yesterday I went to Rodmell to see Virginia. Much to my amusement, they both asked me searchingly whether they were the only people to whom you had written about Lord B [Beaverbrook], the truth being that they were exceedingly flattered and rather touched.

"Are you sure," they asked, "that he didn't consult Raymond? or Eddy? Or anybody?" I assured them that they alone had received your confidence. They are really making Monk's House very nice. Leonard has thrown three rooms into one, and made himself a lovely room to work in. He invited me gravely upstairs to come and see it. I *do* like Leonard.

By the way, I have been induced by him and Dotz [Wellesley] to put together a handful of poems for their series this autumn—and having done so am a little worried about them. I shall have to show them to you before they are published.[1] It is not on the score of their goodness or badness that I am worried, as I think they are quite passable enough, but you see they are love poems, and purely artificial at that—I mean, *very* artificial, rather 17th-century most of them—and although I should have thought this would be sufficiently obvious (that they were just 'literary', I mean), it has since occurred to me that people will think them Lesbian. I should not like this, either for my own sake or yours, more especially as (unlike Shakespeare's sonnets) they are really literary exercises. I shall send you a copy of the complete lot, and would like an honest opinion please.

HAROLD TO VITA   *Berlin*

26 August 1929

You say in your letter that Ernest Gye[2] must have upset me by telling me not to leave the [diplomatic] service. No, my sweet. My perplexity and hesitations are deeper than that. You see, Diplomacy really does give me leisure to do literary work of my own and it *does* have advantages such as leave, nice people etc. Moreover (and this is the essential point), if I stay in diplomacy I am certain of being 'successful', or, in other words, of getting to the top. You say, with justice, that it is not a very glorious top. I quite agree. Yet I have

---

1. They included a series of sonnets addressed to Mary Campbell. Harold advised against publication, but Vita did publish some in *King's Daughter*.
2. Ernest Gye entered the Foreign Office in 1903, and became Minister in Tangier, 1933–36.

sufficient knowledge of human nature to realise that it is more satisfactory to succeed on a small scale than to fail on a big one. If I end up as an Ambassador I shall always feel (and say) what a wonderful career I could have made for myself in the open market. But if I climb down into the open market and then fail to make good there, I shall regret bitterly not having remained in my armchair and ended as an Ambassador. I shall feel that I was absolutely mad to chuck a certainty for an uncertainty, and at an age when my supply of violent energy must shortly begin to give out.

I don't think I shall be affected by the present [Foreign Office] moves, but I shall certainly be affected by the new ones. There is even a prospect, if I stay on, of my being a Minister next year with £4,000 a year.

Naturally I put against this (1) B.M. (2) Being separated from you. In the end these two factors will probably be determinant. But you must understand, my love, that the decision is a grave one to have to take, and you can't quite expect me to chuck my job at my age [43] in a spirit of light-heartedness. I feel *very* heavy hearted about it, and whatever decision I do take will not have been taken without hours and hours of very anxious thought. If I were ten years younger the whole thing would be different.

HAROLD TO VITA   *Berlin*

14 November 1929

Feeling rather miz at the moment as I have been reading three days worth of the *Express* and *Evening Standard*. They really fill me with alarm. I simply shall be unable to write the sort of sob-stuff they want. They seem to have an unerring eye for just the sort of thing I loathe—*Journey's End,* Orpen, *Jud Süss* [1]—all the *faux bon.* There are columns of sob-stuff by R. C. Sherriff about Armistice

---

1. *Journey's End,* R. C. Sherriff's play about life in the trenches of World War I; Sir William Orpen (1878–1931), the fashionable portrait painter; and *Jud Süss (Jew Süss),* the novel by Lion Feuchtwanger about eighteenth-century Germany, published in 1927.

Day and the V.C. dinner. I don't think I am intellectually fastidious but I do loathe slush. Then there is a ghastly article by my colleague Mr James Douglas entitled, "Why do the Heathen rage against me?" in which he explains how he tried to defend "the homespun ideals of humanity" against the new "cloacal school of literature" ('cloaca' is Latin for drain).

Now what shall I do in such a *galère?* I shall be thought highbrow and cloacal. For this reason I shall be glad when my *Express* and *Standard* reach me by post in small doses. I really feel ill when I consume a whole pile of them at a time.

Then about the money. I should really mind if I had tied myself to Shoe Lane [the *Standard's* office in London] and got nothing in return. You see, my sweet, it is rather a blow to my pride to work as a hack on a newspaper, and the only thing that counterbalances that is a gain to my pride not to take money from B.M. So that you must make it quite clear to her that once she has repaid the Knole capital, we shall take nothing more from her. Not one penny. If she insists on paying something, then it must go into a fund for the boys. Also you might take the occasion to hint that she must not tell any lies about us.

VITA TO HAROLD   *Long Barn*

7 December 1929

I wish I knew what you were really feeling these days. I am afraid you will have an awful heart-sink when it comes to the last days; you will look at the red boxes, and the green bootlaces, and the draft-papers, with a real wrench at the heart. But when I open the door of K.B.W.[1] for you, I shall feel as though it were *our* wedding day.

Your own (after 16 years)

Mar

---

1. 4 King's Bench Walk, Inner Temple, London, the flat which Vita had been preparing for Harold's return.

HAROLD TO VITA *Berlin*

16 December 1929

At the Buccaneers [Club] dinner[1] there were nearly 40 people—including old Rumbie [Rumbold] and the American Ambassador. Speech by Rumbie which gave me a lump in my throat. Speech by me—very restrained but gulpy. Musical honours. All went off very well. It is quite extraordinary how nice people are to me here. They really are sorry I am going.

Rumbie made a rather provocative speech saying that the Foreign Office ought to have been able to keep me "had they possessed more imagination." As all the Press were there, this was rather odd.

I was exhausted by the whole thing, and sank into my bed with relief. Luncheon with the [Carl von] Schuberts today. Tomorrow dinner at the Embassy—and then my farewells are over.

My darling, I know what she has done at K.B.W. She has put his modern pictures in the bedroom. Well, I expect she's right. Get a large basin for me to be sick into.

Tomorrow will be my last letter.[2]

---

1. A farewell dinner for Harold given by the British Embassy.
2. He left Berlin, and diplomacy, on 20 December.

Harold joined the staff of the Evening Standard *on 1 January 1930, writing paragraphs for the "Londoner's Diary." He hated the work, finding it trivial and debasing, but enjoyed a little more his weekly talks for the BBC, which made him for the first time a well-known figure to the public. In 1931 he resigned from the Beaverbrook Press, stood for Parliament as a candidate for Sir Oswald Mosley's New Party, and edited its journal,* Action. *From this too he resigned when the paper failed to pay its way and Mosley turned fascist. It was an inauspicious start to his "market-place" career. Vita, on the other hand, wrote two best-selling novels,* The Edwardians *and* All Passion Spent, *and bought the ruins of Sissinghurst Castle, near Cranbrook in Kent, where she and Harold restored some of the buildings and began to create a new garden. They moved there permanently from Long Barn in 1932.*

HAROLD TO VITA   Evening Standard, *London E.C.4*

2 January 1930

My own darling.

I have no pens here and have to do this on Tikki.[1] Just a few kind words, my sweet, to wish you good morning again.

Came up with Desmond [MacCarthy] who was very charming and full of talk. Rather too full of talk as I wanted to do my lessons,

---

1. From now until Vita's death in 1962, Harold almost always typed his letters to her.

which now consists in reading all the papers in the hope of finding a good paragraph. I suppose that I shall get into the way of finding these paragraphs leaping ready-armed to the mind. At present they are rather a bother to think of, rather a bother to write, and terribly feeble when written. But I shall settle down in time.

Got here soon after ten. Found [Bruce] Lockhart fussing about in a rush as usual. I rather like all this rush business. Read French and German newspapers. Wrote three paragraphs. Fiddled about.

The Editor rushed in to say that the Duke of Westminster was engaged to Loelia Ponsonby. He asserted that his information was absolutely correct. I rang up Olive: "Mrs Rubens left this morning for the Continent." Now what does it mean? I begged him to be very careful. [2]

Bless you my sweet. Off to luncheon with Tray.

Your own

Hadji

HAROLD TO VITA   *4 King's Bench Walk,*
London E.C.4

24 April 1930

Well, my view is:—

(a) That it is most unwise of us to get Sissinghurst. [3] It costs us £12,000 to buy and will cost another good £15,000 to put in order. This will mean nearly £30,000 before we have done with it. For £30,000 we could buy a beautiful place replete with park, garage, h and c, central heating, historical associations, and two lodges r. and l.

(b) That it is most wise of us to buy Sissinghurst. Through its veins pulses the blood of the Sackville dynasty. True it is that it comes

---

2. The 2nd Duke married Loelia Ponsonby on 20 February as his third wife. This marriage ended in divorce in 1947, when the Duke married a fourth time.

3. Vita had first seen Sissinghurst Castle (more the ruins of an Elizabethan house) on 4 April, and Harold visited it the next day. They bought it, together with 400 acres of land, on 6 May 1930.

through the female line—but then we are both feminist, and after all Knole came in the same way. It is, for you, an ancestral mansion: that makes up for company's water and h and c.

(c) It is in Kent. It is in a part of Kent we like. It is self-contained. I could make a lake. The boys could ride.

(d) We like it.

VITA TO HAROLD   *Sissinghurst*

23 October 1930

My darling love,

The moat wall is going to be very superb. They have uncovered its foot a bit, and I think there is no doubt that there was originally water there too. There are lovely big stones at the foot of the piers. The piers are going to be lovely—quite a 'feature'. Those nasty little thorns at the end have gone, and it is now open to the view; much nicer. It will be a lovely walk. The wall will look much higher than you think.

The Hayters[1] have cleared a good deal of the nuttery, which now looks like a series of avenues. That is nice too.

I planted a fig, and lots of roses.

I think the yew hedge will be planted by the time you come. The yews are all here, and it won't take long to put them in.

I can see that we are going to have heaps of wall-space for climbing things. I have already ordered some choice shrubs, including a pomegranate and a mulberry.

I am not sleeping in that horrid farmhouse. I have got a bed in the oratory off my sitting room [in the tower], which increases the squalor but also my sense of security. I have also got Canute [elkhound].

Your own Mar

---

1. Tom Hayter and his son George were living in the derelict south wing when the Nicolsons bought Sissinghurst, and remained there for several years as its first working gardeners.

HAROLD TO VITA   Action, *5 Gordon Square, W.C.1*

28 September 1931

I went down to Denham yesterday after writing to you. Tom[1] was alone. We discussed the paper [*Action*] first. He will agree to our taking out shares together. He gives me an absolutely free hand about all editorial stuff. Off we go with a bang on Thursday week. Our orders to date are 110,000 but the advertisements are a bit sticky. We have got six of our twelve pages but shall want six more. This rather worries me, as it is said that one can always get advertisements for the first copy of a paper. But I hope that we are in for a slight trade boom and that may help.

We then discussed the future of the party. The [General] Election has of course caught us bending. We had made all our plans to fight a campaign in February and we are simply not ready to fight one now. I told him that what I dreaded was that no-one would be elected except Mr Kid Lewis [the boxer], and the resultant ridicule would kill the party stone dead for ever. He admitted this but confessed that he was not optimistic about any single one of us being returned to Parliament except perhaps Cimmie.[2] The problem is, therefore, shall we fight a few seats and risk complete annihilation or shall we retire completely from the contest, proclaim that this is a ramp election and withdraw from political life—concentrating our energies upon becoming a movement rather than a Parliamentary party? We still cannot make up our minds on this.

HAROLD TO VITA   Action

1 October 1931

Day of joy and day of good omen [wedding anniversary].

Little one, how young we were those eighteen years ago, how uncertain, how unlike our present selves. And in all these years we have

---

1. Sir Oswald Mosley, leader of the New Party.
2. Cynthia Mosley, a daughter of Lord Curzon and Sir Oswald's first wife. She was also standing as a New Party candidate.

grown into a complete harmony—which seems now so inevitable and so indissoluble but which I suppose was really a very intricate and intelligent thing to have achieved. I have a theory that a happy personal relationship is based upon a dovetailing of the static and the dynamic in people. One day I shall work it out. What I mean is that the active and passive forces in each have to be mingled in equal proportions. There must be an equal proportion of rest (confidence, security, no nagging) and an equal proportion of motion (interest, stimulation of ideas, etc). That's what we have got. We are both static and dynamic in our mutual relations.

Oh my darling, what a lucky man I am to be able to look back on eighteen such years. Whatever happens tomorrow or today nothing can take from us all the great enjoyment we have had together. I do not suppose that two people have ever retained such a high level of happiness for so long a time. I am so grateful to you. It is all your sweetness that has done it. During all those years you have been so loving and gentle. It makes me feel that I have been selfish all the time just to take so much and give so little and then to stand for politics and rush about and be a bother generally.

HAROLD TO VITA　　　　　　　　　　　　　　*Hotel Excelsior, Rome*

3 January 1932

I wrote from Pisa station and sent two postcards to the boys. But after Pisa I got into new territory. For a long time the Carrara mountains flashed above the umbrella pines. Later on we came opposite Elba, and as sunset came we entered the Piombino-Orbetello region— lean flanks of hills and dykes and lagoons catching the sunset. The sun flamed down into the sea and lit up the Isola del Giglio. I insist on going there one day with you. It is small and mysterious and en- trenched. My love, we shall go there one day when troubles have ceased and I do not find my hair crackling to grey with worry.

I read *Mansfield Park* [Jane Austen]. Proust applied to *la petite noblesse de campagne.* I also read Aristotle's Ethics, feeling that it was really high time, before I got to Rome, to know what was meant by 'good'. I arrived at the Terme [station] before I had quite decided that point.

Christopher[1] met me and we drove to this Edwardian caravanserai. They had engaged a suite for us and are charging us absurdly low prices. A vast drawing room replete with palms and little gilt tables. A double-bedded room for me and bathroom. Ditto for Tom [Mosley]. And Christopher in a *chambre de demoiselle* along the passage. Tom arrives tomorrow.

Gladwyn came in.[2] He took us off to dine in his flat. For the moment he is occupying his mother-in-law's little flat looking out on the Castel San Angelo. Very Anglo-Italian. A hard night, steel stars. Not very cold. Christopher has returned from Munich having seen Hitler. He says that the Führer contends that we British Hitlerites are trying to do things like gentlemen. That will never do. We must be harsh, violent and provocative. I do not care for this aspect of my future functions. I fear that it will be very bad for Tom to go to Munich. Oh dear! Oh dear!

Thereafter we had a drink called Nectar which tasted like the sort of hair-wash you would get at the coiffeur at Sauqueville. And then to bed. Being both a little tired.

I woke this morning to find sun pouring in and to see, opposite, a red villa adorned by statues of Emperors and a miffy palm. Above this crenelated cornice swept the deep blue sky. "I am," thus did I address myself, "in Rome." And at that I rang for a *Caffè completo*. Already I am feeling better in the head and heart. My dear—how worried I have been the last three months! How much more worried I *ought* to be now! But there it is—I shall not bother these days and try and enjoy myself.

What a strange expedition this is! Oh my dear, when I saw that Island of Giglio I thought how far better would it have been had I lived there all my life with you. Giglio non Gigolo. But then I have been active—that is something to be said—even if it has given me a sore head and brought me into disgrace with fortune and men's eyes.

---

1. Christopher Hobhouse, aged twenty-one, a New Party devotee, who had just come from Munich filled with pro-Nazi fervor.
2. Gladwyn Jebb, now serving in the British Embassy, Rome.

HAROLD TO VITA   *Hotel Excelsior, Rome*

4 January 1932

My own darling,

I cannot tell you how lovely it was yesterday. A cloudless sky and that light which only Rome can give—a gentle brilliance. We walked in the Borghese gardens observing the equestrians trotting together in the row. Then along the Pincian and down Trinità dei Monti. What a marvellous staircase! Then we went and sat in the sun in the Piazza del Popolo and finally to St Peter's. At an open window on the façade lounged three papal guards in their uniforms. It was exactly like some Velasquez sketch. We went into the Cathedral. Christopher [Hobhouse], who is drawn to Catholicism, was rather shocked. He found it flippant. As indeed it is. And showing off. Which it does. And irreverent. Which it may be. He refused for these reasons either to kiss the pope's toe, or to cross himself.

At 7.45 I went to meet Tom [Mosley]. He arrived looking most unwell. He said that Paris and *réveillon* had knocked him up. He recovered a bit after his bath and we had dinner here at the hotel. They treat Tom with the utmost deference—regarding him as a *duce in erba*. After dinner the editor of the *Lavoro Fascisto* came round to interview Tom. He was not much of a man as editors go, nor did he possess such a knowledge of the English language as might have been helpful to us. But we managed all right, and he told us about the Fascist electoral system which is in fact not electoral at all. We were much impressed.

HAROLD TO VITA   *Hotel Prinz Albrecht, Berlin*

25 January 1932

I did not write yesterday as I was so rushed. It was not a noble rush. It was an ignoble rush. It came from the fact of oversleeping, in its turn induced by too much festivity. For on the previous night I dined at the Embassy. A vast banquet. Rows of state liveries, and the porter going flump with his mace when one came in. The Papal Legate in scarlet, the new French Ambassador with a conceited swing to his head. And all the usual appurtenances of a diplomatic dinner. I wore my little flag [his CMG decoration]. Old Friedländer Fuld was there. She was dressed in a dowdy little shift—none of the emeralds and diamanté of the past. This is because she is afraid of Hitler who has said that if he comes into power he will get rid of all the Jews. Which includes Jewesses. Most disturbing. That little fiend, her daughter, is hiding in the country.

I was warmly welcomed by my ex-colleagues. I sat there looking up the table through the gold candelabra upon those shirt fronts and ribbons. Well, well . . . I keep on reminding myself that if I had stayed in Diplomacy I should now be Minister at Montevideo and not pleased at all. Yet I cannot hide the fact that when I last sat at that table I was a person of consequence. And now I have lost all the reputation that I had. My own fault—and I daresay it is not irremediable. But I certainly have made myself a motley to the view during the last two years. Reckless of me. I had too many irons in the fire. I was in too much of a hurry.

Thinking gloomily of these things I left the banquet having said goodbye to the Papal Legate and proceeded to the Jockey [Club]. There I met Francesco[1] by appointment. He is less wild and extravagant than formerly. He thinks only of his plays—which are doing well. He took me on to the rough bar in the east end. It is pathetic how hungry everyone is here. I stood them all sausages. Their eyes became like wolves.

Yet the result of all this was that I only got to bed at 4.0 a.m.—and that I woke with a start at 10.30 to the telephone saying that the car was at the door. It was to take Christopher and myself to Potsdam. It did. We visited Sans Souci [Frederick the Great's palace]. We walked through the park. We returned to lunch with Francesco. He has constructed a bathroom in a very odd style. The walls are of chromium steel and the bath is a huge Roman sarcophagus. It is spoilt

---

1. Francesco Mendelsohn, a rich, musical lover of the arts and a dramatist, who knew all Berlin society.

in its effect by a neat little white lavatory in the corner. Hitler is the sole topic of conversation.[2]

This sort of life is, I am told, interesting and exciting. Yet I am too old for it. I long for home and quiet. Not that I have been bored. I have learnt a lot.

---

2. Harold recorded in his diary of this visit, "My general impression is that Hitler has missed the boat."

During the summer of 1932 Harold wrote Public Faces, *a novel about diplomacy, which had an instant success, and he and Vita were persuaded, as the best-known married couple in English letters, to undertake a lecture tour of Canada and the United States. They were away nearly four months, January to April 1933. For both of them it was their first (for Vita her only) visit to America, and they stood the physical, mental, and social ordeal with undiminished buoyancy. Sometimes they spoke from the same platform, discussing such subjects as "Marriage" or "How to Bring Up Children," but for much of the time they were lecturing apart, and wrote each other letters that released some of the tensions that they managed to conceal from their hosts.*

HAROLD TO VITA   *British Embassy, Washington*

28 January 1933

My own darlingest,

Tears of a widower—oh my sweetheart—how young you looked as you came down the stairs last night with your little bag. Such a mar. So alone. So wanted and so alone. My heart ached. I talked to the Ambassador[1] for a bit about politics. He is a sensible man. And then dreading it, I went upstairs. There was a cigarette stump in your ashtray and tissue paper about. And the iodine and cough lozenges on my table. Really it is absurd how we go on exposing ourselves to these *déchire-*

---

1. Sir Ronald Lindsay, who had been Harold's first Ambassador in Berlin. He was Ambassador in Washington, 1930–39.

ments. I do not ever want to be separated from you ever again. Not for an hour. My dearest, dearest, dearest marki.

This morning is fine and clear, and I can see the Washington obelisk and the dome of the Capitol. I have finished my breakfast, done my diary, washed, dressed—and here I am settling down to write some letters. Then I go off to Baltimore and the old smile will be set again upon my *pomettes.* But I shall not be really glad till today week when our reunion comes closer.

What an odd life! But it is useful for us not merely as an experience but as a break with vegetationing. I scarcely dare to think of Sissinghurst. I see that they are having very heavy weather in England. Frost and snow. Our poor garden.

Goodbye my own angel—all my love

Hadji

V I T A　T O　H A R O L D

31 January 1933

Hotel General Brock,
Niagara Falls, Canada

Niagara on closer inspection is after all rather more impressive than the waterfall at Sissinghurst. When I wrote this morning I had seen only the American falls, not the Canadian ones. Since then, I have been taken round by Dr Harry Grant. Dr Harry Grant is a darling old boy of 73, with the whitest hair I have ever seen; half scholar, half philosopher, with a real passion for Niagara. He has built himself a house just opposite the Falls, where he lives quite alone, and reads, so he tells me, for ten hours a day sometimes, his only companions being a dog, a parrot, and some pheasants. *Face* [1] is one of his favourite books; so there. He simply loves it. Also your book on your father. He says *All Passion Spent* has had a bad effect on him, in so far as he used to be burdened by 50 nephews and nieces, but now never sees them unless he feels inclined.

I was amused. He began cautiously by asking me to go back to tea with him after seeing the sights. On our way round the sights (driven by a chauffeur called Ben as old as Dr Grant himself, and as

---

1. Harold's novel *Public Faces.*

silvery-haired), he informed me that the way to be happy was to expect only a tenth-part from life; i.e. if you read one book in ten that you liked, or met one person in ten that you liked, you ought to be satisfied, and to feel that you had achieved your quota. After tea, he made me the oddest little bow, and said, "I know now that you are my quota. I trust that you will return to dine with me. The car will call for you at 7.15." So there I am landed with having to go out to dinner. I can scarcely plead a previous engagement in Niagara Falls—although I *have* actually been invited by the Scarlet Quill Club, who in some miraculous way have already nosed me out—and anyhow he is such a darling that I couldn't refuse.

HAROLD TO VITA   *Hotel New Weston, New York*

1 February 1933

We went to Harlem. It is the real thing there—one mass of young black men and black women. They danced the Lindy Hop with intense seriousness. It is unlike any other dancing. The absence of self-consciousness. The absence of any smiles or conversation—grim earnestness. And the subordination of sex to movement. One feels that in this they have a form of self-expression which we whites cannot understand. Something voodooish or religious. Whatever happens Mar must go there. It is a wholly new experience—something which opens out a background which is as alien to us as the real east.

HAROLD TO VITA   *The Drake, Chicago*

7 February 1933

I have just come back from seeing you whirl in a whirl-door into a whirl of blizzard. No, I didn't like it in the least. I wish now that I had insisted on coming to the station as once you are in the train, you will be safe and warm. But then if I had come to the station you would now be fussing about how I would get back—and that would make it all worse for you. Darling, the Mars are really rather silly about each other. I feel now as if a helpless mouse had been turned out into the snow. Whereas really you are the most competent of people and will be travelling in a *train de luxe*. And you feel that a rabbit has been left behind exposed to whirlwinds and gangsters. Whereas in fact I am here in my room tikking away and as safe as safe. But we do love each other so, my dearest. We know that the whole of life is enshrined in the other. I shall see you the day after tomorrow. I shall be separated from you one whole day. I have heaps to do. I feel as if I were a mongoose stuck in the middle of the ice-floes of Lake Michigan.

VITA TO HAROLD   *Minneapolis*

14 February 1933

The whole of Minneapolis seems to be out for Red Lewis' blood; I responded with some mild remark, and that came out in all the papers too.[1] I hope neither he nor Dorothy [Thompson] sees it. There were also several descriptions of my personal appearance; my eyes, you will be pleased to hear, are (1) blue, (2) deep blue, (3) brown, (4) hazel. So you can take your choice. They got very puzzled as to what my name was, and there is a touching reference to my modesty in preferring to be called Miss S-W. instead of Lady "which is her rightful title." I think they thought I was being tactful in a democratic country. I don't feel I can stand many more women. America is rapidly curing me of any weakness I may ever have entertained for my own sex.

HAROLD TO VITA   *British Embassy, Washington*

16 February 1933

Such a miz letter he got from her written in the train. I am not surprised. Wisconsin at 4.30 P.M. on a February afternoon is not *folichon*

---

1. Vita had said, "It is too bad Sinclair Lewis is so widely read abroad and his caricatures are taken as real American people. It is entirely unfair to you."

[festive]. There are few things more depressing in this life than a lonely sunset in a train.

We went to lunch with Alice Longworth.[1] My word! how I like that woman! There is a sense of freedom in her, plus a sense of background. That, I feel, is what is missing in this country. Nobody seems to have anything behind their front. Poor people, they feel it themselves, and hence all those pitiful gropings after Manor Houses in Wiltshire and parish registers and the Daughters of the Founding Fathers. But Alice Longworth has a world position, and it has left her simple and assured and human. Yes, there at least is an American who is unquestionably a woman of importance. It was a pleasant luncheon. You know—those sort of luncheons where one feels mentally comfortable and warm.

After that I walked to the house in S Street where President Wilson died. It is a large neat modern house in good taste. Nothing grim about it. Excellent plumbing, I feel sure. I then walked down to the site of the old [British] Embassy. It has been completely cleared of buildings and the large triangular site is now occupied by second-hand cars standing cheek by jowl in the mud. I felt rather sad about poor B.M.[2]—and those distant happy days when she was young and successful and a belle. I stood there reflecting on the mutability of human affairs, and thinking of that encumbered bedroom at Brighton, and all the rage of disappointment hanging in the air. Oh my sweet!— pray God that you and I will not prepare for ourselves so tragic an old age.

HAROLD TO VITA

18 February 1933

Fort Sumter Hotel,
Charleston, South Carolina

Charleston is really delightful. It has personality—which is a thing most American towns and people lack. It is not merely that there are a few old bits and lovely old houses—it is that the whole place is old in character and southern. The old atmosphere is lazy, untidy, digni-

---

1. The eldest daughter of President Theodore Roosevelt. Her husband, Nicholas Longworth, Speaker of the House of Representatives 1925–27, had died in 1931.
2. As a girl Lady Sackville had acted as hostess for her father when he was British Minister in Washington, 1881–88.

fied, lotus-eating, anti-noise and rush. Even their voices are as soft as
the feet of the negro women selling narcissus in the streets. It is the
most unamerican thing I have met. Mar absolutely must come here.
It would be impossible to understand America's falling off unless one
sees this place.

It is not that they are pro-English, or like the English; it is that
they *are* English of a peculiar sort—a sort of West Indian, plantation
flavour has remained undiminished. They talk of the Americans almost
as of enemies. They dread lest "the Yankees" may come and spoil their
lovely little town. They refer to the Civil War as 'The Confederate
War'. They still long for secession under the British crown with
Dominion Status. Even in details the difference is apparent. They
loathe 'taste' which they call 'Lady's Journal'—and they keep old
Victorian things in their houses so as not to 'become period'. Their
servants are all black nannies like in the magazine stories, but they
refuse to sentimentalize about them. They are infinitely less affected,
more proud, than the denizens of Rye [Sussex].

From my window I look out across the glittering harbour to the
thin line of the Atlantic. Over there, but 500 miles away, is Barbados
and the Bermudas. One is conscious of their proximity. As I write I
can hear soft voices calling 'spring flashers'—all else is padded and
silent. From my other window I look down upon the town. Just low
roofs and white balconies from which emerge white steeples and little
neat lanterns in the Wren manner.

Miss Pinckney picked me up. She is from one of their oldest
families. She writes poetry. She is well-read and intelligent but takes
it as a matter of course. There are gardens everywhere. Public squares
with statues of Pitt among palm trees. Green grass. Azaleas in flower.
No, I mean in bud. Little quiet cobbled streets with the neatest of
houses. Like the back streets of Westminster except that all the houses
have a Barbados feel. And above all they have walls everywhere and
iron gratings and fine iron gates disclosing lovely gardens. And round
it all stretches water.

Dubose Heywood[1] [*sic*] picked us up. A very thin quiet interesting man. He motored us out to Middleton Place—some fifteen miles

---

1. Du Bose Heyward was born in Charleston in 1885. His novel about the Deep South, *Porgy*,
was published in 1925.

away. We drove through avenues of huge ilexes draped in Spanish Moss. This moss is characteristic of the whole country. It isn't moss in the least but a hanging creeper like old man's beard. It drapes every branch, hanging down like huge cobwebs. The effect is as if every tree were draped in widows weeds of grey. In detail it is ugly and untidy: in the mass it is strange and impressive.

Middleton Place was one of the great plantation seats. It still belongs to the family who are cousins of Miss Pinckney. It is as romantic in its way as Sissinghurst. The main *corps de logis* was burnt in the Confederate war. Only the little brick kitchen wing remains. In this they live. But the wide avenue approach and the ensuing terraces and gardens still have their axis on the main frontage, and are on a fine wide scale. Enormous ilexes—eighteen-foot round in the trunk—flank a wide lawn cut up into high beds of camellias in flower. This terrace drops down to dark lakes 30 feet below to right and left. In front stretches a wide marsh intersected by a broad river. The skyline is intersected some fifteen miles away by low hills with forests. The marsh used to be a rice field. Six elderly negroes in blue were mowing the vast lawns with little tiny mowing machines. The camellias blazed. The air was damp and heavy with the smell of *Olea fragrans* or scentive olive—a sprig of which I sent you. I couldn't make out what it reminded me of. We went into the little house. All very simple. Three rooms with Empire furniture and shuttered as if it were blazing hot. Not a touch of *The Lady's Journal.* The gardens were beautifully kept up and when the azaleas are out it must be amazing. I am not much of a one for camellias even in the mass. But there was no nonsense about it. A few old stone benches. No statues. And from every tree hanging shrouds of moss.

We came back, and I came face to face with Elizabeth Lindsay. We fell into each other's arms. I said I had been to Middleton. She said, "Now what did it remind you of?" I said it had reminded me strongly of something but I could not say what. She said, "Well it's Vita's poem—*Sissinghurst.*" Of course it was; she is no fool that Elizabeth.

I gave my lecture in a lovely Adams hall with old pictures. The whole thing is so effortless and unaffected here. No strain. No noise. I delight in it. We MUST come. They are all longing to see you. Great passion-spenters.

HAROLD TO VITA   *Cincinnati*

23 February 1933

Darling, it was so nice settling down into my rather hard little
Victorian bed last night and to feel that when I woke up I should see
you again the day after tomorrow, and that thereafter we would not
again be separated for more than two days at a time. It was also nice
to see that you had traversed your great ordeal without any visible
signs of exhaustion. My sweet—what a strong old horse you are, touch
wood (I gave the desk here such a loud rap at that, that I had to say
"come in"), but really you are a marvel of endurance and good temper.
I confess that I myself find all this slushy adulation very trying, and
irritating in the sense that all unrealities are irritating. Of course I
know that you and I are very gifted and charming. Only we are not
gifted and charming in the sort of way these people suppose.

One should remember however that if we were lecturing at Chel-
tenham, Roedean College, Bath and Harrogate we should be faced
with just the same vapidity of compliment, by just the same uniformity
of faces. I try to concentrate on the really nice people we have met,
who don't gush but are just quietly and competently kind. It is not
that these people are really less civilised than similar sorts of people
in England. It is just that at home we should be bored stiff by that sort
of person, and here we have a feeling (which may or may not be
justified) that there simply does not exist the sort of other person
whom we like. If you cut out the territorial aristocracy and the types
which have gathered round them in England, and also cut out our
scholars and our intellectuals, one would be left with a residue which
would be no better than, and possibly worse than, our audiences. What
appals me is the sense that the only alternative to these audiences is
either the vulgarity of big business or the morons of the farming
community. America seems to have so few alternatives: England so
many.

Anyhow, my sweetest, I slept the first unanxious sleep I have had
for ten days. It was the first night that one way or another I have not
had an anxiety dream about you. I feel this morning so cheerful—a
sense that we have broken the back of our tour, that we have turned
the corner, and that we can now look forward to the second lap, aware

that we have gained a rich experience, much money, a confidence in our own oratorical powers, and that you at least have done some real good for our beloved country. Oh my sweet, I am so proud of you! Your gentleness, your magnificence, your intelligence. You looked so lovely last night with your red velvet and gardenias. They adore your shy dignity, your regal modesty.

*O*n returning from America, Harold devoted the next two *years to his diplomatic trilogy:* Peacemaking, Curzon, The Last Phase, *and the life of the American statesman* Dwight Morrow. *The third of these books took him once to Mexico and several times to the United States, where he stayed with Charles and Anne Lindbergh (Anne was Morrow's daughter) at crucial stages of the trial of Bruno Hauptmann for the kidnapping and murder of their baby. Although they were in frequent financial difficulties, Harold and Vita somehow managed to keep two sons at Eton, employ three domestic servants and three gardeners, travel frequently abroad, and develop ambitious plans for extending the garden at Sissinghurst.*

HAROLD TO VITA

7 November 1933

4 *King's Bench Walk,*
Inner Temple, London

H. G. Wells's dinner party was not, perhaps, an unqualified success. I gather that its intention was to announce his engagement to Moura, but then Odette got nasty[1] and there are breaches of promise in the air and no announcements of immediate marriage. That was the first error. The second error arose from the fact that the titled cousin of Moura who was to play to us on the harp afterwards has an only child, and this child developed a temperature with the result that the titled cousin of Moura failed to come. The harp was there all right as once

---

1. Baroness Moura Budberg, born in Russia, had been the mistress of Maxim Gorki and for many years of H. G. Wells. Odette was Odette Keun, the daughter of a Dutchman and a Greek lady from Constantinople, who was also loved by Wells.

in Tara's Halls[2] but there was no one to play it. The third error was that we dined in a little restaurant called Quo Vadis where there was a large horseshoe table in imitation of the Last Supper. There were also little snippets of lobster in tomato cocktails, which were among the least successful of zakouska that I have ever known. Then the company was mixed in the sort of way that companies could not, or should not, be mixed. There was Emerald Cunard looking like a 3rd dynasty mummy painted pink by amateurs. And there was Christabel who is going to have a baby. And there was Hazel Lavery who looked as though she had stuck on top of her face a caricature mask done by someone else. Very ill she was poor woman. And there was Enid Jones[3] who has an outbreak on her face and arrived veiled like the Beghum of Bhopal. Owing to these disabilities the smarties were not smart enough. The intellectuals were below standard also. There was Stutterheim late of the *Berliner Tageblatt,* David Low the caricaturist, [Sir Frederick] Keeble the botanist, Gip Wells, the son, with his bedint wife, and Brendan Bracken [financier and politician]. After that we adjourned to Wells's flat which is like a fountain-pen box split into cubicles by the designers of Broadcasting House. Maurice Baring appeared and Max Beaverbrook. We sat around looking at the harp. No, it was not a successful party. But I rather enjoyed it. Lady Keeble is hell.

VITA TO HAROLD   *Il Castello, Portofino [Italy]*

31 January 1934

Enchanted, yes; but idiots, no.[4] It is *divine.* You must admit that I acted promptly, for I only fixed it up definitely on the telephone at

2. "The harp that once through Tara's Halls
      The Soul of Music shed
   Now hangs as mute as Tara's Walls
      As if that soul had fled." *Thomas Moore*
3. Christabel McLaren, later Lady Aberconway; Lady Lavery, second wife of Sir John Lavery the painter; and Enid Bagnold, the novelist, wife of Sir Roderick Jones, head of Reuters.
4. Vita and her sister-in-law, Gwen St. Aubyn, had gone to the Italian Riviera, where in a spasm of romantic extravagance they took a fortnight's lease of the castle that overlooks the harbor of Portofino. It was the setting of Countess Russell's novel *Enchanted April,* published in 1922.

7 last night, and by 11 this morning we were here, Gwen's trunk and all, and a demi-john of *vino del paese,* with a complete household of servants waiting for us and mattresses hanging out of every window and the garden-boy with a large bunch of irises at the gate. And if you walked in now, you would not believe that we had not been here for weeks, even to the wireless playing away. Damn, I wish we'd been here on Saturday night to listen to you.

We had luncheon on the terrace and then went down the olive-terraces to the sea. There are bulbs coming up everywhere, but only irises, narcissus, and roses in flower as yet. Oh yes, and we've got a party on Friday. The Beerbohms.[5] In short I can't tell you how perfect it is, and how pleased I am at having been such an idiot.

HAROLD TO VITA   *Munich*

4 February 1934

I have not been very virtuous. I found that Jim Lees-Milne[6] was going over to Paris so I decided to go with him as it was more or less on my way. It was beautiful in the extreme. Cloudless and cold. I have seldom seen Paris looking so crisp and clean. Jim had never been to Versailles so we went out there to lunch. It was quite empty and very cold and magnificent. We walked to the Trianon and then up through the park to the Chateau. I picked up several hints for Sissinghurst. The Bassin de Neptune would do well in Mr Nicolson's rondel. We went over the Palace. I had not been to the Gallerie des Glaces since the great day of 1919. Very odd it was. Then back to Paris.

Jim is such a charming person. He has a passion for poetry and knows masses about it. I like my friends to be well-read and well-bred. Jim is such an aristocrat in mind and culture. You would like him enormously.

Then I walked to James Joyce's flat in the Rue Gallilée. It is a

5. Max Beerbohm, the novelist and essayist, lived close by at Rapallo.
6. The biographer and historian of architecture. In 1980–81 he wrote Harold's biography in two volumes.

little furnished flat and stuffy and prim as a hotel bedroom. The door
was opened by the son. A coarse young man in a huge greatcoat
which he kept on the whole time. A strange accent he had, half
German, half Italian—an accent of Trieste. The sitting room was like
a small salon at a provincial hotel, and the unreal effect was increased
by there being florist's baskets about with arranged flowers—a large
basket of mimosa tied with a broad ribbon. We sat down on little
hard chairs and I tried to make polite conversation to the son. He
got up and offered me an ashtray in the form of a saucer. Then Joyce
glided in. It was evident that he had just been shaving. He was very
spruce and nervous and natty. Great rings upon little twitching fingers. Huge concave glasses which flicked reflections of lights as he
moved his head like a bird, turning it with that definite insistence to
the speaker as blind people do who turn to the sound of a voice. The
son sat there hunched in the chair and his vast greatcoat. Joyce was
wearing large bedroom slippers in check, but except for that, one
had the strange impression that he had put on his best suit. He was
very courteous, as shy people are. His beautiful voice trilled on
slowly like Anna Livia Plurabelle.[7] He has the most lovely voice I
know—liquid and soft with undercurrents of gurgle. He told me
how the ban had been removed from *Ulysses* (Oolissays, he calls it)
in America. He had hopes of having it removed in London also and
was in negotiation with John Lane. He seemed rather helpless and
ignorant about it all and anxious to talk to me. One has the feeling
that he is surrounded by a group of worshippers and has little con-
tact with reality. This impression of something unreal was increased
by the atmosphere of the room, the mimosa with its ribbon, the
bird-like twitchings of Joyce, the glint of his glasses, and the feeling
that they were both listening for something in the house—a shriek
of maniac laughter from the daughter along the passage.

He told me that a man had taken Oolissays to the Vatican and
had hid it in the shape of a prayer book—and that it had been
blessed in such disguise by the Pope. He was half-amused by this and
half-impressed. He saw that I would think it funny, and at the same
time, he did not think it wholly funny himself. It was almost as if

---

7. A character in Joyce's novel *Finnegans Wake*.

he had told me the story in the belief that it might help to lift the ban in England. And yet, being uncertain about it, he smiled deprecatingly as he told it, whereas his eyes behind his glasses were almost appealing.

I suppose that if I had been lunching with him at a restaurant, I should not have felt so strange. But the impression of the Rue Gallilée was the impression of a very nervous and refined animal—a gazelle in a drawing-room. His blindness increases that impression. His shy courtesy, his neatness, his twitching fingers with the rings. I suppose he is a real person somewhere—but I feel I have never spent half an hour with anyone and been left with an impression of such brittle and vulnerable strangeness.

HAROLD TO VITA   *Svenska Lloyd* Suecia *in the North Sea*

13 May 1934

My disinclination to Sweden[1] increased rapidly as Copper [chauffeur] with marked disapproval negotiated the bumps and crevices of our lane. It was so warm and lovely. The horse-chestnuts were beginning to light their candelabra.

This is a nice clean boat with dryad chairs and waitresses instead of stewards. I washed. I brushed my thinning hair. I entered the saloon. *"Skiljetecken Utstrykning sasom sarskilda konditor bud,"* said the head waiter. "That," I answered, "would be delightful." So I sat at the Captain's table. He, poor man, was threading the intricacies of the Thames estuary and did not appear. But two Swedish matrons appeared and a Doctor man, and, I rejoiced to find, Lord Peel[2]—whom I like very much indeed. No food came. *"Gong-gongen gar ej,"* said the head waiter. I translated to Lord Peel (I have picked up Swedish quite quickly), "The gong," I said, "has not sounded yet." We had a nice meal. Then I read. Then I went to bed. The fog-horn hooted in the night. "Danger," I murmured to myself, "drowning and death." But I did not wake.

---

1. Harold was on his way to Stockholm to lecture on Democratic Diplomacy.
2. The first Earl of Peel, Secretary of State for India, 1922–24 and 1928–29.

HAROLD TO VITA   *British Legation, Stockholm*

16 May 1934

I really am a little worried about Tina and Archie.[1] The former has taken Sweden *en grippe*—and I sympathize with her. Apart from everything else, she does not get the admiration she deserves. She is really a museum piece and ought not to be confined to the provinces. It is not merely her very original beauty (which they cannot see) but her intelligence. It is hard luck on her to be in a place for so long where her qualities fail to shine at all. I fear also that she loathes diplomatic life, thinks she is a drag on Archie's career and altogether feels a failure. Archie still treats her as a toy—and you know how bedint and tactless he is. She is far more distinguished and intelligent than he is. I see her squirm when he is snobbish or crude. Yet she still adores him. There are angles in her face which suggest sulkiness, and a spoilt-child ill-temper. There are other angles which are very gentle and rather fine. They both loathe this place with a fierce intensity. I reproved Archie for his sloppy way of living. He has breakfast at 9.30 in his dressing gown and is not dressed till 11.0. Tina stays in bed reading till 1.0. "Well you see," she said, "it makes the day go quicker. The only pleasure we get here is when we feel another day has gone." Archie tells me that she cries a good deal.

HAROLD TO VITA   RMS *Berengaria*
                                  en route *for the United States*
16 September 1934

A male film star approached me rather tight. An ageing Apollo he was, and he said to me, "Where can one get a drink?" I looked at him with marked distaste—pointing with a blunted Royal Sovereign pencil in the direction of the bar. He staggered with an uncertain but still undulating movement of the hips towards a high contiguous stool.

Darkness was descending and the *triste patience des phares* throbbed painfully along the parapets of Europe. Observing that the film star

1. Archibald Clark-Kerr (later Lord Inverchapel) was British Minister in Stockholm, 1931–35. In 1929 he had married a beautiful Chilean girl of nineteen, Maria Salas, nicknamed Tina.

had left his stool, I myself entered the bar and ordered a martini. That made me feel better, and when I felt the throb of engines again I faced my departure with emotion but not in despair. For half an hour I paced the deck seeing the lights fling out sudden appeals. And then I said goodbye to my really beloved continent and retired to my cabin.

I cannot tell you how luxurious and self-satisfied that cabin is. The walls are panelled in chinese silk depicting lotus and dragons. The mirrors flash to concealed lights: the twin beds look like neat little twins; cupboards open on all sides with hangers on which my steward (a talkative man of the name of Emerson) had already hung my clothes. Cameras and binoculars hung upon platinum pegs; a sprig of heather reposed in an ornamental vase; and upon the tables were my books and the Lenare photograph [of Vita].

I then washed in my private bathroom redolent with the rose geranium which B.M. had given me. I then dined at our small table with Victor Cazalet.[1] He has just been motoring in France with Sibyl [Colefax] and cannot speak too highly of her intelligence and charm as a companion. They had ended up at Aix where they had spent the time with Mr and Mrs Baldwin. Teenie [Cazalet] likes Prime Ministers in any form. Mrs B. was hostile to Sibyl and feared she might get hold of her husband. Teenie decided that the visit must not be prolonged and they thus left for the Dordogne.

He is a strange and I fear slightly despicable man. He said, "What I like about journeys such as this is that one can invite people to dinner and not have to pay for their meals." "Yes," I said, "but one has to pay for their drinks." He became thoughtful at this and after a while he said, "We might ask Philip [Lord Lothian] to sit at our table tomorrow evening and then he will ask us to dine with him and the two Astor girls." The whole of Morgan Grenfell and Co rose within me in protest at such meanness. "No," I said, "No, Teenie, we shall ask Philip, Alice Wynn and Nancy Tree to dine with us tomorrow night and we shall give them champagne." He giggled hollow-like.

After dinner (which consisted of grouse and sole ordered fussily by Teenie) we discussed Christian Science which is the centre of his life and the purpose of his visit to the U.S.A. He is not unintelligent

---

1. Conservative M.P. for Chippenham since 1924. A neighbor of the Nicolsons' at Cranbrook, Kent, he was killed in 1943.

about it. But I do feel that a Christian Scientist should not abuse the head waiter because his grouse is an elderly bird and not an adolescent. But he is an agreeable companion full of information about people. His views of things are deplorable in the extreme. He has no ordinary common sense about politics. He advocates an alliance with Japan. Now that is just wrong-headed, and with wrong-headedness I have small sympathy and little patience.

We then went upstairs to the lounge where a band played and where Teenie played piquette with Alice Wynn. She failed to wyn. I talked to Philip about his Knole scheme. He is really keen about it and has gone into the subject thoroughly. His idea is to get the Government to accept certain places (there is a list of some 20 first class and some 430 second class national monuments) as a national possession in their entirety—including park, furniture, gardens and general 'condition'. The Treasury would accept as payment for death duties the transference of an equivalent value in these possessions. The objects thus transferred would belong to the state who would lend them on trust to the owners. Thus Eddie [Sackville-West] could pledge the furniture of Knole as payment in death duties; the furniture would remain there, and all the Government would ask would be that it should not be sold or otherwise dispersed, that the public should be admitted, and that the owners, as guardians, should take all proper precautions for maintenance etc. He thinks he will persuade Neville Chamberlain [Chancellor of the Exchequer] to accept this scheme. It would be a magnificent thing for Knole if he could.[2]

HAROLD TO VITA

20 September 1934

RMS *Berengaria*
One day from New York

We had Professor Catlin and his bright little wife to luncheon. Her name is Vera Brittain. She wrote a book called *Testament of Youth*.[3] He is an austere and vain type. She is like a thin robin pecking with

---

2. Lord Lothian's scheme was carried out by the National Trust Act of 1937. His own house, Blickling in Norfolk, passed to the National Trust in 1940, and Knole in 1946.
3. Her book, published in 1933, was an eloquent exposure of the horrors of the First World War, seen through a woman's eyes. Her husband, George Catlin, was appointed Professor of Politics at Cornell University in 1924 at the age of twenty-eight.

bright eyes. He is lecturing to an American University on political theory. She is lecturing upon the *Testament of Youth* to several women's clubs. I gave her much sound advice. So sound was my advice, so friendly and paternal my attitude, that they both consulted me separately regarding the education of their son aged seven. Catlin wanted to send him to Eton since he feels that it is the best education, being confirmed in that supposition by what his academic friends tell him. She wants more experimental methods and co-education. I said that co-education was calculated to make boys homosexual for life, whereas Eton was only calculated to make them homosexual till 23 or 24. She said she didn't mind about that, but she felt Eton was 'narrowing'. I said, "What do you mean by 'narrowing'?" She had no idea what she meant and made a vague and most unsuccessful gesture indicative of how narrowing the effect of Eton really was. I said it wasn't narrowing at all, and that she could take it from me, and if she didn't want to take it from me she could take it from you. I said that you loathed Eton from the depths of your noble soul, but that if we had a third son now aged seven, I believe that (under much protest and snorting, and after pinching Rebecq [dog] twice, hitting Abdul [donkey] on the nose, removing all food and drink from the budgerigars, sending Tom [gardener] to dig up the rondel and plant artichokes in it, telegraphing "Beast—so there" to Christopher [Hobhouse], and sending Dottie [Wellesley] a small pot of cheese from Woolworth) you would agree.

HAROLD TO VITA

23 September 1934

Deacon Brown's Point,
North Haven, Maine

I woke as we were approaching Rockland.[1] I pinched the clip of the blind and pulled it up. A Scotch mist, and by the railway embankment masses of stunted Golden Rod with rain-drops hanging. Rockland itself is a small place, a sort of log-cabin Shoreham [Sussex]. We

---

1. On the coast of Maine. North Haven is an island off it, where the Morrows had their summer home. This was Harold's first meeting with Elizabeth Morrow, whose husband's biography he had undertaken to write.

were met by the captain of the Morrows' *St Michael*, by a man I could not make out, by another man I could not make out and by a third man I could not make out. The retainers who attach themselves to American millionaires are disconcerting. There are always people hanging about who may be friends or under-gardeners or private detectives. Anyhow I shake hands all round, and if I include a chauffeur here and there, what does it matter in this egalitarian country?

There was a taxi at the station which took us to THE COPPER KETTLE where we breakfasted—George Rublee and I. Now that man George Rublee is an angel. About 63 I should think, huge and lank, the type of an American H.A.L. Fisher. A thoroughly nice man and we got on like anything.

The Copper Kettle was a wooden structure with neat tables in a veranda and a neat proprietress doing accounts at one of them. We had coffee and eggs and dough-nuts. I then walked across to the cable office and sent B.M. a many happy returns cable.[2] The man there was helpful in the best American way. "Now see here," he said, "when exactly do you wish this dame to receive your message?" I said that her birthday was September 23. "Is that so?" he commented. "But you see," I said, "I am not sure whether in England they deliver telegrams on a Sunday." "Is that so?" he said. "Well now, you just leave it to me. With our deferred rate, we can make certain sure that the lady gets her message before she retires for the night." I must say, there is something about this side of American manners which attracts me strongly. It has nothing about it of the prim self-consciousness of the English petty official.

We then went down to the little pier where something between a yacht and a steam launch awaited us. The Scotch mist hung over the little harbour and the spars and rigging of a little yacht at anchor were hung with heavy drops. We hummed out into a satin sea, accompanied by a soft circle of fog. The islands are some eight miles from the mainland and I enjoyed the forty odd minutes which it took us to creep cautiously towards them. We passed a school of porpoises. Among marine monsters, they give me the effect of hawks. They treat their element in so individual a manner, differing from the blind fumblings

---

2. Lady Sackville was seventy-two.

of lesser fish. Sharks are as eagles: porpoises as hawks. They flopped along slowly in the muggy satin sea.

Then a buoy appeared with two cormorants on it, and directly afterwards the dim outline of pine trees stepping gingerly down to the very edge of the rocks where the sea lapped. We swung in between two islands and across to a third where there was a landing stage. There we landed *O venusta Sirmio* [Catullus]. There was a little pier house and an inn with shingle sides. A station car was waiting for us—one of those cars which have yellow wood for sides and give a wagonette effect, and recall the Tyrol and shooting parties in East Prussia. We drove in and out of little bays with pines down to the water and eventually the pines became tidier and there were sweeps of mown grass between the plantations. "That," said Rublee, "is where Lindbergh lands." Then we swept down to the house. It is charming. It is of wood with shingle sides. The views all round (since the fog had begun to lift) are superb. Rocks and islands at every angle and the sea splashing in and out of dahlias.

Mrs Morrow advanced to meet us at the gate. A little woman— neat and ugly. We were given coffee in the drawing room. The whole thing is rather *House and Garden,* but not aggressively so. I have a dear little room on the ground floor with pink curtains and a super-bathroom next door. I had a bath and changed into more untidy clothes. I then went round the place with Mrs Morrow. The lawns run down between quite adequate flower-beds to the sea.

Mrs Morrow was in quite a state of excitement at my arrival. She had not slept all night. I feel that this book means so very much to her. I pray that I shall not disappoint her. She worships her husband's memory, but is intelligent enough not to wish to control what I write. I do not think that we shall have any differences.

VITA TO HAROLD　　　　　　　　　　　　　　*Sissinghurst*

25 September 1934

I am afraid it may be being rather painful for you, living in the Lindbergh milieu with this revived business about the baby going on.[1] It must be so horribly painful for those two nice people to have the whole question re-opened now. Personally, I would like to put the man into the electric chair with my own hands, and give him two minutes agony, to pay him out for the months of mental agony he made them endure. Ben and Gwen both say they can't understand this. But then you know that I am very revengeful when I love, and so I can understand other people being revengeful too. It seems to me that people are mostly very tame—but I daresay I'm wrong. Anyhow I know I would gladly torture anybody who had hurt anybody I really loved. "Revenge is a wild kind of justice."[2] It seems to me a right kind of justice.

HAROLD TO VITA   *Hinsdale, Massachusetts*

27 September 1934

Minna[3] was voluble and informative. She was a great friend of Constance Morrow [Anne's sister] and had often stayed there. She was interesting about Lindbergh. She said he is really no more than a mechanic and that had it not been for the lone-eagle flight [to Paris, 1927] he would now be in charge of a gasoline station on the outskirts of St. Louis. Although the Morrows were themselves of humble origin, yet they were always cultured people and distinguished. Thus Lindbergh is really of a lower social stratum and they treat him with aloof politeness as one treats a tenant's niece. He is himself simple and 'not easy'. Anne has a difficult task. It will be a strange experience being with them all for so long and in such intimate circumstances.

Dwight Morrow junior [b. 1908] is a tragedy in their lives. He was sent to a 'private' school—in fact to the American Eton. He was bullied during his first term there and went off his head. He heard

1. The Lindbergh baby was snatched from his cradle on 1 March 1932. A ransom was paid, but the baby had died within an hour of being kidnapped. The police arrested Bruno Hauptmann, a German carpenter, as a suspect two days before Harold landed in New York.
2. Francis Bacon, *Of Revenge.*
3. Minna Curtiss taught in Northampton College and ran a farm in the Berkshire Hills, where Harold was staying with her.

voices calling him, which is a thing no sane person ought to hear. Remember that, my poppet, and when you start hearing voices you must go to a doctor. Anyhow they shut him up in a private asylum and in the end he recovered. But today he is still nervous and undeveloped and unstable. This is a mortification to Mrs Morrow, who is not really kind to the boy. When the baby was kidnapped one of the news-service people on the radio put out that one theory was that the crime had been committed by the Morrows' 'lunatic' son. This was not a pleasant thing to have broadcast, nor did it diminish the self-consciousness of young Dwight. One way or another, therefore, I expect my three months at Englewood to be rich in human problems.

We climbed up in the heat and it became cooler and gradually the woods increased both in thickness and colour and there were mountain streams tumbling under wooden bridges. We stopped at Archie Mac-Leish's farm.[4] A nice wooden house with green shutters and the shadows of vines upon long deck chairs. It is on the ridge of a hill with fine views over wooded mountains. We sat there on the lawn and had cocktails. Mrs MacLeish was in a bathing dress, and as she looks like Siegfried, Sieglinda and Odin all rolled into one, it was an expansive sight. Archie was in corduroy and a singlet.

He has lost all his money and supports himself by journalism. He is now very famous in this country as he won the Pulitzer prize. He is writing a play in free verse on the subject of the great depression of 1932–33. He says it is the best thing he has ever written. He also experiments in the ballet, and says that it is the perfect form of expression. We discussed the American character. He said that the essential thing to remember was that American men are essentially cerebral. The fact that they are not intellectual makes foreigners think that they are unconcerned with things of the mind. This is a mistake. The brain of an American works all the time, but it works in terms of fact, not in terms of ideas. They have no sensuous perceptions. I enjoyed the conversation. People like Archie are really of far more value to me than the average 'class-mate of '95' who has not noticed the differences between people. I really like that man and admire him. He admires Auden hugely. Stephen [Spender] also.

---

4. Archibald MacLeish, the American poet, then aged forty-two. His poem *Conquistador* had won the Pulitzer Prize in 1933. Harold had first known him in Teheran.

Minna told me her life story after dinner which took place in a very odd room lit by candles in old iron-work stands and off a table painted with the arms of the Curtiss's from a design in the Musée de Cluny. Afterwards we sat in her big room and discussed her life, her brother's life, her father's life, Duncan Grant's life, Miss Bingham's life, Mr Bingham's life (which is indeed odd),[5] Bunny [David] Garnett's life, Stephen Tomlin's life—but NOT, I am glad to say, my life. I went to bed at midnight in the little hut across the lane. There is a bed in the room and a bed outside in the porch surrounded with meat-safe stuff to keep off flies. Frogs croaked from the stream. I could see stars. I slept beautifully.

Today we had arranged to go and see Robert Frost. I discovered however that he lived 60 miles away and that it would take us five hours to go there and back. It was so pleasant here this morning when I woke up—that I struck at Frost. I sent Minna a message to say could we get out of it. She was delighted.

HAROLD TO VITA   *Englewood, New Jersey*

30 September 1934

I confess that these entries into New York [Grand Central Station] are impressive. There was this vast onyx cathedral, bathed in subdued lights, soft to the foot, soothing to the eye, impressive to the sense. Great limousines slid in upon india-rubber flooring, and magnificent lifts moved passengers from one level to the other. It is like the subway at Piccadilly Circus but enlarged to the scale of the baths of Caracalla. The red-caps were, as always, solicitous and fatherly. I did not know where to find the car. "Now don't you worry about that—that'll be all right—you just stay right here." The vast Cadillac of the Estate of Dwight W. Morrow then slid glistening and enormous into my ken. I entered it. It crackled out between onyx and marble into the superb plutocratic canyon of Park Avenue. On and on we crackled, down Fifth Avenue, through Central Park, on the Riverside Drive. The

5. The United States Ambassador in London and his beautiful daughter Henrietta, who was much taken up by the Bloomsbury Group. Stephen Tomlin, the sculptor of Virginia Woolf, was much in love with her.

skyscrapers above the park flashed and winked from a million windows. It is impossible to renounce the exhilaration of such triumphant human energy. London seems in comparison to shrink untidily and to become like Hildenborough Station compared to Versailles. The *metropolitan* can scarcely go further, and on such a scale that the lack of history and organic development does not irritate and depress. After all the Pyramids are standardised, but when you standardise monoliths, their very repetition is impressive. I admit that New York at night is one of the most impressive visions in the world.

A terrific thunderstorm crashed over us as we crossed the Hudson. But it was no good God trying to show off in that way. He cannot do it in New York. I grant you that as a thunderstorm it was one of the best I have ever seen God indulge in. But it just didn't work. It was no more disturbing than the night-flash of a tram wire when a car crosses the points.

We approached Epping Forest (since it is in such terms that you must visualize this place)—the same distance as Epping [from London], the same effect of street lamps in stunted trees, the same idea that in the recesses of those trees lie sardine tins, rain-soaked copies of the *Daily Mirror,* and the corpses of unwanted babies. There is a long approach to the house through a gate. At the gate a man kept guard and waved us on with an electric torch. To be accurate, there is no gate, only two piers and a little hutch in which the detectives group and grouse. The car hummed up the hill between dripping trees, and splattered upon the sweep in front of the house.

Banks, the butler, was waiting. "Mrs Morrow," he said, "is dining out with Mr Lamont. Colonel and Mrs Lindbergh are here." He led the way through the *Home and Garden* hall to the *Home and Garden* boudoir. There were Anne and Charles. Anne like a Geisha—shy, Japanese, clever, gentle—obviously an adorable little person. Charles Lindbergh—slim (though a touch of chubbiness about the cheek), school-boyish yet with those delicate prehensile hands which disconcert one's view of him as an inspired mechanic. They are smiling shyly. Lindbergh's hand was resting upon the collar of a dog.

I had heard about that dog. He has figured prominently in the American newspapers. He is a police dog of enormous proportions. Martin [Vita's alsatian] in comparison is a mere martinette. His name is Thor. I smiled at him a little uncertainly. Not for a moment did

Lindbergh relax his hold on the collar. It is this monster which guards Lindbergh baby no. 2. "What a nice dog!" I said.

"You will have," he answered, "to be a little careful at first, Mr Nicolson."

"Is he very fierce?"

"He's all that. But he will get used to you in time."

"Thor is his name, is it not? I read about him in the papers." I stretched a hand towards him. "Thor!" I said, throwing into the word an appeal for friendship which was profoundly sincere. He then made a noise in his throat such as only tigers make when waiting for their food. It was not a growl, it was not a bark. It was a deep pectoral regurgitation—predatory, savage, hungry. Lindbergh smiled a little uneasily. "It will take him a week or so," he said, "to become accustomed to you." He then released his hold upon the collar. I retreated rapidly to the fire-place, as if to flick my ash away from my cigarette. Thor stalked towards me. I thought of you and my two sons and my past life and England's honour. "Thor!" I exclaimed, "good old man . . ." The tremor in my voice was very tremulous. Lindbergh watched the scene with alert, but aloof, interest. "If he wags his tail, Mr Nicolson, you need have no fear." Thor wagged his tail and lay down.

I had a stiff whiskey and soda and talked to Anne about Mrs Rublee. Feeling better after that, I turned to Lindbergh. "What happens," I asked, "if Thor does not wag his tail?" "Well," he said, "you must be careful not to pass him. He might get hold of you." "By the throat?" I asked—trying, but not with marked success, to throw a reckless jollity into my tone. "Not necessarily," he answered. "And if he does that, you must just stay still and holler all you can." Well, well—I must grin and bear it. By the time you get this I shall either be front page news, or Thor's chum.

HAROLD TO VITA   *Englewood, New Jersey*

1 October 1934

I got your telegram yesterday, bless you. Twenty-one years have we belonged to each other. That is a long period of time. My darling, you know when I pause and look back upon that stretch of time, I feel such gratitude to you. I know you loathe marriage and that it is not a natural state for you. But I also know you love me dearly. And I am grateful to you right inside myself and right through myself and as part of my inner core for having been so gentle to me and so unselfish. Whatever happens, nothing can take from me those twenty-one years. I know that I shall die in agony tomorrow and that Ben will fall down the well and Niggs be run over by a helicopter. I know all that. But there is *la chose acquise*—those twenty-one years of perfect life. You know when I look back upon my life since 1913 I feel almost frightened by my own felicity. Think of it only in terms of laughter, my dearest, how much we have laughed together! Or in terms of the little things we share as memories—the Dolomites and Resht [Persia] and that night at St Cergues and our early gardening efforts and the day at the F.O. when I gave you Turf [a dog]. A million delicate memories which only you and I can share in this world and which will remain with us when the other dies as a ground-swirl of the perished leaves of hope.[1] Just gratitude to fate and you.

Yesterday, I drove out with Mrs Morrow to the Palisades above the Hudson river where Tom Lamont[2] has a villa or home. It was all typically American millionaire. No sign when one had entered the property, just mown grass and neat trees and a tarred sweep. Then as we approached the house there was the detective in his hutch, scrutinising and then taking off a shabby trilby slouchily. Then the sweep in front of the house with four or five grand cars parked. Then the hall, white and black marble floor and a huge coromandel screen. Then the living room, pitch-pine, Raeburns, huge dahlias, *petit point,* the latest books. Then the porch—elaborate deck-chairs and wire-netting to keep off flies. No garden near the house but a bit of Italian nonsense on the way to the swimming pool. Fine views up the Hudson River. All very good taste and depressing. No inner reality.

But what can they do, poor people? After all, nothing is real here except the sky-scrapers. If I were an American I might desire to evolve a domestic architecture on Le Corbusier lines which would bear some

---

1. "The ground whirl of the perished leaves of Hope." Rossetti, *The House of Life.*
2. Chairman of J. P. Morgan and Company, then aged sixty-four.

relation to the sky-scrapers. But would I? I have no wish at all to live among steel arm-chairs. When it comes to comfort, William and Mary goes best with chintz and flowers and books. It is rather like an Atlantic luxury liner. Once one starts going modern it becomes a restless stunt. The only alternative is to copy the English gentleman's home and not mind about the fake. Yet my heart sinks when I think of all those millions of period rooms, correct, tasteful and uniform. We are better at that sort of thing, you and I. I do not see any of these millionaire libraries being diversified by a bit of stone from Persepolis, some bass left about, Martin's latest bone, Tikki, a hammer, a Rodin, a tobacco tin full of seeds, some loose films, a back number of the *New Statesman,* an evening shoe on its way back to the bedroom, and a soda-water syphon. Yet it is these varied and illuminating objects which make our rooms real and personal.

Mrs Lamont is an ass, as you know. Tom Lamont is a nice intelligent man. I walked with him. Norman Davis was there. He is the big noise now in American diplomacy and the adviser of Roosevelt. He is to be their delegate at the Naval Conference [in London, 1935]. At tea, he talked. Now the oddest thing about Americans is that they never listen. Davis was telling us what he felt would be the prospects of the Conference. He was talking seriously and earnestly. His idea is that the Franco-Italian pact and the Russo-French understanding will force Germany to come to heel. He discussed whether the true pacifist should not be strong and forceful rather than weak. What he said was thoughtful, well expressed, and immensely important as coming from him. But did they listen? Not for one moment. "Now let me give you another cup of tea, Mr Nicolson. I am afraid that our tea here is not as good as the tea you get in England . . ." Chatter, chatter; interrupt, interrupt. If I understood the explanation of this, I should understand more about American civilisation. Is it utter frivolity of mind, or merely a complete lack of all sense of real values? I suspect it has something to do with the position of women, or rather with the vast gulf which separates the male and the female in this continent. Women are supposed to discuss art, literature and the Home. Men are supposed to discuss business. Whatever it may be, it irritates me beyond words. It is as though Sir John Simon were lunching at Sissinghurst and explaining his policy to Venizelos and then you interrupted by talking about the Russian ballet. You would not do such things. But why do they?

Mrs Morrow has gone up for two days to Cleveland to see her mother. I am alone with the Lindberghs. He amuses and puzzles me. On the one hand, he is a mechanic and quite uneducated. On the other hand he is shrewd and intelligent. He has also got a sense of humour. Mrs Morrow mentioned that Mrs Lamont, who is not air-minded, said she would only fly if he took her up. "Now that is just like these old dames," he said, "just because I flew alone to Purris they think I am a safe pilot. That's just silly." He has an obsession about publicity and I agree with him. He told me that when [President] Coolidge presented him with a medal after his Paris flight he had to do it three times over—once in his study which was the real occasion, and twice on the lawn of the White House for the movie people. "The fust time," he said, "I was kind of moved by the thing. After all, I was more or less of a kid at the time and it seemed sort of solemn to me to be given that thing by the President of the United States. But when we had to go through the whole damned show over again in the yard, I mean lawn—me standing sideways to the President and looking an ass—I felt I couldn't stand for it. Coolidge didn't seem to care or notice. He repeated his speech twice over just in the same words. It just seemed a charade to me." I asked him whether he also repeated his own little speech. "Well, I mumbled something—but I was kind of sick about the thing and sore about it and I just murmured as low as I could in order to do in the movietone."

He adores that dog. I must say it is a magnificent animal. He trains it in a way I have never seen a dog trained. He says to it, "Now, Thor, you go and be nice to Mr Nicolson," and Thor trots across to me and puts his chin on my knee. He says, "Now, Thor, go and get a magazine for Anne." And off he trots into the library returning with a magazine in his teeth. "Now, Thor, you take Anne upstairs," at which he rushes at Anne, seizes her wrist gently in his teeth, and tugs her from the room.

Another odd thing. We have breakfast together. The papers are on the table. The Lindbergh case is still front-page news. It *must* mean something to him. Yet he never glances at them and chatters quite happily to me about Roosevelt and the air-mail contracts. It is not a pose. It is merely a determined habit of ignoring the press. I like the man. I daresay he has his faults but I have not yet found them. She is a little angel.

HAROLD TO VITA   *Englewood*

9 October 1934

Yesterday Hauptmann was identified by Lindbergh as possessing the voice he had heard calling in the cemetery.[1] Yet this dramatic event did not record itself upon the life here. Lindbergh was at breakfast as usual and thereafter helped me to unload my Leica camera. He is very neat about such things and I am clumsy. He then said, "Well, I have got to go up to Noo Yark—want a lift?" I said no. Then I worked hard at my files and at luncheon there was only Anne and me as Mrs Morrow had gone to some charity committee. Towards the end of luncheon Lindbergh arrived and we chatted quite gaily until coffee came. We had that in the sun parlour, and when it was over I rose to go. The moment I had gone I saw him (in the mirror) take her arm and lead her into the little study. Obviously he was telling her what happened in the court. But they are splendid in the way they never intrude this great tragedy on our daily life. It is real dignity and restraint.

At 3.0 I went out for my walk in the garden. The paths wind in and out of the property and over the stream. Anne and Jon [her younger son] joined me. Jon is bad at going down steps and has to turn round and do them on his tummy. He is a dear little boy, with the silkiest fair curls. I think of his brother's little head being bashed by Hauptmann. They *must* realize that what happened was that the child began to yell and they tried to knock him unconscious. It is a ghastly thing to have in one's life and I feel profoundly sorry for them. The best way I can show it is by manifesting no curiosity. But it is awkward and rather farcical when I take up the paper at breakfast and it is full of nothing else. "Things seem to be getting rather dangerous in Spain," I say. But I am sure that is the best attitude.

---

1. Where the ransom money was handed over on 2 April 1932.

HAROLD TO VITA   *Englewood*

10 October 1934

In odd moments when I am at a loose end (about eleven minutes in the day) I read Emily Dickinson. Now why on earth should your old buttock find such enjoyment in Emily Dickinson I really do not know. She is everything I ought by logic to loathe. She was pretentious, overweening, mystic and fey. Yet my admiration for her mind and personality throbs through this routine treatment. I know why it is. She is Virginia [Woolf] in 1860. "Then," she writes to Colonel T. W. Higginson, "there is a noiseless noise in the orchard which I let persons hear." "And so much lighter than day was it," she writes to Louisa Norcross, "that I saw a caterpillar measure a leaf down in the orchard . . . It seemed like a theatre, or a night in London, or perhaps like chaos." This was when a barn burnt at Amherst. But it is all superb, and gives me the excitement and increased awareness that Virginia gives. Has she read the book? Has she written about Emily Dickinson? Ask her. It is exactly her subject. Beg her to do an article. Really, darling, if there is such a thing as genius as definitive and recognisable as a cigar lighter—then this frail ugly little trout possessed it. "I am no portrait," she writes, "but am small like a wren; and my eyes, like the sherry that the guest leaves in a glass." That is superb. The whole little frail egoist is superb. Mrs [Elizabeth Barrett] Browning is just a charwoman in comparison. She means so much to me here in this instinctive but uneducated country that I wish you were here to talk about her. I know that in England I should loathe her. Over here, she seems Blake without the prophecy stunt. I am deeply grateful to her.

VITA TO HAROLD   *Sissinghurst*

14 October 1934

Raymond [Mortimer] was very sweet. He is a nice person so far as he goes, but soft. Really incorrigibly soft. He said Eddy had invited him to spend the whole of October-November at Knole, but he was afraid that "the beauty of Knole would overwhelm him and make him lazy." Now this seems to me funny, coming from Tray. When has he ever been anything but lazy? You will be surprised to hear that he has actually written two-thirds of his book on suicide. He is inordinately proud of having accomplished this much. I have refrained from asking him how long he has been at it.[1]

Then Charles Siepmann[2] arrived. I know you don't like him much, but really he is a stronger person than Tray, and a more real person. Gwen [St Aubyn] doesn't like him either, but rather came round to him today, which pleased me, because I do like Charles, and I mind when people I love don't like the people I like.

HAROLD TO VITA   *Englewood*

23 October 1934

New York looks superb as you approach it on an autumn evening over the Washington Bridge. It was clear last night and I could see the lights like fire-flies all round me. You know how fantastic is that Christmas-tree effect.

I drove to the club and dressed. I then drove to the River Club to dine with the Kermit Roosevelts. Marthe[3] appeared magnificently dressed and bejewelled. We dined. We drove to the theatre. It was a sort of pre-first night benefit performance for charity. The real first night is tonight. But the theatre was packed and I rather loathed it. I am not good at plays—they *take* so long. Yvonne Printemps was very charming and effective. But she sang rather bad Noel Coward songs rather badly, and there was too much 'charm' about it for my tastes. There was one large young man who wore a tight uniform with white trousers. They were too small for him. His bottom was like the dome of the Salute [Church, Venice]. When he turned round people sniggered, and for the rest of the play the poor man tried to back out of it. My heart went out to him, knowing how gross it is to be too large for one's clothes.

---

1. It was never finished, and consequently never published.
2. He had succeeded Hilda Matheson as Director of Talks at the BBC.
3. Princess Marthe Bibesco (1886–1973) was born in Rumania and married a cousin of Antoine Bibesco in 1901. She was a literary figure of distinction, as much at home in New York, London, and Paris as in her native country.

In the interval Marthe leant across to me. "Harold," she said, "will you take me round to see Yvonne Printemps?" Well you know, I am not good at this sort of expedition. But was I going to leave a beautiful princess in the lurch? I was not. I took her arm, tripping over my great-coat, and forgetting hers. We went out into the street. I asked a policeman. He said, Sur, he didn't know. So we went up an alley where there was much orange-peel, a smell of horses, and a vast iron ladder going up the side of the wall. But no stage door. Then we emerged again and tried the other side of the building. Marthe, flashing emeralds and diamonds, shuddered slightly. I felt like a knight errant— only the errant part of the proceeding was more marked than the knightly part. Anyhow to my astonishment and relief we got to a door marked "STAGE DOOR." I knocked. It was opened by a negro. "We want to see Princess Printemps," I said—being confused by the whole incident. He took that quite naturally and we were taken along a passage. We knocked at a door. An Algerian woman emerged. I said who we were, or rather who Marthe was, since I wasn't anything by that time worth being. And—would you believe it—we were received. Chrysanthemums and a huge mirror and Yvonne in an ivory dressing-gown. She was terribly nervous, on the verge of tears, but so glad to be able to talk French for once. She almost cried. *"Dieu, que c'est gentil de votre part, Madame—je me sentais tellement abandonée."* I was introduced as *"l'écrivain bien connu."* Yvonne swallowed both her tears and her ignorance of that fact, and gave me a hot, still tear-drenched, hand. Then we went back—and the silly billy of a play went on to the end.

HAROLD TO VITA   *Englewood*

5 November 1934 .

I spent the week end on Long Island. I think it was a good thing that your ancestors disposed of their possessions in this continent[1] since

---

1. In 1637 Edward Sackville, 4th Earl of Dorset, obtained a grant from Charles I of Long Island and other islands off the New England coast "not inhabited by any Christians."

I do not feel you would care for Long Island in the very least. You know that I am a social little cove, but I am not, I find, gregarious. I cannot conceive how these people endure the life they lead. Nobody ever seems to know who is lunching with whom and whose house is which. They drift in and out of those white porticoes howling at each other in merriment and neighbourliness.

I stayed with Mrs Kermit Roosevelt. Kermit is away. The house is a typical home, with a nice big library, and more untidy and less heated than other similar homes. I like the whole Roosevelt clan— they are at least thoroughly real people with no affectations or conventions. But they all live in a heap together on this point of Oyster Bay and their friends agglomerate round them. It is all very like Surbiton or Southampton Water. And it poured with rain. But I enjoyed it, and have returned this morning feeling soothed and well. Not that I was nervy or ill before. But of course the atmosphere of incense which floats here above the memory of Morrow is a trifle suffocating at moments. The Roosevelts are fresh air.

Teddy Roosevelt (the eldest of the clan) came to dinner with his wife. He has all the Roosevelt charm. Then on Sunday morning we went across to the Marshall Fields' place to play tennis. It is a huge house in a real park running at the edges down to the sea. The house is William and Mary—like Reigate Priory. There was no one there— but we went in. Very like an English stately home with coromandel screens, wood work, Raeburns and topographical pictures from Legatt. Fine carpets, magnificent massed chrysanthemums, a sense of enormous wealth. There was a closed racquet or tennis court with little rooms opening on to it. Italian gardens, bathing pools—and not a leaf allowed to disfigure the sweeps of grass. But as always in this country a terrible sense of UNREALITY robs it of all meaning. It has just been bought with money. It has never grown an inch by itself. There is none of that sense of the Raeburns having played among the woods as children which gives to our houses the aroma of continuity. Something horribly provisional mars this continent even at its most lovely.

The Marshall Field family itself is a dissolving view. The first wife was got rid of with a pretty little settlement of £200,000 a year. Audrey Coates, the second wife, is now in Reno also being got rid of at an approximate figure. I find all that depressing and unstable.

But the Roosevelts are real all right and rooted. Mrs Kermit took me to Theodore Roosevelt's house to see her mother-in-law, the old President's widow. A gentle, dignified, alert but untidy old lady—her hair in wisps. That in itself was a relief after all the rag-tag, bob-tail white heads I have seen. She was like old Lady Carnarvon. Ungainly and yet beautiful. The house is old fashioned and interesting. Enormous elephant tusks—some shot by T.R., some presented by various African potentates. What thrilled me most was a little case containing snapshots of the famous Döberitz review which Roosevelt attended in the Kaiser's company in 1911.[2] There were about 12 of these photographs mounted between sheets of glass and on the back of each the Emperor had scribbled remarks. These remarks are typical of his arrogance and indiscretion. "The Commander-in-Chief of the German Army and the Colonel of the Rough Riders discuss strategy together. A blow for that old peace-fool Carnegie." "Mr Roosevelt explains to the Emperor how if America and Germany stand together they can defy the world," and so on and so on. Mrs Roosevelt told me that these snapshots were sent round to their hotel by one of the emperor's aide-de-camps. Next morning a man came from the Foreign Office asking if they might have them back as they wanted to mount them in an album. Obviously they had guessed that the Emperor had scribbled indiscretions. T. R. refused to give them up, but said they would never go outside the family. At least he had the decency not to publish them.

I enjoyed all that. And the atmosphere of the place—rather like Clandeboye [Lord Dufferin's house in Ireland]—of an exuberant personality stamping his enormous range of interests upon his house.

HAROLD TO VITA   *Englewood*

13 November 1934

You have been to long barn (not worthy of capitals any more) and hadn't minded in the least. I wonder whether you would have minded

---

2. Theodore Roosevelt, who retired from the Presidency in 1909, reviewed the Imperial Guard at the Kaiser's side, the first civilian to do so.

had the bees been humming in at the big-room door. But Sissinghurst is more your spiritual home since it contains birthright and that sort of thing and a donjeon and a moat and the tower springing like a toolip. By the way, my sweet, in the American edition of Sissingbags[1] there is a Miss Print. At least I think so, but with you one can never tell. "Here," you exclaim, and fittingly, "tall and damask as a summer flower, Rise the brick gable and the *spring* tower." Now the word 'spring' strikes me, being illiterate in such things, as a Miss Print. I think it should be either 'springing' or 'springouth', 'springelth', 'springheld' or some dissyllabic anyway. But of course you may have meant to indicate that you had one tower for each season of the year (a thing of which you are fully capable), a winter tower, an autumn, and a summer tower plus spring ditto. Only, apart from the meaning, the word 'spring' just doesn't scan. Of course you may have felt that to put 'springing' in that line would clash with the next line in which "invading Nature crawls" all creepy crawly. But still I merely refer to the point.[2]

HAROLD TO VITA   *107 East 70th Street, New York*

22 November 1934

I wrote yesterday from Yale. After I had written I walked across to the lecture hall and mounted the tribune. There were about 300 undergraduates there—rows and rows of eager young faces. I talked for 45 minutes and then had 15 minutes for questions, which were intelligent and acute. When I had finished, they started clapping and then they started cheering. Seymour[3] said he had never heard them do that before. I confess to a great pleasure when I can hold the attention and stimulate the ideas of the rising generation. One feels at once that it is really worthwhile and that one is transferring something of one's experience. How different from lecturing to old women in pearls!

I have the definite impression that the new house system as adopted

1. *Sissinghurst,* Vita's poem published by the Hogarth Press in 1931.
2. It was a misprint. The word was "springing."
3. Charles Seymour, Master of Berkeley College, Yale University.

at Princeton, Harvard and Yale is going to revolutionize American education. They are all aware now that the former system, while it imparted superficial knowledge on a great many topics, did not produce educated men. I must say that the young men who asked me questions yesterday were convincingly acute. I have a deep feeling that America is abandoning its old quantitative standards for more qualitative standards. And this will be of immense value to the human race.

After my lecture I visited the university with Seymour. Collegiate gothic can go no further. It is really beautifully done, and I am not sure that this style is not really more suitable to universities than the bright brisk Georgian of Harvard. The Library is superb and all the facilities put at the disposal of these young people are lavish, opulent and not unwise. I went into some undergraduates' rooms. They are better than ours, and the washing facilities are tremendous. But how strange is the gregariousness of the American race! Each boy has a bed-sitter in theory. In practice however they share bedrooms, sleeping cheek by jowl, and keep the other bedrooms as joint studies. In England no undergraduate would willingly share a bedroom with another undergraduate. In America men are never quite happy unless surrounded by other men. This is one of the crude sides of their civilisation. But I like them—especially the professorial and academic class.

HAROLD TO VITA   *Englewood*

14 February 1935

Last night's experience was very strange.[1] Dinner was rather strained. You see, that morning Judge Trenchard had summed up in the Hauptmann trial. He did it very well and his statement was one of which even an English judge need not have been ashamed. Lindbergh tells me that it reads more impartial than it sounded. For instance, he kept on saying to the jury, in going over some of Haupt-

---

1. Harold had been in England during December and January, and now returned to America to complete his book on Dwight Morrow. He reached Englewood on the very day when Bruno Hauptmann was found guilty of murdering the Lindbergh baby.

mann's evidence, "Do you believe that?" Now that sounds all right when read in print. But what he actually said was, "Do *you* believe *THAT?*" Anyhow, the jury had been in consultation five hours when we sat down to dinner and a verdict was expected at any moment. They knew that the first news would come over the wireless so that there were two wirelesses turned on—one in the pantry next to the dining-room and one in the drawing-room. Thus there were jazz and jokes while we had dinner and one ear strained the whole time for the announcer from the court-house. Lindbergh had a terrible cold which made it worse.

Then after dinner we went into the library and the wireless was on in the drawing-room next door. They were all rather jumpy. Mrs Morrow, with her unfailing tact, brought out a lot of photographs and we had a family council as to what illustrations to choose for the book. This was just interesting enough to divert, but not to rivet, attention. Then Dick Scandrett[2] came over to see me. It was about 10.45. The Lindberghs and Morgans and Mrs Morrow left us alone. We discussed Dwight for some twenty minutes. Suddenly Betty [Mrs Morrow] put her head round the huge coromandel screen. She looked very white. "Hauptmann," she said, "has been condemned to death without mercy."

We went into the drawing-room. The wireless had been turned onto the scene outside the court-house [at Flemington, New Jersey]. One could hear the almost diabolic yelling of the crowd. They were all sitting round—Miss Morgan with embroidery; Anne looking very white and still. "You have now heard," broke in the voice of the announcer, "the verdict in the most famous trial in all history. Bruno Hauptmann now stands guilty of one of the foulest . . ." "Turn that off, Charles, turn that off." Then we went into the pantry and had ginger beer. And Charles sat there on the kitchen dresser looking very pink about the nose. "I don't know," he said to me, "whether you have followed this case carefully. There is no doubt at all that Hauptmann did the thing. My one dread all these years has been that they would get hold of someone as a victim about whom I wasn't sure. I am sure about this—quite sure. It is this way . . ."

And then quite quietly, while we all sat round in the pantry, he

---

2. Dwight Morrow's nephew.

went through the case point by point. It seemed to relieve all of them. He did it very quietly, very simply. He pretended to address his remarks to me only. But I could see that he was really trying to ease the agonised tension through which Betty and Anne had passed. It was very well done. It made one feel that here was no personal desire for vengeance or justification; here was the solemn process of law inexorably and impersonally punishing a culprit.

Then we went to bed. I feel that they all are relieved. If Hauptmann had been acquitted it would have had a bad effect on the crime situation in this country. Never has circumstantial evidence been so convincing. If on such evidence a conviction had not been secured, then all the gangsters would have felt a sense of immunity. The prestige of the police has been enormously enhanced by this case.[3]

Poor Anne—she looked so white and horrified. The yells of the crowd were really terrifying. "That," said Lindbergh, "was a lynching crowd."

He tells me that Hauptmann was a magnificent looking man. Splendidly built. But that his little eyes were like the eyes of a wild boar. Mean, shifty, small and cruel.

HAROLD TO VITA   *Cuernavaca, Mexico* [4]

22 February 1935

Such a marvellous morning. I woke up in my little cottage and flung open the door. A blaze of sunshine and plumbago greeted me. The datura in my little patio smells even in day time. There is a feeling of something more tropical than Tangier or Sicily. It is given, I think, by the banana trees which are in fruit. A Gauguin effect with the soft footed gardeners in their huge hats. The hoses have sprinklers, and sparkle on the grass. I go up terrace after terrace on wide tiled steps

3. It is only right to add that considerable doubt has since been thrown on the evidence, and that Hauptmann may have gone to the electric chair an innocent man. See, particularly, Ludovic Kennedy's *The Airman and the Carpenter,* 1985.

4. Dwight Morrow was American Ambassador to Mexico, 1927–29, and he bought this house at Cuernavaca.

edged with huge vases of geraniums and heliotrope. The swimming pool on the central terrace reflects oleander and a blue sky. The awnings are lowered over the upper patios. It is more than summer.

After tea last night we walked in the little town. There is an old baroque cathedral rather tumbled down. There is the palace of Cortes who lived here after the conquest. There are the gardens of the villa inhabited by Maximilian and Carlotta.[5] For the rest, it is exactly like some small Spanish town—Ronda or Algerciras. Along the lane behind the house trot rows of donkeys like at Fez. Thud thud thud thud.

The disadvantage of this place is that it is a weekend resort for Mexico City. I foresee that we shall be overwhelmed with visitors. But here in my cottage (which reminds me of the Villa Pestillini [Florence] cottage) I am detached. I hope to work well here.

We dined out of doors. After dinner we went up to the mirador and looked out over the dark little town to distant shapes of mountains. Popo [catepetl-volcano] was not visible. He is extinct. But what a terrible menace he must have seemed flaming up there among the stars.

Bless you my own darling. I wish you were not six thousand miles away. I cannot get rid of the loneliness and home-sickness which that thought produces. And I hate not to share these vivid pictures with you.

HAROLD TO VITA   *Deacon Brown's Point,*
                                            North Haven, Maine
11 July 1935

We had an almost perfect day yesterday.[6] The sun was very hot but the air was scented with fresh seaweed and pines. I must say this island is a divine spot. It must be exactly like the Western Highlands, with distant mountains, a whole archipelago around one, morning mists, and heavy rain-drops on the pines.

---

5. Ferdinand Maximilian of Austria, Emperor of Mexico, 1864–67, and his wife, Princess Charlotte of Belgium.
6. Harold had returned to the United States to work on his proofs of *Dwight Morrow,* and brought his elder son Ben with him, then aged twenty.

Ben and I worked all morning in our little cottage. He is doing Bismarck. I was doing the final revisions to my proofs and starting on the index. After luncheon we watched Lindbergh doing stunts in his little scarlet aeroplane. It is a divine little instrument, and he plays with it like one plays with a canoe on a swimming pool. Up there in the high air he flashed and dived and circled above the sea and islands just like a boy plunging in the sea. The scarlet wings flashed in the sun and then darkened to shadow.

Then he came down and we played tennis, or rather Ben and the Lindberghs played tennis. I sat and watched with a book. Ben plays a good style but inaccurately. Like my handwriting, it looks efficient from a great distance.

Our dear Benzie—what a strange person he is! He is so absolutely himself. He isn't shy exactly, since he never appears embarrassed or awkward. But he is very silent, intervening but seldom in the conversation. Yet his agreeable smile saves him from appearing morose.

It was a lovely day and we sat on the terrace looking down on the sea and the islands. Anne said to him, "Would you like to come sailing this afternoon?" "No," said Ben, "sailing bores me." I confess that I was rather taken aback. I reproved him afterwards, but he said, "I think it wrong to pretend to like a thing which I don't like. You always say, Daddy, that you hate music." I then explained that he had put on his 'voice', and that his remark sounded not merely like a curt refusal but like a snub. He was terribly distressed by this and brooded over it. I asked Anne afterwards whether she had thought him rude, and what was one to do between telling people to be absolutely frank and yet training them to observe social conventions. She said that she liked him for it. But all the same Ben does lack zest: it is so beautiful here, and the bathing and tennis and general charm of the place render him happy: but he does not show it; he just mouches around looking bored. I know that he is not bored in the very least. But they, who expect high spirits and affability in the young, must feel him very 'dumb' and 'effete'. But perhaps not. One is unduly sensitive about the impression people of whom one is very fond make on other people of whom one is fond. He loves Anne, who is angelic to him. He likes Mrs Morrow. He is thrilled by Lindbergh.

30 August 1935

On the train from Dieppe I found myself in a compartment with three Americans—aged father, middle-aged mother, and much bespotted son. The mother was of the talkative type and kept on drawing the attention of her son Junior to the beauty of France. "Junior," she said to him, "you reeely must look. You remember Mrs Furnivall said that the part between Dieppy and Purris was vurry vurry interesting." Junior merely grunted and went on reading *Time*. And I, pretending to read Charles Lamb, wondered how a woman of over forty could still suppose that Dieppe was called Dieppy. Then the passport man came in. "Les passeports, s'v'plait, M'ssieurs, mesdames." "Junior," screamed the old lady, "go and get your father: he is in the washroom." And in truth the old man had disappeared. "Pass! Pass!", said the conductor breaking into English. When the incident was over, she leant back and with dreamy eyes said, "I reely must learn that word for passport—I reely must—it was 'pass-pass' that he said, Junior. Let's remember that."

Now you know how I always determine to be kind to Americans, especially the dowdy sort. But I did not help on this occasion. I think she thought I was French as I was reading the *Matin*. But when I picked up Lamb which was obviously an English book, she began throwing out leading questions. "My," she said, "look, Junior, that house had Mairie written on it. Now that can't be like our Mary, can it? How I wish that someone could explain these things to me. I find them so *interesting*." But I did not offer to explain.

Then the father came back from the washroom and slept heavily so that the mother had to cease her chatter. I crept out and went and had some tea. When I got back, we were only some forty minutes from Paris. I wanted to smoke my pipe and the father had woken up. I thought it time to emerge from my reserve. "Madam," I said, "would you object if I smoked a pipe?" "Why no," she answered, as if I had pulled the plug of an enormous lavatory, "go right ahead. I always say to my son, don't I, Junior?—I always say, a pipe is a *clean* smoke— now a cigar . . ." and on that she let forth a perfect Colorado River on the subject of cigars. The ice having thus been broken, she paddled ahead exuberantly. They were going to Geneva, for the Conference of course, so difficult to get rooms—so on, so on. I identified him as the rather insignificant correspondent of some Methodist journal in Milwaukee. The old man eyed me sleepily. I had told the old lady that I was off to Venice for a week. "Why," said the husband, "for only one week?" So I explained to him that there was a crisis over a country called Abyssinia, that we took one point of view and Mussolini the other—in fact I explained the whole situation to him in clear, but very simple, terms. "Is that so?", he said from time to time. He was a nice old bedint and my heart warmed to them. I would help them at the station and see them to their hotel—after all I was in no hurry and they would be so utterly lost.

By that time we were running into Paris. "Batignolles," read the old lady on a signal box, "Now whatever can *that* mean?" I assured her that it meant much the same sort of thing as Englewood meant Englewood. "Fancy that, now," she answered, nodding her head wisely. "St Lazare Poste I" flashed by. "Now that, I suppose, means Lazarus like in English, the raising of Lazarus you know, Junior!" "Perhaps," I said, "you will allow me to help with your luggage and things?" "Well that's reel kind of you, mister, but they are coming to meet us."

They were. For as we emerged onto the platform there were three obvious American secretaries from the Embassy and some photographers. The eldest of the secretaries advanced and raised his hat. "Senator Pope?" he enquired of the old man.[1] I bolted to a taxi.

I jumped inside. "Grand Hotel," I shouted. Then I lay back and thought it over. Had I really said anything foolish? Since Senator Pope, as you know, is Roosevelt's Colonel House and has been spending the last three days locked in the embraces of Sam Hoare [Foreign Secretary] and [Anthony] Eden. Had I said anything very foolish? Now why is it that I am exposed so often to situations as absurd as this? I blushed at the thought. I slid the little window aside. "Non pas le Grand Hotel," I shouted, "l'Hotel Ritz, Place Vendôme."

As a matter of fact I did not show off in front of Pope. But ten years ago I would have.

---

1. Senator James P. Pope was then aged only fifty-one. He was a lawyer by profession, U.S. Senator from Idaho, 1933–39, and then Director of the Tennessee Valley Authority. He had married Pauline Horn in 1913, and they had two sons.

*In October 1935 Harold was adopted as National Labour candidate for West Leicester, and on 14 November he was elected to Parliament with the narrow majority of eighty-seven over his Labour opponent. Immediately he became involved in great issues of foreign affairs. Hitler reoccupied the Rhineland and Mussolini invaded Abyssinia. Vita, as the following letter shows, did not share his political interests, preferring her garden and her books (*Saint Joan of Arc, Pepita, *and her poem* Solitude *were published in this period) to the social and political dramas like the King's Abdication, which Harold was experiencing in London. They wrote to each other every day when they were apart, and spent the weekends alone together at Sissinghurst. Lady Sackville's death in January 1936 gave Vita more financial security, and she refurnished much of the house with her mother's treasures.*

V I T A   T O   H A R O L D   *Sissinghurst*

28 October 1935

My darling Hadji—I fear you have gone away hurt—and I mind that dreadfully. It is no good going over old ground, so I won't—only to say that apart from what you called 'principle', I do genuinely think that an isolated appearance [in Leicester] would be worse than none, because of its inconsistency, and that it would lead to bazaars and things *after* the election, if you get in, as I do very truly and sincerely hope you will. Still I am more sorry than I can say to have hurt you, but do remember, darling, that we had always been agreed on this matter even before you got adopted, and I quite thought that your views coincided with mine—as I still think they did, until agents and people started badgering you. Do remember also what I said last night, that I had always cared very very deeply about your writing and even your broadcasting (don't murder me!), and my admiration for your very rare gift, which I rate *far* higher than you do, is great and has always been accompanied by the very deepest interest, so don't run away with the idea that I "have never taken any interest," as you said, in the things which mattered to you. You know as well as I do, if you stop to think, that this is an absurd contention!

Darling, don't let this make a rift?

Mar

HAROLD TO VITA   *Leicester*

10 November 1935

Yesterday I spent the morning canvassing. You know that I am not very good at intruding into other people's lives—and this was in my own interests. "Good morning, Mrs Brown, may I come in for a moment? I hate to disturb you, but as I was visiting round here, I thought you might wish to have a look at the candidate." Mrs Brown has a look in which the emotion of disgust struggles unsuccessfully with the emotion of contempt. "My vote's my own," she snaps. "Good morning, Mrs Brown, and a nice day isn't it? Quite a brisk snap in the air this morning." "My vote's my own, anyway, and I won't tell even the old man which way I'm using it." "Quite right, Mrs Brown, that's the spirit, and I wish all the electors felt the same. Goodbye to you, Mrs Brown." The latter makes no answer, and we then knock next door at Mrs Smith.

Of course I do not have to do much of that side of the business myself, and really only did it as there was nothing else to do at the moment and I wanted to give a good example to my workers. One cannot expect them to do the work one hesitates to do oneself.

Then in the afternoon I attended two football matches. There was tea at half time and my two opponents Crawfurd [Liberal] and Morgan [Labour] came up and talked to me. Crawfurd is hell—very slimy and unreliable. But Morgan is a delicious sturdy man whom I liked at once. I am glad that if I do not get in, he will get in.

I got back late to my office. The woman downstairs said, "Oh Mr Nicolson, a gentleman has just been in to see you—a friend he said he was." "What was he like?" I asked. "Oh, he was very tall and thin and a little blind I should say from the glasses he wore, and he is round at the hotel waiting for you." So round to the hotel I went, and there was Aldous Huxley wearing the strangest clothes. I gave him some tea; and he talked for an hour. I have never heard him talk so readily or so brilliantly. It was like the most perfect hose compared to a tea-pot with a broken spout. He seemed to think it perfectly natural to find me standing National Labour, and he encouraged me enormously just by taking it all for granted and saying that he admired me for doing it. I shall always like him more for that visit. He took me right away from the Turkey rugs of the Grand Hotel and the mud-baths of ignorance and meanness in which I have been wallowing of late.

Then in the evening was one of those bloody working men's clubs and a bright little speech from me.[1]

HAROLD TO VITA   *4 King's Bench Walk*

20 November 1935

We went into dinner. I found that being the only man who has ever *gained* a seat for National Labour I was regarded as a museum piece. I talked to Ramsay.[2] He is a fine battered figure and I love him. He was so *pleased* with my success. "My dear Harrold—that was a grrrand fight—a grrand victory—and mark you, I *know* Weest Leicester—you must have had an ungodly task."

Afterwards over coffee in a private room he discoursed to us in the old campaigner style about the future of the National Labour Party. I confess that it was somewhat like King Charles I addressing

1. On 14 November Harold won the seat, after a recount, with 15,821 votes over Labour's 15,734 and Liberal's 4,621.
2. Ramsay MacDonald, former Labour Prime Minister, now leader of the National Labour Party.

the Cavaliers from the Whitehall scaffold. Yet out of all the muddled truculence of the thing there did in fact emerge an idea. It was this. "In your hands rests the future of Tory Socialism. You eight people are the seed-bed of seminal ideas. The young Tories are on your side. Work hard: think hard: and you will create a classless England."

HAROLD TO VITA   *4 King's Bench Walk*

20 February 1936

When I got to the Londonderry party, there was a dear little patapouf in black sitting on the sofa, and she said to me, "We have not met since Berlin," and I sat down beside her and chattered away all friendly thinking meanwhile, "Berlin? Berlin? How odd? Obviously she is English, yet I do not remember her at all. Yet there is something about her which is vaguely familiar." While thus thinking, another woman came in and curtsied low to her, and I realized it was the Duchess of York.[1] Did I show by the tremor of an eyelid that I had not made her out from the first? I did not. I steered my conversation onwards in the same course as before but with different sails: the dear old jib of comradeship was lowered and very gently the spinnaker of "Yes Ma'am" was hoisted in its place. I do not believe that she can have noticed the transition. She is charm personified.

HAROLD TO VITA   *4 King's Bench Walk*

11 March 1936

Hitler has behaved with a completely reckless regard for morals, and yet he probably thinks he is behaving splendidly. Anthony Eden's statement on Monday was superb and last night we had good speeches from Winston and Lloyd George. There is no doubt that we should refuse to negotiate with Germany until she evacuates the Rhineland and should force her out of it. It is really essential to demonstrate that

---

1. For his first meeting with the Duchess (later Queen Elizabeth) in Berlin, see pp. 214–215.

Treaties cannot be torn up by violence.[1] But the difficulty is that public opinion in this country is really afraid. Terrified of war. Actually frightened. And the result is that we shall give way to Germany and let down France—from sheer lack of courage. Not that I regard courage as a high virtue. But the fact remains that when one country is brave and the other cowardly, the latter is apt to get the worst of it in battle. Anyhow we shall scramble out somehow and achieve peace with dishonour. You can count on that.

VITA TO HAROLD   *Sissinghurst*

29 April 1936

How people can say life is dull in the country beats me. Take the last 24 hours here. An extremely drunken man had left his pony to be tried in the mowing machine. So it was put in the mowing machine; I watched; all seemed satisfactory; I went away. So did the mowing machine. Kennelly [gardener] sent it away without saying a word to me or to Copper [chauffeur] who is supposed to be responsible for it. Copper arrived in a rage in my room and abused Kennelly. I went and cursed Kennelly, who indeed was in the wrong. In the evening at about 9, I was told that Punnett [builder] wanted to see me. I went out. He was in tears, having just found his old father drowned in the engine tank, and a note written to himself saying it was suicide.

Next morning, i.e. today, George [Hayter, manservant] came to fetch me: Copper would like to speak to me. I found Copper in the garden room, covered in blood with a great gash in his head. Kennelly had come into the garage and knocked him down without any warning. He had fallen unconscious, and had come round to find Kennelly throwing buckets of water over him. He had then tried to strangle Kennelly, and they had only been separated by the arrival of Mrs Copper. So I sent Copper to the doctor in George's car, and meanwhile sent for the police. Accompanied by the policeman I went out in search of Kennelly, whom we found very frightened and white. He was

---

1. Hitler's seizure of the Rhineland territories on 7 March 1936 was in violation of the Treaty of Versailles and the Locarno Pact. Britain and France took no action to oppose him.

ordered to go and pack his things and leave at once. So that was that, and we are now without a gardener.

Copper is in bed with a splitting headache, and I fear a touch of concussion. If he hadn't been so knocked out I really believe he and Kennelly would have half killed each other.

HAROLD TO VITA   *4 King's Bench Walk*

11 June 1936

The great event of the day was Sibyl's [Colefax] dinner-party. Poor Sibyl—I had a feeling that it was her swan-song, but nonetheless it was a very triumphant one.[1] I arrived to find everything lit up lovely and the guests assembling—the Stanleys, the Brownlows, the Lamonts, the Rubinsteins, Bruce Lockhart, the Vansittarts, Buck De La Warr. I sat between Lady Stanley and Lady Brownlow. There were two tables. Our young King [Edward VIII] and Mrs Simpson sat at one, and the [Thomas] Lamonts sat at the other. Then when the women went, we all sat at the King's table, and I talked to Stanley about the Navy. Afterwards I took the King downstairs. He said that the Lindbergh dinner had been a great success. Anne had been rather shy at first, "but with my well-known charm I put her at ease and liked her very much."

Then we returned to the party. Rubinstein[2] started to play Chopin. More people drifted in—the Winston Churchills, Madame de Polignac, Daisy Fellowes, Noel Coward, the Kenneth Clarks.[3] Madame de Polignac sat herself down near the piano to listen to Rubinstein. I have seldom seen a woman sit so firmly: there was determination in every line of her bum. It was by then 12.30 and Rubinstein (who is sadly losing his looks) had played his third piece. It was quite clear that he was about to embark upon a fourth, and in fact Madame de Polignac was tapping her foot impatiently at the delay. Then the King advanced across the room: "We enjoyed that

1. Her husband, Sir Arthur Colefax, an eminent lawyer, had died on 19 February, and his widow was selling Argyll House in Chelsea.
2. Arthur Rubinstein, the Polish pianist, then aged forty-eight.
3. Kenneth Clark was Director of the National Gallery, 1934–45.

very much, Mr. Rubinstein." So that was that, and he then said
goodnight all round. But by then more guests had arrived, Gerald
Berners and others, and by the time H.M. had got half through the
guests, we at our end by the piano had forgotten his presence, and Noel
Coward started to strum a jazz tune and to croon slightly. At which
the King immediately resumed His Royal Seat. And I much fear that
Rubinstein and Madame de Polignac must have thought us a race of
barbarians. Nonetheless it was very welcome when Noel sang *Mad
Dogs and Englishmen* and *No, Mrs Worthington,* and even if Madame
de Polignac failed to smile throughout, the rest of us relaxed somewhat. So that when an hour later the King really did leave us, the party
had gone with a swing.

I was glad for Sibyl's sake, since I fear it is her last party in that
charming house and never has it looked so lovely. She managed it well.
She only made one mistake, and that was to sit on the floor with Diana
Cooper to give a sense of informality and youth to the occasion. But
Sibyl, poor sweet, is not good at young *abandon.* She looked incongru-
ous on the floor, as if someone had laid an inkstand there.

But the important part, my dearest, is the following. I talked to
Kenneth Clark. After December there will be a vacancy as Honorary
Attaché at the National Gallery. Would Ben take it? After a year he
could look about for a paid job. Clark suggests that in the interval he
ought to go to Munich, Dresden, Berlin etc. and really master the
galleries of Europe. What do you think about all this?[4]

VITA TO HAROLD   *Sissinghurst*

16 June 1936

While I was at Brighton yesterday I found some papers which
absolutely thrilled me.[5] These were the depositions of the Spanish
witnesses taken before the Knole succession case. They are *exactly* like
the Jeanne d'Arc witnesses: all labourers and suchlike people, living in
a little village in Spain. I have not read them through yet, but have

---

4. The proposal matured. It was the first step in Ben's career as an art historian.
5. Lady Sackville had died in her house near Brighton on 30 January. The papers that Vita
   found formed the basis of her book about her grandmother, *Pepita.*

read enough to make my mouth water. They are all people who knew Pepita and her mother.

VITA TO HAROLD   *Sissinghurst*

2 July 1936

I got such a nice letter from you this morning. I quite see what you mean about not minding if they [The House of Commons] think you dynamic, vitriolic, and violent. But I do think it would be a pity if you gave them any handle for thinking you unbalanced. What I mean is, that judgement is what really counts in the long run—not 'safety first' exactly, but a considered judgement delivered as vigorously as ever you like, so long as it *is* considered. I think that in the long run this is what wins respect in public life, more than any amount of brilliance and wit, both of which you have. And in your case, you have so much of both that people might be liable to mistrust you—you know what English people are. Take Winston as a warning. You see, it is very easy for a person like you to acquire a position and a reputation for brilliance, but very difficult to reverse it later on into a reputation for good sense and sobriety. I think one ought really to start the other way round—build your house first, in fact, and then add the ornamentation. This pi-jaw is not because I think you *have* made any mistakes, but just because I don't want you to do so. You see, again, you have got such a long solid career of work behind you—F.O., Persia, Berlin, and your books—that you have a marvellous foundation to build on. Of course the part of you that I really love best is the part that goes wild, Utopian, and indignant. But everybody doesn't know you as well as I do.

HAROLD TO VITA   *4 King's Bench Walk*

16 July 1936

Lunched with Sibyl [Colefax] yesterday. Somerset Maugham, the Winston Churchills, Mrs Simpson, Prince de Monaco. Mrs Winston talked to me so sadly about Randolph [Churchill], saying he was losing his looks, his mind and his heart. She was very despairing poor woman, and I liked her more than I have liked her before. Willy Maugham was very pleasant as usual. He said (stammering), "I-I-I am the m-m-most interesting person here. I knew Mrs Simpson when she was *a* Mrs Simpson and not *t-t-the* Mrs Simpson."

HAROLD TO VITA

22 September 1936

St Martin, Im Innkreis, Austria

I confess that I find my host and hostess a trifle vulgar.[1] But kind—so kind—so kind to impoverished royalties.

But Chips is really not a snob in an ordinary way. I suppose everybody has some sort of snobbishness somewhere, just like everybody has a few keys somewhere. Even you have a Sackville snobbishness, just like you have a huge key which you put down (together with Sarah's lead and a piece of groundsel and a worm-powder) upon the table in my sitting room. Some people have a whole lot of keys on trusses. But what makes Chips so exceptional is that he collects keys for keys' sake. The corridors of his mind are hung with keys which open no doors of his own and no cupboards of his own, but are just other people's keys which he has collected. There they hang—French keys, English keys, American keys, Italian keys and now a whole housekeeper's room truss of Central European keys. The word 'mediatized' is frequently on his lips: could he pronounce the word *Durchlaucht* [Serenity] that also would figure in his conversation, but the German 'ch' is not within his scope. So it is all Fritzy Lichtenstein and Tuti Festitics and the Windisch-Grätz twins and Cuno Auersperg ("My favourite man, absolutely my favourite man").

Today he goes over to Naziland to lunch with the Törings.[2] They foresaw that I would not want to come. "I am," I explained, "not good

---

1. The host was Henry ("Chips") Channon, the M.P. and diarist, and the hostess was his wife, Lady Honor Channon.
2. Countess Töring was the daughter of Prince Nicholas of Greece and the sister of the Duchess of Kent.

at that sort of thing." "Nonsense, Harold, what do you mean by 'that sort of thing'?" "Greek Royalties." "Well, of course, if you won't, you won't." I think they are rather glad, really, as I expect they want to talk to Countess Töring (who sounds less böring than her bloody father and her shy shambling sister of Kent) about the said Kents. And they might feel that I was looking on and listening in that tiresome way I have.

But how gay and lovely is this rich and ancient country. The villages have baroque frontages in blue and pink with pretty stucco work. A Fürstenstein and a Schillingfürst came to dinner and to sleep. Young men very full of smart English society. I suppose it was always like that, and the Austrians always did regard the *Gräfliches Taschenbuch* [Dictionary of Aristocrats] as the very pillar of life. Chips calls Honor "Frau Gräfin" to the servants. He is not very good at German but he has got that bit quite correct. "Frau Gräfin zurück?" he asks. And they bow. Well, I suppose that's all right, and I do not quite see what else he could call her. All I know is that it would never enter my head to call you Frau Baronin any more than it would enter your head to call me Herr Baron. Shall we start?

HAROLD TO VITA

28 September 1936

*Villa Mauresque,
Cap Ferrat, France*

I do not believe (if I recollect aright) that you have ever been fired out of a cannon. I have. It happened last night in the station yard of Monaco. Having glanced behind him, the chauffeur turned a switch, at which the car trembled slightly and then shook and gave six loud reports like fifty horsemen of the Apocalypse. It then sprang into the air, cleared the barrier, hurtled sideways past a tram, and flung itself with reckless abandon up the hill by Château Mallet. The moon on my left hung over a silent sea and seemed to swing rapidly westwards as the earth flew below us. Snorting furiously with great raucous snorts, the car crashed through Beaulieu and on to the corniche road. Other humbler cars going in the same direction flashed past my window with a woof as if they were in fact going in the opposite direction.

And then we came to the curves. Round we went, the chauffeur leaning out sideways to fling his weight on the inside, in and out, round and round. The precipices, the tunnels, the rock-arches, the great caverns cut above the sea, roared back at us. I thought of you and Ben and Nigel and my poor widowed mother and my little sister. I know I ought to have said, "Please do not go so fast: j'ai une petite *phlébite.*" But I have got Scotch and Ulster blood in my veins. I clenched my teeth. I clung on in grim terror, and suddenly there were the lights of Villefranche swinging round to the right as if someone were swinging them at the end of a string, and with a scrunch of brakes and a rattle of gravel we crashed into the drive and actually stopped at the front door. Staggering slightly, I entered the white hall, and there were Willie and his nephew[1] and Osbert Sitwell.

HAROLD TO VITA   *4 King's Bench Walk*

4 November 1936

I went to a party given by Mr Baldwin [Prime Minister] to the junior Ministers at No. 10. We all sat round the Cabinet Table and old S.B. read out the King's Speech. He then talked to us about what to say, and we had some delicious sherry and it was all rather fun. I cannot conceive how I ever disliked old Baldwin. He is such a dear old thing and so amusing. I asked him whether in my speech I should mention the King. He said, "Yes, but if I were you, I should not mention Mrs Simpson—not in so many words."

I woke up with a sinking feeling and at 12 I went to the opening of Parliament. It is a fine sight. The King looked like a boy of eighteen and did it well. But his accent is really worse than Philippa's [Harold's niece] at her most cockney stage. He referred to the "Ammurican Government" and ended, "And moy the blessing of Almoighty God rest upon your deliberoitions."

I then lunched at a snack bar and got into my [diplomatic] uni-

---

1. Somerset and Robin Maugham.

form. I joined Miss Horsburgh[1] in the Chief Whip's room and we were conducted to seats exactly behind the Prime Minister and Ramsay MacDonald. The Speaker then read the Speech and called upon Miss Horsburgh. She delivered her little piece quite beautifully, in a slow voice and without a tremor. She was very warmly applauded.

The Speaker then called on me. I had been told to follow the precedents, and the precedents prescribe that one must allude to one's constituency and then mention previous holders of the seat who have won distinction. This made it essential for me to mention Ramsay. I knew that this might not go down very well, so I prefaced it by saying, "My constituency, which maybe in a moment of blindness, refrained from electing the Rt. Hon. Member for Epping" [Churchill]. Winston at this flashed out, "They also refrained from electing the Rt. Hon. Member for the Scottish Universities" [Ramsay MacDonald]. At this the Labour Party let forth a hoot of triumph and thereby broke the solemnity which is supposed to reign on those occasions. Thus it became increasingly awkward when I passed on to my eulogy of Ramsay. They yelled. They hooted. Our people shouted, "Order! Order!" On I went, heaping upon Ramsay's head, which was exactly below me and bowed in acute misery, the compliments which I had prepared. Will Thorne, who is a decent old boy, tried to quiet his companions by shouting out, "This is not controversial," but the clamour did not die down until I had finished my bit about Ramsay and passed on to the rest of my speech.

That went well enough. But the incident was unfortunate since it created an impression of a floater whereas it was really an act of courage.

HAROLD TO VITA   *House of Commons*

5 November 1936

All the talk as usual was about Mrs Simpson. The extreme view is that the Cabinet should employ a gangster to murder her. I regard

---

1. Florence Horsburgh, Conservative Member for Dundee. She was the first woman to move the Address, and Harold was to second it.

that view as too extreme. But there is no doubt that they fear his
marriage, and that there will almost be a revolution if it occurs. The
main feeling is one of fury that this empty-headed American who has
twice been divorced should bring this great Empire to the brink of a
very grave crisis. My own view is that I am sorry for her and blame
him. How can one expect a Baltimore girl to appreciate the implications of her action? Sibyl [Colefax] tells me that Mrs Simpson is
getting rattled and that there is terrible ill feeling between her and the
Royal Family. Not only will she split the Empire but she will put her
David [the King] against his brothers and mother. What a mess!

HAROLD TO VITA   *House of Commons*

10 December 1936

We expect the blow to fall today.[1] I dread it. It is horrible. But
I am sure that abdication is the only course. We may have to take a
new oath of allegiance on Saturday. What a little ass the man is to
plunge us into this disorder! I cannot but suspect that Mrs Simpson has
convinced him that she is in a family way. Otherwise he could scarcely
be so obstinate. But none the less, as things have turned out, abdication
is his only card. I feel so sad about it, since it will take years for Albert
the Good [George VI] to build up a legend comparable to that of his
brother, and during those years the socialist feeling in this country will
have grown beyond proportion.

HAROLD TO VITA   *House of Commons*

15 December 1936

I lunched at the Club with Tommy[2] who is so relieved at the fall
of his master that he was almost indiscreet. He said that some disaster

---

1. The King's Abdication.
2. Sir Alan Lascelles, Private Secretary to the Prince of Wales, 1920–29, and to King George
VI, 1936–43.

was certain to arrive sooner or later. He suspects indeed that the King and Mrs S. had laid all their plans to run away together last February and that the death of King George did them in. He says that the King [Edward VIII] is like the child in the fairy stories who was given every gift except a soul. He said that there was nothing in him which even understood the intellectual or spiritual sides of life, and that all art, music, poetry etc. were dead to him. Even nature meant nothing except forms of exercise and his garden at the Fort [Belvedere] meant nothing beyond a form of exercise. He enjoyed nothing at all except through his senses. He had no friends in this country, "nobody whom he would ever wish to see again." He called all respectable people 'Victorian', and all educated people 'high-brows'. When he succeeded, he shirked his duty terribly. The Private Secretaries had a devil of a time. He would disappear every Thursday to Tuesdays to the Fort and they could not get at him. Even when he was in London he shut himself up in Buckingham Palace with Mrs S. and they giggled there together for hours.

Tommy told me of the great row he had had with him when he was his Secretary in Canada and the United States. Tommy resigned the position, and then for one hour and a half he told him what he thought of him. The King took it well. "Yes, Tommy," he said, "I was not made to be Prince of Wales." I really believe that Tommy is glad he is gone. "He was without a soul," he kept on saying, "and this made him a trifle mad. He will probably be quite happy in Austria. He will get a small *schloss;* play golf in the park; go to night-clubs in Vienna; and in the summer bathe in the Adriatic. There is no need to be sorry for him. He will be quite happy wearing his silly Tyrolese costumes (there was a note of fury at that), and he never cared for England or the English. That was all eye-wash. He rather hated this country since he has no soul and did not like being reminded of his duties."

I daresay that this is all true, and it is some comfort to me. Tommy is a very sane and loyal person and I trust his judgement in these things. "The new King," he said, "will be first class—no doubt about it."

Well, thus encouraged I went down to the House and took my oath to George VI.

VITA TO HAROLD   *Sissinghurst*

18 January 1937

I do wish Sissinghurst were not quite so inflammable. It's as bad as Dottie. I was washing peacefully in the bathroom before breakfast this morning, when Pat [Hayter] came knocking at the door to say the tower was on fire. It was. Smoke was pouring out from between the cracks in the bricks, so we sent for Punnett who tore out the fireplace in my sitting room and discovered a huge beam glowing red all through. We poured minimaxes [fire extinguisher] on to it, and the danger was averted, but it has been an awful business getting the beam out and my poor room is in an awful mess.

The smoke has made my room uninhabitable, so I shall spend a useful afternoon doing the books in the big room. It is pouring and blowing a gale, so there's no temptation to go for a walk. The fire insurance people will begin to think we do it on purpose!

VITA TO HAROLD   *Touggourt [Algeria]*

26 February 1937

Darling, I think Touggourt is one of the most magical places I ever struck! On arrival by full moonlight I thought the hotel was white, but next morning discovered it to be the colour of a ripe peach, with bright blue shutters and balconies. It has a big garden, mostly palms, but next door is the *jardin publique,* which is full of flowers—stocks, marigolds, flox, nasturtiums—and also contains wire cages with hyaenas and a little local animal called a fenouk, which is something like a tiny fox only with enormous ears. The town is pure white, and the sand honey-colour; the population dressed almost entirely in white, with occasional cloaks of blue, red, russet, and orange. The sun is so hot that, like everyone else, we have been obliged to buy solar topees, and Gwen [St. Aubyn] is wearing cotton frocks. It is like a hot August in England.

But the best of all was last night. We gave, rather unintentionally, a party. It included Lord Beauchamp,[1] who has turned up here accompanied by a sulky, embarrassed and bored young man called George, whom I take to be the footman you saw on the P. and O. The party came about in this wise: I asked the local guide (a most charming nomad Arab called Dadi), whether there were any dervishes here, and he said that he would get one to come and do his stunts for us in the garden after dinner. It would cost 60 francs. We agreed. But on going out after dinner we found the entire sect of dervishes squatting grouped round little fires, and most of the population of Touggourt as well, with a band of some four or five musicians with drums and flutes—a savage looking lot with their dark faces and white turbans. Even the presence of a Spahi in his scarlet cloak did little to reassure Gwen, who is convinced that there is about to be a revolution.

Then the music struck up, and an old man like a coal-black monkey crept out of the circle and began to dance. Meanwhile the others were heating long needles in the little fires, and when these were red-hot he stuck them into his cheeks, through his ears and into his arms, till as he danced he rattled like a porcupine. Before long he was joined by others; you could see which one was going to creep out next, for they would start to shiver all over, and sway, and crouch. One horribly skinny object flung himself on the ground and started digging with his hands in the soft sand like an animal. They thrust a stick between his teeth. I asked Dadi why. *"C'est pour l'empêcher de mordre quelqu'un,"* he replied casually; *"il est complètement fou, il ne sait pas ce qu'il fait."* Luckily Gwen did not overhear this remark. Then he sprang up and seized two flaming palm-fronds from the fire; he danced and twirled, holding them close to his face, close to his naked chest, close to his throat just under the chin, while the flames streamed all over him in the night. There was worse to come. The young chief of the sect suddenly joined in, stripped to the waist; a piece of wood with about 12 or 15 steel nails, about 5 inches long, was produced, and with a wooden mallet he banged the row of nails right into his stomach. Yet when they had torn it out of him there was not a mark, not a drop

---

1. An immensely wealthy, popular peer, who had been a member of Asquith's Wartime Cabinet. His wife, a sister of the Duke of Westminster, had died in 1936.

of blood. The most horrible of all was when another man plunged a long curved dagger into his stomach.

HAROLD TO VITA *Cairo, Egypt*

27 February 1937

Dear me, I was sorry to leave Khartoum. I found Gordon College fascinating as a problem and the roof of the Palace the best roof there ever was. The administrators were intelligent and friendly, and the weather divine. Now it means farewell to topees and tropical suits, and that cold shiver which will last till June. I was not made for northern climates. I am a child of the Sun—Akhnaton, Ammon, that sort of thing.

I wonder whether you have derived from my [diary] carbons the intense enjoyment I have got out of this commission.[1] Not only has it been enthralling in itself, but it has taught me a great deal that I did not know before. Oh God! Age, age, age! How intolerable it is not to be young. Time's winged chariot has become an aeroplane (not Imperial Airways but a RAF bomber), and I feel that there will not be nearly enough time for me to do all that I want to do. Darling, what a consolation it is for people of fifty to feel that they have at least not wasted one hour of life in the past. Had I strolled through my middle years I should feel enraged today. As it is, I say, "It sinks—and though not in the very least ready to depart[2]—at least I have not dawdled on the way."

Fifty has been a terrible landmark for me. A great gallows upon my primrose path. I suppose I shall get over it. But God doesn't understand somehow that I was not intended to be old. I am a young man by nature. I cannot make him see that. He allows me to get old just as if I was Lord Salisbury. Which I am not. But no grumbles, darling. Only gratitude for being able at the age of fifty to fling into a visit to the Sudan all the energy and zest of a boy of 23.

---

1. He was a member of a Government Commission to report on African education.
2. "I warmed both hands before the fire of life;
   It sinks, and I am ready to depart." Walter Savage Landor

HAROLD TO VITA   *4 King's Bench Walk*

22 April 1937

Poor Mrs Koestler came to see me and cried on the bench of the lobby. She is the wife of a *News Chronicle* correspondent who has been missing for a month in Spain.[1] We suspect that Franco has done him in, although all enquiries are met with, "He is alive and well." But of all atrocities it seems to me that the worst is this keeping of widows in suspense. Anyhow I said I would do what I could, and got hold of Vansittart who was good about it and admitted that our Seville Consul was slack and timid, and sent him there and then a snorter to say, "This must stop. You must insist on seeing Koestler if they claim he is alive." In such matters it is of great advantage being in with the F.O.

Then off I went to a dinner in the French Embassy. Very grand and good. It was in honour of Daladier, the Minister of Defence.[2] He is to be Prime Minister one day. A dreadful little man he seemed, and so bedint in comparison with our own people. There was Halifax, Duff Cooper, Stanley, Philip Sassoon, Derby, Inskip and the rest of our Cabinet, whom I have never regarded as beauties or patricians, looking like Roman Senators compared to this little Iberian visitor.

HAROLD TO VITA   *4 King's Bench Walk*

29 April 1937

The Guernica bombardment was really horrible.[3] It looks as if it had been carried out by the Germans without the consent of Spanish headquarters. They deliberately swooped down on the escaping women and children and machine-gunned them. The feeling in the

---

1. Arthur Koestler (1905–83), author of *Darkness at Noon,* etc. He was imprisoned by Franco for four months, March to June 1937, daily expecting execution. His first wife, Dorothy Asher, campaigned vigorously and successfully for his release. He divorced her in 1950.
2. Edouard Daladier, French Minister of Defense, 1936–38, and Prime Minister, 1938–40.
3. Guernica, a small town in the Basque province of Vizcaya, was totally destroyed by German aircraft on 26 April. 1,654 people were killed and 889 wounded.

House is very bitter—and only that ass Teenie [Victor Cazalet] goes on sticking up for Franco. I could have boxed his silly ears. Anyhow, we are trying to rescue as many women as we can before a similar fate overwhelms Bilbao. The Foreign Office have behaved splendidly.

I do so loathe this [Spanish civil] war. I really feel that barbarism is creeping over the earth again and that mankind is going backwards. It is terrible that the invention of the aeroplane should have given such an advantage to ruthlessness and placed pity and gentleness at its mercy. I feel very deeply about this—right deep down in myself among the hidden shynesses and other things. I wake with it as one wakes with some dread or sorrow.

VITA TO HAROLD   *Sissinghurst*

30 April 1937

I do so agree with your feelings about the war and the other wars for which everyone is preparing. I really feel at moments that Bertie Russell is right and that we ought to retire from the competition, not merely for our own safety but to give a lead away from this insane barbarism. Quite obviously, *in the long run,* we would some day be acknowledged as the first to take a step towards true civilisation—but would anybody follow our example? I doubt it. After all, they wouldn't disarm when we wanted them to. And what about the peoples for whom we have made ourselves responsible? Yet for the sake of civilisation it is the only thing to do. How difficult it is to decide between such things as our national pride and our much advertised sense of responsibility, and our real desire for peace in Bertie Russell's meaning of the word. Would we be really justified in letting other nations partition our Empire, in letting India cut her own throat? Or do we only pretend to ourselves that we wouldn't be justified, just because we want to keep our proud possessions?

It makes me cross when the House spends days discussing Cabinet Ministers' salaries, when there are these appalling problems—and others such as strikes and poverty and cancer and unemployment.

HAROLD TO VITA   *4 King's Bench Walk*

21 July 1937

My speech [on Foreign Affairs] seems to have gone better than I had supposed. Many people have come to congratulate me upon it. It is extraordinary how these things seem to affect temperature. If one makes a good speech even the policemen at the door seem to salute with greater deference. After a failure, it is as if the very pigeons avoided one's eye. This is of course mainly subjective. But I think there really is something in the fact that no institution on earth shows so much barometric variations as the House of Commons. Nor can any triumph be more sweet than a real oratorical triumph in the House. I wonder if I shall ever have one.

I lunched with Mary Spears.[1] Maggie[2] was there like a fat slug. She said, "You know, Harold my dear, the one thing I cannot stand in life is unkindness in any form. Especially people who say unkind things about other people behind their backs." With that little exordium she began to take out her fountain-pen-fillers one by one and inject oily poison into everything. She is now very much the *Reine Mère*. How comes it that this plump but virulent little bitch should hold such social power?

HAROLD TO VITA   *4 King's Bench Walk*

8 December 1937

I breakfasted with old Baldwin[3] at his house this morning. We were alone. He was sweet, and we talked of literature and politics for an hour and a half. He was generous about everyone except Lloyd George who, he said, had done his best to debauch British politics and "had never led a party or kept a friend." He showed me the little

---

1. Mary Borden, the novelist, wife of Sir Edward Spears, soldier and historian.
2. Mrs. Ronald Greville, who from 1906 until her death in 1942 entertained lavishly in London and at her house Polesden Lacey, Surrey, now a property of the National Trust.
3. Stanley Baldwin, Prime Minister, 1923–29 and 1935–37. On his retirement he was created Earl Baldwin of Bewdley. He died in 1947.

pencilled note which was the last communication sent him by King Edward VIII. Such a childish scribble. He is leaving it to the British Museum.

I have never enjoyed a breakfast more. I take back everything I have ever said against that man. He is a man of the utmost simplicity and therefore greatness.

HAROLD TO VITA   *4 King's Bench Walk*

15 February 1938

I had a word with Sibyl [Colefax] about Ben. She said that he had seemed in tremendous spirits, chattered the whole time and was a most delightful companion. She also said that Berenson[1] had said he was the best student he had ever had. I said, "But surely not?" She said, "Those were his words—and you know that B.B. is not apt to be agreeable."

What a mystery Ben is! Wretched at Eton, and one of the greatest social successes Oxford has ever had. Hopelessly lazy, and then he gets so good a second [class degree] that he almost got a first. Incompetent and dreamy, and yet manages to impress Berenson. I can't make him out. Are we too sceptical, or others too credulous? I wish I knew. Bless you, my dearest, who shares with me these worries as no one else does or ever could. Because they are worries to me. I love my sons so deeply. It is my domestic instinct.

HAROLD TO VITA   *House of Commons*

9 March 1938

I had a depressing day yesterday. We had a private meeting at Chatham House[2] to discuss the present situation. We came to the

---

1. Bernard Berenson, the American art historian, with whom Ben had been working at I Tatti, his house outside Florence.
2. The Royal Institute of International Affairs.

unhappy conclusion that now that Russia has dropped out we are simply not strong enough to resist Germany. Or rather we did not come to so extreme a conclusion. But we did feel that 80 million fully armed Germans plus the Italians were more than we and France could safely take on. What tremendous things have happened in these five years! We are suddenly faced by the complete collapse of our authority, our Empire and our independence. Poor England.

Then I dined with [Sir Edward] Spears. Vansittart[3] was there. He was most gloomy. He thinks that we can scarcely prevent Germany collaring Eastern Europe, and that when she has done so, she will turn round on us and demand our submission. Well, it may not work out like that. But opinion is at the moment as gloomy as in the days after Austerlitz [1805]. Nobody who is well informed believes that there is any chance of negotiations with Germany leading to anything at all. We may get some little scrap out of Italy but it will be a mere crumb of comfort and quite unreliable.

Jolly, isn't it? My dearest, do not worry about these things but cultivate your lovely garden. I wish you were here nonetheless. You always soothe all my ruffled feathers, and make me as sleek and gay again as any Bantam.

HAROLD TO VITA   *British Legation, Bucharest*

17 April 1938

As I walked upstairs I felt strangely giddy.[4] The staircase seemed to shift and wobble. I was appalled. Supposing I came over faint during my luncheon? That would be hell. I arrayed myself miserably in the tail-coat of Rex Hoare [British Minister] which would not, I regret,

---

3. Robert Vansittart, who had been permanent Undersecretary at the Foreign Office since 1930, was demoted to "chief diplomatic adviser" to the government, after he lost the confidence of the Prime Minister, Neville Chamberlain, for opposing the policy of appeasing the Dictators.
4. Harold was on a lecture tour of the Balkans on behalf of the British Council, and had been invited to lunch with King Carol of Rumania. Having left his own frock coat behind, he was obliged to borrow that of his host, the British Minister in Bucharest.

meet in front. But it looked all right. Then I espied the bottle of Sal Volatile which I had bought at Cambridge when I had to deliver the Rede Lecture after an all-night sitting. I corked it tightly and put it in my pocket. Then off I went.

At the Palace an aide-de-camp in stays and aiguillettes arrived and made polite conversation. Then a lift hummed and two little pekinese darted in barking followed by the King in naval uniform. I bowed. He greeted me with affection and respect. We passed into the dining-room. I sat on his right. The aide-de-camp sat on his left. The pekinese sat on his knee. We started conversation.

He had ordered, he said, a purely Rumanian luncheon. God, it was good! In spite of my feeling so faint, I gobbled hard. I sat there on my pink plush chair and ate the *marimagi* and the *olovienic* and the *gruzaka*. We talked agreeably. He is a bounder but less of a bounder than he seemed in London. He was more at ease. His Windsor-blue eyes wistful, and he had something behind them. Was it sadness, or overwork, or mysticism? He spoke with intelligence about Chamberlain and Eden and the Italian Agreement and the French Cabinet and the League of Nations. He was well-informed and most sensible. We kept all debating topics away.

I had been asked nonetheless to try and tackle him about his dictatorship and the Hungarian minorities. I got on to the former subject by saying how difficult it was for us not having a good Opposition; how the basis of a democracy was an alternative Government; how the Labour people did not offer a possible alternative; and how bad that was for everyone concerned. He rose to the bait. He said that he also was experiencing that difficulty. It had been necessary for him to clear away the old party politicians (and indeed they were a poor lot), and he must now build up again three more parties. "Why three?" I asked, my mouth full of *lutchanika*, "Your Majesty," I added. He replied that two parties were apt to share the spoils between them, and a third party was necessary to restore the balance. Quite a good idea.

I was beginning to enjoy my conversation when I became aware of a cold trickle and the smell of ammonia. I thrust my hand into my pocket. It was too late. The Sal had indeed proved Volatile and my trousers were rapidly drenched. I seized my napkin and began mopping surreptitiously. My remarks became bright and rather fevered, but quite uninterrupted. I mopped secretly while the aroma of Sal Volatile rose above the smell of *gruzhenkoia*.

This was agony. I scarcely heard what he was saying. "Have you," he was asking, "recovered your land-legs yet? After three days in the train one feels the room rocking like after three days at sea." So that was it! Why on earth had he not told me before, and now it was too late. I recovered my composure and dropped my sodden napkin. The conversation followed normal lines. At 2.45 he rose abruptly. I rose too, casting a terrified glance at the plush seat of my chair. It bore a deep wet stain. What, oh what, will the butler think? He will only think one thing.

HAROLD TO VITA   *4 King's Bench Walk*

2 May 1938

My luncheon to meet Ethel Smyth[1] was not really successful. She arrived in a state. Her hair was coming down and she mistook her muffler for a handkerchief. I knew that she was frequently and inordinately committing this mistake, but I forebore to say so. One must forebear on such occasions, since it is difficult to say, "Do you realise you are blowing your nose on your muffler?" when one has to say it through a machine that looks like a cinema apparatus. She is really stone deaf. She carries this machine about, but she always turns it the wrong way round, and she interposes between her head-phone and her ear a whole wad of untidy grey hair. Not one word does she hear. Moreover, her train had arrived one-and-a-half hours before luncheon, so she had gone to the Paddington Hotel and sat in the lounge reading P. G. Wodehouse. She had drunk sherry after sherry and was quite biffed. But what a magnificent fighter all the same! It is like a Moscow veteran in 1852 telling stories of Borodino.

---

1. Dame Ethel Smyth, the composer and suffragette, was then eighty.

HAROLD TO VITA   *4 King's Bench Walk*

30 May 1938

It was nice seeing those hulking young men[1] together. I am always impressed by their relations with each other. Although utterly different in character, they have for each other a sort of amused respect. Isn't it ghastly to imagine that two people who deserve and get so much from life may be nipped off by a bullet? That is a terrible thing.

I cannot really believe that humanity will not see before it is too late that there is nothing heroic about war but only a foul foolishness. To that extent the Canton bombings are a lesson. I do not mean that I wish this lesson to be inculcated upon the Chinese, but I do think it is less fatal to civilization that Canton should be bombed than London or Paris. I do really believe that we shall unite in this country and in other countries to say, "This thing must cease." But the anomaly of it all is that we can only do so by arming. Strength and justice has worked in the Czech crisis. Perhaps we can extend it.

HAROLD TO VITA   *Waddesdon Manor,*
                                               Aylesbury
17 July 1938

Oh my God, how odd my arrival here was! I was all untidy after a long train journey, and I was ushered into a vast saloon sprinkled with bridge tables occupied by the racing set—Hillingdons, Bessboroughs[2] and God knows what. There was not a soul I really knew. I was greeted warmly by Mrs Rothschild and then presented to Princess Mary who was gracious—gracious me she was gracious. Then I sat down and watched them playing poker. Hillingdon was tight, which was rather awkward.

I can't tell you what this house is like. It is vast, 1870, Italianate stucco. But hardly a thing has been changed since the old Baron's

---

1. Ben, now twenty-three, was Deputy Surveyor of the King's Pictures under Kenneth Clark; and Nigel, twenty-one, was still at Balliol College, Oxford.
2. 3rd Lord Hillingdon, banker, soldier, former M.P.; and 9th Earl of Bessborough, Governor General of Canada, 1931–35.

time.[3] There are marvellous pictures and Sèvres, but execrable taste. Jimmy[4] hates anything being altered, and the lavatories still have handles you pull up instead of chains you pull down. There is no running water in the bedrooms, and although it is all very luxurious as regards food and drink and flowers, it is really less comfortable than our mud-pie in the Weald.

I came down to breakfast. Hillingdon was there, very red about the gills. Then Harry Lascelles[5] came in. Hillingdon asked him if he minded a cigarette. "Yes I do," answered Lascelles. "Well now I know," said Hillingdon, continuing to puff his cigarette. A slight strain descended upon the breakfast room. I think on the whole (miserable as your decision was in its consequences) that it would have been even more fraught with disaster if you had married Harry Lascelles instead of me. Oh my dear Mar, really you would not have liked it in the very least.

HAROLD TO VITA   *4 King's Bench Walk*

26 July 1938

My own dearest,

I had time yesterday to read your poem.[6] In fact I read it three times. Once in the train. Once after luncheon in the library. And once before I went to bed.

I had rather dreaded that I should find it vague and metaphysical. I also had a sort of fear that it might be too ambitious in the way that *Genesis* [Dorothy Wellesley's poem] was too ambitious. That was silly of me. Your greatest gift is perhaps an extraordinary sense of propor-

3. In 1874 Baron Ferdinand de Rothschild built this elaborate house on a Buckinghamshire hilltop, and surrounded it by a Victorian formal garden. It is now a property of the National Trust.

4. James de Rothschild, M.P. for the Isle of Ely, 1929–45, and a Trustee of the Wallace Collection.

5. Henry Lascelles, 6th Earl of Harewood, who had been much in love with Vita before her marriage, and married Princess Mary, daughter of King George V, in 1922. He was a Steward of the Jockey Club and a Trustee of the British Museum.

6. *Solitude.* Hogarth Press, 1938. Its themes were reflections on love, God and the universe, beauty and truth, life and death.

tion in all important things. It is very odd. In little things your s. of p. is almost as bad as B.M.'s. But in big things it is the best I know.

Now instead of a metaphysical or didactic poem, I get one of the loveliest things I have read for years. It is 'pure poetry' in the sense that it makes no appeal to sentimentality or mere lilt. When I say 'pure poetry', I mean a passage like that on page 16, "Then strength and beauty came into my hands . . ." That very sentence is pure poetry. The use of simple words in the right order, so that each one takes on a special value. The whole of that passage is superb.

But what a strange thing poetry is! Why are the first four lines on page 12 so lovely?[7] I mean they might so easily be ridiculous— Brendan Bracken and a bird. And yet somehow they are lovely lines. Absolute poetry.

It is a lovely sombre poem, beautifully written, absolutely sincere, and poetry rather than verse. I should put it No. 3 of your poems. *Sissinghurst* comes first. *The Land* second. This third.

I am so proud of you, my darling. I think you are someone apart from all the rest of the world. But I don't think that blurs my judgement. If I had read this poem as if it were by someone else, I might have approached it in a more critical mood. But I should certainly have felt when I had finished it that I had had a new experience—something as sombre and sincere as a meadow at night.

Bless you my dearest,
Hadji

VITA TO HAROLD   *Sissinghurst*

3 August 1938

I went to Rodmell last night, and very nice it was too. We sat out in the garden watching the late sunlight making the corn all golden over the Downs. Then I had a long talk this morning with Virginia

---

7. "As once Saint Brendan cast his harp aside
    When he had heard
    Gabriel in the plumes of a white bird
    Singing within the Temple as day died."

[Woolf], who was in her most delightful mood. Tell your host [Somerset Maugham], if you think it would please him, that she much admired his autobiography, *The Summing Up.* She had liked the clarity of his style, and also the honesty with which he tried to get at the truth. She liked his analysis of his own methods of writing. And you know that she is *peu facile,* so, as he knows it too, he might be pleased.

She went so far as to say that although she had first got his autobiography out of the circulating library, she now intended to buy it for herself for keeps, but for goodness sake don't tell him this, or he will send her a presentation copy, and I shall be *blamiert* for having repeated what she said.

Oh my dear, what an enchanting person Virginia is! How she weaves magic into life! Whenever I see her, she raises life to a higher level. How cheap she makes people like Teenie [Cazalet] seem. And Leonard too. I know he is tiresome and wrong-headed, but really with his schoolboyish love for pets and gadgets he is irresistibly young and attractive. How wrong people are about Bloomsbury, saying that it is devitalised and devitalising. You couldn't find two people less devitalised or devitalising than the Wolves—or indeed more vitalising than Roger Fry for example. I think where Bloomsbury has suffered is in its hangers-on like Angus Davidson[1] and equivalent young men, and of course the drooping Lytton [Strachey] must have done its cause a great deal of harm. I hated Lytton.

HAROLD TO VITA

4 August 1938

Villa Mauresque,
Cap Ferrat, France

I am glad I came here. It really is the perfect holiday. I mean, the heat is intense, the garden lovely, the chair long and cool, the lime-juice at hand, a bathing pool if one wishes to splash, scenery, books, gramophones, pretty people—and above all, the sense that it is not going on for long.

I was met by the car and told the man that my *phlébite* was very

---

1. He had worked for the Hogarth Press for three years until 1927, and was now living in Cornwall writing a biography of Edward Lear.

bad this year, so would he go slowly. He did. Then I was met by Willy
[Maugham] at the door. He has an old-fashioned courtesy about these
things. Rather bedint about it. There has been a terrible drought and
I expect Willy is selfish about water. Anyhow the garden was as cool
and as green as could be and I had a lovely bath. I sat and read for
a bit as Willy went off to work. Then the Paravicinis appeared. He
is Willy's son-in-law and really beautiful. The daughter is just a mar.[1]
I have not made her out. Very pretty in a way.

I am afraid that this household is on the capitalist side, and they
do not feel for Leon Blum[2] those emotions of respect and admiration
which are felt by others. They regard Communism as the greatest of
all dangers, and their conception of the German menace is, "Well, why
not give Hitler Togoland and the Cameroons and Tanganyika if only
he allows us to keep our yachts and villas." Of course I may exaggerate
all this. On the one hand my loathing for fascism is due to the fact
that I hate the type of mind that believes in brute force. It is not
nobility on my part but a sort of physical loathing which I suppose
is based on cowardice. Conversely, we doctrinaires have not come
across Communism in fact. Willy and Gerald Haxton[3] have. Down
in the harbour at Villefranche there is acute Communism and they see
what harm it does to the decent people. For instance, the Italian boats
used to put in here on their way back to America. The dockers refused
to handle their stuff so that they now cut out Villefranche—with the
result that the whole port loses about £200,000 a year. This means real
loss to all the little people. I think Gerald Haxton (who knows the
people here intimately) is quite sincere in hating the reds for this alone.

I had a lovely afternoon. I went out in his little yawl to bathe.
We crossed the bay, anchored under the rocks opposite, got out the
harpoon gun, gazed into the depths for fish, found none, bathed in
warm water, sat on deck and drank in the sun and the sea and the sky.
I do not want to do that for ever, and I should die of ineffectiveness
if I spent my whole time in delights of the body. But really, when one
has a clear conscience about public work and so on, it is a halcyon thing
to do just to sit and bask. We had with us Jojo and Lulu. Jojo's function

---

1. Elizabeth (Liza) Maugham, aged twenty-one. Her husband, whom she had married in July
1937, was Vincent Paravicini, son of the Swiss Minister in London.
2. Socialist Prime Minister of France, 1936–38.
3. Somerset Maugham's companion and secretary until Haxton's death in 1944.

I understand—he is the sailor who works the boat. Lulu's status in life was less evident. Gerald Haxton described him as "a friend from Nice." But when Gerald was swimming round with his harpoon, Lulu told me that he had been a miner in Lens, that Gerald picked him up, brought him down here, and he was now very happy training to be a tailor. *"Oui, monsieur, et quand je dis tailleur, c'est bien entendu de la haute couture que je parle."* He was himself exquisitely dressed or rather undressed. Perfectly manicured and decapilatorised.

When we returned to the shore, Lulu leaped into a beautiful little two-seater and buzzed off. "Tailors' apprentices," I murmured to Gerald, "must be very well paid in Nice." "They are," he answered.

HAROLD TO VITA   *Villa Mauresque, Cap Ferrat*

5 August 1938

I had a bath, shaved, and put on my best clothes. Because the late King of England [the Duke of Windsor] was coming to dinner. Willy Maugham had prepared us carefully. He said that the Duke gets cross if the Duchess is not treated with respect.

When they arrived Willy and his daughter went into the hall. We stood sheepishly in the drawing-room. In they came. She, I must say, looks very well for her age. She has done her hair in a different way. It is smoothed off her brow and falls down the back of her neck in ringlets. It gives her a placid and less strained look. Her voice has also changed. It now mingles the accents of Virginia with that of a Duchess in one of Pinero's plays. He entered with his swinging naval gait, plucking at his bow-tie. He had on a *tussore* dinner-jacket. He was in very high spirits. Cocktails were brought and we stood around the fireplace. There was a pause. "I am sorry we were a little late," said the Duke, "but Her Royal Highness couldn't drag herself away." He had said it. Her (gasp) Royal (shudder) Highness (and not one eye dared to meet another).[1]

---

1. King George VI had informed his brother that the Cabinet had advised him that the title Royal Highness could not be extended to the Duchess.

Then we went into dinner. There were two cypresses and the moon. I sat next to the Duchess. He sat opposite. They called each other 'darling' a great deal. I called him 'Your Royal Highness' a great deal and 'Sir' the whole time. I called her 'Duchess'. One cannot get away from his glamour and his charm and his sadness, though I must say he seemed gay enough. They have a villa here [at Cap d'Antibes] and a yacht, and go round and round. He digs in the garden. But it is pathetic the way he is sensitive about her. It was quite clear to me from what she said that she hopes to get back to England. When I asked her why she didn't get a house of her own somewhere, she said, "One never knows what may happen. I don't want to spend all my life in exile."

HAROLD TO VITA   *4 King's Bench Walk*

10 October 1938

My Leicester speech went off well. There were 2,500 people in the de Montfort Hall which is its full capacity. I was very loudly cheered. I spoke on democracy and made no allusion to the crisis.[1] But the audience were all Workers Educational Association and that sort of person. Left-wing and therefore pro-me. The people against me are the ladies of Leicester. Isn't it terrible that the destinies of the Empire should rest in the hands of such as them? I feel terribly sad about democracy. I do not think we can survive. And now Hitler tells us what Ministers we are to have and what Minister will be disagreeable to him. What a terrible speech and what a slap in the face! That is the worst of Germans. Once they have knocked you down they cannot resist kicking you.

I found Bertie Jarvis[2] very distressed. There is a meeting of the Association on Thursday and I shall have to come up for it. A frightful bore. They will probably ask me to pledge myself to support Cham-

---

1. The crisis provoked by Hitler's threat to annex Czechoslovakia, and the meeting at Munich on 29 September between Hitler, Mussolini, Chamberlain, and Daladier. Hitler had obtained almost everything he wanted without a war. Harold strongly criticized Chamberlain.
2. The Chairman of Harold's Constituency Association.

berlain. I shall do nothing of the kind. It is just possible that the women will turn me out. If that happens, I think I shall regret not having resigned my seat as a noble gesture. But Bertie seems confident he can keep me in. I expect I shall get away with it.

VITA TO HAROLD   *Sissinghurst*

14 November 1938

I know you will never forgive me, but I *can't* go to this party.[1] I wrote to Jay's and discovered that an evening-dress would cost at least £30, and the adjuncts (shoes, underclothes, gloves etc.) another £10. Well, that seems to me wicked to spend on personal adornment for one evening. It was silly of me ever to say that I would go to it. Gwen [St. Aubyn] says that it would be wrong of me to funk it, and that I *must* go. But I am too shy. And if I went to this party, I should be being false to myself. I am writing this letter with my jewels littered all around me—emeralds and diamonds, just taken out of the bank— and they make me feel sick. I simply *can't* buy a dress costing £30 or wear jewels worth £2,000 when people are starving. I *can't* support such a farce when people are threatened that their electric light or gas may be cut off because they can't pay for their arrears.

HAROLD TO VITA   *4 King's Bench Walk*

7 February 1939

Really Chamberlain [Prime Minister] is an astonishing and perplexing old boy. This afternoon (as you will have heard) he startled the House and the world by proclaiming something like an offensive

---

1. A dinner at Buckingham Palace on 16 November in honor of the King of Rumania. At her death in 1962, only one evening dress was found in Vita's wardrobe. It dated from 1927.

and defensive alliance between us and France. Now that is the very thing that all of us have been pushing for, working for, writing for, speaking for, all these months. And the old boy gets up and does it as if it was the simplest thing on earth. The House was absolutely astounded. It could not have been more definite.

Now what does it all mean? Is he really so ignorant of diplomacy as to assume that this means little? I cannot believe that. The F.O. would never have allowed him to make the statement without his being quite certain what it meant. Moreover, he spoke so resolutely and so deliberately. The House cheered loudly. It was superb. I felt happy for the first time for months.

But this is a complete negation of his 'appeasement' policy and of his Rome visit. He has in fact swung suddenly round to all that we have been asking for. What does it mean? I think it can only mean that he realizes that appeasement has failed. It is at this stage that his value as a diplomatic asset becomes operative. No ordinary German or Italian will ever believe propaganda telling him that Chamberlain is a 'war-monger'. I feel so pleased about it since I feel that our constant unexpressed opposition has had some effect. I am so glad that we all lay low all this time and allowed facts to speak for themselves.

Yet still I have the awful doubt lest he (being so abysmally ignorant of foreign policy) may not have understood what was meant by his statement. But if he did understand what he said, and if he did mean what he said, then all differences are over. I know very well that he will say, "But how foolish of you to doubt me." I know very well that in saying this he will be talking rubbish. There must have been some very unpleasant information that drove him to make this statement. But how odd these things are. My line was, "You are mad to trust the Dictators." His line was, "Appeasement is the only policy." Now that he sees we were right and he was wrong he can say, "Wasn't it clever of me to try appeasement first? I always knew that it would come to this. You tried to force me into a breach before I had convinced the world how pacific I really was!" He may say that. But it isn't true. He is a convert—not an original believer. But so long as he does the right thing, God knows all personal scores or triumphs mean nothing.

Happy for once—since I think *this* may give us peace.

VITA TO HAROLD   *Sissinghurst*

13 February 1939

I have really nothing to say at all except that Mr Armstrong is coming to look at the orchids this afternoon. And that's of no interest, compared with the full life you lead.

I do feel so dull always, compared with your life.

I like my life, and don't envy yours, but at the same time I often feel how dull and rustic I must appear to you.

Anyhow, I have spent the whole morning writing poetry (though no doubt Spender, Auden, etc. wouldn't call it poetry at all), and that gives me some sense of justification. *"On fait ce qu'on peut,"* as the French priest said.

Je fais ce que je peux—which is very little, I know, but if I can write a few decent respect-worthy verses I am doing of my best. And I suppose that if one means to be "a good sweet pea," in your phrase, one must be the best sweet pea one can.

Darling, you are such a very *right* person in everything you do. I was so struck by your saying you had re-written your review last Saturday, because you thought it was slops. How many people would have let it go, even though slops, when they were as tired as you must have been? *How* I respect you for that probity! It is one of the many things that makes me respect you as I do. You know, or perhaps you don't know, I respect you (quite apart from loving you) as the most respect-worthy person I have ever known. I think you go wild and injudicious on occasion, but fundamentally I know that your values and standards are permanent and honest and indeed noble.

HAROLD TO VITA   *House of Commons*

7 March 1939

I had to dash up to Leicester yesterday. Jarvis wanted me to take an early opportunity of saying that I agree with the Government's present policy. Which indeed I do. So up I went and spoke to a woman's meeting.

Harold Nicolson in 1930, the year when he abandoned diplomacy for journalism and politics. (Photo courtesy Howard Coster)

The entrance range of Sissinghurst Castle, built in 1490 and restored by the Nicolsons in the 1930s.

The Nicolsons at Sissinghurst in 1932.

Vita and Harold at Smoke-Tree Ranch in California, 1933.

The Elizabethan tower at Sissinghurst. Vita's writing room was behind the first big window above the archway. (Photo courtesy Country Life)

With her dog Rollo in the orchard at Sissinghurst.

Charles and Anne Lindbergh, 1934. (Photo courtesy The Bettmann Archive)

The yew "rondel" at Sissinghurst in the center of the rose garden, which Harold designed and Vita planted. (Photo courtesy L. & M. Gayton)

Harold with Bertrand Russell (left) and Lord Samuel at a broadcast discussion on the BBC's Overseas Service in 1951. (Photo courtesy BBC)

Vita in 1955, aged sixty-three.

Vita and Harold outside the South Cottage, Sissinghurst, in a photograph taken in 1959, three years before her death.

Three generations in 1962, in a photograph taken a few days after Vita's death. Harold, Nigel, and Nigel's son Adam. (Photo courtesy Edwin Smith)

They do not really understand what it is all about, and I spoke more for the local press than for my audience. What it really boils down to is that the ordinary elector does not want to be worried. He *loathes* fuss, anxiety, apprehension or even being obliged to think. Thus what he really wants to do is to say, "Leave it all to Chamberlain," and he is therefore annoyed if anyone throws doubt upon Chamberlain's infallibility. Moreover (and this is what inflames peoples' tempers) they have a subconscious feeling of guilt. They feel dimly that we behaved badly to the Czechs and that we did not conduct ourselves with our usual courage and calm. Now Chamberlain has rendered cowardice and treachery respectable. This is why people get so cross.

HAROLD TO VITA   *4 King's Bench Walk*

8 May 1939

How lovely it was this week-end! It was such a happy time for me, beginning with my silly little boat[1] (oh my dear—how I love the sound of foam against a boat!) and fortified by the fact that squalid little tub though she be, she is really quite habitable, and has taken a distinct liking for myself—and then the beauty of the garden afterwards. I really do think that you have done a great work in that garden. It is so like yourself.

I have got an up on Benzie. He is so keen on his present job[2] and so determined not to be dilettante about it. He says he will get to know every print and picture in Buckingham Palace before his little Queen [Elizabeth] comes back. I thought it rather moving all the descriptions of their departure.[3] They are a great asset. Just think how miserable we should all feel today if our national feeling were symbolised by Wallis Simpson. The Queen (and he also in a way) are really representative of what is best in our national character. I have always been a

---

1. Harold bought a yawl, which he christened *Mar,* and hired a crew of two to sail her at weekends.
2. Deputy Keeper of the King's pictures.
3. It was the first visit of a reigning British monarch to the United States.

monarchist. And when I saw the *Europa* creep into Southampton against all the background of the *Victory* and the *Repulse* and the flags and the simple people feeling so happy, I felt that we were in fact invincible.

VITA TO HAROLD   *Sissinghurst*

19 June 1939

I must write to tell you how excellent your speech was yesterday afternoon.[1] It was really a work of art in the beauty of its construction and development; its simplicity, logic, and reasonableness in the sense of the 'reasonable man'. I was deeply impressed. It was like watching a beautiful piece of architecture grow before one's eyes, in a quick-motion way, rather like those films which show one a nasturtium attaining its full development in an hour. As I listened to you, I felt that you were not only my charming Hadji, but also a creative artist moulding your clay into a shape like a chalice.

I don't think I had ever realised before how deeply you reflected the truly Greek and also the Christian spirit.

Darling, what a combination! What an influence you are, and ought, to be! 'The Good Pagan'—yes, you are that, but also the Good Christian although you don't subscribe to any orthodox religion. How far more Christian you are than many so-called Christians!

Of course I have always realised this about you, but it is odd that a speech of 40 minutes should have made me realise it even more vividly after 25 years. I suppose it was because I was seeing you and listening to you objectively, as 'the speaker', not as Hadji who takes Martin down to bathe and folds his pyjamas neatly before catching the 8.50 train. It produced a queer division in my mind—you, so familiar, standing on the platform, dressed in the neat stripey suit I know so well, the handkerchief I have so often rescued from the laundry sticking out of your pocket, and then the public Harold Nicolson

---

1. At the Barn Theatre, near Tenterden, Kent, on "Foreign Affairs and Public Opinion." Harold wrote in his diary, "I did not enjoy it at all."

standing up to address an audience, becoming a stranger, a public figure, and yet remaining Hadji just the same, blinking at the lights.

Darling, it was a beautiful speech. I say 'beautiful' with intention. You will laugh, because you make similar speeches all the time, and this letter will sound to you like fan-mail. But I do mean it; out of the deeps of my soul.

HAROLD TO VITA   *4 King's Bench Walk*

17 July 1939

Benzie rang up. He said, "Daddy, I have been asked to the Buckingham Palace Ball on Wednesday and I suppose it is all right to refuse?" I said, "No, you cannot possibly refuse." He said, "But I am dining out that night for another dance." I said, "Well, that may be, but you had better not refuse." He said, "But couldn't I go to the Master of the Household and ask to be let off?" I said, "No—any hostess will understand that a command is a command, and that you as a member of the household have got to go." He said, "But I shall be so *bored.*"

That fairly got my goat, and for once in my life I cursed him. I said that if he had a first class appointment he must put up with the rough and not merely take the smooth. That if he did not do his duty in every way he would lose the job. That in any case to describe a court ball as something odious and intolerable was showing lack of intelligence. Anyhow, it proves that he has some qualms of conscience that he should have consulted me at all. But what are we to do about the boy? He has no *savoir faire* at all.

HAROLD TO VITA   *Yacht Mar, Guernsey*

15 August 1939

We had a gay time in Cherbourg since there was a fair on and we watched the merry-go-rounds and fired at the shooting galleries. Niggs was rather good at it and won a little woolly monkey. Then this morning we put out of the harbour and came on here on our way to Brest. It was without question the perfectest of sailing days that I have ever seen. A light following wind, blue dancing seas and not a cloud in the sky. We read and joked and basked in the sun and were wretched when we began to see the outline of the Islands in front of us. We passed very close to Sark and it is in truth a fine sight. Then we passed Herm and I smiled rather sadly at the thought we once had of taking it. I do not think we should have liked it. Then in we came to the harbour here and while Niggs and John [Sparrow] are busy tidying up the deck, I am here in the little cabin writing to my dearest eponym.

HAROLD TO VITA   *4 King's Bench Walk*

25 August 1939

Yesterday's meeting of the House was glum in the extreme.[1] None of the speeches reached the level of the occasion. Chamberlain was like a coroner summing up a murder case.

I had a long talk with Lloyd George and Winston. They said that it was hopeless to expect Parliament to speak out except in a secret session. We should have such a session at once and tell the P.M. what a hopeless old crow he was. I gather that he at last realizes that fact and has offered to resign, but the King (rightly) has refused to accept his resignation. Obviously the man cannot leave the ship which he has run on to the rocks. He must for the moment remain in command. But the reception which he had in the House yesterday must have convinced him that we know how much he is personally to blame for this disaster. Naturally I feel sorry for him. Who would not? but his refusal to take into the Cabinet those who had criticised appeasement has demonstrated his mean and vain side and has lost him all sympathy. The reception yesterday (compared to the ovation last September) was so cold that he must have felt it as a douche. Poor man! Poor man!

1. Parliament had been recalled when Russia announced a Pact of mutual support with Germany.

I cheered as much as I could, having a weak spot for lost causes. But it is a lost cause. Nor is it concerned with personalities. It is concerned with realities. We have said since 1935, "Be careful, Germany is plotting our destruction." He said, "Trust me and I shall make friends with Germany." The result is that we are today in the most dangerous position we have been in since after Austerlitz.

The Second World War began on 1 September 1939 with Hitler's invasion of Poland. Britain and France declared war on Germany two days later. Harold's first wartime task was to write, in two weeks, a 50,000-word book, Why Britain Is at War, which was published on 7 November and soon sold over 100,000 copies. He was immensely active in this period, broadcasting regularly, writing a weekly column for the Spectator, reviewing books for the Daily Telegraph, and speaking at meetings all over the country and sometimes in France. Vita remained at Sissinghurst and joined the Kent Committee of the Women's Land Army. Both their sons were soon in uniform, Ben with an anti-aircraft battery at Chatham and Nigel as an officer cadet at Sandhurst. After Hitler's conquest of Poland in less than a month, there was a lull (the "Phoney War") throughout the winter, while the British Expeditionary Force manned a section of the fortified Franco-Belgian frontier. Hostilities began in earnest in April 1940 when the Germans invaded Denmark and Norway.

VITA TO HAROLD   *Sissinghurst*

28 September 1939

I very much enjoyed seeing the Wolves. It was a lovely day and the Downs looked very beautiful in the sunshine. Virginia seemed well in health, though naturally unhappy in mind. She says the only good thing which has come out of the war for her so far is that Ethel (Smyth) has fallen in love with her next-door neighbour, who, like herself, is aged 84. For years they have lived side by side avoiding each other, but the war caused them to talk over the garden fence, with the result that they discovered they were twin souls.

Leonard told me to warn you about Kingsley Martin.[1] He says he is the worst scare-monger and rumour-monger in London, far worse in talk than in the N.S. and that half the 'stories' that go about originate with him. Allowing for wolfish exaggeration, I daresay there is something in it.

I do like the Wolves so much. They always do me good. Virginia was so sweet and affectionate to me. I was touched. She told Ethel that she only really loved three people: Leonard, Vanessa and myself, which annoyed Ethel but pleased me.

HAROLD TO VITA   *4 King's Bench Walk*

2 November 1939

We had Lord Trenchard[2] to dinner last night. He is angry with the Air Force for not attacking Germany. He says we have an immense geographical advantage and ought to use it. It is very difficult indeed for them to bomb us across the North Sea and very easy for us to bomb them across France. For instance a great many machines which get away, get away 'wounded'. Now our wounded machines can land in France. The German wounded machines have to go back across the North Sea and a very large proportion must drop into the sea before they get home. It is for this reason that he thinks the Germans are almost certain to attack Holland. But they have mighty little time to do it in. The weather has been on our side. If they do not start their attack at once they will have to wait till the Spring by which time we shall have more aeroplanes than they have.

He was most optimistic.

---

1. Editor of the *New Statesman*, 1931–60.
2. The Marshal of the Royal Air Force, who was appointed its first leader in 1918 when it became a service independent of the Army.

VITA TO HAROLD   *Sissinghurst*

12 December 1939

The Lion Pond is being drained. I have got what I hope will be
a really lovely scheme for it: all white flowers, with some clumps of
very pale pink. White clematis, white lavender, white Agapanthus,
white double primroses, white anemones, white camellias, white lilies
including *giganteum* in one corner, and the pale peach-coloured
Primula pulverulenta. [1]

HAROLD TO VITA   *4 King's Bench Walk*

1 March 1940

I had such a rush yesterday I couldn't write. I had to revise my
speeches for France, dictate a speech for Glasgow, dictate a broadcast
for France. I also had to go and see Vansittart. He is worried about
the Home Front. Not merely are the Peace Pledge Union people and
the Communists creating much havoc, but the rich right-wing appeas-
ers are getting active. Both are being much assisted by Jo Kennedy and
Maisky[2]; particularly Kennedy (who is about to return) is very dangerous. He is essentially a stupid man but he has a swollen head and
thinks he can play a great part in world politics. I see the danger of
such people. Everything is so hush and secret that the rulers can really
dictate policy without question and it is very difficult to have a good
parliamentary opposition.

I lunched with the lobby correspondents. Winston made a magnificent speech. I have never seen him in such form. He did not speak
about the war but about the House of Commons. The Prime Minister
[Chamberlain] was there and Winston could not resist teasing him. He
did not like it at all.

---

1. This idea was carried out after the war, not in the Lion Pond, which was small and sunken,
   but in the old rose garden beside the Priest's House. The "White Garden" is now the best
   known of many separate gardens at Sissinghurst.
2. The Ambassadors of the United States and the Soviet Union.

On 10 May 1940, the day when Hitler attacked in the West,
Chamberlain resigned and Winston Churchill succeeded him
as Prime Minister. Harold Nicolson was promoted from the
back benches to become Parliamentary Secretary to the Ministry of
Information, under his friend Duff Cooper as Minister. Thus during
the critical retreat of the British Army to and from Dunkirk, the
collapse of France, the air battles over southern England, and the
bombardment of London, he was in the center of events and in
considerable danger, as was Vita at Sissinghurst, which lay in the
path of the German bombers and on the route to the capital which
the Germans would have taken if they had invaded Kent. Harold's
main duties concerned civilian morale, war-aims, relations with
France and the United States, and advice to the public on how to
act if invasion came. His short period as a junior Minister (May
1940 to July 1941) was ended by Churchill's curt demand that he
vacate his office in favour of a Labour Member.

HAROLD TO VITA   *Ministry of Information*

19 May 1940

Things seemed a little better this morning. Duff [Cooper] went off
to luncheon in the country and Winston dashed down for two hours
to Chartwell. I went to lunch at the Travellers and then returned here.
In the hall I met Ronnie Tree and saw from his face that something
awful had happened. He took me to my room and then said that he
had been to No. 10 to pick up Brendan Bracken for luncheon, and just
as they were leaving, Anthony Eden and Ironside[1] flew up with

---

1. Field Marshal Sir Edmund Ironside, Chief of the Imperial General Staff, 1939–40.

haggard faces and said that Winston must be summoned back immediately. It is all terribly grave. We know no details as yet.[2] Poor Winston—having to speak on the wireless tonight!

Darling, we share together this unutterable sorrow.

VITA TO HAROLD   *Sissinghurst*

22 May 1940

My darling

How ghastly it all is. How thankful I am to think of your dug-out.[3] I begin to wonder when I shall ever see you again. Supposing Kent is evacuated, as seems increasingly likely, and I have to go? In that case I suppose the Government would be evacuated too, so we may next meet in Bristol!

I dread the possibility of Niggs being sent out [to France]. But what's the good of going on like this?

Darling, to think we should come to this! And the eventual outcome—victory, or defeat? Anyhow, you and I have always foreseen the possibility of defeat, since the beginning of the war and even before that. The only thing for us to do now is to reverse that idea and make the most of such poor hope as remains to us.

HAROLD TO VITA   *Ministry of Information*

22 May 1940

We hope to pinch the German bulge and to throw them back from the Channel. They are not there in strong force and we have already retaken Arras.[4] But you are right to feel we should be prepared. I do not know whether the Government have prepared any scheme for evacuation [of Kent] but I shall find out and you can be certain that

---

2. The Germans had broken through the French defenses and reached the Channel coast on 20 May, thus cutting off the British Army.
3. The reinforced basement of the Ministry of Information.
4. Arras was not "retaken," since it had not yet been captured by the Germans, but Allied attempts to pinch out the bulge ended in failure and the retreat to Dunkirk continued.

I shall let you know. Meanwhile you should think it out and begin to prepare something. You will have to take out the Buick and get it into a fit state to start with a full petrol tank. You should put inside it some food for 24 hours and pack in the back your jewels and my diaries. You will want clothes and anything else very precious (Barbara?), but the rest will have to be left behind. After all, that is what the French did in 1915 and we have got to do it ourselves. You might make for Devonshire. This all sounds very alarming, but it would be foolish to pretend that the danger is inconceivable.

VITA TO HAROLD   *Sissinghurst*

24 May 1940

Beale[1] came here yesterday with the officer in charge of all the searchlights in this district. He wanted to inspect the country from the top of the tower. He was very frank. It is not only parachutists that they are afraid of, but troop-carrying planes landing on our own Sissinghurst fields and the fields at Bettenham. If this happens, our tower-guard rushes downstairs, informs Beale who telephones, and shock troops are produced. They have pickets all over the district. The officer was obviously longing for German planes to choose Sissinghurst or Bettenham to land on; personally I wasn't sure that I shared his longing. Nor was Beale. "My wheat . . ." he remarked ruefully.

HAROLD TO VITA   *Ministry of Information*

27 May 1940

I am afraid that the news this afternoon is very bad indeed and that we must expect the Germans to surround a large proportion of our army and to occupy the whole of the area of Belgium and Northern France. We must also face the possibility that the French may make a separate peace, especially if Italy joins in the conflict. I warn you of

---

1. Oswald Beale, the tenant farmer at Sissinghurst.

this so that you will prepare your mind for the bad news when it comes and be ready to summon all the courage that is in you.

VITA TO HAROLD   *Sissinghurst*

29 May 1940

I am so appalled by thinking of the Belgians that I don't know what to say.[1] Not only is it a major disaster, but a real soul-hurt. I could no more have believed it of him than I could believe it of our own King. One is so shocked and incredulous that Duff's [Cooper] plea to suspend judgement is scarcely needed. He *cannot* have been a merely 5th column traitor to his own country and his allies. Yet it looks horribly like it.

VITA TO HAROLD   *Sissinghurst*

3 June 1940

Last night was one of the most beautiful nights I ever remember. I was out late by myself getting some of Beale's sheep back into the field from which they had escaped. One lamb got *égaré* into another field and I pursued it through the long wet grass, led by its bleatings and the faint glimmer of its little body. The rim of the sky was still pink with sunset, Venus hung alone and enormous, and the silhouette of the sentry appeared above the parapet of the tower.

HAROLD TO VITA   *4 King's Bench Walk*

4 June 1940

I was terribly rushed yesterday as I had to get out a memo for the Cabinet about invasion. We do not know whether to warn people

---

1. The Belgian army, on the instructions of King Leopold, capitulated on 27 May.

now or to wait until it becomes likely. It is 80 per cent probable that the enemy will attack France first and only go for us afterwards. Yet we must be prepared for the invasion when it comes and the public must be told what to do. We have got a long list of instructions, but do not like to issue them without Cabinet orders. As Duff was over in Paris I had to do all this myself.

My dearest Viti—I suppose it is some comfort to feel that it will either be all over in August or else we shall have won. Hitler will not be able to go on into next year. The whole thing is, "Shall we be able to stand it?" I think we shall. And if we do win, then truly it will be a triumph of human character over the machine.

I force myself to see things at their worst. I do not really believe in my soul that the Germans will make a successful invasion of this country, but I do think they may bring off a smash and grab at several points. But I force myself to foresee what will happen if they land at Hastings and Faversham and make a pincer movement to cut off our forces in Kent. This will mean that there will be fighting at Ashford. It means that you will be in danger. Now that thought makes my heart stand still with a sick pause. But then it beats again. You are a brave person and you have a sense of responsibility. It would not be you to run away and leave your people behind. If you are told to do it, then you must go. But I see, and you see, that you must stick it out if you are allowed to. And finally there is the bare bodkin.[1] That is a real comfort.

But actually I do not think it will come, especially if the French are able to put up some show of resistance on the Somme. How I long for the spirit of Verdun to revive! It may—you know what the French are. I feel so deeply grateful for having hard work to do in these days. And now comes Italy.[2] My dearest, what a mean and skulking thing to do. The French have offered them practically all that they want in Tunis etc., but they want more and more. They are like the people who rob corpses on the battlefield. I forget what those people are called. The Greeks had a name for it [Necrosylia].

Bless you my poppet—courage and hope.

---

1. The "bare bodkin" was a lethal pill that Harold and Vita had acquired from their doctor, for suicide in the case of capture by the German army. See *Hamlet,* Act III, Scene I: "He himself might his quietus make with a bare bodkin."
2. Mussolini declared war on 10 June.

HAROLD TO VITA   *4 King's Bench Walk*

10 June 1940

I looked in at our Duty Room to see how the map of the battle was getting on.[1] To my horror I saw that the Germans had got to Pont de L'Arche on the Seine. But it must only be a thin spear of armoured columns and we must try to cut them off. The French, we hear, are fighting absolutely magnificently. But it is dreadful that we cannot help them. We simply must do something. It is all very well getting the announcer to say, "This is our battle," and so on. We must do more than that.

If the French can only hold them up, what a triumph it would be! The Italians are playing the dirtiest game ever played. I sat down in my bath last night and said to myself, "Now be a sensible person and try and see the Italian point of view." But try as I could, I could see nothing more than the point of view of a man who waits till the merchant drops on one knee before attacking him and stealing his goods.

Darling, do you feel as I do? Never have we been threatened with such separation as we are threatened with today: and never have we been closer to each other. I feel no need to say anything to you. I just know that you and I think the same. I have found in these weeks that a love such as ours really is above space and time.

HAROLD TO VITA   *4 King's Bench Walk*

19 June 1940

We still do not know what terms the Germans intend to impose on France.[2] If they were wise they would give good terms and treat the French population very well. This will not only enable them to exploit French resources but also increase defeatism over here. I think it is practically certain that the Americans will come in in November, and if we can last till then, all is well. Anyhow as a precaution I have

---

1. The Germans had crossed the Somme to renew their attack on the French Army, and entered Paris on 14 June.
2. The French Government had sued for an Armistice on 17 June.

got the bare bodkin. I shall bring down your half on Sunday. It all looks very simple.

How I wish Winston would not talk on the wireless unless he is feeling in good form. He hates the microphone and when we bullied him into speaking last night he just sulked and read his House of Commons speech over again.[3] Now as delivered in the H. of C., that speech was magnificent, especially the concluding sentences. But it sounded ghastly on the wireless. All the great vigour he put into it seemed to evaporate.

HAROLD TO VITA   *Ministry of Information*

26 June 1940

I must say that the French have behaved with intolerable cowardice and treachery. They gave us their word of honour that whatever happened they would not allow the French fleet to fall into the enemy's hands but they seem to have surrendered it already. We have taken steps to prevent the rot going further. But what a collapse for a great nation! Henri Bernstein[4] told me that most of the upper classes were almost delighted at Hitler's victory since they imagined it would save them from communism. He said that nothing in Shakespeare could equal the complete moral collapse of French society. He feared that this would mean the end of France. *"Ils nous ont trahis avec une bassesse inconcevable."* They are of course trying to excuse themselves on the grounds that it was all our fault.

VITA TO HAROLD   *Sissinghurst*

9 July 1940

The army came here yesterday, looking for large country houses to use as headquarters if necessary. They were much taken with Sissing-

---

3. The "finest hour" speech.
4. The French dramatist. After the fall of France he lived in New York until 1946.

hurst, I fear, for this purpose. I don't at all relish the idea, as headquarters are apt to become the favourite target of German bombers. The army was two young officers and an N.C.O. in a lorry. One of the officers was an absolute dream of beauty and elegance, in a black cloth beret and pale tight riding breeches. Very polite they were, and I left them talking to Beale.

HAROLD TO VITA   *4 King's Bench Walk*

15 July 1940

I had such a curious and distressing experience this evening. André Cheradame came to see me. In the period before the last war he was a famous journalist and wrote books about Pan-Germanism and was quite a figure. What he wanted was that we should get him a passage to the U.S.A. and arrange about his money. Now getting him a passage means that we have to requisition a berth and turn out some wretched person whose claims may be greater than we know. Arranging his money means trouble with the Treasury. It all boils down to influence and favouritism which I loathe. Thus when Cheradame came to see me this evening, I was none too well disposed. He tottered in and said that he must take his secretary with him. All he wanted was a letter from me to say that he and his secretary were essential for national service. There was no real reason why he should not remain here.

I then realised that I had lost all sense of pity. Having adjusted my mind to the loss of my own life, I had become so hard that I did not care for the lives of others. I felt only contempt for a person twenty years older than myself who could not *"faire la mort du loup."* [1]

Anyhow this smelly trembly old man came and fiddled with papers at my desk. I was correct and calm. But I was as hard as nails. And then I felt a beast and the memory of it hangs round me. I feel ashamed of myself. It is easy to be brave if one suppresses one's own sensibilities. But it is not so easy to be brave if one tries to keep a perfect proportion between one's hardness to oneself and one's softness to other people.

---

1. Alfred de Vigny's poem (1838), which proclaims that man has a lesson to learn from the wolf, which, when cornered, licks its wounds and dies silently.

There is a tendency to feel that Hitler may hesitate to attack us now that we are so strong. But I do not believe this. I think he is bound to attack us.

VITA TO HAROLD   *Sissinghurst*

17 July 1940

I was amused by your story of Cheradame. But I am sure you were right, and what you call your hardness was merely a sense of proportion induced by the changed scale of values by which we now order our lives. Not that our essential values would ever change, but the top ones do and must. We are forced to become less soft and sentimental about personal convenience and safety. This is one effect of Nazi theories raging through Europe, and I am not at all sure that it is not a salutary effect. It may lead us to consider our personal security and prosperity a little less, and to realise the insecurity and anxieties of other people a little more. (By 'our' I mean the well-off classes.)

I see that the invasion is now announced for Friday. Don't worry about me down here if we should get separated. If the worst comes to the worst, well, there it is. Like you I have adjusted myself to the idea of losing my own life. I don't in the least want to lose it; but if I must, I must. I should worry about you, naturally. But we both have the bare bodkin. I prefer the idea of doing a Jeanne Hachette[1] on the top of the tower with Dada's shot-guns.

HAROLD TO VITA   *Ministry of Information*

19 August 1940

It was fun yesterday wasn't it—watching the aeroplanes fighting for Britain in the sunshine.[2] Our people here (I mean our air experts)

---

1. Jeanne Hachette saved Beauvais in 1472 when it was under attack by Charles the Bold. One of his soldiers had scaled the battlements, when Jeanne cut him down and flung him into the moat, thus reviving the courage of the garrison.
2. The Battle of Britain started on 13 August, and much of it took place above the Weald of Kent.

think it the best day we have had mainly because we brought down so high a proportion of German fighters in which they are weaker than bombers.

I got caught by the siren at Tunbridge Wells. We were herded into the waiting room. There were all types of people and many women and children, but there was no trace of nervousness. Generally people when they are frightened talk and laugh abnormally, but there was no sign of that at all. They read their magazines and newspapers quite quietly. Eventually my train came in and I looked out to see if I could see any damage. But none at all. There was a bomb at Dunton Green but I saw no signs of it. Also one at Tenterden. People are beginning to feel that there is no possibility of even seriously impeding this country by air bombing. I whisper to myself, "Yes, but he will start gas." But really yesterday he had 600 over, and for the damage created, we could stand 6,000. Our losses were really very slight. In this week we are as good in the air as Drake's men were at sea. It is a heartening talk. God! I feel so proud of my country! Bless it.

VITA TO HAROLD   *Sissinghurst*

28 August 1940

We had such a raid last night: the whole of the South Cottage shook, and I am told that 6 bombs were dropped at Frittenden falling in fields only but making a horrible row. The sky over towards Tenterden was lit up with a red glow—so I suppose they must have started a fire there—I saw flares falling through the darkness.

Today, so far, we have had 3 warnings and some bursts of machine-guns overhead this morning behind the clouds.

Darling, I am appalled by something which has happened. You know I told you Violet [Trefusis] was coming here today—well, she rang up this morning to say she couldn't because her mother was returning to London, but might she come on Saturday for the night instead? I lost my head and said yes—but you will be here, and you didn't want to meet her. Anyhow I daresay it won't come off. I devoutly hope so.

HAROLD TO VITA   *4 King's Bench Walk*

3 September 1940

I read the Keats letters coming up in a belated and dawdling train. His letter to [Charles Armitage] Brown from Naples is one of the most terrifying things that I have ever read. The knowledge of his own genius ("an intelligence in splints") and the certainty of his approaching death are bad enough—but one has to add to these the obsession about Fanny Brawne. What a beast one feels her to be! The whole story is obscure. When he was staying next door to her at Hampstead she seems to have been kind; she visited him regularly and showed herself at the window since it gave him pleasure; but thereafter she appears to have become irritated by his passion, and it is clear that from his bed of sickness he writhed in agony at the thought that she was going out into the world and seeing people whom he did not know. But what essential dignity he had! That fierce integrity about poetry and his own art. He is too great even to be jealous of Byron.

Darling—if only one could have told Keats that one hundred and twenty years after his death people like you and I should in a great crisis (with death hurtling at us through the skies) write to each other in respect for him? That, I suppose, is one of the benefits of war. One ceases to think of the topical or the fashionable or even the contemporary, and falls back for comfort (which one finds) upon the beauty and the dignity of the human imagination and character. One feels the sinews of one's soul grow hale. It may be this factor which in this year of suffering has made my love for you tower like Everest above the shabby hills of self-indulgence.

HAROLD TO VITA   *Ministry of Information*

16 September 1940

We did far better yesterday than was given out. Our people decided to throw in a proportion of their reserve fighters. We got down 185 for certain but there were another 80 'probables'. This excludes the further 40 'possibles'. One can be certain that of the 60 probables, fifty were done for. That means a loss to them of 235.[1]

Everybody here is rather cocky today. It was a real defeat for the Germans yesterday and the American press is taking it up hot and strong. My dear, what a world we live in. Ugly, heroic and mad. I am ugly but I am not mad. Therefore I shall be heroic. It is very odd that I should not be more frightened. It rather worries me, since I fear I may be suppressing fear and will end in a nervous collapse. But truly I am not conscious of any fear. I am conscious only of immense curiosity and a strong desire not to die.

I shall be careful, dearest, truly I shall. I saw Vansittart today. He was 5 to 1 on invasion three weeks ago. Today he is not so sure, if it does not come tonight or tomorrow.

HAROLD TO VITA   *Ministry of Information*

2 October 1940

I attended the Cabinet Committee on Home Policy this morning. We all had to go down to the basement at one moment. We should have been a big bag as six Cabinet Ministers were there. The odd thing is that the people in the East End refuse to budge. We had expected something like panic evacuation and in fact the infidels ran away as quick as they could. But the cockney sticks to his ruins to an embarrassing degree. He doesn't want to be given a basement in Belgravia. Not he. He just wants to stay put.

HAROLD TO VITA   *Ministry of Information*

8 October 1940

I went to supper with Julian Huxley[2]. Poor man, he is rather worried by his animals. They are always bombing round Regent's

---

1. This was the day when the Luftwaffe made their supreme effort to overcome the RAF. The true figure of their losses was not 235 planes but 56.
2. The author and scientist. He was Secretary of the London Zoo, 1935–42.

Park, and the other day they hit the Zebra cage and one of the Zebras bolted as far as Marylebone. "At any rate," he said, "I think the carnivores are pretty safe." But he saw no humour in the situation. He was clearly much worried.

I like him so much. We discussed peace aims and a raid began in the middle. The whole flat shook. I was relieved when he offered to drive me home. We walked round to his garage. It was a perfect night. The moon showed through mackerel clouds and the guns were booming splendidly. The streets were all silent under the noise of the bombardment and suddenly the whole sky was lit up by a flare which sailed down gently under a parachute with tracer bullets after it. It was beautiful in the extreme but I was glad when I was safe again inside the Ministry.[3] One really cannot dine out these days.

VITA TO HAROLD *Sissinghurst*

8 October 1940

Lord! we have had a lot of raids this morning. They began at 8.30 and are still going on at 11. There was a most lovely sight: ten white machines climbed absolutely sheer, leaving perfectly regular white streaks of smoke like furrows in a cloudless blue sky, while a machine lower down looped smoke like gigantic spectacles before shooting up to join its friends. We saw one catch fire and fall. "That's one less to go after Hadji," I thought.

HAROLD TO VITA *Ministry of Information*

16 October 1940

Last night was the worst I have had. Bombs boomed all round. The whole place shook. I slept fairly well but it was none too good. When

---

3. At this most intense period of the night raids on London, Harold slept in the tower of the Ministry of Information, where he was less exposed to the bombs than at King's Bench Walk.

I walked down to K.B.W. this morning there was a smell of burning in the air.

There had been a heavy bomb on the poor little Temple. The whole of Middle Temple Lane was down and the Middle Temple Hall (where Shakespeare acted in front of Queen Elizabeth) was badly hurt. Not destroyed but just knocked about and the windows blown out. My own little K.B.W. was all neat outside, but when I got in, I found that two of the pictures had been blown down and that the panelling behind them had been splintered. Nothing bad really, but I was glad I had not been sleeping there at the time. The whole place was full of soot and ashes like Pompeii.

I had a Cabinet Committee in the morning and then the House. People were grim but not in the least gay. The new tactics of the Germans in sending over fighter bombers in twos and threes all night certainly faces us with a problem.

In the afternoon I had to address the American correspondents. It did not go well at all. They are enraged by our censorship. Poor people, they feel that the bombardment of London is the hottest news ever and they get furious at our stopping their stories. I am not good at coping with that sort of thing.

HAROLD TO VITA   *Ministry of Information*

6 November 1940

I was so happy this morning when I heard of the Roosevelt result.[1] I had steeled myself to pretend not to mind either way, and I think it was true that three months ago it would not have mattered so much if wee Willy Winkie had got in. But in the last month Roosevelt had become identified with our cause and Willkie (unfairly perhaps) with the German cause. Although the German papers have been very cautious about it all, the French papers in occupied France have not been so cautious at all. They have openly rejoiced at the apparent decline

---

1. President Roosevelt was elected for his third term with a majority of five million votes. He carried thirty-eight States, and Wendell Willkie, his Republican opponent, ten.

in Roosevelt's popularity and said that it shows that America has no faith in our victory. Now they will have to swallow their words.

HAROLD TO VITA   *Queen's Hotel, Leeds*

7 January 1941

We had a ghastly drive here, or rather the country through which we drove [from Manchester] was hell. Great rolling moors under a grey sky, not unhedged or unvintaged enough to be magnificent, but like soiled grey counterpanes. Then in between and all along the valleys dark mills belching smoke. God, how I wish man had never invented the machine! I sympathise with the Nottingham frame-breakers. They saw the light.

I dined with Billy Harlech,[1] the Regional Commissioner. He had been spending the day with the Queen visiting Sheffield. He says that when the car stops, the Queen nips out into the snow and goes straight into the middle of the crowd and starts talking to them. For a moment or two they just gaze and gape in astonishment. But then they all start talking at once: "Hi! Your Majesty! Look here!" She has that quality of making everybody feel that they and they alone are being spoken to. It is, I think, because she has very large eyes which she opens very wide and turns straight upon one.

HAROLD TO VITA   *Ministry of Information*

21 January 1941

I wonder whether you fully realize what it means to me coming home. It is like what a motor must feel having fresh water in its radiator. I have got enough petrol. But it is the cooling drafts I need.

---

1. Lord Harlech, the North-East Regional Commissioner for Civil Defence. He had been Secretary of State for the Colonies, 1936–38.

Your love for me is a thing which always surprises and delights me as the beauty of Knole takes one by surprise.

I got to what remains of the station[1] in time. It poured with rain and we cowered in a tin hut looking out on the remains of the snow as if we were refugees on the Finnish frontier.

I lunched with de Gaulle. He is less horrible with his hat off since his hair is young and spruce and his eyes look tired although not benevolent. He attacked me on the ground that the Ministry were not sufficiently anti-Pétain. I held my ground. [Hugh] Dalton and [Clement] Attlee were there. De Gaulle told me that he had received a letter from unoccupied France telling him that the whole country was with him. His correspondent had put at the top in red ink that he had written the letter from a desire to express himself, but he well knew that the Vichy Censor would not approve it. Written across was a message in violet ink—*"La censeur de Vichy approuve totalement."*

HAROLD TO VITA   *Ministry of Information*

25 February 1941

Winston came here today to inspect us and to see some of our films. We showed him 'Cambridge'. That was my idea. He loved it. He said, "That is fine stuff." He also saw all our posters and stuff and was very kind about them. We had kept his visit dark, but the whisper went round and all the typists leant out of the windows and cheered and cheered. He was rather touched. The Press cheered him also. What popularity that man has got!

Kenneth Clark and I took Sibyl [Colefax] to dinner. It was not really a success. She wanted to talk gossip, and we wanted to talk shop. In the taxi coming back, I asked K. whether Sibyl was becoming a bore or whether we were so deeply concerned with the war that all trivial conversation seemed tiresome. He said that it did not work out that way. He loved nothing more than getting away from the war and

---

1. Staplehurst station (five miles from Sissinghurst), which had been destroyed by a fighter plane that crashed on it in flames.

talking about other things. I said that was why I looked forward to coming to Sissinghurst, as you never bothered me about war subjects but talked about the boys or the garden. You always listened when I wanted to talk my war things. So then we decided that Sibyl was not as intelligent as we thought. Then we corrected that, and said that why she bored us was that she was really out for inside information, and wanted us to tell her things the repetition of which would increase her self-importance. Then we felt we had been unkind about her. But were we? There is such a greedy look in her eyes when she scents inside information. I think this war is like a sieve. All the dross appears. I suppose that really K. himself is an ambitious and worldly person. But all that has gone. He works twelve hours a day[1] for purely impersonal reasons. So do I. Although I was pleased at the little pat Winston gave me on my bald head. But that is not ambition. It is just admiration for a great man.

HAROLD TO VITA   *Ministry of Information*

31 March 1941

It is always a gloomy moment for me when I unpack the *panier* which we packed together. I take out the flowers sadly and think of you picking them and putting the paper round them. But today it was worse, as I feel such a failure as a help to you. I do not know what it is, but I never seem to be able to help you when you are in trouble. I loathe your being unhappy more than I loathe anything. But I just moon about feeling wretched myself, and when I look back on my life, I see that the only times when I have been really unhappy are when you have been unhappy too.

I wonder whether you would have been happier if married to a more determined and less sensitive man. On the one hand you would have hated any sense of control or management, and other men might not have understood your desire for independence. I have always

1. Kenneth Clark was not only Director of the National Gallery, but Director of the Film Division of the Ministry of Information.

respected that, and you have often mistaken it for aloofness on my part. What bothers me is whether I have given way too much to your eccentricities. Some outside person might imagine that I should have made more of my life if I had had someone like Diana De La Warr to share my career. There are moments when I think you reproach yourself for not having been more interested in my pursuits and for not having pushed against my diffidence. I never feel that myself. I have always felt that the struggle in the market-place was for me to fight alone, and that you were there as something wholly different.

But what has always worried me is your dual personality. The one tender, wise and with such a sense of responsibility. And the other rather cruel and extravagant. The former has been what I have always clung to as the essential you, but the latter has always alarmed me and I have tried to dismiss it from my mind—or, rather, I have always accepted it as the inevitable counterpart of your remarkable personality. I have felt that this side of you was beyond my understanding, and when you have got into a real mess because of it, you have been angry with me for not coping with the more violent side in yourself.

I do not think that you have ever quite realised how deeply unhappy your eccentric side has often rendered me. When I am unhappy, I shut up like an oyster. I love you so much, darling. I hold my head in my hands worrying about you. I was nearly killed by a taxi today. I only missed an accident by a hair's breadth. And my first thought was, "If I had really been taken to hospital in a mess, then Viti would have been shaken out of her muzzy moods." I love you so much.

VITA TO HAROLD   *Sissinghurst*

31 March 1941

My darling

I have just had the most awful shock: Virginia has killed herself. It is not in the papers, but I got letters from Leonard and also from Vanessa, telling me. It was last Friday. Leonard came home to find a note saying she was going to commit suicide and they think she has drowned herself as he found her stick floating on the river. He says she had not been well for the last few weeks and was terrified of going mad again. He says, "It was, I suppose, the strain of the war and finishing her book and she could not rest or eat."

Why, oh why, did he leave her alone knowing all this? He must be reproaching himself terribly, poor man. They had not yet found the body.[1]

I simply can't take it in—that lovely mind, that lovely spirit. And she seemed so well when I last saw her, and I had a joky letter from her only a couple of weeks ago.

She must have been quite out of her mind or she would never have brought such sorrow and horror on Leonard and Vanessa.

Vanessa has seen him and says he was amazingly self-controlled and calm, but insisted on being left alone—I cannot help wondering if he will follow her example. I do not see him living without her.

Perhaps you better not say to anyone that it was suicide, though I suppose they can't keep it out of the papers. I suppose there will have to be an inquest.

What a nightmare for L. to have to go through. When they find her body, and all that.

Your Mar

HAROLD TO VITA   *Ministry of Information*

2 April 1941

I am glad I came down last night since I was so worried about you and it was a relief to see you taking the shock so well. I hope you can manage to dismiss the physical aspect from your mind and to concentrate only upon the great joy that friendship has been to you. But, my dearest, I know that Virginia meant something to you which nobody else can ever mean and that you will feel deprived of a particular sort of haven which was a background comfort and strength. I have felt sad about it every hour of the day.

---

1. Virginia Woolf's body was found three weeks later in the River Ouse, Sussex, a short distance downstream from where she had drowned herself.

17 April 1941

The Blitz last night was the worst we have had. Even I slept badly listening to the chatter and jabber of the bombs and guns. There was a moment when I thought I should never get to sleep and that it would be interesting to go down and see what was happening. But that meant putting on bedroom slippers and a British Warm [overcoat] and I felt that I might look foolish. The alternative was to dress completely, but I knew that if I did that I should remain up all night. With the result that I stayed in bed and slept fitfully. I am sorry now. On the one hand the view from our upper stories was superb. And on the other hand we had some 40 casualties from the Victoria Club opposite who were carried in. Five of them died in our hall.

London today is rather muzzy and distraught. The damage is very bad indeed. Selfridges has gone and most of Jermyn Street and the R.A.C. and other clubs. Windham's has collapsed, and the London Library has escaped by a hair's breadth. In fact it is a Coventry and has made people half angry and half worried.

30 April 1941

How difficult this world is! I quite like it in a way, but I wish the Germans were less successful. And I wish our own people were less foolish. Bless their hearts.

I have got into a row with Herbert Morrison [Home Secretary] because Lady Astor lost her head at Plymouth and started screaming. [1] I quite see that Lady Astor had survived five raids in nine nights and had the right to be unstrung. But why the censor should have stopped her ululations I do not quite see. Anyhow I am to be put on the mat by Morrison tomorrow and it amuses me having to defend Lady Astor. I think she was wrong. Plymouth as a result is almost totally destroyed.

---

1. She had said publicly that Plymouth, her constituency, had been so badly bombed that the people were panicking, with the result that the Germans bombed it again.

Kingsley Martin came to see me this evening and talked defeatism. He wants to make peace with Germany. He calls my opposition to that suggestion 'emotionalism' whereas his panic point-of-view is called 'facing realities'. He is a shattered worm. I left him feeling that I could fight the whole panzer divisions of Germany armed only with a fountain pen. Nothing does me so much good as cowardice in other people.

VITA TO HAROLD   *Sissinghurst*

4 June 1941

My darling,

I write this after dinner. A big thunderstorm is circling round somewhere: a pale flash comes, and then a dim rumble some appreciable time later. I was up in the potting shed, getting out the dahlias from under the bench. (I have not dared to plant them out before now, because of the frosts.) I was thinking to myself, as one does think when one is alone and doing something mechanical like putting dahlias into a trug, I was thinking, "How queer. I suppose Hadji and I have been about as unfaithful to one another as one well could be from the conventional point of view, even worse than unfaithful if you add in homosexuality, and yet I swear no two people could love one another more than we do after all these years."

It *is* queer, isn't it? It does destroy all orthodox ideas of marriage?

Yet it is true, so true that I know our love to be like a great oak tree with lots of acorns, or like a tulip-tree with lots of flowers.

I do think we have managed things cleverly.

I was sorry I had said to Cyril[1] that I wanted you to divorce me for the sake of economy; I thought he might misunderstand so I wrote to him and put it right. I don't think he would misunderstand, but I wasn't taking any chances.

Goodnight, my darling.

Your

Mar

---

1. Professor Cyril Joad, the philosopher, and one of Harold's partners in the popular radio chat-show *The Brains Trust*.

In compensation for his loss of office, Harold was appointed by Churchill a Governor of the BBC, and this was his only public duty until the war ended. He resumed his journalism (mainly book reviews and his weekly Marginal Comment *for the* Spectator*) and found time to write two books,* The Desire to Please *and* The Congress of Vienna. *Politically his chief concern was in reconciling de Gaulle and the Free French to the British Government. Vita remained at Sissinghurst, writing* The Eagle and the Dove *and her long poem* The Garden. *Both their sons went overseas as serving soldiers, Ben to the Middle East and Nigel to Tunisia.*

HAROLD TO VITA   *4 King's Bench Walk*

22 July 1941

I dined with James and Guy Burgess.[1] I do not think that that affair is going very well, and James looks white and drawn. I am seeing him alone on Wednesday and he will tell me all about it. Guy is a bit of a scamp, and James is far too sensitive and affectionate for that sort of relationship.

Well here I am in K.B.W. as a private individual.[2] If only it were not for the raids I should be glad to be back, but it is really impossible to stay here when the bombing begins since the shelters are quite inadequate and the place exposed. I shall go to Atheneum Court and

---

1. Guy Burgess had resigned from the BBC in 1938 and joined the Secret Service. He defected to Russia with Donald Maclean in 1951. James Pope-Hennessy, the author, had been Nigel's friend at Oxford, and now became Harold's.
2. He meant losing his job in the Ministry of Information.

see if I can get a room there. It is by far the largest and strongest of those sorts of building.

The Times has a rather disobliging paragraph today suggesting that a job had to be found for me and that this was invented.[3] I really do wish that I could have afforded to refuse it. I hate the idea that I should be bought off with favours. Dearest Mar—such a nice letter from you today. What should I do in life without you? I would be lost and lonely, like a jam-jar floating in the North Sea.

HAROLD TO VITA   *4 King's Bench Walk*

21 August 1941

I went to the funeral.[4] It was moving and short. But please, at my funeral let there be no moaning at the bar,[5] and no anthems. I cannot abide anthems. When one thinks that they are all over, suddenly some fool starts yelling out the opening words all over again. They had Cecil Spring-Rice's, "I vow to thee my country." I should like that at my funeral. It is not so much my attitude towards foreign policy. Is it not strange that that brilliant man who lived so long and did such good work will be remembered only because he wrote a really rather ordinary little poem one morning at Government House, Ottawa, after he had been sacked and only a fortnight before he died.[6]

HAROLD TO VITA   *4 King's Bench Walk*

12 September 1941

I have had Dylan Thomas [the poet] to see me this morning. He wants a job in the BBC. I told him that he must not drink if he wanted a job there. They did not care for drunkards. He took it well.

---

3. The Governorship of the BBC.
4. The funeral of Lord Willingdon in Westminster Abbey. He had been Governor General of Canada and Viceroy of India.
5. "And may there be no moaning at the bar
    When I put out to sea." Tennyson, *Crossing the Bar*
6. Sir Cecil Spring-Rice (1859–1918) had been British Ambassador in Washington, 1913–17, and was on leave in Canada when he died suddenly.

HAROLD TO VITA   *4 King's Bench Walk*

22 October 1941

I have got so fond of my Leicester people. They are glum and shy and rude; but so loyal. If there were an election tomorrow, I should get in by a large majority entirely upon my Munich stand.

I went to see Maisky.[1] How you would like that little man! He talked to me with the utmost frankness, and I think he feels that I am safe and sympathetic. He does not think they will surrender, but they may be knocked out for a bit.[2] He said that of all our statesmen Anthony Eden was the one he trusted most. He said, "He understands. Churchill does not wholly understand." Now isn't that odd?

I like life being odd. I like hearing Maisky praise Eden above everybody. But one must not allow one's liking for strange patterns to develop into a taste for the arabesque. But truly, how odd it is. Brendan Bracken[3] had a long talk with me in the House about the Ministry and the BBC. Suddenly he said, "God! Harold, how I wish you were at the Ministry still—what fun we would have!"

That's pretty odd.

HAROLD TO VITA   *4 King's Bench Walk*

10 December 1941

I lunched with de Gaulle yesterday. I cannot make out whether I like him or not. There are sides of him which are as attractive as a Newfoundland dog. There are other sides which are arrogant and hostile. He is obviously a clever and a powerful man. He thinks the Germans have failed badly in Russia and that they will have to compensate their public opinion by an early and large success elsewhere. This can only be in the Mediterranean and we must expect heavy fighting in North Africa.

---

1. Ivan Maisky, Ambassador of the Soviet Union in London.
2. Hitler's attack on Russia had started on 22 June. Few experts had thought that the Red Army could resist for more than a few weeks.
3. He had succeeded Duff Cooper as Minister of Information. Harold had been succeeded as Parliamentary Secretary by an insignificant Labour Member, Ernest Thurtle.

The Americans were badly caught. I gather that the damage done to their fleet at Pearl Harbor and above all to their sea-planes was serious.[1] But not really serious enough to make it worth Japan's while to have put upon the American people so vast an affront. They will not rest until they have avenged it. But I hope that whoever was responsible for the light-hearted way in which they allowed the Japanese fleet to approach so near to Honolulu will get it hot. I am sure that the Japanese trick, however successful for the moment, was a mistake. People here think that Japanese intervention will do us much harm and bother for six months, but after that its advantages will be greater than its disadvantages.

HAROLD TO VITA   *4 King's Bench Walk*

28 January 1942

I wish you had been in the House yesterday. There really had been considerable opposition[2] and many members had been boasting openly that they would vote against the Government unless Winston changed his Cabinet. But after Winston had been speaking for five minutes one actually felt the opposition dropping like a thermometer. He also sensed it, and began to enjoy himself more and more. He thrust his hands deep into his trouser pockets and turned his tummy now to the right and now to the left, revelling in his own mastery. He is so sturdy and so lucid. He told us that further horrible blows were to come, and we loved it instead of being depressed. It is like a doctor in whom one has got total confidence saying, "I expect your temperature will go up to 104 tonight and tomorrow night, after which it will drop." In a way it was his most successful speech although it contained no fireworks. But if the purpose of a Parliamentary speech is to change the opinion of one's auditors, then surely Winston did it. He was so patient, so polite, so modest. I revelled in it.

---

1. The Japanese attack on Pearl Harbor on 7 December sank four of the finest American battleships.
2. The campaign in North Africa had been going very badly. Rommel's attack on 21 January had led to a rapid British retreat and the loss of Benghazi.

HAROLD TO VITA   *4 King's Bench Walk*

24 February 1942

The debate today went on and on. Running through it was the idea that our troops had not fought well in Malaya.[1] There were only two Japanese divisions engaged and our men retreated and surrendered more readily than they ought to have. This is a most alarming thought. It gives me cold shudders in my heart. The left-wing people say that it is because we have not got a cause. The right-wing people say that it is because we have not got sufficient discipline. Cause be hanged! What keeps men in the front line is fear of being shot if they run away. On the other hand we have the behaviour of the civil population in London, the conduct of the Air Force, the Navy and the Mercantile Marine, and the real guts shown by our people in Libya. We have captured a German army order there saying that our generals may be stupid but our men fight well. But Malaya is the blackest mark in the whole history of the British army. Why? Why?

Some people think that it is because we have allowed the Press to put such stress upon equipment. That gives the private soldier an excuse for cowardice. He can always say, "But we had not enough aeroplanes or tanks: what else could I do?"

HAROLD TO VITA   *Dublin*

16 March 1942

The High Commissioner's car picked me up and I drove with him into the Wicklow mountains. Rain and sunshine over moors and streams gushing. We drove to the famous waterfall in the Powerscourt demesne which I remember so well from childhood. Behind us in another car rode four detectives, since Maffey[2] has to be guarded. It was lovely by the waterfall and the grass all around is springy and

---

1. Singapore had fallen on 15 February and 60,000 men surrendered to the Japanese.
2. J. L. Maffey, later Lord Rugby. He had been "British Representative" in Eire since 1939. The Irish did not use the term "High Commissioner."

green from the spray. Then we turned back and drove to Powerscourt House[3] where we lunched. A great ostentatious eighteenth century mansion with a most elaborate Italian garden and a superb view of the Wicklow mountains. Viscount Powerscourt, whom I remember as a young guardee forty years ago, took me into the garden. We leant upon a gilt balustrade over the fountains looking down upon the great pool between the statues. He said, "Here I am marooned—the last of the Irish aristocracy with nobody to speak to." And I remembered when the place was the centre of social life in Ireland and when two brass bands played upon the terrace and the great marquee seemed to provide innumerable ices for little boys. My granny[4] would not let me have more than one ice. She was a firm woman.

I gave a lecture in the evening. It went well. There was one man afterwards who made an impassioned speech saying that there was only one thing which should be subject to government censorship and that began with the letters 'c.o.n.' I imagined of course that he was attacking the cruelty of Great Britain and all the wrongs that we were still doing to Ireland. I looked down my nose. I merely said, when panting with passion he had resumed his seat, that I did not wish to comment on controversial matters. It was only when I was walking away that I was told what he had meant was 'contraceptives'.

HAROLD TO VITA   *House of Commons*

23 April 1942

I am feeling cheered tonight. We have had our secret session and although I must not say what transpired, yet I can say that Winston had a great personal triumph.[5] He spoke for nearly two hours and he avoided all oratory, jokes or brilliance. He just stood there at the box telling us one alarming thing after the other and piling up a huge

---

3. The great house and Italianate garden of the Slazenger family, twelve miles south of Dublin.
4. Catherine Rowan Hamilton, who died in 1919 in her ninety-ninth year.
5. His speech dealt with the surrender of Singapore, retreat in the Libyan desert, and losses in the Battle of the Atlantic.

pyramid of adversity, mischance and danger. And then like some God of War he stood, stout and stubborn, upon the pyramid he erected and the House knew that he was far greater than themselves. To do them justice they rose and cheered as I have never seen them cheer since that dreadful Munich scene. He must feel that whatever the country may think, he has re-established his ascendancy over the House. It was a magnificent triumph.

After that the debate really collapsed. Nobody felt they could speak after that and the thing petered out.

HAROLD TO VITA   *House of Commons*

24 September 1942

Ben said to me today, "How happy I have been these days!"[1] I said, "But you have done nothing." He said, "But I am always happy when I am at home with Mummy and you."

Now truly that is a compliment (fresh with all his great sincerity) which I cherish more than any other. It is really an achievement on our part to have created an atmosphere which is more congenial to a fastidious young man like Ben than all the glitter of the Gargoyle [a London club]. It gives me pleasure that he should have said this so spontaneously, since I know that it was true. Of course one can modify it by saying that he is sedentary by nature and likes his files and books. But the fact does remain that poor old Sissinghurst (which offers no entertainment) does offer something which his sensitive and exacting criticism enjoys.

It is you, my darling, who have made this atmosphere (a) by great integrity; (b) by hating rows; (c) by a sense of real values. I do not think that, except for Winston, I *admire* anyone as much as I admire you.

I remember you saying (years ago) that you had never established a complete relationship with anyone. I don't think you ever could—

---

1. Ben was then on embarkation leave, but did not leave England for the Middle East till 4 October.

since yours is a vertical and not a horizontal nature, and two-thirds of you will always be submerged. But you have established, with your sons and me, a relationship of absolute trust and complete love. I don't think that these things would be so fundamental to the four of us were it not that each one of us four is a private person underneath.

I have often wondered what makes the perfect family. I think it is just our compound of intimacy and aloofness. Each of us has a room of his own. Each of us knows that there is a common-room where we meet on the basis of perfect understanding.

If Ben were killed or drowned, I should always remember that remark. And I should know that from the difficult web of human relationship (now a spider's web, now a mass of steel hawsers) we—thanks to you only—have made a pattern which is taut where tautness is wanted, and elastic where we need to expand on our own.

HAROLD TO VITA   *4 King's Bench Walk*

2 October 1942

Benzie has had instructions to leave [for Cairo] early on Sunday morning. He is rather excited. Lists all over the place—socks 3, pants 2, and so on. But the point is that he will not see you again. I do not suggest your coming up to London. What is the point of these last farewells? We four understand and love each other so deeply that there is no need for conventionalities. Ben will telephone.

The three of us dined at the Greek restaurant. Nigel seemed in very good form. But I was sad and Ben was sad and it was not the gayest evening I have passed. And then this morning they are both here together—enormous khaki shapes in my little room—cleaning their buttons and chaffing. Then it is time for Ben to go to Paddington. "Well, goodbye Niggs—we may meet somewhere." Then it is Nigel's turn to return to Perth. "Goodbye Daddy." His voice was gay but he had tears in his eyes.[1]

---

1. Nigel embarked at Gourock, Scotland, on 14 November to take part in the invasion of Algeria and Tunisia. Both sons remained overseas for nearly three years.

VITA TO HAROLD　　　　　　　　　　　　　　*Sissinghurst*

10 November 1942

The American invasion [of North Africa] is indeed wonderful. One does feel that anything may happen now anywhere and at any moment. What a superb moment of history to be living at! It makes one feel again as one felt during the Battle of Britain, only the other way round—the exhilaration of victory, not of a high despair. But in quality the feeling is the same.

One understands the feelings of St George when he saw the dragon beginning to bleed, the black-blooded worm of evil oozing under his lance.

HAROLD TO VITA　　　　　　　　　　*4 King's Bench Walk*

24 November 1942

I came up from East Grinstead with Mr Dewar and his charming daughter. She is to be married on Saturday to Michael Astor,[1] and he is a lucky man. She is gay and clever and charming. Dewar is rather a stiff sort of man, but it may be that he is averse to M.Ps. We had to change at East Croydon and get into a bedint train which had only one class and no corridors. As soon as I realised that I was stuck with no possibility of escape, I began to suffer from agonies of Secret Sorrow. I felt that the worst was bound to happen. A cold sweat broke out upon my highbrow. The train stopped at Norwood Junction, and in despair I murmured to Mr Dewar that I must get out. "Not here, surely?" he said, perplexed as well he might be. "Yes, here," I wailed, and as I wailed, the train started again. "How far is it," I murmured to him with clenched teeth, "to the next station?" "It depends on the fog," he answered—and shame and disaster danced before my eyes. I summoned up all the moral courage and physical muscles of which I am capable. The train stopped because of fog. In an agony of mind and body I made feverish conversation. The train went on. After an

---

1. She was Barbara McNeill (her mother subsequently married a Dewar) and her fiancé was the son of 2nd Viscount Astor.

aeon of internal pangs it stopped at London Bridge. I bumbled out. But my Secret Sorrow (which is a sneak and a thief) ceased to be a sorrow at all the moment it saw GENTLEMEN. I just ignored it, and replaced in my pocket the penny which I had held there, anxious that there should be no slip between the slot and me. Then I took a taxi to King's Bench Walk and spoke quite calmly to Miss Niggeman[2] on various matters before I retired to that place which but half-an-hour before had glimmered as the bourne of all human desire.

VITA TO HAROLD   *Sissinghurst*

2 December 1942

I wonder what you thought of the Beveridge Report?[3] I think it sounds dreadful. The proletariat being encouraged to breed like rabbits because each new little rabbit means 8/–a week [in Family Allowances]—as though there weren't too many of them already and not enough work to go round, with 2 million unemployed before the war, and everybody being given everything for nothing, a complete discouragement to thrift or effort, and not a word said about better education. Lloyd George gave them old-age pensions, and what do they do? They grumble about having to contribute to the stamps, and then grumble because they don't get enough money. Oh no, I don't hold with Sir William Beveridge, and it all makes me feel very pre-1792.

HAROLD TO VITA   *4 King's Bench Walk*

9 December 1942

Why do you say "it is silly to think that anything in life matters much"? I think everything in life matters terribly. I feel that this war

---

2. Elvira Niggeman, Harold's secretary from 1938 till 1965.
3. Sir William Beveridge's plan for universal social security, which was largely implemented by postwar governments.

is a test of our character and I rejoice that all those I love have come through it enhanced and not diminished. I want to live through this war with my courage unabated, my faith firmer, my energy increased, and my hopes and beliefs lit by a sun that has never lit them before. I have much pride in my own people and much faith in the future. I really do believe that we in England have set an example to the world. I think that we may solve the social and economic problems of the twentieth century with as much wisdom and tolerance as when we solved the political problems of the nineteenth. Surely this is worthwhile? Surely your dignity and calm and uncomplainingness and courage are an example to all who see you? Not worthwhile! Why, everything is ten times more worthwhile now than ever before!

VITA TO HAROLD   *Sissinghurst*

10 December 1942

When I said that it is silly to think that anything in life mattered much, I suppose I meant one's personal life. Of course I think with you that the war and after-the-war matter. But, darling, you are a goose to talk about my "uncomplainingness and courage," because (a) I have nothing to complain of, and (b) my courage is a very poor thing. I am sure it would go phutt if put to the test. My calm is really my cabbagey nature. Luckily for you, you have never seen the more tempestuous side of my nature. You have only seen an occasional bubble rising to the surface, which has startled you and made you realise vaguely that I feel passionately, and am vindictive and uncontrollable when my emotions are aroused, but as you do not like that sort of bubble, you have always wisely looked the other way. The emotions I give you are deep and strong. You are about the only person in whose love I trust. I know that we will love each other till we die.

By the way, you said we ought to ask de Gaulle to luncheon. Shall we give a joint luncheon party? You ask the guests, and I will go shares with you. Shall we?

V I T A   T O   H A R O L D   *Sissinghurst*

3 February 1943

I am rather excited about this book[1] which entirely absorbs my mind. I think that you will like it even though the subject is not at all your cup of tea. I think that I am dimly beginning to understand the saints and what they were after, far better than I did when I was writing about Joan of Arc. It is rather like trying to grasp relativity, and every now and then getting a flash of understanding. It is such a totally different world, and the first point to understand is that all ordinary values are reversed. You will understand better what I mean when you come to read it; and if you don't, it will merely mean that I have done the job badly.

I have got a grand phrase as an epigraph for the beginning, by Cardinal Newman: "There is a God—the most august of all conceivable truths."

H A R O L D   T O   V I T A   *4 King's Bench Walk*

12 May 1943

I wish you had been in the House yesterday. Attlee had to make a statement on Tunisia.[2] It would seem almost impossible to render that amazing campaign dull—but he succeeded fully. It was as if, when one expected an eagle-swoop, one had the pecking of a tiny quail in a bamboo cage. It was so extraordinary that a man could be so ineffective that if he had gone on for another five minutes, the good manners of the House would have broken down. One felt that a *fou rire* was about to burst, and had one man tittered, the whole House would have rocked with guffaws.

Anyhow, it is all practically over—and if Niggs is alive he has had

---

1. *The Eagle and the Dove*, a study of the two Saints, St. Teresa of Avila and St. Teresa of Lisieux.
2. The British First Army had captured Tunis and Bizerta on 8 May, and on the 12th forced the capitulation of the entire German-Italian Army in Tunisia. 250,000 prisoners were taken. Clement Attlee was deputizing for Churchill, who was in the United States.

the satisfaction of delivering the *coup de grace*. What the *Daily Telegraph* calls "the famous Sixth"[3] broke through at Hammam Lif by sending their tanks into the sea and just splashing through the waves.

VITA TO HAROLD   *Sissinghurst*

12 May 1943

Violet [Trefusis] is here. It is extraordinarily unreal and rather embarrassing. It is rather like speaking a foreign language that one has once known bilingually and has not used for years: idiomatic phrases, and even bits of slang, come back to one suddenly, yet one finds that the foundation has gone.

She discovered that she would be alone in the Priest's House and declared that she would be terrified, so I gave her my room (but did not share it with her). It was all very odd, and we were both acutely conscious of the oddness. Luckily we were able to say so, which eased it into amusement instead of embarrassment.

VITA TO HAROLD   *Sissinghurst*

26 August 1943

I am glad that we see so completely eye to eye about the new world. I am not a very public-minded sort of person, as you know, but this is a point on which my personal idiosyncrasies and public tendencies touch and correspond with yours. The reason they correspond is of course that we have fundamentally the same standard of values. And this is probably one of the reasons why we are so happy together. Over essentials we invariably agree—and indeed over minor matters too. We differ only in that you are a more public and active person than your skulking old stodge of a Mar.

---

3. 6th Armoured Division, of which the First Guards Brigade (in which Nigel was serving) was the infantry element.

Darling, I love you so much—so very, very, very, very much—more than anything—so dearly, so protectively, so respectingly, so much more than anything else, so eternally.

I do hope that you will like my new book [*The Eagle and the Dove*]. I think it has some merit, but of course, as one always does, I wish that it were better. I do so want you to have the leisure to write another book yourself. I have such enormous belief in your writing, and regret always that you should by force of circumstances regard it always as a sort of sideline. My idea of heaven on earth would be for you to live here and bury yourself all morning and evening in your room and write, with perhaps one very interesting job that took you to London once every six months. But you would not like that. Perhaps when you are eighty you may come round to my point of view.

HAROLD TO VITA   *House of Commons*

23 September 1943

Darling,

I shall be rushed tomorrow, so I write to you late tonight. I thought this evening that supposing I were killed in a raid, the nurse would lean over me and I would feel a block of cold cement rising from my knees to my thighs. Before it reached my heart I should want to send you a message. Yet (even if I had been as detached as Socrates) how could I compress into a few minutes of obituary communication what I would really feel? You admit that this is an interesting conundrum.

I worked it out as follows:—

a) Your knowledge of what I feel (and how gawky and slipfaced I am about it) is the axiom.

b) Therefore I need never *explain* anything.

c) Therefore I need never *express* anything.

d) Therefore if (to my nurse taking down my dying words) I merely gasped out the family phrase, "Loving thoughts," you would see that phrase not as a small map of the environs of Ventnor, but as Mercator's Projection.

And having realised that my last words could (without offence, disappointment or misunderstanding) be reduced to this code-formula, I thought just this, "Hurray!" Because, my saint, after thirty years that does really imply a certitude of understanding. And God knows I am muddled and confused enough!

Your own,
Hadji

HAROLD TO VITA   *Stockholm*

19 October 1943

On all fours I crept below and out of the aeroplane to be met by a blaze of arclights.[1] A neat little man came up to me and took off his hat: "Good evening, Mr Nicolson. I am Leadbetter of the Legation. I hope you had a good journey." I shuffled across to the adjoining customs shed and got rid of my beastly [flying] clothes. I was passed through immediately and taken to a huge car with a kettle on the luggage-rack which makes gasoline out of wood. We drove into Stockholm through brilliant peacetime streets.

I was shown to my rooms [in the Grand Hotel]. It is a royal suite. Anyhow, I don't have to pay for it. There are five windows looking out on the Palace and the river, with a view of the tower of the town-hall, surely the loveliest thing in modern architecture. I had a bath. I dined. I went to the flat of the Press Attaché, Peter Tennant, where I found many other members of the Legation. The Minister [Sir Victor Mallet] is away, having gone to Gothenburg for the exchange of disabled prisoners with the Germans. I sat talking till midnight.

It is really very odd sitting in this palatial room looking out on Stockholm. I feel as if my body had been flung through space and that my mind had been left in Dundee. I suppose it will follow on later.

---

1. Harold had flown from Dundee to Stockholm in a RAF Mosquito to give a series of lectures for the British Council.

HAROLD TO VITA   *British Legation,*
                                                        Stockholm
27 October 1943

The coast of Denmark—the coast of the enemy—glimmered in
the sunshine and the towers of Elsinore stood up above the woods. I
went to see the graves of our airmen who have been washed up on
the coast. Four little white crosses. The Consul who was with me had
lost his boy off Pantelleria [near Malta] and seemed to be distressed that
his body has never been found. I do not understand that. I should not
feel any better about a dead person if he or she were put in the ground
than if they melted gradually into the great purity of the sea. I should
far rather be buried in the Mediterranean than in earth. But the poor
man minded, and he cried as he looked at the neat graves.

I fear that the Swedes regard me as far more important than I am.
My meetings have all been crowded and people who do not know a
word of English come to honour. I have met with more than kindness;
I have met with enthusiasm. I am sure it was worthwhile. They are
flattered that a middle-aged buffer like myself should have faced the
discomfort and danger of a Mosquito to come and talk to them. They
do *admire* us so. I am glad I came. Tremendously glad.

VITA TO HAROLD   *Sissinghurst*

5 January 1944

My own darling Hadji,

I cannot tell you how touched I was by the letter Elvira [Nigge-
man] brought me, nor how pleased I was that you should have liked
that little poem,[1] written with so much love. I was so extravagantly
pleased, too, by your saying I had got control of such literary powers
as I possess, and was writing better than I ever had. I was pleased about
this, because I do feel that something has happened—or is in process

---

1. The poem, addressed to Harold, began, "I must not tell how dear you are to me. / It is
unknown, a secret from myself / Who should know best." It was read by the Poet Laureate,
Cecil Day-Lewis, at their joint memorial service in 1968. For the full text, see *Portrait of
a Marriage*, pp. 192–3.

of happening—within me, and that I may write better in future. It is as though something had gone, or was about to go, click. I think that this possibly happens to people of talent in their middle age; I mean, flaming genius may be a thing of youth, e.g. Shelley, Keats; but failing that, experience teaches, only it takes a long time to come to fruition. Like *Chimonanthus fragrans* (Winter sweet) which doesn't flower till it is years old. I *know* that in the little poem I wrote for you I was setting myself to compress a complicated story into a short space, and that in its small way it was a tour de force to do so with any clarity. I feel like a juggler who has hitherto been able to spin only three plates into the air at a time, and who now can spin twenty. But this is only one thing. This is merely getting control of one's medium. Apart from this, I feel I have lost my shallowness; and if I can put both gains together I may yet do something worthwhile.

Oh darling, what an egotistical letter—but you will forgive me. Your own letter provoked it.

Your Mar

VITA TO HAROLD *Sissinghurst*

18 January 1944

My own darling Hadji

Considering that Niggs will be twenty-seven tomorrow and Ben thirty in August, it is remarkable, isn't it, that I should love you so much more now than I did when we made them? And you me, I think. Of course I was much in love with you then, in a very young and (also) uninformed way; it was young and fresh like Greek poetry, (I have just been reading some translations from the Greek Anthology), but it was like a spring then, like the mountain springs we used to drink from in Persia; but now it is like a deep deep lake which can never dry up. Darling, I don't honestly think that as much can be said for most marriages, do you? Of course I suppose it could be said of the bourgeois bedint marriage founded on habit; but not for a difficult unorthodox marriage like ours, with rather subtle and difficult people involved. Of course it is largely due to your own sweetness of nature;

I don't think any man but you would have put up with me; but there is something more to it than that even. Oh I don't know and I can't express myself—and this letter will reach you on a busy morning—and Hadji sheers off from anything like emotional expression anyhow—and my quiet room with the pink tower seen through the window is so different a place from London—but I did want to say these things to you on Niggs' birthday somehow, when everything is so precarious and we may either of us get killed at any moment, and Niggs too. A little record of thirty-one years of love.

from Mar

VITA TO HAROLD   *Sissinghurst*

16 February 1944

Darling, Knole has been bombed. All the windows on the front of the house and in the Green Court and Stone Court, and on the garden side (including a window in the chapel) have been broken. A special sort of bomb fell just in front of the wicket—no, not just in front, but slightly to the left. Eddy [Sackville-West] rang me up to tell me. Then I rang up Uncle Charlie [Lord Sackville] who says he has written me a long letter about it today, which I suppose I shall get tomorrow. I mind frightfully, frightfully, frightfully. I always persuade myself that I have finally torn Knole out of my heart, and then the moment anything touches it, every nerve is alive again. I cannot bear to think of Knole wounded, and I not there to look after it and be wounded with it. Those filthy Germans! Let us level every town in Germany to the ground! I shan't care. Oh Hadji, I wish you were here. I feel hurt and heartsick.

VITA TO HAROLD   *Sissinghurst*

23 February 1944

As I read the *New Yorker* article (getting more and more indignant) I thought, "This man, although he is saying some exceedingly foolish things, is a man of intelligence who also writes very well."[1] Then I looked for a signature and found Edmund Wilson. It is of course absurd to say that you are shocked by Byron or Swinburne, and where he goes wrong over criticising you for so obviously belonging to a definite class, by birth, education, experience and consequent outlook, is that he ought to have stated it as a fact and not as an adverse criticism. He is falling into a common error of critics, which is to demand that a writer shall be something he is not. It is no good expecting a gentle person of sensibility and culture to care for the rough and tumble. I think that your almost morbid dislike of emotion is at the root of much of what E. Wilson is trying to say.

VITA TO HAROLD   *Sissinghurst*

13 June 1944

"One enemy raider was destroyed during the night." It was indeed. I thought it was going to destroy Sissinghurst Castle in the process. We had a series of warnings and all-clears (three, to be exact) and then a solitary plane came along, with a sudden burst of machine-gun fire, so close that I leapt from my bed and rushed into your bedroom to look out of the window; and there, beyond the roses, was a stream of scarlet tracer-bullets rushing up into the sky and a plane all in flames, apparently about to descend on Beale's stock-yard.

VITA TO HAROLD   *Sissinghurst*

4 July 1944

Poor old Rosie has been killed.[2] I got a telegram from Jack Lynch, and then I saw it in *The Times,* as no doubt you did too. Well we

---

1. The article, by Edmund Wilson, was titled "Through the Embassy Window; Harold Nicolson" and was published in *The New Yorker* of 1 January 1944.
2. Rosamund Grosvenor, Vita's first love, had married Captain Jack Lynch in 1924. She was killed, with many others, when a bomb fell on the Savoy Chapel.

always teased her about her passion for attending memorial services, and now she is going to have one for herself. It has saddened me rather, that somebody so innocent, so silly, and so harmless should be killed in this idiotic and violent way.

V I T A   T O   H A R O L D   *Sissinghurst*

19 December 1944

I have lost all pleasure in the lake and indeed in the woods, since soldiers came and invaded them and robbed them of all the privacy I so loved.

I shall never love the lake or the wood again in the same way as I used to. I mind about this—more than you would believe. It was a thing of beauty, now tarnished for ever—one of the few things I had preserved against this horrible new world.

I wish I could sort out my ideas about this new world. I feel one ought to be able to adapt oneself—and not struggle to go back to, and live in, an obsolete tradition.

All this makes me very unhappy, Hadji. And my back worries me too.[1] I don't mind its hurting—but the *weakness* it brings to my limbs worries me. You see I used to be so strong, but now I dare not make a rash movement and am also frightened of falling down.

If only I thought I could write good poetry I should not mind anything, but even over that I have lost my convictions.

H A R O L D   T O   V I T A   *4 King's Bench Walk*

21 December 1944

I do so understand your unhappiness at the moment. I think that everyone in these dark autumn days is truly unhappy. Partly war

---

1. She had arthritis in the spine.

weariness, partly sadness at things not going right, and partly actual malnutrition. But I also know that yours is a deeper unhappiness. You do not ask much from life but you do desire passionately privacy and the respect of your independence and quiet. The tanks in the wood were a real symbol; the boats being sunk by carelessness or actual malevolence is another symbol. The world for people like you and me is becoming a grim place. Then of course added to this is your arthritis which makes everything seem dim through a cloud of pain. I pray to God that the treatment will improve it.

But there is one thing which I do not agree about—namely your poetry. I do not think you have ever written better than you are writing now. Even if you never wrote another line of poetry your fame as a poet is anchored to *The Land*. Not a day passes almost in which someone does not mention that poem to me. At the Club on Tuesday Tommy Lascelles said, "I suppose *The Land* is about the only truly classic poem written in our times." But I believe *The Garden* will be as good and certainly the cradle poem is among the finest you have ever written.

Oh my sweet sweet Mar—how it hurts me that you should be unhappy. You are all my life to me. The thought of you is a little hot water bottle of happiness which I hug in this cold world. When people behave meanly and badly (as they did in the debate yesterday) I think of you—so serene and lovely—and it all seems to smooth itself out. As I said to Duff [Cooper] the other day when he said that he thought the Government had treated me rather shabbily, "Well you see someone who has had my happiness in life has no right to feel bitter about anything." "You mean Vita," he said. He understands.

V ITA TO H AROLD   *Sissinghurst*

7 February 1945

Darling, listen; there is an agitation on foot to get a bus service between Biddenden and Cranbrook. This is horrid for us, as it would pass along the road skirting our wood, but it would be nice for the inhabitants of Biddenden and Three Chimneys who are entirely cut off from the world—the world in this case being Cranbrook. We cannot resist it, so we had better co-operate. Why people have this passion for moving about passes my understanding, but there it is.

What a world! It's like drawing up one's own death warrant and is all on a par with the tanks coming into our wood.

Manifesto: I hate democracy. I hate la populace. I wish education had never been introduced. I don't like tyranny, but I like an intelligent oligarchy. I wish la populace had never been encouraged to emerge from its rightful place. I should like to see them as well fed and well housed as T.T. cows—but no more thinking than that. (It's rather what most men feel about women!)

Oh—à propos of that, I've been absolutely enraged by a book about Knole, in which Eddy is described as "author and musician," and I am described as "the wife of the Hon. Harold Nicolson C.M.G."

I don't grudge Eddy being described as an author and musician—but I do resent being dismissed as merely somebody's wife—with no existence of my own—especially in connexion with Knole, and my name.

Very very cross about this. You know I'm not a feminist, but there are limits . . .

HAROLD TO VITA   *4 King's Bench Walk*

9 May 1945

The whole of Trafalgar Square and Whitehall was packed with people and I had some difficulty in pushing my way through.[1] At last I got to Palace Yard and as it was a few minutes to three I thought it would be a good thing to stand there and listen to Winston's Broadcast before entering the House. And then as the clock struck 3.0 an immense hush descended on the crowds and Winston's voice boomed out over the loud-speakers. When it was finished the B.B.C. played God Save the King and I went into the House. They were going through questions at the ordinary pace and when 3.15 came they kept

---

1. May 8 was Victory in Europe Day.

them going by sham questions. All that was amusing and dignified. Then there was a slight bustle at the door and Winston, a little shyly, came in. The whole House rose and yelled and yelled and waved their order papers. It was by far the most triumphant demonstration I have ever seen.

H A R O L D　T O　V I T A　　　　　　　　　　　　　*Leicester*

21 June 1945

The election campaign continues. Yesterday I had a deputation from the anti-vivisectionists in the morning. They are also anti-vaccinationists. I said that to my mind the life of 10,000 guinea-pigs was less important than the life of one human. They contend that we have imposed "untold agony" on millions of guinea pigs without having discovered a cure for cancer. So there!

In the evening I had one bad meeting and one not so bad. The first one was small and sparsely attended. But it was dominated by a slightly intoxicated workman who kept on yelling, "You're a liar, you are!" That meant that I had to raise my voice. But what was worse was a sort of Madame de Krüdener[1] and Lady Macbeth all in one who rose all the time and waved her arms aloft and uttered incantations. One of her incantations was that I was a bloated landowner who lived in a Castle and ground his tenants down for rent. No good at all my saying that Sissingbags wasn't a castle but only the remains of it; that it didn't belong to me but to you; and that Beale was not being ground into the earth. But I did not at all like Sissinghurst, that shrine of quiet and loveliness, being dragged into this squalid controversy. It was like seeing a piece of Tudor embroidery in the mud.

Darling, truly it is not as bad as last time [the 1935 Election]. In the first place I have far more experience and am not in the least nervous at meetings. I have infinitely more self-confidence as a speaker. In the second place it makes a difference to know Leicester people well. On the one hand it makes me feel that the apparent animosity, hatred,

---

1. The Russian mystic (1764–1824) who conceived a passion for Czar Alexander I.

scolding etc. is confined to a tiny minority. And in the second place I am surrounded by friends and supporters who really do want me to get in. I have been allotted a LOVELY girl to be my chauffeuse; she has white hair but is quite young.[2]

2. Polling day was on 5 July 1945, and the result was declared on 26 July. Labour won a majority of 180 seats, and Harold lost his seat by over 7,000 votes.

The war ended. Ben (damaged by a road accident in Italy) and Nigel (unwounded) returned to Sissinghurst, and for some years Harold shared a house with his sons in Kensington, having been obliged, to his great chagrin, to give up his flat in the Temple. Having lost his parliamentary seat in the General Election, he hoped for a peerage, which to some extent would restore it. In this he was disappointed, and he joined the Labour Party in a moment of aberration. His income, mainly from journalism and broadcasts, was more modest than his tastes, and it was Vita who again came to the rescue of the family finances by her weekly articles on gardening for The Observer *and a novel,* Devil at Westease, *which she would only allow to be published in America. Harold was the more active of the two. He lived a vigorous social life in London, went to Nuremberg to witness the trial of the Nazi war criminals, and to Paris in 1946 to broadcast twice weekly for the BBC about the Peace Conference. His books of this period were* The English Sense of Humour *and* Benjamin Constant.

HAROLD TO VITA   *4 King's Bench Walk*

14 July 1945

Ben said that he was going to the Ordinary.[1] I cut in at once as if the idea had just occurred to me: "I pray to God, Benzie, that you will, if you find yourself next to a dull person, not just sit in a heap

---

1. The "Ordinaries" were large dinner parties at the Dorchester Hotel organized by Sibyl Colefax for friends, who were discreetly asked to contribute to the cost.

with your mouth open." Here I gave him an imitation of himself that made him laugh. I went on to say that such an attitude was unkind to the dull neighbour, and unkind to Sibyl who would spot the well of loneliness sitting over there. Moreover there was always something interesting in everyone, and a man who could talk as well as he could when aroused could always, with a very little effort, find something at least to get out of even the dullest neighbour. He would be surprised, if he once tried, to find how easy it was, and how afterwards it gave one a small satisfaction to have made what might have been a dull dinner-party interesting by one's own efficiency in talking to bores. Then (such is my tact) I immediately changed the subject and asked him to help me with an article on the National Gallery pictures. I proposed to mention only three pictures which I specially liked, and I explained to him what I was going to say about them. He lit up at once. He agreed with my comments and added a whole mass of fascinating detail to complement them. I do not think I ever met a man who can talk so interestingly as Benzie does about pictures. So thus I was able (a) to reprove him for being a well of loneliness; (b) to stimulate him by showing how brilliantly he could talk.

HAROLD TO VITA   *British Embassy, Athens*

27 October 1945

After luncheon the Leepers drove me out to Penhelicon.[1] There are Mediterranean pines and little byzantine chapels and slim autumn croci in the pine-needles. And a view, darling, such as only Attica can give. The great sweep of the Attic plain and then the mountains of the Peloponnesus and the islands. And below, Athens bathing in a clear light. My God! I am not surprised that from this wonderful air and setting should have come the greatest lucidity of mind.

---

1. Harold had flown to Greece to give two lectures, on Byron and democracy, and stayed in Athens with the British Ambassador, Sir Reginald Leeper.

HAROLD TO VITA　　　　　　　　　　*4 King's Bench Walk*

29 November 1945

Look here, my sweetest. Madame Massigli[1] is giving a "small but interesting dinner" for Winston and Clemmie [Churchill] on December 19 and wishes us both to go. Now Mar will say that she does not go out and that she has no clothes. That is rubbish. She can easily evolve the sort of tea-gowny stuff that women wear for dinner parties. There is no need of an *ausgeschnittenes kleid.* Mar must have some sort of draperies she can affix or get the Belgian seamstress to affix. I think she would regret it if she missed the chance of meeting Winston again in congenial surroundings. So be firm with yourself and not a cabbage stalk. You could stay the night here. I should have telephoned had it not been that I knew such a suggestion would fling you into a flutter, and it was best to put it to you calmly and in writing so that you could recover from your first panic-stricken instinct to say "No."

Oh my love! what a crazy loon she is, bless her![2]

HAROLD TO VITA　　　　　　　　　*10 Neville Terrace,*
　　　　　　　　　　　　　　　　Onslow Gardens, London S.W.7
14 February 1946

I went to Beaconsfield to lecture to the Germans there. It is a sort of course which they arrange at which selected prisoners are to be taught civic values. A mansion in the park surrounded by wire and huts and more wire. All very grim and grey.

We started by having dinner in mess. The Commandant, who is an elderly Australian, had been there ever since it was a prison camp in 1940, and it was astonishing to him to find himself surrounded suddenly by professors and school-masters and odd visitors like me. He had not yet recovered from his bewilderment with which mingled a touch of resentment at he knew not what. Anyhow he was

---

1. Wife of the French Ambassador, René Massigli.
2. Vita did go to the party at the French Embassy, and in his diary for that day Harold described her as "looking quite beautiful in diamonds and emeralds."

polite to me and even offered me a glass of port (which was not forthcoming) and then I walked through the barbed wire and into an enormous hut which was packed with Huns. The idea is to get together some of the older ones (who are anti-Nazi) and some of the cleverer Hitler Jugend. It is a good idea. I spoke to them about "An Englishman's View of the German Character," and they listened entranced. They laughed very loud indeed at my jokes. Then there were questions for one hour and a half! Poor people—I felt so sorry for them. I had a feeling that I had cheered them up by treating them as civilised human beings.

HAROLD TO VITA   *10 Neville Terrace*

25 April 1946

I am afraid I have a nasty for you. It is now confirmed that I am to go with George Clerk to Nuremberg next week.[1] We fly there on Tuesday morning and ought to get back late on Friday. I am sorry about this as I know it casts over you a cloud of anxiety. But I should always blame myself if I funked going to Nuremberg (which quite honestly I do) since it would be like having a chance to see the Dreyfus trial and refusing it. But I do dread it so. I know I am squeamish about that sort of thing, but I hate the idea of my sitting all comfy in a box with George Clerk and staring at men who are certain to be hanged by the neck and who are in any case caught like rats in a trap. You know as well as I do that my feelings for Ribbentrop have always been cold feelings. But I do not want to see the man humiliated. And Schacht was a friend of mine.[2] I do not want to see him a prisoner in the dock. Nor really do I want to see Germany in its present state. But I should never forgive myself if I shirked this opportunity.

---

1. He went there, at the invitation of the Foreign Office, to write about the trial of the major Nazi war criminals. George Clerk had been British Ambassador in Paris, 1934–37.
2. Dr. Hjalmar Schacht, Hitler's Finance Minister, had been President of the Reichsbank when Harold was Counsellor in the British Embassy.

HAROLD TO VITA   *10 Neville Terrace*

15 May 1946

I went to the Flower Show yesterday. I could not see any *Cheiranthus* displayed at all. What really happens is that things become fashionable and nurserymen concentrate on such things and ignore the other things. I mean there were no herbaceous things at all except for Delphiniums. The azaleas were no good, the rhododendrons good but not up to Bodnant standard, and the Alpines no better than what we have got. In fact I saw little there which we could envy or even desire. But there were very beautiful tulips. I enclose the list of those I ordered. When you see "24" or "three dozen" do not be upset. It means that half goes for my life's work[1] and half for Mar's garden. The Barr parrot tulips were really wonderful, enamelled like Battersea china. Then there was the finest delphinium I have ever seen—a most beautiful Eton blue with a dash of Oxford blue. It was expensive. It was 30/– a plant. But I ordered two plants as a birthday present and we can take seeds from them.

I like spending money in this way. I mean, I believe that before we die we shall make Sissinghurst the loveliest garden in Kent. And we can only do this by getting better and better varieties of things we like. It is no good trying to have things which we do not get on with. Rhododendrons are to us like large stock-brokers whom we do not want to have to dinner. But there are certain things which are adapted to Sissingbags and those things should be improved and improved and improved until they reach the perfect standard.

HAROLD TO VITA   *10 Neville Terrace*

5 June 1946

I lunched with the Walter Elliots to meet Smuts.[2] He is an amazing old man—so gay, so young, so full of optimism and faith.

---

1. The Lime Walk, or spring garden, at Sissinghurst, which Harold designed and planted himself.
2. Field Marshal Jan Christian Smuts, who was then seventy-six, was still Prime Minister of South Africa, and had been in San Francisco helping to create the United Nations.

He greeted me as if I had been his oldest friend. He talked well. He spoke of his visit to Germany and of how the Germans had not yet acquired repentance. Hatred and self-pity enervated their will. He had, arrayed as a Field Marshal, addressed the Senate at Hamburg. He had told them that Germany would in all certitude perish if they did not help themselves. "I also," he said, "have belonged to a defeated nation. I also have looked around and seen the ruins of my country and felt that no human energy would ever suffice to repair them. But we set to work. We made friends with our enemies; and God has spared me to witness the birth of a country more rich and prosperous than we ever dreamed. A great South Africa which is now a power in the World."

He said, "Your England is not an old country; she is a young country—far younger than the United States or Canada. And I shall tell you why. Because you absorb new ideas into your blood stream; you keep your arteries elastic; you change the whole time. Never have I seen so many gifted and energetic young men as I have in England. You have a great future before you."

Oh yes, darling, a lovely man, a lovely man. He asked in a funny old-fashioned bowing sort of way about you. I said you were thriving, and then I put my hand behind me to touch wood in case some fatal illness had attacked you during the night.

HAROLD TO VITA   *Ritz Hotel, Paris*

30 July 1946

You will see that I have been busy enough and very happy and passionately interested.[1] Looking down upon Gladwyn [Jebb] sitting as a delegate in a plush armchair did give me a slight twinge; but not of envy; merely the 'elderly failure' twinge. But as a matter of fact I am glad to be free of responsibility and these slight twinges at being out of official life are as nothing to the great tugs of misery which I feel when I go to my beloved but unwanting House of Commons.

---

1. Harold had gone to Paris to report the Peace Conference for the BBC, and remained there till mid-October, when the Conference ended.

What is odd is that I am not lonely or depressed. Now why is this? Partly I suppose because I am surrounded by friends and fans, that I love Paris, and that I am doing something which I know to be important and which I believe I do well. That I take for granted. But there is something more than that. The ghastly home-sickness and depression which usually assail me when you go, are not present this time. My God! how I suffered at Lausanne (why on earth was that the worst barring Persia?), and how I suffered in Berlin! But this room is in an odd way more friendly to me since you have been there, and with the rosemary and the sweet geranium and the violas in front of me. Of course it is mostly because I am active and interested and surrounded. But I think it is also because your coming gave me such extraordinary pleasure that the pleasure lasts even after the cause of it has been removed. I feel I am so lucky to have you and Niggs and Benzie in my life. How empty poor little Pierre de Lacretelle[2] is compared to me! Nobody really cares if he is run over or not.

VITA TO HAROLD   *St Antonin (Tarn et Garonne), France*

5 September 1946

We did not get to Albi today after all. We got to Toulouse instead—and by mistake. After we had driven for about 50 miles we reached a village, and Tray [Raymond Mortimer] said, "Where are we now?" "Caussade," I said, having just seen the name in the *poteau.* Tray collapsed into a heap with his face in his hands. "My God," he said, "so it *was* the wrong bridge we went over. We have gone west instead of east."

So then we decided to go on, and we got to Montauban where there is a vast episcopal palace entirely devoted to the culte of Ingres. We arrived there to find, much to my relief, a notice on the gates saying, *"Le musée Ingres est fermé."* But did that defeat Tray? Not a bit. He got hold of the concierge and sent in his card to the director, with the result that an enormous *trousse de clefs* was produced and the

---

2. His old bachelor friend whom he had first met in Constantinople. Harold called him "one of the most brilliant people I have ever known." Opium and gambling were his undoing.

gates unlocked and we were admitted. Now of all great painters Ingres is the one I most dislike. And then a bright young woman appeared and said she was working on a complete catalogue of Ingres in eight volumes, and would we like her to show us over? There were about 3,000 drawings by Ingres in the museum which she would be delighted to show us . . .

When, exhausted, I emerged two hours later into the street again, Tray exclaimed *"Wasn't* that a bit of luck?" Personally, I thought it a disaster.

HAROLD TO VITA   *10 Neville Terrace*

6 March 1947

I must break the fact to you that I have joined the Labour Party. I have done this because in the end it was inevitable and I had better do it when the night of misery is on them rather than when they are basking in the sun of popular acclaim. I did it quite quietly by joining the local branch. They registered me as 'H. Nicolson', and it is probable that there will be no publicity. I told Elvira [Niggeman], who emitted a short sharp scream. I told the boys, who received the news in horrified silence. I shall get into a real scolding when I come down on Saturday. But I know I was right. This is NOT (repeat NOT) an impulsive gesture. I have been worrying over it for months.

VITA TO HAROLD   *Sissinghurst*

7 March 1947

I am not sure about the Labour Party, though not wholly hostile, especially if it leads eventually to Lord Cranfield.[1] Of course I do not really like you being associated with these bedints. I like Ernest Bevin [Foreign Secretary], I have a contemptuous tolerance of Attlee, but I *loathe* Aneurin Bevan, and Shinwell is just a public menace. I do not

---

1. The title that Harold had decided to assume if he was offered a peerage.

like people who cannot speak the King's English. The sort of people I like are Winston and Sir John Anderson. I like Jowitt personally, but now think him to be a windbag and a broken reed.

HAROLD TO VITA   *10 Neville Terrace*

22 May 1947

I went to the Salisburys' party at Montpelier Square. We were told to be there at 6.0 as the Queen was coming. There was the American Ambassador and Mrs Lou Douglas and lots of younger people. The Queen arrived on the stroke and remained for two solid hours standing the whole time. She was looking radiant. She said in her lovely clear voice, "How nice to meet old friends again." Then she shook hands with us one by one. Then she established herself in the corner of the room and we were brought up for a chat. She asked after you and I said we had been down to Panshanger. Then we got on to St Helena. She is all very easy and simple. Lady Harlech, who went round South Africa with her, said that she possesses a sixth sense. She can tell when someone is feeling hurt or left out or frightened. She can spot them even when they are skulking or sulking at the back of a crowd. She will pass through the crowd and talk to them and all is sunshine again. She says it is some magnetic faculty. The one thing wrong with the Queen is that she is a bad leaver. "Like Pharaoh," said Lady Harlech, "she won't let the people go."

VITA TO HAROLD   *Sissinghurst*

5 June 1947

I am amused. You know the absurd thriller story I wrote in 4 weeks for an American magazine and got £3,000 for? [*Devil at West-ease*] not that it was £3,000 by the time Dr Dalton [Chancellor of the Exchequer] had finished with it. Well, I said on no account was it to be published in England but I didn't mind it being published by Doubleday in the U.S.A. (I have got copies; but I won't inflict it on you.) And now I hear from Curtis Brown [literary agent] that they have applications for translation rights into Spanish, Portuguese, Italian, German, and 'English Continental' whatever that may be. I think they must have had even more than those, because they say "numerous enquiries, *including*" . . . the ones mentioned.

I re-read it. It is quite readable, and as I had completely forgotten it, I was able to read it quite objectively. But it is only a nonsense.

HAROLD TO VITA   *10 Neville Terrace*

22 July 1947

No darling—I do not agree about the azaleas. And why is that? First because I don't feel that azaleas are very Sissinghurst in any case. They are Ascot, Sunningdale sort of plants. Not our lovely romantic Saxon, Roman, Tudor Kent. I know you will say, and rightly, that nor are magnolias. But you know what I mean. Anything with the suggestion of suburbia should be excluded. But secondly because I think we want something formal. You have the wall; you have Dionysus [statue]; you have the strip of mown grass; you then have the bank; and along the top I want something different from the bank and different from the nuttery. Something dividing the formality of the moat walk from the comparative informality of the nuttery. I should rather have a row of stiff Irish yews than a flurry of azaleas. But we may find something. It is a very important site.[1]

HAROLD TO VITA   *Hotel Richmond, Geneva*

7 September 1947

I spent most of the time in the library of the University poring over their amazing collection of manuscripts.[2] They were frightfully

---

1. Harold did not get his way. The bank was planted with azaleas, underneath which wild bluebells were allowed to flourish.
2. Harold was in Switzerland gathering information and impressions for his book on Benjamin Constant, the French intellectual banished by Napoleon for his political activities.

kind and I sat in the librarian's room at a little table and had in front of me all the letters from and to Constant that they possessed. I had of course not time to read more than a small percentage of them, nor in fact do I want my book to be a work of research. I have no time for that. I want it to be a study. An 'interpretation' if you like. But of course to handle all these letters gave me added insight. As a child Constant was a regular calligraphist. He wrote to his grandmother at the age of ten in a hand which is like that which B.M. used to affect when she wrote the names of guests for the bedroom doors. I was lucky, I think, as each of the letters I selected for special reading gave me some information of value.

The librarian was a nice man and an intellectual. He had read several of my works. He did not call me "cher maître," which I thought remiss of him, but in other respects he was waggy-tail, and handling things with neat fingers, and pointing out things I might miss. Then he showed me the manuscript of the *Contrat Social,* and what was more interesting, that of the *Confessions* [both Rousseau]. The latter is written in the tiny hand which people adopt when they want to write the Sermon on the Mount on a five-shilling piece. Beautiful it was in its neatness. *"On voit bien,"* said the librarian, *"qu'il était fils d'un horloger."*

Well I enjoyed that and thereafter I strolled through this Calvinistic city and had luncheon alone with Lysistrata (a fine strapping girl),[3] and then went to the museum where there is an extraordinary picture called 'Le Lever de Monsieur de Voltaire'. Voltaire has just tumbled out of bed and is struggling out of his night-gown. White naked thighs stamp in impatience, and with his free hand he is dictating furiously to a secretary sitting all prim at a table by the window.

HAROLD TO VITA   *10 Neville Terrace*

19 November 1947

I had foreseen the Violet [Trefusis] difficulty and ought to have discussed it with you before I left. I remember that she is frightened

---

3. Not a person but a book, the play by Aristophanes that described a women's revolt.

of sleeping alone. The solution is that she should have my room and I will go into Ben's. I should really loathe feeling I was alone with her in the cottage, and I do not think she would like it either. Why I should hate it so much I cannot begin to say. But the idea fills me with horror. Real horror. In fact I refuse absolutely to do it. So Violet has my room and I go to Ben's. I will not truly accept any other solution. But why the idea of sharing the cottage with Violet should make me tremble with real panic I have no idea. I shall have to be psychoanalysed about it. But make no mistake at all. I would rather walk the fields all night.[1]

HAROLD TO VITA   *10 Neville Terrace*

11 December 1947

I met Tommy Lascelles in the Club. He said to me, "Was Vita pleased?" I said, "Yes," not wishing to expose to the private secretary of the fountain of honours [King George VI] that my own beloved is a nit-wit about such things. But I did say to him, "Tommy, who was it who suggested V. should get the C.H.?"[2] "The Prime Minister," he said. I said, "Yes of course I know that formally it has to come from the P.M., but who was at the back of it?" "The Prime Minister," he repeated grinning—and then he told me that Attlee had a passionate admiration for THE LAND and had tried to get you this last year but the list was full. So the little rat whom you so despise is a persistent little rat.

I wrote our names down at the Palace. I told Tommy that if he was a true friend he would see to it that the announcement was V.S.W. with (Mrs Hadji) in brackets. He said it would have to be Victoria in any case as full names have to be given. He did not know about the V.S.W. coming first. But he promised to see what he could do. I hope

---

1. Violet Trefusis did not come to Sissinghurst after all.
2. Vita was made a Companion of Honour in the New Year's Honours of 1948.

he will. He will be all friendly about it I know, but I doubt whether he realizes the importance you attach to it. Poets still and patriots deck the line.[3] But I couldn't explain all that to Tommy at the Beefsteak. But I did my best.

---

3. "And patriots still, or poets, deck the line." Pope's epitaph on the tomb of Charles Sackville, 6th Earl of Dorset, at Withyham, Sussex.

Harold was nominated by the Labour Party to contest a bye-election in North Croydon. He did himself no discredit, but failed to win the seat, and the experience effectively ended his political career. Vita (who was on a lecture tour in North Africa during the election) was secretly delighted, particularly when Harold was invited to write the official biography of King George V, his magnum opus, *which occupied him till 1952 and gained him a knighthood. In the intervals of his researches in the royal archives at Windsor, he continued his weekly journalism, his membership of several committees including the National Trust and the London Library (of which he became Chairman), and gave many lectures, three of them in the devastated city of Berlin. Vita became a local Justice of the Peace, and explored the idea of a White Garden, her greatest horticultural triumph at Sissinghurst.*

HAROLD TO VITA   *10 Neville Terrace*

19 December 1947

It was nice of you to telephone about Croydon. Niggs also telephoned on his return from Leicester. I was touched by this solicitude. I meant to treat Croydon as my own private worry and not impose it on my family. Like a dog going into the dark when ill. But I was touched by their interest and sympathy. Niggs is so sweet about it all.[1]

I dined with Rab Butler last night. He says that Winston is a grave

---

1. The problem was that Nigel was standing as Conservative candidate in Leicester while his father was the Labour candidate in Croydon.

liability to the Party. He does not consult them and is always making speeches which let them down. But they can't get rid of him. "It is a question of which dies first, Winston or the Tory Party."

HAROLD TO VITA   *10 Neville Terrace*

8 January 1948

I went yesterday to hear Chaim Weizmann give an address on Palestine. He is a fine man, like a large Lenin, and with a sort of sad dignity which is impressive. He was more optimistic than I expected. He says that we are apt to judge the Zionists by the Stern gang which is nothing but a tiny gangster minority. That is all very well, but Haganah is not a minority and they do nothing at all to control the Stern gang. Poor Weizmann—he will live to see his independent Jewish State—but instead of it being a nice comfy little home like Luxembourg, it will be a fierce camp, riven with hatred, and red with blood. A sad thing to achieve the aim of one's life and find it a thing of horror.

VITA TO HAROLD   *Algiers*

19 February 1948

Well, I went to Radio-Alger and did my little piece in a strange studio whose walls and floor were made of cork. It had a vaguely Egyptian look, like a chamber in the centre of the Pyramid. You could poke holes in it with your fingers; and as everybody had apparently amused themselves by doing so, it had a honeycomb appearance. I expect you went there too, when you were here.

Darling, I go on scribbling my little doings to you in spite of realising how silly and remote they must seem in the middle of an election campaign. Listen, I wish you would get yourself a really good tonic for this election. Will you? To please Mar? Metatone is as good as anything, I think, if you can get it; unless you would like to ask

Dr Goadby to prescribe something which he knows would suit your make-up. Do, *please,* Hadji. You will need it. Oh my darling, you're going to be so tired and bothered, I can't bear to think of it.

HAROLD TO VITA   *The Queen's Hotel, North Croydon*

24 February 1948

This is, or was, a hydro—like one of those many hydros in Tunbridge Wells—but has fallen on evil days. There is no heating, no running water, a bath along the passage with a tepid drip, a gas-fire in my room which I have to work by inserting a shilling into the metre. I know that I shall return frozen to find that I have no shillings. The other inhabitants of this hotel consist in broken old ladies and epileptics.

My Committee Room is a disused and requisitioned building. Most of the windows have holes in them, the doors won't shut, and it is very cold and draughty. I have to sit all day in my greatcoat with a muffler. But they are getting me another electric stove and the thaw has begun. Great icicles drip from my window-ledge. Huge posters of myself decorate the walls with exclamatory gestures. No, I do not like it one little bit.

The staff are charming and gay and efficient, and that makes a great difference and relief. But the hours are ungainly. I mean, I don't know when I get my meals. There is a tiny bedint restaurant near here where one can get fish-and-chips and a cup of coffee. But somehow that is not a diet to which I am accustomed.

I met my opponents.[1] Harris is stout, common, naive, young, rather attractive I thought. Bennett is young-looking, smart, determined, speaks with a faint Australian accent, very composed. Harris speaks glibly but evidently he has learnt one gramophone record and will play it over and over again. Bennett made a set speech quite well. I follow with an ordinary little talk. The whole theme is, "What, in

---

1. Harold was the Labour candidate; F. H. Harris (who won) was the Conservative; Air-Vice-Marshal Donald Bennett, a war hero, the Liberal.

your opinion, should be done for the smaller trader and businessman?" Now, the Croydon Chamber of Commerce are entirely composed of small retailers and businessmen, and are enraged by all the restrictions and forms which the Government have imposed. Thus Harris and Bennett were very popular when they said, "We are for freeing the small man," and I was not at all popular when I said, "We must retain controls." But up to that point it went well enough.

Then came questions. They were all addressed to me. As always happens, they were based upon a detailed grievance and not upon a definite principle. "Why has the Croydon Council requisitioned a house at the corner of the Bellevue Road?" "Why was I not allowed to get hides from Sweden?" "Why does one not have a rebate on purchase-tax for unexpended stock?" Now, of course, I could not answer these questions, but Harris could. So in the end he and Bennett scored heavily.

I drive back at 9.45 to my hotel. It is bitterly cold. I find the whole place in semi-darkness and cannot get anything at all to eat—not even a glass of water. I go up to my room and light the gas-fire. It is not a cheerful contrivance. I then go to bed, but I sleep badly, as I am cold and nervous. And rather hungry. I shall buy some Ovaltine tomorrow to drink when I get back from meetings.

Well, that is the end of the first day. I found such a sweet letter from you here, darling. It did cheer me up. I have got the Lenare photograph [of Vita] in the office, and all the Sissinghurst ones in my hotel bedroom. The silver pot is in the hotel, as it will be useful for the Ovaltine.

HAROLD TO VITA   *Croydon*

1 March 1948

I am so glad I belong to the [Labour] Party now. I really feel much more comfortable as a Labour man than I ever did as a hybrid. There is a quality of mutual confidence which is moving and rare.

The Tories are evidently very frightened of losing the seat. I do not think they have any cause for alarm. Air-Vice-Marshal Bennett is not cutting very much ice. And unless he seriously splits the Tory vote, then Harris is bound to get in. You know that I shall not mind much being beaten although it would be a terrific triumph to win. What I do not want to do is to make a fool of myself. But the Tories have gone all out. They have imported cinema vans, and loud-speaker vans, and the whole of their Central Office, and the whole of their shadow Cabinet. Anthony Eden is coming, and Oliver Lyttelton, and Harold Macmillan, and Rab Butler and all the rest. I am glad of that. It will make my defeat less humiliating and my victory more triumphant.

HAROLD TO VITA   *Croydon*

10 March 1948

Well the battle is over and I am alive and well. It has been the most lovely weather and promises to be fine tomorrow. Quite summer warm it has been and I am thinking of the Magnolia and almonds at home. I shall see them on Saturday. And then on Saturday week we are united again, thank God, and resume our happy private life without publicity or angry crowds.

I can honestly say, darling, that there has not been one moment in the last three weeks which I have not hated to a large or small degree. The only contented moments I have had is when I have got back to my room and my Ovaltine and written to you. However much one tries, there is always a falsity about elections. I mean, one simulates friendship and matiness with people whom one does not wish ever to see again. My hands are still aching (and have to be washed) after shaking hands with a hundred enthusiastic workers. Something of their excitement does communicate itself. But it does not go deep down. And always the censor watches and murmurs in my ear, "Hadji—you are putting it on and showing off."

But truly, darling Viti, I can look back with some satisfaction upon this campaign. I have not spared myself and have not shirked a single odious task. I have spoken well enough and answered questions frankly. I have not descended to any abuse or tricks; I have not made a single pledge or promise which I shall be unable to fulfill; and I have not, even in the heat of controversy, said a single word which, in the after vacancy, need cause me shame.

Of course I am aware that there have been those among my supporters who feel that I have exaggerated the superior and noble line and that a more dynamic and popular candidate might have done better. I do not regret the line of moderate decency which I have taken. From the practical point of view, the Labour vote was mine anyway; the reason I was chosen was that they felt I might attract some floating votes. I think I might have done so and may have done so. But I do not think I shall get in.[1]

HAROLD TO VITA   *10 Neville Terrace*

7 May 1948

Another lovely May morning and I think of the view over the lilacs to the azaleas which I get from my bedroom window. I think I gain more from Sissinghurst than anyone else. (1) My sitting room is the nicest room in the estate. (2) My bedroom is the nicest bedroom in the castle. (3) My Life's Work is the finest part of the whole garden.

Anyhow I go to Oxford today and it will be nice to see it on a May evening. I am going for the opening meeting of the Oxford Philhellenic Society. A most inauspicious moment to have chosen, since the Greek Government are massacring their [Communist] prisoners by the shoals. So conscious of this was I that I went and saw the Greek Ambassador who was to have presided and told him he must contract an immediate diplomatic illness. It would not do at all if there were to be boos at the Greek Ambassador. He was much relieved at my insisting that he should chuck.

On my way there I called in at the Roosevelt memorial.[2] The statue itself is a nightmare but the surround with its two pools and little fountains is quite successful. But how difficult the proletariat are! In principle I like to see such gardens thrown open to them. But they destroy the grass and there were little ragamuffins sailing cigarette

---

1. The result was declared next day: Harris (Conservative) 36,200; Nicolson (Labour) 24,536; Bennett (Liberal) 6,321. Conservative majority 11,664.
2. In Grosvenor Square. The Memorial (by Sir William Reid Dick) had been unveiled by the King in April.

cartons in the two pools. Yes I fear my socialism is purely cerebral; I do not like the masses in the flesh.

10 Neville Terrace

14 May 1948

I went to [Laurence] Olivier's *Hamlet* yesterday. It is built on the theory that Hamlet was a man of weak decision. But I agree with [Salvador] Madariaga that this is not possible as an interpretation. He was a tough. After all he murdered Polonius and Ophelia and Rosencrantz and Guildenstern without a qualm. But in any case Olivier cannot act a *weak* man. He is himself a tough. So the thing is more unconvincing than ever. It remains an insoluble problem. Shakespeare must have known it was one of his finest plays, and yet he was terribly careless about it. For instance Hamlet is 20 when the play opens and then one discovers that he is really 30. And all those stiffs at the end are pushing it too far. Anyhow the film is a very competent piece of work—but not more. It lacks that touch of April which made *Henry V* so unforgettable a film. I went three times to see *Henry V*.

10 Neville Terrace

8 June 1948

I walked across the park to Buckingham Palace. I was taken at once into Tommy Lascelles's room. He had been delegated to approach me to write the life of George V. I said that in principle I did not like writing biographies when I could not tell the whole truth. Tommy said (well, I thought), "But it is not meant to be an ordinary biography. It is something quite different. You will be writing a book about a very ancient national institution, and you need not descend to personalities." He said that I should not be expected to write one word that was not true. I should not be expected to praise or exaggerate. But I must omit things and incidents which were discreditable.

Well, that is the proposition. I have not got clear in my head what I really feel about it. I see the balance-sheet as follows:

Advantages: A definite task, taking me three years at least and bringing a large financial reward. Access to papers of deep interest and importance. Close collaboration with charming people such as Tommy and Morshead.[1] The opportunity of writing the history of my own times. Added to which, I suppose, is the compliment of having been chosen.

Disadvantages: To have to write an 'official' biography. The lack of charm in the King I am dealing with. My inability (and indeed my unwillingness) to poke fun at the monarchy. My not being allowed to mention discreditable or foolish things. My having to be mythological.

I shall like to hear your reactions to all this. What you will hate, as I hate, is the idea of having to write 'to order'. Rather like a painter being forced to paint the official royal portraits. But being a writer, you will also see the fascination of the challenge. Is it possible to write such a life in a way that will be really interesting, really true, while keeping to the convention of royal portraits? I do not feel that my integrity is involved. I need not say one word in praise. All I have to do is leave out the funny bits. Nor shall I consent to distorting a single passage.

I told Elvira [Niggeman]. She was delighted and as usual most intelligent. She said, "But it is just what you need—an anchor. It will keep you busy for three years and prevent you doing silly things like Croydon. People say that young men need anchors. That may be true—but people of later middle age need anchors far more than the young."

After we had discussed this, Tommy said, "Must you rush off at once? Can you spare me another ten minutes?" He then gave me the speech he had been writing for the Duke of Edinburgh at the Guildhall. I pointed out that certain phrases would be difficult to get across clearly. He then took up the telephone and said, "Get me the Duke of Edinburgh." "Could you come down, Sir, for a moment?" So the young man came in like a schoolboy. He is far better looking than his photographs. We made him go through it. He did it so seriously and so well. "What a bit of luck," said Tommy when the boy had gone, "such a nice young man, such a sense of duty, not a fool in any way,

---

1. Sir Owen Morshead, the Librarian at Windsor Castle, 1926–58.

so much in love, poor boy—and after all, put the heir to the throne in a family way all according to plan."[2] Yes, Tommy is the least courtly courtier I have ever known.

VITA TO HAROLD   *Sissinghurst*

8 June 1948

I am divided in my mind about George V. I do see that he would be a good solid peg on which to hang a very interesting study of the period. Very interesting indeed, if you were allowed a free hand. But would the King want you to concentrate principally on his father? Or would he allow you excursions all round? Tommy L. of course would understand exactly how you wanted to write it, but Tommy's employer probably has a Divine Right attitude, and might not understand. Anyhow it was a great compliment, and I expect Queen Mary was the originator.

VITA TO HAROLD   *Sissinghurst*

26 September 1948

It was such a relief to get that telephone message to say that you had arrived safely in Berlin.[3] It was just like you to have taken the trouble to get it sent, but really you would have been rewarded for your trouble if you could have known the relief it gave me. I slept soundly all night, whereas I hadn't slept much the night before. It is a perfect day here. Hot, like summer, and you among the ruins. You will hate all that: I know how much you will mind it. Oh Hadji, how much I wish you were here instead of in Berlin! With the world in such a mess, I cling more and more to the serenity and happiness of Sissinghurst and our life—our way of life, as we have made it.

---

2. Prince Philip, Duke of Edinburgh, was then twenty-seven. He had married Princess Elizabeth on 20 November 1947, and Prince Charles was born on 14 November 1948.

3. He had flown there via Hamburg, since all other forms of transport were cut off by the Russian blockade of West Berlin. Harold had been asked to give four lectures as a demonstration of British solidarity with the Berliners.

29 September 1948

I had a long talk alone with Lalli [Horstmann] yesterday, and she told me the whole story. She says that we have no idea of the extent of rape the Russians carried out. She herself had to jump out of her window and hide in the hay in the barn night after night. The officers made no pretence at all to stop their men. Not a single woman, whatever her age, in her own village was not raped some ten or twelve times by different soldiers. Then after a month of these nightly orgies, discipline was reestablished. But for that month the thing was hell. Lalli, who has endured so much, now feels that she must really get away to safety. She hopes to go to Portugal and remain there a year.

I lunched with the Acting Lord Mayor of Berlin [Friedenburg] in a clubhouse on the Wannsee. I met most of the leading Berlin politicians and was glad to find that my German was coming back to me. They were delighted that their city was the centre of world attention. But except for one of them [Reuter], I thought them a poor lot.

When I got back, old Graf Limburg Stirrum was waiting for me. He used to be a very rich landowner, but all his properties are beyond the iron curtain and he is left with one room in Berlin, a Boucher, and not a bob. He is dreading the winter. He has no light except for two hours a night. No candles. He just sits in the dark. And what happens when the cold comes? The prospect for them is really terrible.

26 October 1948

How cold and lovely it was this morning. I walked about the platform of Staplehurst station and watched the leaves turning. I thought how much nature has meant to me in life. I do derive intense pleasure from the loveliness of my whole world of Kent, and above all of Sissinghurst. I am sure we are right about that. Sissinghurst has a quality of mellowness, of retirement, of unflaunting dignity, which is just what we wanted to achieve and which in some ways we have achieved by chance. I think it is mainly due to the succession of privacies: the forecourt, the first arch, the main court, the tower arch, the lawn, the orchard. All a series of escapes from the world, giving the impression of cumulative escape.

VITA TO HAROLD   *Sissinghurst*

9 November 1948

Darling, it was such a lovely rich sunset this evening—the woods looked like tapestry, all brown and green, and the poplars on the way to the lake were bright gold. Then there was an extra bit of enchantment, because all the younger Jacob's sheep were playing a game round the big oak. They scampered round and round after each other, and sometimes they tried to run up the trunk of the oak, and then fell off again, and ran round again, and butted each other when they caught each other headlong. They played the game not knowing that I was watching them, all unselfconscious they were—it was like a Greek thing, an idyll, or like a frieze—it reminded me of Keats and the Grecian urn, only there was no urn, just our Sissinghurst field and the woods beyond.

Oh how happy I was—oh how happy—for that brief suspended moment. I felt so wildly happy that I had to tell you about it—like a sort of sharing.

Your Mar

HAROLD TO VITA   *10 Neville Terrace*

7 January 1949

I sent you a wretched little scribble yesterday as I was hurrying off to Windsor. My visit there was a great success. I climbed up the hill and the policeman directed me to the entrance to the Library. There I met Owen Morshead, who was kind indeed. He first showed me the diaries [of George V]. They are really little more than engage-

ment books and not at all revealing. But they are invaluable for
checking dates. There are also those extracts from Queen Victoria's
diaries which Princess Beatrice preserved. She burnt all the rest.
Wicked old woman. Morshead tells me that he does not think that the
King or the Queen or even Queen Mary will be difficult so long as
I do not attack the principle of monarchy, which I assuredly have no
intention of doing. But he fears that all the old aunts and people will
descend upon them and bully them. Luckily there are few aunts left.
He says that the difficult thing to treat will be King George's handling
of his children. "The House of Hanover, like ducks, produce bad
parents—they trample on their young."

Thereafter he took me to the Round Tower, to the muniment
rooms where I was received by Miss Mackenzie, a formidable woman
who has all the appearance of being the Principal of Girton [College,
Cambridge]. There is one room devoted entirely to George V. It has
a small window with a lovely view over the river. This will be my
room, and Elvira [Niggeman] can come and type with me. The
documents are sufficiently numerous to provide me with masses of
original material but not so vast as to be unmanageable. If I go there
three days a week, I should be able to get through the lot in four
months. I was cheered by this. I then lunched with Morshead and his
wife and daughters. A happy, decent, cultured family. I came back here
feeling zest about the book. It will really contain material of importance.

VITA TO HAROLD   *La Tour St Loup,*
                                         Longueville, France
1 March 1949

Violet's [Trefusis] car met me at the Gare du Nord. We drew up
at the Meurice, and there was Violet herself, with plumes waving all
out of her hat, looking like a dowager duchess. So we drove out to
St Loup together and had a perfectly delicious dinner (champagne),
and talked. What worries me is the way that V. persecutes her charming old maid. It reminds me of B.M. It's really more than a little mad.
She curses her *all* the time. If I spoke to Rollo [her dog] like that, he
would run away and never come back. She (Alice the maid) poured

it all out to me this morning, says her health is breaking down (V. even wakes her up at all hours of the night), and that she will have to leave. Of course V. doesn't believe it, but the day will come when Alice will really go, and I don't know what V. will do without her. It is a sort of lust for power, I think: she must have someone to bully. I cannot explain it in any other way, but it is most painful and horrid.

VITA TO HAROLD   *Parador de San Francisco, Alhambra,*
                  Granada, Spain
10 March 1949

I have had an odd experience today. I have been to the street where Pepita was born.[1] Oh such a slum it is—very narrow, you could almost shake hands from one little balcony to the other overhead—crowded with people and children, but there can be little doubt that it was exactly the same when Pepita played there as a little girl. A Malaguerian poet called Munoz Rojas took me there. He has been looking up all the places and found the hotel where the Consul locked Granpapa into his room.[2] We lunched with Rojas after seeing the cathedral and the Alcazar. He was at Cambridge, and is now a farmer as well as a poet.

HAROLD TO VITA   *10 Neville Terrace*

1 June 1949

The Brains Trust was not, I felt, a very good one.[3] Such silly questions. Enid was so terrified of saying something silly that she scarcely said anything at all. I had to jab at her. Crowther was angry that the question about the devaluation of the pound was left in. He thinks that it is something that should not be mentioned. He is quite

---

1. In Malaga in 1830. Her mother was gipsy-born and her father a barber.
2. Lionel Sackville-West was so desperately in love with Pepita that he intended to marry her although he knew that she was already married. The British Consul prevented him by locking him into a hotel bedroom for three days.
3. Harold was a frequent quest on the BBC's prestigious radio program, "The Brains Trust." On this occasion his partners were Geoffrey Crowther (editor of the *Economist*), Enid Bagnold (the novelist), and Julian Huxley. Donald McCullough was always the Chairman.

sure that it will be of no benefit to anyone. I said that people had felt exactly the same in 1931 and that when we devalued, everybody was delighted and trade revived. He said that this was due to special circumstances. I said that it was odd that a terrible crisis arose in order to keep us on the gold standard, and that when we were off it, everybody was delighted. "It is a familiar experience," he said. "When we were boys we were told that certain practices were worse than death. And when we at last indulged in those practices, we found them rather pleasant." "I am glad you didn't say that on the air," Donald McCullough said: "It would have meant the end of the Brains Trust for ever."

VITA TO HAROLD   *Sissinghurst*

5 July 1949

I am not at all sure that we oughtn't to make the Erechtheum garden all grey and white.[1] It would then be nice all the year round. This would entail millions of cuttings, but I think it would be worthwhile, and by 1951 the cuttings will have grown into reasonably large plants. We will talk about it. It would mean leaving the *Night* roses there for another summer, or it would really be too empty, so we must make 1951 the year of triumph.

HAROLD TO VITA   *10 Neville Terrace*

6 July 1949

I agree with you about the Erechtheum garden being all grey. For next year we must keep *Night* where she is and prick in grey things all round her. We shall also have to take a vast amount of *regale* seed this year although it will not make big bulbs till 1952. We must think this out carefully. It will require *some* colour. I incline to pink as in the China roses. You prefer yellow. I am quite prepared to agree to

---

1. This was the White Garden, the most original and best known of all the separate gardens at Sissinghurst. The Erechtheum was a columned outdoor dining room that they made in a corner of this garden.

yellow since I feel that it is more original, and you have a better colour taste than I have. I quite see that those big pale yellow things in the cottage garden (Evening primroses?) would look very well. They must be faint pallid yellow—nothing that shouts or raises its voice. Yellow roses perhaps here and there. But all faint. We must aim at making it look pretty by 1951.

VITA TO HAROLD   *Sissinghurst*

28 September 1949

Darling, I did so enjoy reading *George V*. Not only because it was by my favourite author, but because it was so skillfully done. I do like good craftmanship in literature, even as I like it in a good carpenter or thatcher or bricklayer. I like things well made. I feel only, if I may speak as a reviewer and not as your worshipping fan, that you are getting a bit too frightened of what you regard as the too-personal touch. I know what is producing this cautiousness in you: it is the flood of cheaply vivid biography of recent years, the Philip Guedallas and so on. You are reacting; and it is a wholesome reaction. Think, all the same, of Stefan Zweig's life of Balzac: there was nothing cheap about that—he got the solidity as well as the highlights, the little points of light that touch up the character as in a Rembrandt. You are getting cautious and I think it is a pity because you are denying your own special gift. I know that *George V* is a serious book, so don't imagine that I am judging it from a light, frivolous, or what is called 'feminine' aspect. I am only asking you not to abjure your own particular genius, which you seem in some danger of doing because you are frightened of it.

VITA TO HAROLD   *Sissinghurst*

8 November 1949

The two people I miss most are Virginia [Woolf] and Geoffrey [Scott]—not that Geoffrey wasn't an awful nuisance to me—he was—and an anxiety—but I still think sometimes, "How that would amuse

Geoffrey!" and then I remember that I can't tell him. And Virginia even more so, because she was never a nuisance, only a delight. An anxiety of course—and I still think I might have saved her if only I had been there and had known the state of mind she was getting into. I think she would have told me, as she did tell me on previous occasions.

VITA TO HAROLD   *Sissinghurst*

14 December 1949

I am somewhat agitated, because the police telephoned for me to take a rather complicated case this morning.[1] I rather hate these cases, although the human aspect of them always interests me objectively. I don't like it when I am the only Justice, as I was this morning, and have to sit in a large armchair behind a table, while the wretched delinquent stands before me, and the room is full of police officers and the Clerk of the Court and his Clerk and the Detective Superintendent, all bringing charges and evidence against the prisoner, and all the ponderous weight of the Law and its apparatus of which I am a part. I always feel that here is a wild animal trapped and caged, and that if it sprang suddenly at my throat it would be seized and restrained by a dozen strong hands; and above all I feel, "There but for the grace of God and B.M.'s Marriage Settlement, go I."

"Take your hands out of your pockets when Her Worship speaks to you!" Oh darling, it makes me feel like a character in a Galsworthy play.

VITA TO HAROLD   *Sissinghurst*

7 March 1950

It has turned into the heavenly day we anticipated. Oh how I wish you were here! I walked down the spring garden and all your little

---

1. Vita had been appointed a Magistrate (Justice of the Peace) for the Cranbrook Bench in October 1948.

flowers bit and tore at my heart. I do love you so, Hadji. It is quite simple: I do love you so. Just that.

I look forward to the weeks when you will be here, loaded as a bee, and will stay put for a bit.

I faintly regret the French party.[1] I would have liked to see all the nobs—e.g. the Cabinet ministers, and the Queen for whom I cherish a scullery-maid passion, and I would have liked to wear my little medal [the C.H.] with its cherry-coloured ribbon, but on the other hand I wouldn't have known anybody there and I would have felt and looked oafish and been ashamed of my hands. No, it's better for me to stay down here and talk to the Women's Institute in Sissinghurst.

One has to choose.

SITWELLS

HAROLD TO VITA   *10 Neville Terrace*

26 July 1950

Oh my God! Those Sitwells! Edith made the main speech at the London Library meeting yesterday. It was more conceited and egoistic than anything I have ever heard. She began by saying how shy and frightened she felt. She then launched an attack on people who made anthologies. And she then said something about how one was bound to suffer if one wrote great poetry. She then sat down suddenly. It was about the most incompetent thing I have ever seen. What made it all worse was that Lord Ilchester (who in his best moments is not good at managing a meeting) is getting I fear terribly gaga.[2] He made a deplorable chairman and I am sure everyone left the room feeling that the whole thing had been embarrassing and confused. I hate those things being muddled. It requires so very little arrangement to make them go properly.

I asked Edith how Osbert's gout was. She said, "Gout? That is but

---

1. A reception given on 8 March at the French Embassy for Vincent Auriol, the French President, who was on a State visit to England. Vita had been invited, but pleaded that she had nothing suitable to wear.
2. Harold succeeded Lord Ilchester (who was seventy-six in 1950) as Chairman of the London Library in November 1951.

a slight matter. What worries me is the state of his nerves. And can one wonder when one thinks of the ceaseless persecution to which he has been exposed these thirty years!"

VITA TO HAROLD   *Sissinghurst*

27 July 1950

I was amused by your description of Edith Sitwell—you remember that they are true neurotics; only, unlike most neurotics, they have got away with it, and have managed to impose a reign of terror on their contemporaries. Even Stephen Spender told me he would not dare to write a not-agreeable review of any of them. Thus the persecution of thirty years has been reversed.

All the same, Edith is a fine poet—I took down her *Song of the Cold* a day or two ago, and was uplifted in the way one is uplifted only by the best. You know, that sense of exhilaration . . . which has its counterpart in the sense of depression induced by bad poor thin stuff.

HAROLD TO VITA   *10 Neville Terrace*

17 August 1950

"What fun for you to go by river to Windsor and sleep on a boat." That was what Mar thought. But this is what happened.

Robin Maugham[1] had told me on the telephone that he specially wanted me to come that Tuesday as there was a Tangier friend of his coming who wanted to talk to me. The plan was that the Tangier friend and her little daughter should come down for tea and be taken a trip on the river; that I should arrive by train at 7.45 after they had got back; that we should all dine at the Hotel and then see the Tangier friend into her train; that we should sleep at Wargrave and start at

---

1. The novelist, playwright, and nephew of Somerset Maugham. He succeeded his father as 2nd Viscount Maugham in 1958.

dawn next day. He promised to get me to Windsor or at least Maiden-head by 10 a.m. But fate willed otherwise.

When I reached Wargrave Station I was met by Ken Long, who is Robin's assistant. Such a nice youth. He told me that on their return from their trip up the river the engine had conked out and the house-boat was stranded some miles up the stream. He had come to row me there. So I got into the tiny dinghy, draped myself in oil-skins and sat there in the pouring rain while he rowed me up the stream. The battery had run out and the only light on board were three candle stumps. The Tangier friend was a Mrs Dunlop—a nice woman—with a darling little daughter aged eleven of the name of Hughine. Had Robin and Ken realised in time that the boat was immovable and that the only thing was to row the Dunlop pair across to the hotel while there was still some light in sky and on river, all might have been well. But they conceived the *idée funeste* of towing the houseboat itself across the half mile of open stream which separated it from the hotel on the opposite bank. It was pouring with rain and there was a strong wind blowing up the river. Therefore after two hours grunting and towing by the dinghy they were obliged to abandon the project.

It was by then 10.0 at night and very dark. There was no food in the boat except bread and cheese and a cake. They decided to get some supper, and then to embark Mrs Dunlop and the child in the dinghy and row them across to the hotel where with luck they could get a taxi to take them to the station. Thus after supper they dressed the child up in Robin's huge army coat and lowered her gingerly into the dinghy. Her mother then handed down her coat and bag and climbed down herself. The night was wet and dark and they had no torch. Ken was in the boat helping them in. As Mrs Dunlop disappeared into the darkness I felt a bit uneasy and immediately there was a loud splash and spluttering and shouting.

The dinghy had capsised and there was the child weighted by this enormous coat in the water. Luckily they were not far from the bank and Ken was able to rescue her, and Mrs Dunlop swam to the shallow edge. The dinghy had meanwhile righted itself and drifted away down stream. By pulling on ropes hard we were able to edge the houseboat into the shallow water and Mrs Dunlop walked and the child was carried to the point where their dripping clothes wetted everything

around. They went into the wash-place and took off all their clothes
and dried with towels. They were then lent Pyjamas and wrapped in
blankets (of which luckily there were a huge quantity), were put in
the cabin and given coffee and hot rum. Mrs Dunlop behaved splendidly as did the child. The only remark that the little elf made was,
"This is what comes of knowing Robin." But Mrs Dunlop had lost
her bag in which was her passport and her savings bank-book for £150
and loose cash. The accommodation problem was serious. Mrs Dunlop
and her child were put in the cabin which had been meant for me. I
had to share Robin's cabin and the boy had to lie on the floor. It was
all very wet. Robin snored all night. I did not sleep very well. At 6.0
the next morning Robin got up and plunged into the river. He came
back towing the errant dinghy. He had also rescued the oars. Then in
the cold light of dawn he again plunged into the water and came up
after a few minutes clasping Mrs Dunlop's bag—muddy, sodden but
still intact. Ken rowed himself ashore in the recovered dinghy and from
there ran across to a boat-house and obtained a motor boat. With that
we started to tow the houseboat back to its base. It took a long time.
At one moment the dinghy sank, but we were able to recover it as it
was tied on to us by the tow rope. Finally at 10 a.m. we got back to
the landing stage. I left them drying their clothes. I caught the 10.28
and was in my room at Windsor by 11.30.

HAROLD TO VITA   *10 Neville Terrace*

12 December 1950

    I went down to Shaw's house yesterday.[1] We drove down in a
car which was very rich and American—a Plymouth, bouncy seats,
central heating and so on—and we lunched at a Road House near.
Then we went to the Shaw's Corner house. It is a loathesome little
building. A small red brick 1880 vicarage with a sloping lawn, some
conifers masking the road, and some elongated flower-beds in the shape

---

1. Bernard Shaw died on 2 November 1950, and bequeathed his house, Shaw's Corner, near
   Ayot St Lawrence, Hertfordshire, to the National Trust.

of kidneys. A large kitchen garden to provide Shaw with his food. In the garden a hut in which he worked. The furniture was lodging-house. Not a single good piece. In every room pictures of himself everywhere. The Public Trustee was there and then Mr Löwenstein arrived, and Mr Horowitz representing the Shaw society. I took against them.

The Trustee man told me that Shaw had left the whole of his fortune to the Spelling Bee.[2] He was a discreet man, but he just hinted that it might be contested. Not on the grounds that Shaw was mad, but on the grounds that the spelling bee is not a charity. You heard the story of the man in 1650 who left £10 to accumulate for ever at compound interest? It was discovered that if that Will held, he would own something like £200,000,000,000 by 1850. Thus they brought in an Act to prevent that sort of legacy. It is under that Act it seems that Shaw's will could be contested.

But darling, it was thrilling. Shaw was there, in the garden. Still in the shape of ashes. It was difficult and indeed impossible to tell which was Shaw and which was Mrs Shaw as their ashes had been mixed.[3] But there on the rose bed and garden paths were these white ashes— just like the stuff Mar puts down for slugs. I could easily have picked some up and taken it home in an envelope. But I do not admire Shaw all that. Besides Jim [Lees-Milne] might have thought it in bad taste. But it is a lesson not to leave in one's will that one's ashes must be scattered over the garden. They remain there for weeks and weeks.

VITA TO HAROLD   *Sissinghurst*

19 October 1950

Wasn't Ben charming this weekend? I go such a see-saw over him: he gets me into a state when he arrives in one of his moods, and then when he is in a good mood I *love* him. I often feel I should be nicer

---

2. A great part of his fortune was left to a society for the propagation of a new English alphabet.
3. His wife, Charlotte, had died in 1943, and her ashes had been preserved until they could be mixed with his.

to him, and I long to be, but he makes me so dreadfully shy some-times—I can't feel at ease with him, I feel like a motor-car with a clutch that won't get into gear. It grinds and nothing happens—the car won't start off.

VITA TO HAROLD   *Sissinghurst*

4 January 1951

I have been writing all morning. I re-read the beginning of my book [*The Easter Party*], and it doesn't seem so bad as I had thought. You know what ups and downs one has. Perhaps one is never able to judge oneself. One gets so easily dejected and then so readily elated, but the elation goes and the dejection returns. And of course the fact that one's own book, during the process of writing it, is so living and absorbing a part of one's existence, is in itself misleading: one has so immense a background of ideas that never get down on paper (because one must be severely selective) that one is apt to imagine that the reader will be sharing the whole of this cloudy experience, and will under-stand what is implicit as well as what is explicit.

I suppose this would not apply to a biographical or historical work like George V, but it certainly applies to fiction.

HAROLD TO VITA   *10 Neville Terrace*

17 January 1951

My mother is too pathetic for words. She just sits and cries. She is also rather irritable and suspicious. In fact, I fear her mind is giving way. People ought not to live over 85. I think it such a terrible thing that one should go on living and cease to be oneself—leaving a different picture of oneself behind. Life can be very hard and tragic.[1]

I have no news. I went to Windsor yesterday. The Thames was

---

1. Lady Carnock died on 23 March, aged ninety.

very full and quick and angry. I am reading Roy Harrod's book on Keynes[2] which I find entrancing. Really that Cambridge set were more gifted than anything we have seen since. They make Balliol look like an old cart-horse.

HAROLD TO VITA *10 Neville Terrace*

12 June 1951

No my darling, I am not hiding anything from you. I have not become involved in a spy ring nor have I become connected in any way with Guy's disreputable habits.[3] I have not seen or heard of or from him for two years.

If I was depressed this weekend it was due to a combination of circumstances. In the first place my visit to the South of France showed me that I had really become an old man [he was 64]. I did not want to bathe, being so fat, and I was clumsy and slow getting in and out of boats. That depressed me, but I shall get over it. Then I was depressed by my conversation with Roland de Margerie[4] and others. They really feel that France is done for as a Great Power. Then, above all, I was upset by the Maclean-Burgess business. It is not only that I hate my old profession being made a fool of and degraded. It is not only that I am really sorry for Anthony [Eden] and all Guy's friends. It is not merely that I hate to think that Philip Toynbee had the same sinister effect on Donald Maclean (politically and morally) as he might have had on Benzie. It is that I am shocked to see how this terrible infection assails even the most well informed people. It is as if, during a cholera epidemic, even those who were immune began to contract the disease. If people such as they with education and a position in the country can throw over everything in their hysterical love for holy Russia, then what can one expect will be the effect on less informed people? Guy and Maclean KNEW that most of the Russian stuff was

[margin annotations: Burgess; Fr. Foreign office]

---

2. *The Life of John Maynard Keynes,* 1951.
3. Guy Burgess had defected to Russia with Donald Maclean in May 1951.
4. Of the French Foreign Office. He had been in the London Embassy before the war.

lies. Why should they have become infected? It will do such dreadful harm. And in the third place, I am constantly, persistently, deeply worried by the fear that the cold war may turn into a hot one.

That is all, my sweet. Niggs has rather cheered me by saying that he dined with Ben on Friday and found him really "speechless with horror and disgust." He feels of course that Guy has betrayed Anthony and the boy Jackie. I do not think that Ben would be as horrified as I am by someone betraying his COUNTRY, but it is terrible to him to think of someone betraying his friends.

So I feel a little easier about it. But what a curious mystery it all is!

HAROLD TO VITA   *10 Neville Terrace*

2 January 1952

I dined with Raymond [Mortimer] yesterday at the club. I asked him whether he thought it would be wise to get an injunction against the publishers to prevent them republishing the Roy Campbell attack, or at least to threaten the publishers with a solicitor's letter saying that we would take action if the passage were reprinted.[1] He begged me earnestly to do nothing of the sort. A libel action would be insane since it would lead to nothing and create a vast scandal. But if we were rightly determined not to bring a libel action, then any action short of that would do more harm than good. Roy would be able to boast, "They tried to frighten my publishers with vague threats, but they never dared to bring an action." Tray begs us very earnestly to do nothing at all. I think he regrets now that he ever reviewed the book. He thought it the best way of saying what he thought. But on *second* thoughts I think he wishes he had left it unmentioned. Anyhow he is perfectly certain that all we can do is to adopt an attitude of silent

---

1. In 1931 Roy Campbell had published in his poem *The Georgiad* a satire on Vita and Harold, which was particularly vitriolic about Vita's affair with Roy's wife, Mary. They took no action at the time. Then, in 1952, Campbell returned to the attack in his autobiography, *Light on a Dark Horse*. Harold wrote a letter of protest to the publisher but took the matter no further.

disdain. I shall bring the book down with me. I would rather you did not read the passage, which is fiendish, but after all I suppose you must read it. What a bother for you, my poor darling Mar.

HAROLD TO VITA   *British Embassy, Copenhagen*

21 January 1952

It was dull and drizzly yesterday, but none the less I did some expeditions. The coast of Sweden appeared shining through the rain and finally we got to Elsinore. Mr Jerichow[1] is quite sure that Shakespeare came there himself with a company of English players and acted before the Royal Court. Does not the reception of the Mummers suggest personal experience? And how else could Shakespeare have known those two Danish names Rosencrantz and Guildenstern? I admit that the latter point always struck me as strange. Anyhow we went on to the bastions where a Danish soldier in a tin hat was gazing fixedly at a tanker steaming slowly across the Sund. The wild swans that frequent these waters had come into the moat of the castle since the open sea was too rough. Those that remained (and one could see them from the bastion) had their feathers all blown backwards by the howling N.W. wind. I thought of my return journey on Wednesday night.

In the inner bastion there is a plaque with a reproduction of the portrait of Shakespeare in the first folio. Underneath an inscription in Danish records that the saga regarding the Prinz Amleth of Juitland was used by Shakespeare in such a manner that the name of Elsingore or more accurately Helsingør became famous throughout the world. A true statement and to me, in the drizzle and the gale, with the wet swans struggling with their feathers, rather moving. Mar would have been moved; my mind and heart flashed out to her.

Then we visited the palace of Fredensborg, celebrated in the early diaries of George V; the little palace of Sorgenfri or Sans Souci; and the huge castle of Fredericksborg. We only descended from the car at

---

1. Harold's host. He was a very wealthy Anglophile Danish brewer.

the last place and then only visited the Chapel where are hung the shields of the Knights of the Elephant. Then we arrived, a little late, at the house of Mr Per Federspiel (or Peter Featherplay). He was educated at Harrow, got a C.B.E. for his assistance during the German occupation, and is legal adviser to the Embassy. There were many Danes there. A nice wife. The two little boys helped to hand round the food and drink. I noticed that the younger (aged 10) held the beer bottles in a most ungainly way. His mother whispered to me to explain. The beer they contained came, not from the brewery owned by Mr Jerichow, but from that of the rival Carlsbad Brewery. Thinking that Mr Jerichow might be hurt, the boy had decided to hide the label by putting his hand over it even at the risk of splashing beer.

I then retired and read a few pages of *Les Ambassades* [by Roger Peyrefitte]. It ought to be suppressed by the French censorship. It confirms everything I hate about the French: their meanness, their lasciviousness, their graspingness, their disloyalty, their cruelty, their egoism, their belief that anything said brightly and smartly must be true. Moreover I think it terrible to write about one's own amorous adventures in so stark a way, merely pornography. It is a revolting book; one cannot put it down.

HAROLD TO VITA   *Hotel Internazionale, Brindisi*

25 February 1952

I took the train [from Rome] for Brindisi. I had a first class compartment and luckily the British Council had reserved a seat as the train was packed. For nine hours, until ten thirty at night, did I sit tight on a hard red velvet seat. I read Simenon. I read Agatha Christie. I looked at the scenery, which really was not too good after one left the coast. It was of course dark when we reached the Adriatic Coast and I munched the cold chicken the Mallets[1] had given me and sipped the bottle of Chianti they had provided.

Oh my darling! How vivid to me was that journey we took

---

1. Sir Victor Mallet, British Ambassador in Rome.

thirty-nine years ago![2] Do you remember the sick woman and the husband who kept on jumping up and giving her sips of medicine? And how when in the autumn dawn we reached Bari and they got out, how you said with your sweet gentle smile, "I hope you will soon be better." And she cast back at you a look of utterly resigned despair? There we were, my sweet, so young, so healthy, embarking on what was a long life of love and action and success—and she must have been dead now these almost forty years and no more than a pinch of dust!

I walked out into the station square at Brindisi to find only a one-horse brougham. Anyhow, I bundled into it and drove through straight streets to this hotel. It was the last Sunday of Carnival and a few youths and maidens were parading the boulevards dressed in fancy dress and masks. But how dead it all was! Never have I had such a sense of absence of *stimmung* and *entrain*.

V I T A T O H A R O L D   *Sissinghurst*

27 February 1952

At the R.H.S. show there were the most lovely little spring things, crocuses, irises, scillas—in fact, a sort of idealised My Life's Work at its very best. I felt completely intoxicated.

People didn't begin to arrive for about twenty minutes. It was heaven.

At dinner I sat between the Chairman, Patrick Synge, whom I don't like; and David Bowes-Lyon,[3] whom I do. He wants us to come and see his garden. I met heaps of gardening friends and enjoyed myself very much. Jim Russell then gave a talk, with lantern slides, on the old roses; Graham Thomas was to have given it, but was ill. I was made rather a fuss of; they made me speak—but you know, Hadji, *I don't like it;* I hate getting credit for the wrong things; and I felt that there I was, an amateur amongst real experts;

2. On their honeymoon.
3. Sir David Bowes-Lyon was President of the R.H.S. His garden was at Hitchin, Hertfordshire.

and all because of my thin little *Observer* articles I had an undeserved reputation, also because a lot of people in the audience had been to the garden here. I felt a fraud.

H A R O L D   T O   V I T A   *British Embassy, Athens*

10 March 1952

Oh my word there was such a posh dinner in the evening! The King and Queen of the Hellenes, the Queen of Rumania and Princess Nicolas, with attendant gentlemen and ladies in waiting. I sat next to the Queen. You know, she was a German (a Hanover princess, I think, name of Frederika), and she is generally supposed to be rather bossy and managing. Although they agree that she has been excellent in charitable work and in encouraging industries and so on, they feel she interferes too much in politics. I daresay that is all very true, but the Greeks are never contented with anyone. She is pretty for a Queen, not very well dressed for a Queen, easy to get on with for a Queen, out-spoken for a Queen. But I did not really like her. I suppose she had been told that people said she bossed the King, so she was doing the silly but devoted little wife stunt which always makes me want to yell aloud. She told me she liked being a Queen; she told me that she would not mind being poor if she could have two hot baths a day; she told me that she has a cushion which fits onto her bath; she told me she believed in God; she told me that Queens could always tell when people were flattering them.

After dinner I had a talk with King Paul. He is an old pansy really, I suspect, but he adopts the manner of a bluff and hearty sailor. He tried on me the stunt that the Americans interfered too much with Greek politics. I did my stupid stunt of not knowing anything about nothing. But I rather liked him, I must say.

After dinner we had a film of the King's funeral[1] as Princess Nicolas had asked to see it. Then we had *cercle* again. They stayed on till twenty minutes to two, regardless of my bed-time. But after the

---

1. King George VI had died at Sandringham on 6 February 1952.

film I had a long talk with the Queen of Rumania, who really is a nice woman, and who is coming down to lunch at Sissinghurst.

You can imagine how glad I was to get to bed.

HAROLD TO VITA   *10 Neville Terrace*

12 June 1952

In the morning we had the Historic Buildings Committee of the National Trust. We have a new member, the Earl of Euston. You know I am always rather worried that this Committee, which actually decides whether we take a house, is composed almost entirely of peers. Well, we are now to have a man called Mr John Smith. When his name was put up Esher said, "Well it's a good thing to have a proletarian name on the Committee—anybody know the man?" "Yes," said Lord Euston, "he is my brother-in-law."[1]

Then I had the Royal Literary Fund which rather depresses me. It is what people on the Actors Benevolent Fund must feel when they give assistance to the broken down chorus girls of the 'nineties': "I may end that way."

I dined at the Beefsteak and sat next to Richard Molyneux.[2] He had decided that his courtier days were over and all that remained was to retire to his rooms in Pall Mall and die. But then he was summoned to Windsor for a whole fortnight by the young Queen, just as an old family friend. He was beside himself with pleasure, and said that of all his many visits to Windsor he had enjoyed this one most. He says the Queen is very much the sovereign. She enters the room at least ten yards ahead of her husband or mother. I asked him whether the Queen Mother objected to being thus put in the shade. "Not at all," he said, "her attitude is one of adoring admiration." He says he asked the Queen whether Winston treated her as Lord Melbourne treated the young Queen Victoria. "No, not a bit of it. I find him very obstinate."

1. Viscount Esher was Chairman of the National Trust; Harold was Vice-Chairman; the Earl of Euston (later 11th Duke of Grafton) was Chairman of many amenity societies; John Smith became Deputy Chairman of the National Trust in 1980.
2. Sir Richard Molyneux (1873–1954) had been a soldier and Equerry to Queen Mary.

HAROLD TO VITA   *C.1. Albany, Piccadilly*

30 July 1952

My George V is to be published on August 14. They sent me round four copies. One I gave to Tommy Lascelles; one I sent with a really charming letter to the Queen Mother at Sandringham; one I sent with a rather stiff letter to the Queen herself at Buckingham Palace; and one I wrapped up in brown paper and took out to luncheon with Tony Rothschild. He always hurries one out at 2.30 as then the work begins again and the great wheels of the Maison Rothschild revolve. So grasping my brown paper parcel I went by bus to the Travellers. I washed and tidied there (I had got on my best suit with a white shirt) and went on to Marlborough House to which I had been summoned. The dear old lady [Queen Mary] is rather groggy on her pins now. She tottered across the room. I bowed and presented the book, bowing. She sat down with me in the window seat and looked at every page. "What a lot of hard work!" she said from time to time. "How dignified," she said. She looked at the picture of the King when he was a young boy. "How like he was then to my poor silly son [Edward VIII]." Then she chattered away for half an hour and then Princess Margaret came in. So I went away. But it was a strange visit and the last time I shall see the old monument.

Never in my life have I been as comfortable as in my son's flat.[1] It really is delicious in itself and so convenient in its location.

HAROLD TO VITA   *C.1. Albany*

4 September 1952

I brought myself to tell Niggs about the K.C.V.O.[2] He was absolutely horrified. He said that it would be "so unlike you, Daddy, and even less like Mummy—poor dear Mummy," he said, as if you

---

1. Harold had left Neville Terrace, and was now sharing rooms with Nigel in Albany, the Regency apartment building off Piccadilly.
2. Harold had been awarded a knighthood for his biography of King George V.

had lost an arm. "Oh my God!" he said. "That is a frightful thing to happen." But being a sensible lad he quite saw that it would not be possible for me to refuse without appearing churlish, snobbish and conceited. But how much more I would have liked a Regency Clock.

HAROLD TO VITA   *C.1. Albany*

25 September 1952

I went to the Aberconway party. I was rather late in arriving, and the Amadeus string quartet had started playing Mozart's K.464 Quartet in A. So as not to interrupt, I sat on a little chair by myself outside the door. On and on they went. Mozart is just like Bunny.[1] He says, "Well, I must be going now," and then thinks of something else to say, and goes on and on till I could have struck the door with angry fists. Then the Amadeus were let out for a drink, and I was found by Christabel [Aberconway] on my little chair alone. So she dragged me into the room where there was a large selection of the nobility and gentry. The Amadeus quartet returned and I bolted, foregoing a rich supper awaiting the guests and taking my hat and coat away with me. I did not feel that I had dealt with this situation with much skill. I felt an untutored boob, a rustic, provincial.

1. Mrs. Cynthia Drummond, a Sissinghurst neighbor.

The success of King George V *gave Harold Nicolson more pleasure than the knighthood that resulted from it, and Vita was displeased at being addressed as Lady Nicolson when she wished to remain V. Sackville-West. Harold immediately began research for his next book,* Good Behaviour, *and as soon as it was finished, he embarked on his biography of the French critic Sainte-Beuve. He ceased writing his weekly column for the* Spectator *but continued his broadcasts on Foreign Affairs for the BBC's Overseas Service. He stood unsuccessfully for the Oxford Professorship of Poetry. Vita, meanwhile, was writing* Daughter of France. *Both their sons married, and in 1954 their first grandchild, Juliet, was born. The most important public events of these years were the death of Stalin, Anthony Eden's succession to Winston Churchill as Prime Minister, the end of the Korean War, and the coronation of Queen Elizabeth II.*

HAROLD TO VITA   *C.1. Albany*

20 November 1952

Oh my darling, when you get this I shall be 66, the mark of the beast. I do so hate growing old and the only thing to do is to bear the calamity with calm and resignation. But I was not intended to be old. I mean, for me there are no compensations at all in being a veteran and a grand old man of letters. I have no pleasure in being grand or important, or a K.C.V.O. Not that I am anything but delighted at the success of *George V*, or that I do not enjoy praise and being taken seriously as a writer. Of course I do. But I do not like being 66, so there.

James [Pope-Hennessy] gave a farewell party last night. He is off today in a cattle or at least a cargo boat to Dominica in the Antilles. He will be away five months. He told me such a funny thing about Gerry [Duke of] Wellington, who really is going mad with avarice. After dinner Gerry asked James to drop him on his way home. So they shared a taxi. James said to the driver, "Go to Apsley House," but Gerry said crossly, "No—certainly not, stop opposite on the park side." He then explained that if he drove to his own house, the taxi had to go round by St George's hospital which meant another 6d on the metre. Then when they reached the point opposite where Gerry was to be dropped, he jumped out quite crossly and said, "You would have taken a taxi in any case, so I needn't contribute." I really think avarice is the strangest of all obsessions. It can give no pleasure to oneself, and is a cause of dislike and contempt to others. I am not an avaricious man.

VITA TO HAROLD   *Sissinghurst*

31 December 1952

Well, when you get this letter you won't have time to read it, because your telephone will be starting to ring.[1] What a funny day for you, my darling. *I* know you don't like it. But what you must surely like, my sweet, is the realisation that you have made a real, solid, monumental contribution to English biography. I know that external appreciation means very little to you (except in so far as you are human, and praise from the right people is always acceptable, as they say in hospitals when one sends a brace of pheasants), and that the only true satisfaction one ever derives comes from within oneself, in the knowledge that one has done a job of work to the very best of one's ability and made a respect-worthy job of it, and given of one's best, both in conscientiousness and effort and even a kind of self-dedication to the task imposed.

This you have done, and you must know it, *dans ton foi intérieur,*

---

1. On the following day Harold's knighthood was announced in the New Year's Honours.

whatever you may pretend even to me, in your so-loveable diffidence and reserve and modesty. Then you must also know that *Marginal Comment* [his weekly article for the *Spectator*] has been a remarkable achievement.

Yes, looking back on this going year, I see what an enormous stride you have made, not only in your public reputation but in the satisfaction you must have given to your curly self.

And then, as you say, there are the boys: Niggs getting into the House and Ben happy at the Burlington[2]—and their affection for us, and the ease we all found together over Christmas. My only sorrow, and it is a deep one, is Nigel's appalling hair-cut.

VITA TO HAROLD   *Sissinghurst*

17 February 1953

Oh my darling Hadji, how much one dislikes growing older! I know how you hate it. You know how much I hate it. But I think the reason we both hate it is a double reason: the superficial reason is the physical reason, that one gets fat and bald and what-have-you, in the American phrase, but the real deep reason for us, you and me, is that we hate the idea of leaving Life, as we must, twenty to thirty years hence, and we both love life and enjoy it.

HAROLD TO VITA   *C.1. Albany*

7 May 1953

I lunched with the Austrians and the Queen of Spain[3] was there. After luncheon she took me aside and sat me down on a sofa and talked

---

2. Nigel was elected M.P. for Bournemouth East on the day the King died, 6 February 1952, and Ben became editor of the *Burlington Magazine,* the leading journal on the history of the fine arts. He remained editor until his death thirty years later.
3. The daughter of Princess Beatrice (youngest daughter of Queen Victoria) and wife of King Alfonso XIII of Spain. In 1953 she was aged sixty-six.

for half an hour much to the fury of everybody else. The odd thing
is that she reminds me the whole time of Violet [Trefusis]. She has the
same sort of waddle and the same sort of voice. I am writing to Violet
to tell her how like the Queen of Spain she is—but I shall not use the
word 'waddle': I shall say 'Démarche'.

When I got back from the clutches of the Queen of Spain, Elvira
said, "Honours are showering upon you." And there was a letter from
the Master of Balliol saying I have been elected an Honorary Fellow.
How strange and impossible that would have seemed when I was there!
But if there was one honour I should like above all else it is to be an
Honorary Fellow of Balliol. I was so pleased that I telephoned to you
three times but each time it was number engaged.

HAROLD TO VITA   *C.1. Albany*

10 June 1953

I lunched with Violet yesterday. It was not a success. She has a
maddening habit of summoning the waiter, and forgetting all about
him when he stands beside her awaiting instructions, but launching
out on a long and boring story of her own. Pat Balfour was there
and Osbert Lancaster and Loelia [Duchess of] Westminster. But it
was not an easy luncheon somehow, and they spent their time telling
mean little stories about their friends. Only one of them amused me.
It was Maurice Bowra's[1] comment on being asked whether Rosamund Lehmann [the novelist] was as beautiful as reputed. "Me-
ringue-outang," he answered. But my darling, life is such a difficult
and cruel thing, so why make it more difficult by gossiping about
people's faults? There is beauty, and love, in this world, and intelligence and faithfulness, and happiness and virtue—why lunch at the
Ritz and spend your time picking out the ugly things? I felt all
angry.

---

1. The Warden of Wadham College, Oxford, 1938–71

HAROLD TO VITA   *C.1. Albany*

3 November 1953

My own darling Mar,

Oh it was a gale, and rain slopped among the bricks—but I was so happy with my home and my darling and dear Benzie. I know Sissinghurst to outsiders may seem a bleak and ruined sojourn, but to me it is mellow and warm and welcoming always and the haven of peace.

I can't get over Virginia's diary—so self-pitying, so vain in a way, so malicious.[1] The envy is difficult to understand. One realizes that she must have been far more mad than that calm exterior suggested. It doesn't make me admire or like her less. But it will surely create a bad impression on those who never saw her great dignity or witnessed the wit and curiosity that rendered her animated. It really has left me with a puzzle.

VITA TO HAROLD   *Sissinghurst*

2 June 1954

Never again will I write in *The Observer* about being ill. Besides I wasn't ill; it was simply that I couldn't think what to write about. It brought me so many deeply concerned letters of sympathy and enquiry. How false and fleeting is journalistic popularity! I often think how empty and lonely some people's lives must be, that they project themselves into the lives of unknown people. One can understand the glamour appeal of film-stars or Princess Margaret. But why us?

VITA TO HAROLD   *Sissinghurst*

31 August 1954

I miss you! It is dreadful, getting so used to your daily companion-ship, my most perfect companion, whether travelling or at home.[2] But

---

1. Extracts from Virginia Woolf's diary had just been published by her husband, Leonard.
2. They had been on a motoring tour of the Dordogne in search of literary and historical sites, including the Lascaux caves and the Château de Montaigne.

we *were* happy weren't we? And we can think back on that lovely country with the poplars and the green grass and the hanging woods and the quiet river and the strange caves and the patient pious oxen and the castles and the *manoirs*. I can't tell you how happy it makes me to think that you liked and understood the Dordogne in exactly the same way as I do. It is horrid to have to communicate with you by letter instead of just shouting "Hadji!" whenever I want you. But as a result we have stored up a great cellar-full of vintage happiness and love—as we always do when we get away together alone.[3]

V I T A   T O   H A R O L D   *Sissinghurst*

14 September 1954

I got into such a rage. I listened to a BBC Home Service programme about myxomatosis, and it was all from the point of view of the farmer or the tame-rabbit breeder whose trade might be threatened. And *not one word* about what the rabbits might suffer—just profit, profit, profit, or loss of profit. That is all men think of—just their purses—and I do think it is disgusting. It makes me sick with life. I know you will think me silly and sentimental, but I don't care if you do. I *know* there is something beyond material profit in this beastly utilitarian world. You can't deny this. It is the thing that makes me love you, and you love me. It is what takes the place of religion in people who are not that way inclined. It is all the same thing: all paths meet at the end of a long converging perspective—whether the end of it is what is called science, or God, or the Creator—that is what I profoundly believe.

Sorry, darling, I got carried away on a storm of temper, thinking of those wretched swollen rabbits I had seen in our lane. I think I had better stop now. You don't like it when I take up lost causes, although you can take them up with violence sometimes yourself. Only then it is something like Cyprus and ENOSIS, or the reconstruction of Germany—shaking hands with bloodstained murderers, who would start it up all over again if they saw a chance.

---

3. Harold wrote on the top of this letter, "Keep this dear letter, always."

HAROLD TO VITA   *C.1. Albany*

13 January 1955

I went to give the first of my Mau Mau talks.[1] Miss Fuller presided
and I was cross (a) because they had put a huge picture of me on *London
Calling* without asking my consent; (b) because it had been cold at
Stationers Hall; (c) because Miss Fuller had asked me to come 15
minutes earlier in order to "settle down," whatever she meant by that.
Then when I arrived, she asked me primly if I would change the
opening words. They were, "When a man reaches the age of 68." She
explained that my talks in this series were being put on discs and sent
to the Mau Mau to play over to themselves on winter evenings and
must thus have no date-mark. Would I say instead, "When a man is
approaching the age of 70"? Then having gained my consent to this
outrageous mistatement, she mumbled something about "having left
my handkerchief upstairs" and left the room. So to pay her out I
climbed under the table and hid there. Unfortunately the young man
in the control room saw me doing this, and when Miss Fuller came
back he said to her, "He has got under the table." So when she entered
the room she said coyly, "I see you," and I had to climb out looking
Oh! so foolish.

HAROLD TO VITA   *C.1. Albany*

9 February 1955

At the Literary Society I sat next to Tommy Lascelles. He says that
your Queen made a wonderful job of her dull shy husband. But he
would willingly commit suicide for her daughter. He admits that she
has not got the public charm of the Queen Mother, but says that she
is really a sweeter nature and a far better mind. He says people will
not realize for years how intelligent she is, but that eventually it will
become an accepted national fact. He says that Winston always comes
away from an audience with tears in his eyes. Silly old buffer.

---

1. His overseas talks for the BBC, which he called Mau Mau after the Kenya tribe that was
   then in revolt against the British.

VITA TO HAROLD *Sissinghurst*

5 April 1955

My very own darling Hadji

You have gone away again, and oh the difference to me! I have got so used to having you here safe, that I cannot re-orientate life without you at all. Somehow I feel that these 3 weeks have brought us so close together; so although of course I hate your suffering pain, I cannot help feeling that something valuable has come out of it.[1]

All I hope is that Dr Hunt will urge you to spend as much time as possible down here in future. I do so love having you here, and being able to look after you in little ways—and you would be better able to write your books instead of Mau-mauing[2] so much—I know you like your London Library, National Trust, National Portrait Gallery, and your London life, *grand lever* and so on, and I would be the last person to want you to stop all that—you know that, don't you?—but I do estimate your own books so high, the Manners book [*Good Behaviour*] is one of your very best, and if you spent more time down here you could write another book—oh please, Hadji, consider my plea, which is half selfish and half reasonable. The selfish part is that I do so love having you here; you are all my happiness; the reasonable part is that I think you ought not to drive yourself so hard as you do, and waste your wonderful gifts on Mau-mau when you might be writing a book on—Bad behaviour?

Anyhow, darling, you know I love you absolutely and completely and for whatever remains of our lives.

Your Mar

HAROLD TO VITA *C.1. Albany*

24 May 1955

I got a simply frightful supertax demand, approaching £2,000. It does mean that no author can save for his old age in these days unless

---

1. Following visits to Germany and Portugal, Harold had suffered two minor strokes, on 11 March and 15 May. He was less affected by them than by an acute attack of sciatica.
2. See note, p. 414

he lives in a garret in Soho. I have no wish or desire or intention of living in a garret.

Oh my dearest, how lovely it was when we went out into the orchard last night! So calm. So gentle, and the ducks following. And now my dear silly Fanny [duck] has returned! What happiness you and I have derived from that garden—I mean real deep satisfaction and a feeling of success. It is an achievement—assuredly it is. And it is pleasant to feel that we have created a work of art. It is all your credit really. Mine was just rulers and bits of paper.

HAROLD TO VITA   *C.1. Albany*

16 November 1955

But I *do* know about the R.H.S. Medal in gold.[1] I know it is among the highest honours one can receive in the shrub world. It is like being made a Fellow of All Souls. Now it is nonsense you saying it is owing to *The Observer* articles. They may have helped, since people know that they have been uniformly instructive and have exercised a wide and long influence. But it is really that my darling is a very very good gardener and that at Sissinghurst she has planted so wisely and so well. I cannot think of anything that has pleased me so much since you got your C.H. and I was made a fellow of Balliol. It is a long long time since the day when you and I dug up a primrose in full flower and shoved it into the bank at Long Barn.

VITA TO HAROLD   *Sissinghurst*

31 January 1956

My Hadji

Such a cold, white Sissinghurst—but I'm so snug in my tower with your lovely fur tippet round my shoulders, keeping me warm like

---

1. Vita had been awarded the Veitch Gold Medal of the Royal Horticultural Society.

love—so I thought I would write you just one last January word before retiring in the somewhat Amazonian embraces of Mademoiselle [*Daughter of France*] for the evening—and tomorrow it will be February, and although we may be in for a horrible wintry time we shall know that spring is always round the corner.

Darling, I love you so; you are my eternal spring.

I suddenly thought, supposing you were found poisoned one day when we were here alone together, and I was accused of poisoning you. Then there's an inquest, and it is discovered that I have been buying cyanide of potassium, ostensibly to destroy wasps' nests, but I cannot account for it: where did I put it? what have I done with it? did I give it to the gardener? wouldn't that have been the natural thing for me to do? people aren't so careless as all that with a deadly poison, surely, Lady Nicolson? Come now! You can't expect us to believe that . . .

And then my Counsel produces our letters to each other, years and years of letters full of love.

What a silly story. That's what comes of reading too much [Georges] Simenon.

Your Mar

HAROLD TO VITA   *C.1. Albany*

8 February 1956

Oh I had such fun just now! A woman telephoned asking whether I was Fergus & Fergus, and would I have her fiancé's kilt ready by the first of March without fail? I said that we were an old Scotch firm, perhaps a wee bit old-fashioned, but we did not think that a young woman should mention her fiancé's kilt. She gasped in astonishment. I said, "I am afraid that I cannot answer so delicate a question, and you must get your fiancé to write to us himself." "But he is in the Cameroons!" she wailed. "Oh," I answered, "I thought you said he was in the Black Watch." By then she was getting suspicious, so I replaced the receiver.

HAROLD TO VITA   *C.1. Albany*

29 May 1956

Alas—May is leaving us and how superb it has been. I walked round the garden last night between 7.0 and 7.25, absolutely drinking in the beauty of the sunset and the soft lights playing across the Weald towards the downs. I felt that no garden has ever been so beautiful as our garden, no May ever so beautiful as this May, no duck ever possessed of such personality as Fanny, and nobody ever so showered with love and happiness as I am. So I entered into a mood of UNIVERSAL GRATITUDE and then a little worm came and said I was being selfish about the Canaries.[1]

But, darling, it really is a combination of negatives, of which my extreme prejudice against Franco is the easiest to abandon. We must face the fact that it is probable that before long and at any time I shall have a serious stroke. I have got so much out of life that the prospect of death fills me with no apprehension. Of course I want to live to see Carlo become a person, Juliet a little girl,[2] and our relations with Greece placed upon a footing of amity. Of course I loathe the prospect of being separated from you and all those really very numerous people whom I love. But I shan't be there to feel sorrow. Thus I concentrate my worry on the situation I shall leave behind and dread a complicated death or extreme squalor at the end. That is the worst of those who have no belief in the life hereafter: they do not want to say goodbye ungainlily, since death-bed scenes and circumstances may leave sad memories and I should wish to be remembered only as a person who was alive and happy. It is for this that I fuss about crematoria, not wanting my darling to be faced, as Diana[3] was faced, with the problem of how to dispose of the corpse. Thus if we went to some remote island in the Canaries, I should be worrying about this corpse business even as I worry about wasps. I know this is irrational, but one is irrational

---

1. He and Vita had discussed taking tickets for a cruise to the Canary Islands, which had been a Spanish possession since 1476.
2. Carlo was Ben's putative son (in fact, a daughter, Vanessa, was born on 8 August) and Juliet was Nigel's actual daughter, born in June 1954.
3. Duff Cooper died on 1 January 1954 while on a voyage to the West Indies. His body was landed in Vigo and buried at Belvoir Castle, the home of his wife's family.

about some things, and my holiday would be clouded by my fuss and I should feel only that we had spent more money than we can afford and derived no pleasure. Thus I do not want to go to southern islands and would much prefer to remain even in February at home where there are lovely quick crematoria waiting to receive me. I should like us to have a motor trip in France or even Spain in October when the wasps are few. And then face the winter at home with solemn resolution.

HAROLD TO VITA   *C.1. Albany*

15 August 1956

I do so love it when you come to London and bless these rooms with your presence. You are like a country-bred puppy on a lead, seeking to escape up some side street from the crowds upon the pavement and the fierce traffic in the streets. Your hand was trembling with panic when we crossed Piccadilly. Oh my dear dear Mar! How one does love the odd corners of people whom one loves!

I did not dare to ask Ken[1] how *Good Behaviour* had sold in the U.S.A. Now why was I so gawky about that? Was it just shyness and a feeling that when one lunches with a man one should not talk business? Or was it an odd pride, which made me suggest to this dollar magnate that as a Knight of the Victorian Order I was indifferent to money? I really do not know. All I know is that I am an ODD FISH.

---

1. Ken McCormick, the president of Doubleday, the New York publisher.

*I*n 1957 Harold, then aged seventy-one, described himself as "getting very old, decrepit, gaga, forgetful, deaf and aphasic [speechless]." In fact he wasn't. His slight deafness never became a serious problem, though it caused him to retire from the chairmanship, not membership, of his Committees, and the two minor strokes he suffered in 1955 scarcely diminished his social, literary, and gardening energy. Politically he was aroused to his former fervor by the Suez crisis of 1956, and he wrote three more books, The Age of Reason, Monarchy, and Journey to Java. The latter took the form of a diary written on one of the winter cruises that he and Vita enjoyed during the last six years of her life, and she based her last novel, No Signposts in the Sea, upon another. It was during the last of these cruises, to the West Indies in January–February 1962, that she first noticed the symptoms of abdominal cancer, from which she died at Sissinghurst on 2 June of that year.*

HAROLD TO VITA   *C.1. Albany*

30 October 1956

I read in the newspapers this morning as the train sped through Kent the statements made by Anthony and Selwyn Lloyd on Hungary.[1] I was revolted by their cant. When people rise against the Russians they are hailed as heroes and patriots; but when they rise against us, they are called terrorists and hanged. I do not see that it was

---

1. On 29 October, Israel launched their attack against Egypt (in collusion, as it later transpired, with Britain and France), and the Soviets crushed the Hungarian revolt in Budapest. Anthony Eden was Prime Minister, and Selwyn Lloyd his Foreign Secretary.

at all necessary for Anthony to indulge in such hypocrisy. He went out of his way to do so. He is a rotten creature, vain and purposeless, and I hope he is soundly defeated at the next election. A Prime Minister should give some idea of principle and consistency; Anthony is just all over the place all the time.

HAROLD TO VITA   *C.1. Albany*

15 November 1956

Eden's policy was not only morally wrong but a costly failure as well. People will talk less about keeping the Canal open and safeguarding our oil supplies when they have to have petrol coupons. But for the moment all Tory opinion, bemused though it be, is in favour of Eden. Simple minds work simply. The ladies of Bournemouth do not like the Russians, the Americans or Nasser; Eden has dealt a blow to these three enemies; therefore Eden must be right. It is as simple as that. Nigel and I have always believed that there was some collusion between the French and the Israelis to which we were a consenting party. It now seems that some American journalist[1] has got hold of the story and has obtained documentary proof. If the story gets out I do not see how the Government can survive. It is an utterly disgraceful tale.

HAROLD TO VITA   *C.1. Albany*

11 July 1957

The Prime Minister [Harold Macmillan] appeared at the Grillions [Club] dinner last night. He seemed bursting with energy and high spirits. One of his many headaches is that under the new scheme for

---

1. Not American, but the French brothers Merry and Serge Bromberger, in their book *Secrets of Suez* (1957). Nonetheless, the revelation did nothing to change opinion in Bournemouth, and Nigel was disowned by his constituents for his opposition to the Suez operation and eventually lost his seat.

economising on the army, some county regiments will have to be fused and this will arouse fierce resistance. Will the West Kent agree to being called the Kent and Surrey? No they will not. Macmillan is thinking of dropping the county names altogether and inventing new regional names such as "The Weald Regiment," "The Regiment of the Tweed" and so on. But he says that the life of a Prime Minister is spent between successive waves of indignation, and that he must accept that fact.

VITA TO HAROLD   *Sissinghurst*

1 October 1957

I write to you on this the 44th anniversary of that happy day [their wedding], and love you even more now than I did then (which is saying a lot) and please forgive me all my trespasses.

I have finished those American proofs and am filled with loathing for my *Observer* articles, but must now finish arranging the latest lot for publication in a fourth book—but what on earth am I to call it?[1] It makes me rather cross to have had this (may I say?) success with those wretched articles and to have gained a reputation of a kind I never desired or deserved. You will understand this, so I needn't enlarge. It's rather like you not liking to have your voice recognised by taxi-drivers who have heard you on the wireless.

And so goodbye, my precious most precious Hadji—I return to my galleys—a galley slave, in fact—but you are there in the background always, filling my heart with love.

VITA TO HAROLD   *The King's Arms, Hadleigh, Suffolk*

9 October 1957

We went to Layer Marney[2] which I had always wanted to see. It is *very* odd, but far bigger and less ugly than I expected and there

---

1. *Even More for Your Garden,* 1958.
2. In Essex, where there is an eight-story Tudor brick tower, the tallest in England. Vita was motoring with her friend Edith Lamont.

is a lovely little church next door, of the same date, with Crusader tombs, and all the decorations of their harvest festival—sheaves of corn, marrows, apples, masses of flowers, baskets of eggs—very charming and real.

Then we went to Lavenham [Suffolk], famous as a beautiful village, with a really magnificent church like a small cathedral—the churches everywhere are beautiful as I had always heard—and through other unknown villages, all perfectly charming—and on to Hadleigh with a red sunset on one side and a full moon on the other—by lanes, through absolutely *uninhabited* country, Hadji, except for an occasional farm homestead—it might be France, you see nobody, and no new houses, and lots of water in little streams and lakes, and a church tower on a distant hill.

This is a very nice tiny hotel, spotlessly clean, boiling hot water, no other guests, very nice people, Rollo a great success ("you can leave your dog behind when you go, madam"), and as it seems quite near everything I want to see, we have decided to stay here the next two nights.

HAROLD TO VITA   *C.1. Albany*

13 November 1957

Oh my sweet, I had such a bloody afternoon yesterday. I told you I was doing my advert on independent T.V. for *The Observer*. [1] So I went to the studio in Ebury Street at 2.0. My piece was only to last 3 minutes but it took three hours and a half !!!!! First a man in a green jersey made me up—smearing beige grease over my poor face and then powdering the surface lightly. He touched my eyebrows with kola and then smeared my eyelashes which have never in seventy long years required such surrogation. Then the interviewer arrived and we had to rehearse the piece four or five times. Then the lights were turned on and they measured distances with long tape-measures and kept on fuss, fuss, fuss. It was 3.30 before they had arranged the thing to their

---

1. A television commercial, for which Harold was not paid. He contributed to it out of loyalty to the newspaper, where his weekly book reviews were published.

liking, moving the property ornaments backwards and forwards along the property chimney piece, and then I and the interviewer began our silly little dialogue over again. At 4.0 the lights were turned out and the electricians and camera men left us alone. That was the ten minutes tea interval. At 4.20 they came back and I thought that it would be terrible had I been doing a love scene, and made to rehearse passionate embraces over and over and over again. The falsity of that world is really terrifying. Anyhow at 5.20 I got away into a darkened Ebury Street with all those arc lights making brown circles in the pavement and on my retina. But one must learn to suffer without complaint.

VITA TO HAROLD   *Sissinghurst*

26 February 1958

Oh Hadji, my book [*Daughter of France*] is so bad. It really is. I am not imagining this: I *know* it is bad.

I am writing this to you late at night. I haven't been over to have my supper yet.

I did take trouble over that book. I read a lot, but I haven't been able to synthesise or compress it as I hoped. It is just a mess. I had a clear picture when I started, but now it has all got muddled up with detail and the outline has got lost.

HAROLD TO VITA   *C.1. Albany*

9 April 1958

As my train drew out of Etchingham station I looked down on the graveyard and there were three men in greatcoats and cloth caps shovelling clay on top of Eustace's box.[1] It struck a cold horror to my heart. I felt the whole thing was the grimmest, coldest funeral I had

---

1. The funeral was that of Lord (Eustace) Percy, who had died at Etchingham, Sussex, on 3 April, aged seventy-one. He was one of Harold's oldest friends, his contemporary in the Foreign Office, and became Rector of the Newcastle division of the University of Durham.

ever attended, and at least to be cremated (apart from other advantages) is warm. I thought how terrible it was to be dressed in a night-shirt, nailed in a box and then put deep in the cold clay. And I thought back on the days when Eustace was young and regarded as among the most gifted and promising of my generation. What has he done with his life? I daresay he did much good at Newcastle, but what pleasures or adventures has he enjoyed? His life has been as cold and bare as the church in which he was funerated (by the way, the Church as seen from the Railway is a truly splendid bit of architecture). At least when I die nobody will think I failed to make the most of life.

VITA TO HAROLD   *Sissinghurst*

10 April 1958

I drove back from Sevenoaks through the park at Knole. I had taken my key with me, and let myself out by the Mast-head gate.

Oh Hadji, it was such an odd experience—it seemed as though I had never been away—it was all so familiar. I think I had better not go on writing about it, because it is making me cry, but I might tell you some time. I hadn't really meant to go and yet I think I must have or I wouldn't have taken my key. Edie [Lamont] was so tactful, she never spoke—she just let me look.

Oh Hadji Hadji—why do I love Knole so much? It's stupid—and I hate that beastly Nat. Trust symbol. Knole should have been mine, mine, mine. We were meant for each other.

VITA TO HAROLD   *Sissinghurst*

23 September 1958

I am sorry I was tiresome to you, getting upset about Edie [Edith Lamont] yesterday morning. I know you hate emotional manifestations, and shy away. But sometimes one's feelings overcome one, and one bursts out. You see, if Edie died, I should really feel rather desolate.

For one thing, she is about the only person who understands how much I love you, and would know what I would feel if you got ill or died. She is my only close friend. I haven't got many friends, and I don't want them, but it is nice to have one friend to whom one can talk openly, and if I lost Edie, I should have nobody left.

VITA TO HAROLD   *Sissinghurst*

12 May 1959

You have been so good to me,[1] so patient, taking trays away, taking Dan [dog] out, sending me champagne and God knows what else, and then your readiness to trot about fetching Aristotle. You and I are so unaccustomed to being ill, that when illness does descend on us, we regard it with astonished resentment and don't quite know what to make of it.

HAROLD TO VITA   *C.1. Albany*

14 July 1959

I have still not disinfected myself from the slime of *Lolita*.[2] It is nonsense for Niggs to assert that it is a "great" work of literature. Literature will not experience any loss if it is not published. I think it a very clever book and well written. But I also think it 'obscene' in the sense of 'liable to corrupt'. It is absurd for Niggs to contend that it is a 'cautionary tale' and will deter those who have this temptation from wishing to practise it. Perverts of that sort are obsessed by the physical appeal and do not mind if Lolita was a horrid little minx. Nabokov has stressed the physical appeal with such licentious insistence that the pervert will be encouraged in his passion rather than discouraged.

---

1. Vita had been ill for two months with viral pneumonia.
2. The novel by Vladimir Nabokov, which Weidenfeld and Nicolson published in 1959 in defiance of much controversy. Vita and Harold were among those who considered it obscene. Today it is regarded as a minor classic.

HAROLD TO VITA   *C.1. Albany*

8 September 1959

What a lovely morning! Sun coming through mist. It was pleasant sitting on the catalpa bench with my darling and discussing why so many of our friends were discontented or unhappy. I still maintain that it is worse to muck up one's life by one's own fault than owing to an act of God or someone else's fault. You see, it adds self-reproach and guilt feelings to misfortune. Thus I am sure Cyril Connolly is more unhappy at being lazy and wasteful of his own great gifts if he could attribute his indolence to anything but himself. You and I can at least feel that we have got the most out of such talents as God gave us. But I believe what I appreciate most about my gifts is the gift of seeing beauty. Why should I experience such a spurt of pleasure at seeing the tower of Staplehurst church catch the sun through the fog? And why should that pleasure be doubled if you are there to share it? Oh bless you my saint for giving me such a happy life.

VITA TO HAROLD   *Sissinghurst*

27 October 1959

My own darling Hadji,

I was thinking this morning how awful it would be if you died. I do often think that; but it came over me all of a heap when I looked out of the bathroom window and saw you in your blue coat and black hat, peering into your scoop.[1] It is the sort of sudden view of a person that twists one's heart, when they don't know you are observing them—they have an innocent look, almost as a child asleep—one feels one is spying on some secret life one should not know about. Taking advantage as it were, although it is only the most loving advantage that one takes.

Anyway, the scoop would be the most poignant coffee-cup [relic after death] ever made.

I often think I have never told you how much I love you—and

---

1. The "scoop" was a hollow in one of the paving stones in the Cottage Garden at Sissinghurst, and Harold used it as a rain gauge.

Tuesday
Oct. 27.
'59

Keep

Mon darling Hadji

I was thinking this morning how awful it would be if you died. I so often think that; but it came over me all of a heap when I looked out of the bathroom window and saw you in your blue coat and black hat, peering into your scoop. It is the sort of sudden view of a person that twists one's heart, when they don't know you are observing them — they have an innocent look — almost as a child asleep. One feels one is spying on some secret life one should not know about — taking advantage as it were, although it is only the most loving advantage that one takes.

Anyway, the scoop would be the most poignant coffee-cup ever made.

I often think I have never told you how much I love you — and if you died I should reproach myself, saying Why did I never tell him? Why did I never tell him enough?

I am Mar.

if you died I should reproach myself, saying, "Why did I never tell him? Why did I never tell him enough?"

Your Mar

HAROLD TO VITA   *C.1. Albany*

22 March 1960

I may see you during the course of today but I do not count on it. I rather want to see you, more than usual, as I want your advice on what literary figure should be awarded the O.M. Edith Sitwell has been suggested and I repress all jealousy and try to view the proposition wholly objectively. I feel that the O.M. should only be given to poets likely to be esteemed by successive generations, and I cannot rid myself of the idea that Edith is just a momentary or contemporary fashion. I should prefer, if the Arts are to be considered, to give it to Kenneth Clark.[1] The O.M. is a tremendous order and I do not wish to diminish its prestige.

I dined at the American Embassy. We were twelve at dinner. The two Whitneys[2]; the Queen Mother and lady; the Prime Minister and Lady Dorothy [Macmillan]; Heathcoat Amory, the Chancellor of the Exchequer; Mr and Mrs Profumo[3]; and Jeremy Tree, the racing son of Ronnie: he is a great race-course friend of the Queen Mother's. I sat between Mrs Whitney and Mrs Profumo, and thus was able to talk to the P.M. who was on Mrs Whitney's other side. He was delighted by what I had said to the *Daily Express* about his election.[4] He was in splendid form and really talked sense about the summit conference. He is annoyed at people calling it 'the' summit conference, and would prefer it to be called 'a' summit conference. He foresees that if we can have these summit conferences say once in every four years, we shall not perhaps achieve a complete settlement, but shall avoid momentary blocks and disagreements. He quoted me as saying (I suppose I did

---

1. Kenneth Clark was awarded the Order of Merit in 1976.
2. John H. Whitney, the Ambassador, and his wife.
3. John Profumo was then Minister of State for Foreign Affairs. His wife was Valerie Hobson, the actress.
4. As Chancellor of Oxford University.

somewhere) that the greatest of all diplomatic assets was the passage of time. If we could, by recurrent summit conferences, gain twenty years of peace, then by that time Africa and Asia may have settled down and Russia become more bourgeois. He dreads the disappearance of Khrushchev, since he is personally pledged to peace and his successor might be more militarist.

I had a long talk with Lady Dorothy afterwards. She says that at Rambouillet[5] there was a wonderful chef and about fifty servants with silver chains, but no soap in their bedroom and so cold that she had to sleep in a woolly. She asked Mme de Gaulle whether there was anything special she wanted to do when she comes on a State Visit and she said she wanted to go to Gorringes. I talked to the Queen Mother for about half an hour. I had to leave in the middle to go wee wee, but she took it well. As always, she asked after Mar and the garden. She did not offer to come down again and I did not press the suggestion. She was wearing a superb necklace of diamonds and pearls and a lovely pink taffeta dress. She really has the most wonderful skin I have ever seen. I could not detect in it a wrinkle. I enjoyed my dinner very much.

I have written to Mrs Whitney to say so.

They are nice people.

VITA TO HAROLD   *Sissinghurst*

13 April 1960

What a delightful article about de Gaulle. Darling, there's nobody like you for doing that sort of thing so gracefully, so amusingly, so originally; and, in the conclusion, so nobly. You always achieve the perfect balance between the light and the serious. Your article reminded me of Virginia's remark that a phrase ought to be like casting a line in fishing, which I have quoted to you before now: it should describe a graceful parabola and come to rest in a solid plomp. Only Virginia was talking about a phrase; and I am talking about a whole article. Her metaphor (or simile?) applies to both.

---

5. The imposing château outside Paris where François I died and Macmillan met de Gaulle to discuss Britain's entry into the Common Market.

HAROLD TO VITA *C.1. Albany*

1 June 1960

No darling—the reason I was depressed was not financial worry (an obsession to which I am not addicted) but merely that I had felt exhausted in the morning and too slack to write. Hitherto I have got tired when standing or walking too much, but have never been tired by reading or writing. I felt it a portent, and that I might cease to be able to earn my living and might have to fall back on my heiress and become a charity child. That prospect is enough to sadden any man. But I recovered all right and yesterday I felt quite spry again.

In fact I did a lot. I had myself shaved and manicured at Delhez. I lunched at the American Embassy. They have erected on the terrace a shamyana or palenquin or tent, the paving stones covered by a thick grey pile carpet and tables with drinks. The occasion was the conferment on Maurice Bowra of the diploma as honorary Academician, such as I have got. I wore my button in my lapel. The Ambassador made a halting allocution and Maurice said nothing—not a single word of thanks—in reply. There were leading university figures there—Noel Annan, Dadie Rylands, Mortimer Wheeler[1] and so on. I told Wheeler that I regarded him as a traitor to sacred Greece for extolling the harsh Romans. "I do it," he said, "with my tongue in my cheek." Now people ought not to discuss and expound such serious subjects unless sincerely. I always thought Wheeler a fraud.

VITA TO HAROLD *Sissinghurst*

23 November 1960

I don't really look forward to our trip this year[2]—and I don't believe that you look forward to it either. Anyhow, I am sure we shall get some pleasure out of it—as we always do.

---

1. Sir Mortimer Wheeler, the most distinguished archaeologist of his day.
2. Their cruise in January–February 1961 was to Rio de Janeiro and Montevideo. Violet Trefusis did not, after all, join them.

I pray to God that Violet does not really come, whether escorted by a new prince or not. I simply cannot envisage Violet on a ship with us. We should have to control her very strictly, and bolt our cabin doors against her all through the morning and evening when we want to be quiet, you with Tikki and me with foolscap.

Isn't life odd?

There was once a time when Violet and I were so madly in love, and I hurt you so dreadfully—and now how dead that is, passion completely spent—and the true love that has survived is mine for you, and yours for me.

I think it was partly your fault, Hadji. You were older than me, and far better informed. I was very young, and very innocent. I knew nothing about homosexuality. I didn't even know that such a thing existed—either between men or between women. You should have told me. You should have warned me. You should have told me about yourself, and have warned me that the same sort of thing was likely to happen to myself. It would have saved us a lot of trouble and misunderstanding. But I simply didn't know.

Oh what a very unexpected letter to write to you suddenly. You won't like it, because you never like to face facts.

HAROLD TO VITA   *C.1. Albany*

30 May 1961

Did you see that Sidney Bernstein[1] has sold some of his shares for four million pounds? Lucky person. We could pay all our wages, clean the moat, have a forester and mate to clear up the wood, and live happily ever after. But I don't believe that money brings happiness although it may diminish worry. I am a happy man. I have you and Niggs and Benzie, and Juliet and Adam [Nigel's children]. I shall never forget Juliet running down the path between the big yews and flinging her arms round me. The charm of those two children is hot sunshine to me. I do like good manners. I do like affection. I feel all comfortable

---

1. The film producer, who had rented Long Barn in the 1930s.

inside when I think of that happy, happy day. Oh my darling, how lucky I am!

HAROLD TO VITA   *C.1. Albany*

23 August 1961

I went to see your grand-children in Limerston Street. The door was opened by Juliet in her dressing-gown and pyjamas. She bounded down the staircase and flung herself into my arms. She insisted on showing me her homework, and I must say she seems to have done very well, scarcely ever getting a sum wrong. Then Adam came in very solemn in his new scarlet dressing-gown. They clambered onto my knee as usual, and made me tell them stories. Most of the tales of my youth end up by my being beaten by my father. "Dadda," they chimed in chorus, "has never beaten us. He has never said cross things to us." "I don't believe it," I said, but they nodded their little fair heads in unison and repeated, "He never gets cross"—implying that Mumma often does. I am afraid that Niggs is what you call 'mild'—you think it a beastly thing to be. But I should like to see you with someone who wasn't mild. It would be hammer and tongs all the time. It is merely because I submit patiently that no crockery is broken in anger at Sissinghurst.

The children were still on my knee when the following conversation took place:—

Adam: Grandpapa, I shall be four next month.
H.N.: Yes, I know, Adam.
Adam: I shall soon be quite grown up.
H.N.: Yes, but don't hurry to get as grown-up as I am.
Adam: You are very very old, aren't you, Grandpapa?
H.N.: Yes, Adam, I am very very old.
Adam: You will die soon, Grandpapa, won't you?
H.N.: Yes, Adam, very soon. And I hope you will always remember me.
Adam (a look of devil mischief on his face): No I shan't. I shall forget all about you at once.
Juliet (flinging her arms round my neck): But that's rude, Adam. I shall remember Harold all the rest of my life.

Adam continues to grin like a little imp. He truly is adorable, since
he has so unconventional a mind. They were both looking so well.
Juliet's teeth have returned, and she is much better-looking and as
graceful as ever.

H A R O L D   T O   V I T A   *C.1. Albany*

27 February 1962

My darling,

I enclose the order for Daimler saying they will be waiting in the
forecourt. I am so relieved that dear Edie [Lamont] is coming with
you. I could not abide the idea of Mar with her little suitcase going
alone to Holloway Prison. Edie's tact and discernment and reticence
about the tragedy in the boat-train has wiped out all trace of jealousy.[1]
It was ridiculous of me to feel jealous, and Edie, I know, suspected
it and was wonderfully considerate. But I *was* jealous, idiot that I am.

I do not allow myself to get worried, and in the watches of the
night I forbid myself to brood in misery and concentrate my mind on
our happiness together, on great moments like Kermanshah [in 1926],
and above all on our deep love for each other which no catastrophe
can ever take away.

Thus my heart is filled with pity for you, knowing how you hate
hospitals and bedint sisters, and hospital beds and foods, and being
mucked about, and leaving our lovely house. We have both got to go
through a nasty time and must face it like square-jawed Janes. You are
so brave that you can be calm and self-contained. But I am not as brave
as you are, and I miss my Mummy who could comfort me. Knowing
your secrecy, or more accurately your love of privacy, I shall not tell
anyone and merely say that you are in hospital 'for observation'. Even
that I hate, since I know how you loathe being spied on.

I doubt whether you will get this, but I shall come to the hospital
soon after six tomorrow.

---

1. Vita had suffered a haemorrhage in the train at the outset of their cruise to the West Indies
with Mrs. Lamont, and on her return she was advised to undergo an operation at the Royal
Free Hospital, Canonbury, in north London.

VITA TO HAROLD   *Canonburg Hospital*

27 February 1962

My own darling Hadji,

 This is not a nice patch for us to be going through, but I think the only way to take it is to realise that as one gets older these bothers do come upon one.

 I am not going to indulge in self-pity, and I am not going to be more of a bore and a worry than I can help. I have an absolute horror of being a bore and a worry to anybody, but more especially to you, my sweet, who are not a person who ought to be worried.

 So I hope that within a few days I shall be home, and all gay and happy again.

              Your Mar

HAROLD TO VITA   *C.1. Albany*

24 April 1962

 I am sorry to have annoyed you by insisting on a night nanny, but I do so dread the idea that you might fall down in the night and be ill for another six months.[1] She is a competent woman and I don't really mind her. But I am seeing far more television than ever before since it aids conversation at meals. Oh dear, I hope it is warm today and that you sit a bit under the catalpa. It is so lovely there.

 I feel that people are under the impression that I don't know how ill you have been, or that, if I do know, I don't care. How little they understand! Why bother poor old Hadji? As if I hadn't been worried enough! But they *mean* well—how astonishingly well they mean! What is odd is that Bunny [Drummond] is the least hysterical of the lot. But all the others say that I have never been accustomed to grave operations and don't UNDERSTAND. I wish Glen [dog] could be taught to bite all well-wishers.

---

1. Vita had survived the operation for abdominal cancer, and returned to Sissinghurst in a very weak condition.

VITA TO HAROLD   *Sissinghurst*

2 May 1962

My own darling Hadji,

    I am going to get up and go into the garden: it is quite warm. I am glad that you have got away from all those boring nurses and atmosphere of sickroom: poor Hadji, you are so uncomplaining. My handwriting is better, don't you think? I shall try to get as far as your life's work [Spring garden] today, and can take one of the nice light garden chairs along with me. Also I shall put on some clothes which may make me feel a little more human. What I find one grudges is the appalling waste of time and not seeing to the things one wants to see to.

HAROLD TO VITA   *C.1. Albany*

24 May 1962

    I hope it is all right about Philippa, Niggs and the children coming to luncheon on Sunday. I shall see to it that they do not trouble you too much. Oh my sweet, how I long for the day when you get well again. I don't like the idea of that vast dog keeping you awake. He means so well, but he can't reduce his size nor does he understand how ill invalids can feel. I shall be down by tea tomorrow and shall remain all the week.

Vita died at Sissinghurst on 2 June 1962 at the age of seventy, and her ashes were placed in the Sackville family vault at Withyham in Sussex. A tablet to her memory is in the church above.

Harold was profoundly shaken by her death. Although he continued to write his weekly book reviews for two more years, and once traveled to Greece, once to Italy, and once, for two weeks, to the United States, his energy slowly declined. He gave up writing and gardening, and in his last years scarcely read more than newspaper headlines. He became very silent, but would occasionally reveal flashes of his old, self-mocking humour, as when he said to me after the success of his published diaries, "It is rather sad to think that of all my forty books the only one that will be remembered is the one I didn't realise I'd written."

Of course this wasn't true. Scarcely a week passes when I do not see quoted by a journalist, politician, or fellow author some saying of his, and Some People, his biography of Tennyson, and King George V: His Life and Reign have in their different ways become classics. Vita's reputation, too, has long survived her death, far more of her books remaining in print than Harold's, and her garden at Sissinghurst, now a property of the National Trust, has become one of the best known in England.

They are remembered, too, for their unusual marriage, which since their deaths has been celebrated in print and film, but never more sympathetically than in the present volume, where they tell their own story. My fear has been that some readers might find it sentimental. Reiterated expressions of mutual love between husband and wife are said to be unnecessary if it is genuine and strongly rooted, but Vita and Harold felt the need to reassure each other constantly of what both profoundly believed, so amazed were they that *their marriage had survived its first traumatic ten years to become for both of them a life-enhancing success in the remaining forty.*

Harold died at Sissinghurst, aged eighty-one, on 1 May 1968 of a heart attack as he was undressing for bed, and his ashes were interred in the cemetery of Sissinghurst parish church, which looks across the woods, fields, and orchards of the Weald of Kent toward the rose-red house where both had given and experienced so much happiness.

INDEX

Abbreviations: V.S-W or Vita for Vita Sackville-West, HN for Harold Nicolson

Abadan (Iran) 183
Aberconway, Christabel 245, 407
Aberdeen 106
Abyssinia 276
Action 226, 229
Adenauer, Konrad 211–12
Adrianople 38
Albany, Piccadilly 406 & *n*
Albert, Dr. and Mrs. (Berlin) 186–7
Albi (France) 370
Algeria 291–2
Algiers 76, 378
All Passion Spent (V.S-W) 226, 236
Amadeus Quartet 407
Americans: HN's attitude to, 11–12; on American character, 242, 253, 270; loves Charleston, 239–40; grand houses, 260–1, 267; position of women, 261, 275–6; universities, 270; HN misjudges, 275–6; and London bombing, 332. *See also* United States
Amiens 108*n*, 109*n*, 116
Amman (Jordan) 129–30
Amory, Heathcoat 429
Anderson, Sir John 372
Annan, Noel 431
Aphra Behn (V.S-W) 182*n*
'Appeasement' 309, 314–5
Aristophanes 374 & *n*
Aristotle 230, 426
Armistice Day (1918) 73

Arras (France) 320
Asquith, Herbert 124
Asquith, Margot 126
Astor, Michael & Barbara 348
Astor, Nancy 45, 338
Atchley, S. C. 123 & *n*, 124
Athens 123–4, 221, 365
Attlee, Clement 334, 351, 371, 375
Auden, Wystan 256, 310
Auriol, President Vincent 393*n*
Austen, Jane 177–8, 230
Austria 32, 58, 285–6
Auxerre (France) 204
Avignon 73*n*

Bagdad, 130–1
Bagnold, Enid (Lady Jones) 146 & *n*, 245, 389
Bakhtiari Mountains (Iran) 182*n*
Baku 139, 157–8
Baldwin, Stanley 250, 287, 296–7
Balfour, A. J.: Foreign Secretary, 59 & *n*; praises HN, 70; at Paris Peace Conference, 76, 84, 97; at Colefax party, 152
Balfour, Patrick 411
Balfour, Ronald 165
Balliol College, Oxford 399, 411, 416
"Barbara" See St. Barbara
Bari (Italy) 403
Baring, Maurice 245

Battle of Britain 327–8, 329–30
BBC: V.S-W broadcasts, 209–10; HN broadcasts, 226; HN as Governor of, 341; "Brains Trust," 389–90; overseas broadcasts, 408, 414
Beaconsfield, 366
Beale, Oswald 321, 322, 326, 362
Beauchamp, Lord 292 & n
Beaverbrook, Lord 219, 221, 245
Beerbohm, Max 246 & n
Belgium 322
Bell, Clive 119n, 135, 152, 154, 182, 199
Bell, Gertude 131 & n
Bell, Julian and Quentin 135, 154
Bell, Vanessa 135–6, 152, 204, 317, 337
Bennett, Donald 379–80
Bentinck, Charles 123
Berenson, Bernard 297
Berlin: HN in Embassy, 11, 185ff; V.S-W in (1926), 140, 142; HN returns to (1932) 232–3, (1948) 385–6
Berners, Lord Gerald 283
Bernstein, Henri 325 & n
Bernstein, Sidney 432
Berry, Walter 126n
Bessborough, Earl of 301
Bevan, Aneurin 371
Beveridge, Sir William 349 & n
Bevin, Ernest 371
Bialystok (Poland) 140
Bibesco, Princess Marthe 265–6
Biddenden (Kent) 360
Bingham, Henrietta 257 & n
Blackboys (Sussex) 96 & n
Blake, William 217
Bloomsbury Group 152, 304
Blum, Leon 305
Bournemouth 421
Bowes-Lyon, David 403
Bowra, Maurice 411 & n, 431
Bracken, Brendan 245, 319, 342
"Brains Trust" 389–90
Brawne, Fanny 329
Bridges, Robert and Mrs. 148–9, 172
Brighton 79, 113, 138, 183

Brindisi 403
Brittain, Vera (Catlin) 251–2
Bromberger, Merry & Serge 421n
Brontë, Charlotte 177 & n
Brown, C. A. 329
Brown, Jane 3
Brownlow, Lord and Lady 282
Buchan-Hepburn, Patrick 160 & n, 161
Bucharest: HN in, 298–300
Budberg, Baroness Moura 244–5
Burgess, Guy 340, 399–400
Burlington Magazine 410
Butler, R. A. 377–8, 381
Buxton (Derbyshire) 47
Byron: The Last Journey (HN) 117n, 123–4, 124–5, 358

Cambridge 399
Cameron, Julia 119
Campbell, Roy and Mary 10, 187 & n, 222n, 400 & n, 401
Canada (V.S-W in) 236–7
Canary Islands 418 & n
Cannes 76, 111
Cap Ferrat (French Riviera) 286–7, 304–7
Cardinal, Vera 149 & n
Carnock, Lady 37, 398 & n
Carnock, Lord (Sir Arthur Nicolson) 11, 197, 206 & n, 207
Carol, King of Rumania 298–300, 308n
Catlin, George 251–2
Cazalet, Victor ("Teenie") 250–1, 295
Cecil, Lord Hugh 88
Cézanne, Paul 207
Challenge (V.S-W) 96 & n, 100, 101
Chamberlain, Neville: Chancellor of Exchequer, 251; and appeasement, 298n; Munich Crisis, 307–9, 311; "hopeless old crow," 314; resigns, 319
Channon, Henry ("Chips") and Lady Honor 285–6
Charles, Prince 385n
Charleston (South Carolina) 239–40

Charleston (Sussex) 135
Cheradame, André 326–7
Cherbourg 313
Chicago 237–8
Churchill, Clementine 284–5
Churchill, Randolph 285
Churchill, Winston: esteems "mettle,"
  12; interrupts HN's speech, 288;
  criticizes Chamberlain, 314;
  "magnificent speech," 318; becomes
  Prime Minister, 319; "finest hour"
  speech, 325; visits Ministry of
  Information, 334; parliamentary
  confidence in, 343, 345–6; war ends,
  361–2; dinner for, 366; "a grave
  liability" to Tory Party, 377–8;
  with Queen Elizabeth II, 405, 414
Chute, Rev. J. C. 203 & n
Cincinnati 242
Clark, Kenneth 14, 282–3n, 334–5n, 429
Clark-Kerr, Archibald 21 & n, 26, 249
  & n
Clemenceau, Georges 76, 83, 92–4
Clerk, Sir George 58 & n, 367
Clifford, Lady Anne 196
Clive, Sir Robert and Lady 169–72
Coates, Audrey 267
Cocteau, Jean 199
Colefax, Lady (Sibyl) 152 & n, 174,
  250, 282–3, 297, 334–5, 364–5
Cologne 211–12
Connolly, Cyril 195, 201–2, 214–15,
  427
Constant, Benjamin 373–4
Constantinople (Istanbul) 18ff, 34,
  38–9, 50
Coolidge, President 262
Cooper, Lady Diana (Manners) 19n,
  65 & n, 283, 418
Cooper, Duff 294, 319, 323, 360, 418n
Cooper, Reginald 31 & n, 43, 125
Cooper-Willis, Irene 166
Copenhagen 401–2
Copper, J. 281–2
Corfu incident 122n
Cornwall 61–5
Cospoli 50
Coward, Noel 186 & n, 265, 282–3

Cowper, William 64n
Cragg, Rev. 217
Cranbrook (Kent) 360, 392
Crawfurd, H. E. 278–9
Crewe, Marquess of 45
Critic, The 85 & n
Crowther, Geoffrey 389–90
Croydon bye-election (1948) 377–82
Cuernavaca (Mexico) 272–3
Cunard, Emerald (Maud) 188, 245
Curtiss, Minna 255–7
Curzon, Marquess George: at Lausanne
  with HN, 115n, 116, 118; HN's
  admiration for, 120; admires
  V.S-W's novel, 122–3
Curzon, 2nd Lady 116, 118, 132
Curzon The Last Phase (HN) 244
Czechoslovakia 307n: See Munich
  Crisis

Daladier, Edouard 294
Dalton, Dr. Hugh 334, 372
Dansey, Pat 149 & n
Daughter of France (V.S-W) 417, 424
Davis, Norman 261
De La Warr, Diana 336
Denman, Lord 69–70
Denmark 355, 401–2
Desborough, Lady 25n
Devil at Westease (V.S-W) 364, 372–3
Dickinson, Emily 264
Dickinson, Oswald 34 & n, 99
Dieppe 205, 275
Dilijan (Iran) 164
Dolomites, the 127 & n, 260
Dordogne (France) 412–13
Dostoyevski, Fyodor 101
Douglas, James 224
Douglas, Lou 372
Dover 108
Draper, Ruth 152, 183
Drinkwater, John 166
Drummond, Cynthia ("Bunny") 407
  & n, 435
Dufferin, Lord 268
Dunkirk 319
Dunlop, Mrs. 395–6

Eagle and the Dove, The (V.S-W) 340, 351, 353

Easter Party, The (V.S-W) 398

Ebury Street (London) 57*n*, 85

Eden, Anthony (Earl of Avon): Abyssinia crisis, 276; Rhineland, 280; Maisky praises, 342; opposes HN in Croydon, 381; in Suez crisis, 420-1

Edinburg, Duke of (Prince Philip), 384-5

Edward VIII (Prince of Wales, Duke of Windsor): at London party, 282-3; opens Parliament, 287; abdicates, 288-9, 297; "without a soul," 290; at Maugham party, 306-7

Edwardians, The (V.S-W) 10, 226

Einstein, Albert 213-14

Eliot, T. S. 177-8, 196

Elizabeth, Queen (Duchess of York, Queen Mother): in Berlin, 214-15; HN fails to recognize, 280; visits USA, 311 & *n*; her "very large eyes," 333; her "magnetic quality," 372; defers to her daughter, 405; HN gives her copy of *King George V,* 406; "wonderful skin," 430

Elizabeth II, Queen 385*n*, 405, 414

Elliot, Walter 368-9

Elsinore 355, 401-2

Emery, Winifred 125

Englewood (New Jersey) 258-9

Enver Bey 34*n*

Esher, Lord 405

Etchingham (Sussex) 424-5

Eton College 252

Euston, Earl of 405

Evening Standard 219-20, 223-4, 226-7

Façade (Sitwell) 151-2

Fairbanks, Douglas 152

Farman, Farma 134

Fascists (in Rome) 232

Federspiel, Per 402

Fellowes, Daisy 282

Fergus & Fergus, tailors 417

Feuchtwanger, Lion 223*n*

Field, Marshall 267

Florence (Italy) 20, 273

Foch, Marshal 94, 95

France: surrenders in 1940, 324-5; French character, 402; V.S-W and HN holiday in, 412-13

Franco, General 294-5, 418

Frankfurt 211

Fraser, Capt. and Mrs. 137

Frazer, Sir James 155*n*

Fredensburg (Denmark) 401-2

Frost, Robert 257

Fry, Roger 163, 304

Fuld, Friedländer 233

Gallipoli 119

Galsworthy, John 177, 200, 212, 392

Garden, The (V.S-W) 11, 340, 360

Garnett, David 257

Garrick Club 124-5

Gaulle, General Charles de 334, 342, 430

Geneva 373-4

Genoux, Louise 149 & *n*, 194*n*

George V: His Life and Reign, King (HN): HN commissioned, 383-5; reads documents, 387-8; V.S-W reads drafts, 391; published, 406; copy for Queen Mary, 406; V.S-W praises, 409

George VI, King: HN meets in Berlin, 214 & *n*, 215; becomes King, 289-90; denies Mrs. Simpson a title, 306*n*; dies, 404

Giglio, Isola del 230, 231

Glendinning, Victoria 3, 60*n*

Good Behaviour (HN) 408, 415, 419

Gosford, Lady 201

Gosse, Sir Edmund 166-7

Grajewo (Poland) 141

Granada (Spain) 389

Granby, Marquess of 21 & *n*, 26 & *n*

Grant, Duncan 135, 152, 204, 257
Grant, Dr. Harry 236–7
Greece: HN's visits to, 123–4, 365; might be offered Athens Legation, 221; warns Greek Ambassador, 382; meets King and Queen of Greece, 404
Greville, Mrs. Ronald 296 & *n*
Grey of Fallodon, Lord 120 & *n*
Grey Wethers (V.S-W) 114 & *n*, 115, 123
Grosvenor, Rosamund 17 & *n*, 23, 36, 44, 51; dies, 358–9
Gstaad (Switzerland) 117–18
Guedella, Philip 166, 391
Guernica (Spain) 294–5
Gye, Ernest 222 & *n*

Hachette, Jeanne 327 & *n*
Hadleigh (Suffolk) 423
Haig, Field Marshal Douglas 95
Hambourg, Mark 45
Hamilton, Lady 88
Hamlet 383, 401
Hammam Lif (Tunisia) 352
Hankey, Sir Maurice 84 & *n*, 98
Hardinge, Lord 59 & *n*, 94 & *n*, 95
Hardy, Thomas 154
Harlech, Lord and Lady 333, 372
Harris, F. H. 379 & *n*, 380
Harris, Robert 196
Harrod, Roy 399
Hatch, Lady Constance 51
Hatfield House 18, 20
Hauptmann, Bruno 244, 263, 270–2*n*
Haworth, Colonel 164
Haxton, Gerald 305 & *n*, 306
Hay, Algy 71 & *n*
Hayter, Tom and George 230, 281
Hellenes, Queen Frederika of the 404
Heneage, Dorothy 25, 51
Herbert, David 214 & *n*
Heritage (V.S-W) 87 & n, 114*n*
Herm (Channel Islands) 68 & *n*
Heyward, Du Bose 240–1
Hillingdon, Lady 149

Hillingdon, Lord 301–2
Hindenburg, President von 196–7
Hitler, Adolf: advises British Fascists, 231; HN forecasts Hitler "has missed the boat," 233–4*n*; seizes Rhineland, 280–1*n*; Munich Crisis, 307; invades Poland, 316; attacks France, 319; attacks Russia, 342
Hoare, Rex 298
Hoare, Samuel 276
Hobhouse, Christopher 231–2
Hogarth Press 119 & *n*, 137*n*
Horder, Sir Thomas 191 & *n*
Horsburgh, Florence 288 & *n*
Horstmann, Frau Lalli 188–9, 386
Hudson, Nan 204 & *n*
Hungary (1956) 420–1
Hunter, Mrs. Charles 41 & *n*, 42
Hutchinson, Mary 199 & *n*
Huxley, Aldous 279
Huxley, Julian 330–1, 389*n*
Hyères 111
Hymns 217, 341

Ilchester, Lord 393 & *n*
India 164
Ingres, Jean 370–1
Ireland: HN visits, 344–5
Ironside, Sir Edmund 319 & *n*
Ismet Pasha 120 & *n*
Israel 378
Italy: V.S-W's love for, 20, 23–4, 31, 41–2; HN's, 402–3

Japan 343–4
Jarvis, Bertram 307 & *n*, 310
Jebb, Gladwyn (Lord Gladwyn) 132, 156, 160–1, 231, 369
Jerichow, Mr. (Denmark) 401–2
Jerusalem 129
Joad, Prof. Cyril 339
Joan of Arc, Saint (V.S-W) 13, 277, 351
Joffre, Marshal 95
John, Augustus 151
Johnson, Edward 106

Journey to Java (HN) 420
Joyce, James: HN visits, 246–8

Keats, John 329, 387
Keeble, Sir Frederick and Lady 245
Keeling, Edward 26, 30, 45
Kennedy, Joseph 318
Kent, Duchess of 286
Kephisia (Greece) 123
Keppel, Mrs. George (Alice) 46, 67, 96–7
Keppel, Sonia 96–7
Keppel, Violet: *See* Trefusis, Violet
Kermanshah (Iran) 131, 164, 434
Keun, Odette 244 & *n*
Kew Gardens 183
Keynes, Maynard 152, 399
Khartoum 293
King's Bench Walk (London) 224 & *n*, 225, 364
Kitchener, Lord 50, 126
Knole: Sackvilles at, 16; V.S-W decorates room, 19, 21; alone there, 22; Christmas at, 179; V.S-W's father dies, 191; V.S-W revisits, 195–6, 425; her love for, 218, 361, 425; inheritance tax, 251 & *n*; bombed, 357
Knole and the Sackvilles (V.S-W) 110, 114
Koestler, Arthur and Mrs. 294 & *n*
Königsberg 140, 142

Lacretelle, Pierre de 370 & *n*
Lamb, Charles 275
Lamont, Edith 422, 425–6, 434
Lamont, Thomas 260–1, 282
Lancaster, Osbert 411
Land, The (V.S-W): V.S-W writes, 127, 129*n*, 135, 136–7; proofs, 143; Bridges praises, 148, 172; V.S-W thinks good, 163; Gosse praises, 166–7; HN's opinion, 167–8, 360; wins prize, 168*n*; Attlee praises, 375; Lascelles praises, 360
Lascelles, Sir Alan ("Tommy"): on

Edward VIII, 289–90; award of CH to V.S-W, 375; HN's life of George V, 383–5; on Queen Elizabeth II, 414
Lascelles, Viscount 30 & *n*, 302 & *n*
Lausanne: Conference at, 113ff; V.S-W at, 118*n*
Lavenham (Suffolk) 423
Lavery, Sir John and Lady 45, 245
Layer Marney (Essex) 422
League of Nations 84 & *n*, 85, 94, 299
Leeper, Allen 115, 122
Leeper, Reginald 365 & *n*
Lees-Milne, James 3, 246, 396–7
Leicester 277–9, 288, 307, 342, 362–3, 378*n*
Lewis, Kid 229
Lewis, Sinclair 192 & *n*, 238 & *n*
Lichnowski, Princess 188–9
Lilly Library, Bloomington, Indiana 3
Lincoln 107–8*n*
Lindbergh, Charles and Anne: baby kidnapped, 254–5*n*; "not easy," 255; HN first meets, 258–9; on his flight to Paris, 262; Hauptmann case, 262–3, 270–2; in Maine, 273–4; meets Edward VIII, 282
Lindbergh, Jon 263
Lindsay, Sir Ronald and Lady: in Berlin, 196 & *n*, 197, 198; in Washington, 235 & *n*, 241
Lloyd, Selwyn 420
Lloyd George, David: on Armistice Day, 73; at Paris Conference (1919), 76, 83–4, 98; signs Treaty of Versailles, 92, 94; Baldwin on, 296; criticizes Chamberlain, 314
Lockhart, Robert Bruce 218–20, 227, 282
Lolita (Nabokov) 426 & *n*
London, bombing of 330–2, 338
London Library 393 & *n*
Long, Ken 395–6
Long Barn: purchased, 50; happy in, 57, 67, 113–14; garden at, 114–15, 143, 162, 166, 180–1; air crash at, 165–6; V.S-W's love of, 216; she revisits, 268–9

Longden, Robert 201 & *n*
Long Island (NY) 167–8
Longworth, Alice 12, 239 & *n*
Loraine, Louise 149 & *n*
Loraine, Sir Percy 132, 134 & *n*, 150
Lothian, Lord 250–1*n*
Low, David 245
Lowther, Lady 26 & *n*, 76
Ludwig, Emil 208 & *n*
Lutyens, Sir Edwin and Lady Emily 59 & *n*, 60
Lynch, Jack and Rosamund 358–9
Lytton, Lord 60*n*, 117

MacCarthy, Desmond 152, 168, 178, 183, 226
McCormick, Ken 419
MacDonald, Ramsay 279–80, 288
McFadyean, Lady 189–91
Maclean, Donald 399–400
MacLeish, Archibald 256 & *n*
McCullough, Donald 389–90
Macmillan, Lady Dorothy 430
Macmillan, Harold: opposes HN at Croydon, 381; Prime Minister, 421–2; Oxford Chancellor, 429 & *n*, 430
Maffey, J. L. (Lord Rugby) 344–5
Maisky, Ivan 318, 342
Malaga (Spain) 389
Mallet, Victor 354, 402
Manchester 333
Mann, Thomas 212 & *n*, 213
Mar (HN's boat) 311 & *n*, 313–4
Margaret, Princess 406, 412
Margerie, Roland de 399 & *n*
Marginal Comment (HN, *Spectator*) 410
Marsh, Edward 178
Martin, Kingsley 317 & *n*, 339
Mary, Princess 301
Mary, Queen 388, 406
Massigli, René and Mme. 366
Matheson, Hilda 10, 185, 209–10, 220
Maugham, Liza 305 & *n*, 306
Maugham, Robin 287, 394–6

Maugham, Somerset 285, 286–7, 305–7
Maurois, André 188*n*
Mendelsohn, Francesco von 233 & *n*
Mexico, HN in 272–3
Middleton Place 241
Minneapolis 238
Missolonghi (Greece) 124 & *n*, 125
Molyneux, Edward 10, 98
Molyneux, Sir Richard 405 & *n*
Monson, Edmund 137
Montague, Venetia 137
Montauban (France) 370–1
Monte Carlo 73ff, 98ff
Morgan, John 278–9
Morrell, Ottoline 151
Morrison, Herbert 338
Morrow, Dwight 244, 254, 271
Morrow, Elizabeth 254, 271
Morshead, Owen 384 & *n*, 387–8
Mortimer, Raymond ("Tray") 10: essay on marriage, 138–9, 145; criticizes HN, 150; consoles V.S-W, 194; in Berlin with HN, 201; laziness, 264–5; in France with V.S-W, 370–1; on Roy Campbell affair, 400
Moscow 139
Mosley, Lady Cynthia 229 & *n*
Mosley, Sir Oswald ("Tom") 226, 229, 232
Mozart 48, 407
Müller, Hermann 197
Munich 207, 212
Munich Crisis (1938) 307–9, 311
Murray-Scott, Sir John ("Seery") 20*n*, 39 & *n*, 46*n*
Mussolini, Benito 122*n*, 276, 323

New York 237, 257–8
Nicolson, Adam (grandson) 432, 433–4
Nicolson, Sir Arthur (Lord Carnock, father) 16, 32, 46, 67, 132*n*, 197, 206*n*
Nicolson, Benedict ("Ben," son): relationship with Vita, 14, 397–8;

born, 50; his name, 54; misses
V.S-W, 79–80; his reticence, 106; as
a baby, 137; at school, 149;
character aged twelve, 179; told
facts of life, 202–3; with HN and
Lindbergh in USA, 274; on staff of
National Gallery, 283 & n; adult
character, 297, 313; Deputy
Surveyor King's Pictures, 301n, 311,
313; happiness at Sissinghurst, 346;
in army in Africa, 347; HN's advice
to, 364–5; influence of Philip
Toynbee, 399; disgusted by Burgess,
400; edits the *Burlington,* 410 & n
Nicolson, Catherine (Lady Carnock,
mother) 37, 166, 398 & n
Nicolson, Eric (brother) 166
Nicolson, Harold:
  Life: meets V.S-W, 16; in
    Constantinople Embassy, 18ff;
    marries, 49; honeymoon, 50; in
    Foreign Office in WW I, 50ff,
    69–70; Paris Peace Conference,
    74ff; Treaty of Versailles, 91–4;
    Lausanne Conference with
    Curzon, 113ff; in British
    Legation, Teheran, 127ff; in
    British Embassy, Berlin, 11,
    185ff; decides to leave diplomacy,
    218–20, 221, 222–3; leaves
    Berlin, 225; *Evening Standard* and
    Action (Mosley), 227–9, 232;
    American lecture tour with
    V.S-W, 235–43; stays with
    Lindberghs, 244, 259ff; elected to
    Parliament, 277–9; in Africa, 293;
    opposes Chamberlain, 307–8;
    promoted Minister, 319; suicide
    pill, 323; in bombing of London,
    330–2, 338; loses office, 340;
    Governor of BBC, 341; in
    Sweden, 354–5; loses seat in
    Parliament, 362–3; at Nuremberg
    trial, 367; broadcasts from Paris,
    369–70; joins Labour Party, 371;
    stands at North Croydon
    bye-election, 377–82; writes Life
    of King George V, 383ff; returns

to Berlin, 385–6; knighted,
    406–7, 408; suffers strokes, 415 &
    n; V.S-W's illness and death,
    434–7; death, 438; made most of
    his life, 425, 427
  His marriage: summary, 6–7, 13,
    437–8; his homosexuality, 10,
    60n, 98, 161; engagement to
    V.S-W, 18ff; insists he will be
    master, 35; crisis in engagement,
    42–5; marries, 49; honeymoon,
    51, 402–3; happiness in WW I,
    57–8; contracts venereal disease,
    60 & n; V.S-W in Cornwall
    with Violet Trefusis, 61–5; HN's
    reaction, 69, 70–1; wishes Violet
    dead, 71–2; reproaches V.S-W,
    74–8, 82, 100; appeals to her
    love, 105–7; retrieves her from
    Amiens, 109n; fears renewal of
    Violet affair, 111–13, 126; misses
    V.S-W terribly, 128, 138, 183,
    370; on infidelity, 138–9;
    analyzes success of his marriage,
    184, 230, 260, 335–6, 347,
    353–4
  Character and tastes: not weak, 8;
    not a snob, 11–12; as a diplomat,
    70, 185; as a politician, 12–13,
    284; hates electioneering, 379–81;
    dislikes smart society, 285–6; his
    Socialism 'cerebral,' 383; courage
    in war, 330, 339; on Negroes,
    237; idealism (League of
    Nations), 84–5; patriotism, 95–6,
    119, 150, 350; no religion, 13,
    153, 155–6, 186–7, 203, 217;
    "good pagan," 312; gentleness,
    66, 105; capacity for anger, 119,
    173; dislikes affectation, 170;
    hates talking sex, 202–3;
    clumsiness, 189–91; unmusical,
    407; love of nature, 67, 181–2,
    386, 427; gardens (at Long Barn),
    180–1, 416; (at Sissinghurst), 368,
    373, 386, 390–1; skis, 117–18;
    rides, 182; sails, 311, 314; hates
    growing old, 293, 399, 408, 420;

"Secret Sorrow," 348–9; relationship with his sons, 274, 297, 317, 346–7; and with his grandchildren, 432–4

Books, etc: his letters, 3, 5; diaries, 437; radio and television broadcasts, 226, 389–90, 408, 414, 423–4; on Keats, 329

Verlaine, 110*n*; Tennyson, 114*n*; *Byron: The Last Journey*, 117*n*, 123–4, 124–5, 358; *Some People*, 115*n*, 128, 195, 215; *Lord Carnock*, 11, 207–8; *Public Faces*, 11, 235, 236; *Peacemaking*, 244; *Curzon, The Last Phase*, 244; *Dwight Morrow*, 244; *Why Britain Is at War*, 316; *The Desire to Please*, 340; *The Congress of Vienna*, 340; *Good Behaviour*, 408, 415, 419; *Benjamin Constant*, 364; *George V: His Life and Reign*, qv.; *Sainte Beuve*, 408; *Journey to Java*, 420

Nicolson, Juliet (granddaughter) 408, 418*n*, 432, 433–4

Nicolson, Nigel (son): relationship with V.S-W, 14; she prefers Ben to him, 80; at school, 149; character aged nine, 179; at Oxford, 301; in army in WW II, 347, 352*n*, 357; stands for Parliament, 377*n*; reaction to HN's knighthood, 406–7; elected to House of Commons, 410*n*; opposes Suez operation and loses seat, 421 & *n*; publishes *Lolita*, 426; relations with his children too mild?, 433

Nicolson, Philippa (Nigel's wife) 433, 436

Nicolson, Vanessa (Ben's daughter) 418*n*

Niggeman, Elvira (HN's secretary) 349 & *n*, 355, 371, 384, 388

Norman, Sir Montagu 95 & *n*

North Haven (Maine) 252–4, 273–4

Novello, Ivor 10, 192–3

Noyon (France) 91

Nuremburg trials 367

Oates, Lawrence 118 & *n*

Observer, The V.S-W's articles in, 11, 404, 412, 422

Olivier, Laurence 383

Orchard and Vineyard (V.S-W) 162

Orde, Cuthbert 47*n*

Orlando (V. Woolf) 9, 205–6

Orpen, William 223 & *n*

Oxford 149, 382, 399, 411, 416

Pansa, Mario 188 & *n*

Paris: Peace Conference (1919), 74ff; Treaty of Versailles signed, 91–4; Victory Parade, 95–6; HN broadcasts from (1946), 369–70

Pashkolé (Iran) 144

Passenger to Teheran (V.S-W) 127, 163–4

Pater, Walter 69*n*, 114

Peacemaking (HN) 244

Pearl Harbor 343 & *n*

Pearson, Harold 16

Peel, Lord 248 & *n*

Pepita (V.S-W) 16, 277, 283–4, 389

Percy, Lord Eustace 424–5

Persia (Iran) 127ff, 181–2

Peyrefitte, Roger 402

Pickford, Mary 152

Pietri, Dr. 211–12

Pinckney, Miss 240

Pirie, Irene 51, 125

Plank, George 154, 165, 166

Plymouth (Devon) 338

Poincaré, Raymond 120, 123

Poland 140, 316

Polignac, Madame de 282–3

Polk, Frank L. 97 & *n*

Polperro (Cornwall) 61–5

Pope, Senator James P. 275–6

Pope-Hennessy, James 10, 340, 409

Portofino (Italy) 245–6*n*

Possingworth Manor (Sussex) 96

Powerscourt (Ireland) 345

Printemps, Yvonne 265–6

Profumo, John 429 & *n*

Proust, Marcel 133, 177, 201

Public Faces (HN) 11, 235, 236

Ramadi (Iraq) 130

Resht (Iran) 215, 260

Reza Khan (Shah of Persia) 133–4, 144

Rhineland crisis (1936) 280–1

Ribbentrop, Joachim von 367

Richardson, Miss 153–4

Richmond (Surrey) 119, 182

Robey, George 152 & *n*

Rockland (Maine) 252

Rodin, Auguste 45, 47–8

Rodmell (Sussex) 145–6, 150, 303–4, 316–17: *See also* Woolf, Virginia

Rojas, Munoz 389

Rome: V.S-W in, 41–2; HN in, 230–2

Roosevelt, Edward 267

Roosevelt, Franklin D. 332–3, 382

Roosevelt, Kermit 265, 267–8

Roosevelt, Theodore 268 & *n*

Rothschild, James de 302 & *n*

Rothschild, Tony 406

Rousseau, J. J. 374

Royal Air Force 317, 330

Royal Horticultural Society 416

Royal Literary Fund 405

Rubens, Mrs. Walter (Olive) 51 & *n*, 69, 79, 227

Rubinstein, Arthur 282–3

Rublee, George 253–4

Rumania: HN in, 298–300; Queen of, 404–5, 308*n*

Rumbold, Sir Horace 198 & *n*, 199–200, 208, 225

Russell, Bertrand 159, 295

Russia: V.S-W in, 139; attacked by Germany, 342; behaviour in Germany, 386; Burgess and Maclean, 399–400

Sackville, Anne 195 & *n*

Sackville, Charles (4th Lord, V.S-W's uncle) 195, 357

Sackville, Lionel (2nd Lord, V.S-W's grandfather) 389 & *n*

Sackville, Lionel (3rd Lord, V.S-W's father): at Knole, 23; in V.S-W's will, 52; she finds him sympathetic, 79; hates his wife, 80; at smart party, 152; dies, 191

Sackville, Victoria ("B.M.", Vita's mother): youth in Washington, 239 & *n*; attitude to Vita's engagement to HN, 18, 29; quarrels over Ben's name, 54–5; and Lutyens, 59*n*; scolds Vita, 79; leaves Knole, 80*n*; learns Vita's sex secrets, 99; in Paris with HN, 102; anxious to help Vita, 104; V. Woolf visits her house, 146; terrible row with Vita, 193–4; reason why HN leaves diplomacy, 223–4; death, 277, 283*n*

Sackville-West, Edward ("Eddy," V.S-W's cousin): heir to Knole, 24 & *n*, 251; at Long Barn, 168; V.S-W fond of, 180; succeeds to title, 195*n*; in Berlin with HN, 208; at Knole, 357; author and musician, 361

Sackville-West, Victoria Mary ("Vita," Mrs. Harold Nicolson): *Life:* her childhood at Knole, 23; affair with Rosamund Grosvenor, 18, 23, 36, 44; meets HN, 16; engaged, 18; the Scott case, 20 & *n*; social life as debutante, 25–6, 45–6; in Spain and Italy, 41–2; marries HN, 49; Ben born, 50, 53; second son born dead, 56; affair with Violet Trefusis, 61ff (see next section); rescued by HN from Amiens, 108–9; first journey to Persia, 138*n*; adventurous journey back, 139–43; second visit to Persia, 182*n*; her father dies, 191; terrible row with her mother, 193–4; American lecture tour with HN, 235–243; affair with Geoffrey Scott, 9, 110, 136; *Orlando*, 205–6; buys Sissinghurst, 226–8; Women's Land Army, 316; suicide of Virginia Woolf,

336–7; awarded C.H., 375, 393; Justice of Peace, 392; Gold Medal of RHS, 416; illness, 434–5; death, 437

Her marriage: summary, 6–7, 13, 437–8; what is the point of marriage?, 180; a bad wife for HN?, 210; their affairs, 9–10; crisis in engagement, 42–5; marries, 49; happiness in WW I, 53, 55–6, 58; affair with Violet Trefusis, summary, 7–8, 432; affair begins, 61–5; her excuse, 66–7, 72; to Monte Carlo with Violet, 73ff; feels guilty, 88–9, 90–1; second Monte Carlo visit with Violet, 98ff; defends herself to HN, 101–3, 104–5; elopes with Violet to Amiens, 108–9; with Violet abroad again, 111–12; "I was mad," 117, 158, 437–8; misses HN terribly, 128, 159, 215–16; affair with Virginia Woolf, 134n, 135, 150, 158–9, 178–9; with G. Scott, 136; with Mary Campbell, 187–8, 400 & n; Vita on infidelity, 145, 339; her love for HN, 215–16, 277–8, 310, 353, 356–7, 412–13, 427

Character and Tastes: analyzes her character for HN, 29–30; the streak of violence in her, 8–9, 255, 350; dual personality, 336, 350; a wanderer, 6, 24, 66; love of solitude, 10, 145; love of gipsy life, 41; love of nature, 387; and animals, 413; her conservatism, 10, 349, 360–1, 371–2; dislike of diplomacy, 28, 33, 186, 198; and of politics, 277–8, 295; patriotism, 10–11; religion, 13, 351; love of aristocracy, 45; 'bedint' prejudice, 13; love of Knole, 22, 195–6, 218, 357, 425; hates smart parties, 308, 393; attitude to sex, 9, 432; relationships with her sons, 13,

137, 149, 160, 162, 179, 202, 397–8; gardening (at Long Barn), 114–15, 143, 162, 166, (at Sissinghurst) 230, 318, 390, 403, 416; courage in war, 327, 348; few friends in later life, 426

Books and writing: her letters, 5–6; "I will never write a good book," 101; "no vibration in her writing," 173–4; on the English poets, 177–8, 196; on her own poetry, 310, 356, 360; her fiction, 398; broadcasts, 209–10; her *Observer* gardening articles, 404, 412, 422

Heritage, 87 & n, 14n; *Dragon in Shallow Waters,* 94n; *Poems of West and East,* 52; *Constantinople,* 52n, 82; *Grey Wethers,* 114, 115, 123; *Orchard and Vineyard,* 162; *Knole and the Sackvilles,* 110, 114; *Challenge,* 96 & n, 100, 101; *The Land,* qv. *Seducers in Ecuador,* 9; *Passenger to Teheran,* 127, 163–4; *Aphra Behn,* 182n; *The Edwardians,* 10, 226; *King's Daughter,* 22n; *Sissinghurst,* 241, 269; *All Passion Spent,* 226, 236; *Joan of Arc,* 13, 277, 351; *Solitude,* 9, 277, 302–3; *Pepita,* 277, 283–4; *Eagle and the Dove, The,* 340, 351, 353; *Devil at Westease,* 364, 372–3; *The Garden,* 5, 11, 340, 360; *No Signposts in the Sea,* 420; *Easter Party, The,* 398; *Daughter of France,* 408, 417, 424

St Aubyn (Lady St Levan) 44, 51, 245–6, 265, 291–2, 308

St. Barbara (statue) 19 & n, 52, 114, 156, 321

Sadleir, Michael 85n

Salisbury, Lord 372

Sand, George 71

Sandilands, Colonel J. W. 188

Sands, Ethel 204 & n

Sans Souci (Potsdam) 233

Sargent, J. S. 45
Saulieu (France) 203
Sauqueville (France) 205
Scandrett, Richard 271
Schacht, Dr. Hjamlar 367 & n
Schubert, Carl von 197, 225
Scott, Geoffrey 9, 110, 136 & n, 149 & n, 391
Scott, Sir John ("Seery"): See Murray-Scott
Scott-James, Anne 3
Seducers in Ecuador (V.S-W) 9
Seville 41
Seymour, Charles 269–70
Shakespeare, William 383, 401
Shaw, G. B, and Mrs. 396–7
Shaw-Stewart, Patrick 21, 25
Sheffield 333
Shelley, Percy Bysshe 196
Sherriff, R. C. 223 & n
Shinwell, Emmanual 371
Siepmann, Charles 265 & n
Simenon, Georges 417
Simpson, Mrs. Wallis (Duchess of Windsor) 282, 285, 288–90, 306–7
Singapore 344 & n
Sissinghurst (Kent): V.S-W buys, 226, 227–8; dramas at, 281–2; catches fire, 291; threat of invasion, 321, 323, 327; Battle of Britain, 327–8, 331; near-miss by German bomber, 358; no guest rooms, 10; Garden at, summary, 14; early plantings, 230; White Garden, 318, 390–1; Lime Walk, 368, 436; azaleas, 373 & n; HN analyzes its virtues, 386–7, 416; its fame, 437
Sissinghurst (V.S-W) 241, 269
Sitwell, Edith 151–2, 393–4, 429
Sitwell, Osbert 152, 287, 393–4
Sitwell, Sacheverell ("Sachie") 151
Smith, John 405 & n
Smuts, Jan Christian 368–9
Smyth, Ethel 208 & n, 209, 300, 316–17
Solitude (V.S-W) 9, 277, 302–3

Some People (HN) 115n, 127, 128, 195, 214–5
South Africa 368–9
Spain: V.S-W in, 41, 389; civil war, 294–5; Queen of, 410–11
Sparrow, John 314
Spears, Sir Edward and Lady 296 & n, 298
Spender, Stephen 256, 310, 394
Stambolisky, Alexander 121–2
Staplehurst (Kent) 334, 386, 427
Stirrum, Graf Limburg 386
Stockholm 248–9, 354–5
Strachey, Lytton 176 & n, 304
Strang, William 68 & n, 69
Strick, John 10
Suez crisis (1956) 420–1
Summer Fields (Oxford) 149, 202n, 217
Summers, Rev. Alphonsus 182 & n
Sweden 248–9, 354–5
Sweet Waters (HN) 110
Sykes, Christopher 214 & n, 233
Synge, Patrick 403

Tardieu, André 97 & n
Teheran 132ff
Television, HN on 423–4
Tennant, Peter 354
Tennyson (HN) 114n
Tenterden (Kent) 328
Therapia (Istanbul) 32 & n
Thomas, Dylan 341
Thomas, Graham 403
Thomas, Hugh 132
Thompson, Colonel 157–8
Thompson, Dorothy (Mrs. Sinclair Lewis) 192, 238
Thorne, William 288
Tomlin, Stephen 257 & n
Töring, Countess 285 & n
Touggourt (Algeria) 291–2
Toynbee, Philip 399
Tree, Jeremy 429
Tree, Nancy 250
Tree, Viola 147 & n

Trefusis, Denys 71*n*, 91*n*, 96*n*, 108–9, 111

Trefusis, Violet (Keppel): summary of Vita's affair with, 7–8; "my erratic friend," 22; early friendship, 36; in Vita's will, 52; begins affair in Cornwall, 61–5; in Monte Carlo, 74ff; marries Denys, 81 & *n*, 87–8, 91; HN reproaches, 71–2, 86; at Possingworth, 96–7; in Monte Carlo with Vita again, 98ff; elopes with Vita to Amiens, 108 & *n*, 109; abroad with Vita again, 111; in London, 115; "unscrupulous," 116; Vita renounces, 116–17, 149, 158; 'mesmerises' Vita, 125–6; visits Sissinghurst in WW II, 328, 352; HN's 'horror' of her, 375; persecutes maid, 388–9; gossipy lunch with, 411; Vita reflects (in 1960) on their affair, 432

Trenchord, Lord 317

Trieste 127

Trott, Alan 154, 155

Tunisia 351 & *n*, 352

Turks 119, 120

Tyrrell, William 122 & *n*, 123

Ulysses (James Joyce) 247–8

United States: HN's attitude to, 12; HN's and V.S-W's lecture tour in (1933), 235–243; writing *Dwight Morrow,* 252ff; with Lindberghs, 258ff; in WW II, 324; Pearl Harbor, 343; HN's last visit to, 437. *See also under* Americans

Vansittart, Robert 17 & *n*, 25, 282, 294, 298 & *n*, 318, 330

Venizelos, Eleutherios 97 & *n*

Verlaine (HN) 110*n*

Versailles, Treaty of 91–4, 246

Vézelay (France) 204

Victoria, Queen 388

Victory Parade, Paris (1919) 95–6

Vienna 32, 33, 35

Villefranche (France) 305

Voltaire 374

Wace, Alan 124 & *n*

Waddesdon Manor 301–2

Walpole, Hugh 209–10

Walton, William 151*n*

Warner, Christopher 132, 156

Warren, Dorothy 149 & *n,* 187

Warsaw 140

Washington DC 235–6, 239

Weidenfeld & Nicolson Ltd 426*n*

Weimar, Duke of 208

Weizmann, Chaim 378

Well of Loneliness, The 200

Wellesley, Lady Eileen 47 & *n*

Wellesley, Lady Gerald (Dorothy) 113*n*, 117, 142, 162, 165, 166, 222

Wellesley, Lord Gerald (Duke of Wellington, "Gerry") 39, 68, 113*n*, 133, 302, 409

Wells, H. G. 213, 244–5

Westminster, Duke and Duchess of 227, 411

Wheeler, Mortimer 431 & *n*

Whitney, John H. 429, 431

William II, Kaiser 268

Williams, Dr. Cyril 202 & *n*

Willingdon, Lord 341 & *n*

Willkie, Wendell 332 & *n*

Wilson, Edmund 358 & *n*

Wilson, President Woodrow 76, 83, 93–4, 239

Windsor (Berks) 387–8, 394, 396, 405

Windsor, Duke and Duchess of: *See under* Edward VIII and Simpson, Wallis

Withyham (Sussex) 376*n*, 437

Woolf, Leonard 134, 138*n*, 146, 155, 168, 182–3, 198, 317, 336–7

Woolf, Virginia: summary of Vita's friendship with, 9; Vita first meets, 119; love affair with Vita, 134*n*, 135; they sleep together, 150,

158–9, 178–9; Vita at Rodmell, 145–6, 198, 222; in London, 147; HN on their affair, 136, 175–7; at Sitwell party, 151–2; sees Thomas Hardy, 154; on being mad, 155; at Vita's lecture, 166–7; stimulates Vita, 168–9; criticizes Vita's writing, 173–4; Vita's feeling for, 169, 174–5; kind to HN, 176–7; learns to drive, 182–3; goes with Vita to France, 203–4; Memoir Club essay, 204 & *n*, 205; *Orlando*, 205–6; compared to Emily Dickinson, 264; Vita again at Rodmell, 303–4, 316–17; loves only Vita, Leonard and Vanessa, 317; suicide, 336–7; Vita might have saved her, 391–2; her diary published, 412

Wordsworth, William 153, 174, 177
Wynn, Alice 250–1

Yale University 269–70
York, Duke and Duchess: *See* George VI and Elizabeth, Queen Mother

Zionism 378
Zweig, Stefan 391